Formission Ltd
Rowheath Pavilion
Heath Road
Bournville
Birmingham B30 1HH

Spreading Fires

The Missionary Nature of Early Pentecostalism

Allan Anderson

Formission Ltd
Rowheath Pavilion
Heath Road
Bournville
Birmingham B30 1HH

scm press

The Author has asserted his right under the Copyright, Designs and Patents
Act, 1988, to be identified as the Author of this Work

British Library Cataloguing in Publication data

A catalogue record for this book is available
from the British Library

Maps by John Flower

ISBN 978-0-334-04063-7

First published in 2007 by SCM Press
9–17 St Alban's Place,
London N1 0NX

www.scm-canterburypress.co.uk

SCM Press is a division of
SCM-Canterbury Press Ltd

Typeset by Regent Typesetting, London
Printed and bound in Great Britain by
William Clowes Ltd, Beccles, Suffolk

Contents

Acknowledgements

This study would have been impossible without the assistance and inspiration of many people, not all of whom I have been able to name personally. There are, of course, my missionary predecessors in the Salvation Army and the London Missionary Society: parents Keith and Gwen Anderson, grandparents William and Sheila Anderson and Thomas and Lily Starbuck, and three generations before them. I have been stimulated by the willingness of friends to share their insights and resources from their global research and here in particular, I appreciate immensely the advice, critique and practical support of Michael Bergunder, Mark Cartledge, Dale Irvin, Hugh McLeod, Mel Robeck, Edmond Tang and Amos Yong, each of whom read earlier drafts of the book in whole or in part. I have benefited enormously from the marvellous digital collection of early periodicals of the Flower Pentecostal Heritage Center in Springfield, Missouri, from the archives of the Donald Gee Research Centre in Mattersey, England, those of the International Pentecostal Holiness Church in Oklahoma City, and from the Revival Library in Bishops Waltham, England for other digital periodicals. SCM Press and especially Barbara Laing, commissioning editor, enthusiastically supported the project from the beginning and were always a pleasure to work with. Bill Burrows, managing editor of Orbis, read the completed manuscript and enthusiastically supported the book's publication in the USA.

The love of my life partner Olwen – her foundational support for almost three decades, her cheerfully enduring the maintenance of our home through her own personal affliction while my research and trips abroad have sometimes distracted from important family matters; and our two grown children Matthew and Tami, who in different ways make their father proud.

Thank you.

Selly Oak, Birmingham, England
September 2006

Abbreviations

Advocate	*The (Pentecostal Holiness) Advocate*
AF	*The Apostolic Faith* (Los Angeles)
AFM	Apostolic Faith Mission of South Africa
AG	Assemblies of God (USA)
AJPS	*Asia Journal of Pentecostal Studies*
AV	Holy Bible, Authorised (King James) Version
BM	*The Bridegroom's Messenger*
CE	*The Christian Evangel*
CEM	Congo Evangelistic Mission
CG	Church of God (Cleveland, Tenessee, USA)
CIM	China Inland Mission
CMA	Christian and Missionary Alliance
CMS	Church Missionary Society
Conf	*Confidence: A Pentecostal Paper for Great Britain*
DPCM	Burgess, *New International Dictionary of the Pentecostal and Charis-matic Movements*
FF	*Flames of Fire*
JEPTA	*Journal of the European Pentecostal Theological Association*
JPT	*Journal of Pentecostal Theology*
LMS	London Missionary Society
LRE	*The Latter Rain Evangel*
MPC	Methodist Pentecostal Church (Chile)
NIV	Holy Bible, New International Version
PE	*The Pentecostal Evangel*
Pent	*The Pentecost*
PHC	Pentecostal Holiness Church (USA)
PMU	Pentecostal Missionary Union for Great Britain and Ireland
Pneuma	*Pneuma: Journal of the Society for Pentecostal Studies*
TF	*Triumphs of Faith*
THW	Overy, *The Times History of the World*
TJC	True Jesus Church (China)
WE	*The Weekly Evangel*
WW	*Word and Work*
WWit	*Word and Witness*
UR	*The Upper Room*
YMCA	Young Men's Christian Association
YWCA	Young Women's Christian Association

Dedicated to
Brigadiers Keith A. Anderson (1917–2006)
and Gwenyth Anderson (1916–2006).
African missionaries, devoted to God and each other,
much loved parents.

Formission Ltd
Rowheath Pavilion
Heath Road
Bournville
Birmingham B30 1HH

Part One

Context

1

Spreading Pentecostal Fires: Introduction and Sources

A little band of native Christians in India were gathered in a revival meeting, con-fessing their sins. Suddenly a kerosene oil lamp fell to the ground and broke to pieces, so that the bench, matting on the floor, etc., were soon in a great blaze. The Lord miraculously saved all the people from being injured, and enabled them to extin-guish the fire. In a short time they were all again down on their faces before God, and the old preacher prayed, 'Dear Lord, we thank Thee for sparing our lives, and we thank Thee for the object-lesson Thou hast taught us. When that flame was confined within the lamp chimney, what a small thing it was, but the moment it was all smashed up, how great was the blaze. Lord, break us all to pieces, that the Pentecostal fire may spread.'

(Weekly Evangel, 1917)[1]

One of the prominent convictions of early Pentecostals expressed in the above excerpt from India was that their experience of Spirit baptism was a 'fire' that would spread all over the world, a last-days universal revival to precede the soon second coming of Christ. As the first issue of the Azusa Street revival newspaper *The Apostolic Faith* in 1906 put it, 'The fire is spreading'. People were writing from different places to find out what was happening in this new Pentecostal revival, and were now 'beginning to wait on God for their Pentecost'. God was 'no respecter of persons and places', the paper continued, 'We expect to see a wave of salvation go over this world'.[2] Samuel Otis, the founder of the Christian Workers' Union and a newly convinced Pentecostal, asked the readers of his *Word and Work* periodical in 1907 to 'pray that the Holy Fire may spread'.[3] The May 1908 issue of *The Apostolic Faith* had as its first-page banner headline: 'FIRES ARE BEING KINDLED By the Holy Ghost through-out the World'. It described the spread of Pentecostalism in Ireland, England, China, West Africa, Palestine, Sweden, India, Scotland, and Australia. All this had happened within two years of the beginning of the revival in Los Angeles in April 1906.[4] And a testimony published in the English Pentecostal periodi-cal from All Saints Church in Sunderland, *Confidence*, told of similar con-victions following their experience of Spirit baptism. The fire would spread, they declared, 'until all the world shall know the salvation of God'.[5] This book discusses the processes and implications of these 'spreading fires'.

Before discussing this further we need to ask, who exactly *are* these early Pentecostals? Although the term 'Pentecostal' was used widely in the early twentieth century it was neither an exclusive nor the usual expression used to describe the people we call 'Pentecostals' today. The more common term used in these years was 'Apostolic Faith'. I take the position that from their

beginning, Pentecostals are best defined broadly to include both their historical connections and theological focus. Furthermore, Pentecostalism was in a
process of formation that was not seen as a distinct form of Christianity at least
until a decade after the revival and missionary movements in which it was
entwined. This is an important distinction because, seen from this perspective,
Pentecostalism is not a movement that had a distinct beginning in the USA or
anywhere else, or a movement that is based on a particular doctrine – it is a
movement or rather a series of movements that took several years and several
different formative ideas and events to emerge. Pentecostalism then as now is
a polynucleated and variegated phenomenon. I remain convinced that it is best
seen from its pneumatological centre as historically related movements where
the emphasis is on the exercise of spiritual gifts.

The early Pentecostals were not wrong in their expectations about spreading
global fires. Although they may not have spread as suddenly as they had
thought, within less than a century Pentecostal and Charismatic Christianity in
all its diversity had expanded into almost every country on earth. By the late
twentieth century Pentecostalism in its many forms had become extremely
significant movements both inside and outside the older, 'historic' churches,
possibly the fastest growing religious movement/s of the twentieth century.
With up to a quarter of the world's Christian population, Pentecostalism had
become predominantly a non-western and independent church phenomenon
with a significant Catholic component.[6] Of course, statistics of such magnitude
are controversial and require very careful analysis, particularly when it comes
to defining what we mean by 'Pentecostal'. In all probability, no one actually
knows with any certainty how many Pentecostals and Charismatics there are
in the world or who they are. But there can be no doubt that Pentecostalism is
proliferating and that during the twentieth century it has contributed to the
reshaping of the nature of Christianity itself and become 'globalized' in every
sense of the word. This has enormous ecumenical, social and interreligious
implications, as its adherents are found in every Christian denomination and
are often on the cutting edge of the encounter with people of other faiths. That
this global expansion of Pentecostalism has occurred simultaneously with the
inexorable globalizing forces unleashed by the imperialist cultures of Western
Europe and the USA is a coincidence that must not escape our attention.

Just how these 'fires' spread throughout the world is one of the most amazing stories in the history of Christianity. To tell some of the details of this story
is one of the purposes of this book. A number of scholarly works on
Pentecostalism have appeared recently, including important books on the first
years of American Pentecostalism.[7] However, little attention has been given so
far to the theology, culture and praxis that made these primarily migratory
and missionary movements, nor to the motivations and processes of expansion into Africa, Asia and the Pacific, Europe, Latin America and the
Caribbean. This book explores the early history and activities of Pentecostals
through the writings of these missionaries (western and national) and draws
out some of their theological and missiological principles in order to better
understand the subsequent growth and mission theology of Pentecostalism.
My perspective is that of an insider who has been involved in Charismatic
Christianity all my adult life and to a large extent I share the theology and

worldview of these missionaries. Over 40 years spent in intercultural contexts in southern Africa and three decades in ministry, and latterly teaching students from every continent, has given me empathy with and understanding of those often not adequately represented in the existing literature.

What were the origins of this tremendous surge in the growth of Christianity in the Majority World during the twentieth century? This book is based on the conviction that the present proliferation of Pentecostalism and indeed its inherent character result from the fact that this was fundamentally a missionary movement of the Spirit from the start. At the beginning of the twentieth century, we can already discern the roots and trends of the subsequent dynamic expansion of this movement from 'classical' churches into historic, independent and 'postdenominational' churches. The rapidly 'spreading fires' that characterized the growth of Pentecostalism are directly attributable to the efforts and vision of its pioneers – who were by no means always westerners. The early years of Pentecostalism represent more than its infancy. This period was the decisive heart of the movement, the formative time when precedents were set down for posterity – whatever happened later was because of the founders who blazed the way. This study traces some of the features of the history, theology, social structures and patterns of early Pentecostal missions in the hope that it will help us more adequately understand the present. Based on the whims of the Spirit, missionaries scattered themselves within a remarkably short space of time to spread the 'fires' wherever they went – and these fires were somewhat unpredictable and out of control. When human organizations attempted to quench the flames – as they often did – more often than not, this resulted in new fires breaking out in other places and the further proliferation of new churches.

Bias in Pentecostal Historiography

No historian is without bias of some kind. Historians select, sift and arrange their evidence according to criteria or biases predetermined by their particular ideological, cultural and religious values and personal attitudes. This may create further discrepancies between written history and the actual past – although biases do not necessarily always have detrimental effects. When historians thoroughly seek evidence to support their own beliefs, the value of their written histories is sometimes enhanced. I hope to have done this. But it is impossible to write a value-free account of the past; it is always a selective and subjective interpretation of it. As a researcher I enter into the history myself and influence its character.[8]

So, biases and presuppositions always influence the writing of history, and the writing of Pentecostal history is no exception. Historians of Pentecostalism have often interpreted this history from a predominantly white American perspective, adding their own particular biases of denomination, ideology, race and gender. They often tended to write either hagiographies seeing their particular movement or central characters in glowing terms that overlooked or minimized historical realities, or (less frequently) polemical treatises designed to illustrate the deviant or heretical nature of Pentecostalism. Bearing in mind that many studies are intentionally American in focus – and at the risk of oversimplification – most histories declare or imply that Pentecostalism, fanning out from the western world and particularly from the USA, grew and expanded in Asia, Africa, the Pacific, the Caribbean and Latin America because of the work of a number of white missionaries who carried the 'full gospel' to the ends of the earth. In these histories, the various presuppositions of the writers are often transparent and now easily dismissed.[9]

At least as far as the origins of Pentecostalism are concerned, according to these histories the heroes and heroines are westerners regarded as the main role players responsible for the global expansion of Pentecostalism. The commencement of the movement is situated in the USA, whether in Cherokee County, North Carolina in the 1890s (according to some Church of God historians), Charles Parham's movement in Topeka, Kansas in 1901 (where many histories start) or the Azusa Street revival led by William Seymour in Los Angeles, 1906 (which most agree was the driving force behind the rapid spread of the movement). Although the exact place of origin is disputed, the primacy of Azusa Street as the heart or cradle of Pentecostalism was reaffirmed in the 1970s largely through the influence of Walter Hollenweger and his researchers at Birmingham. Writers began to assert the important role of this predominantly African American church as the generator of Pentecostal churches throughout the world. Most recently, Robeck has definitively sealed for posterity the significance of Azusa Street and William Seymour in global Pentecostal history.[10] Histories of Pentecostalism usually begin with American pioneers like Parham and/or Seymour and then emphasize the beginnings of Pentecostalism in other countries with reference to male missionaries sent from the USA or other western countries. So for example, John G. Lake is credited with the founding of Pentecostalism in South Africa, Alfred Garr and George Berg with India, Gunnar Vingren and Luis Francescon with Brazil, William Burton with the Congo, and so on. Without wanting to underestimate the important role of these pioneer missionaries or of the Azusa Street revival, it remains true that many historians – some of whom have attempted to correct errors of the past – have ignored, overlooked or minimized the vital role of thousands of national workers in early Pentecostalism.

The very significant role of women in the global expansion of Pentecostalism has also often been neglected. The first histories of the movement exhibited not only a 'white racial bias' but also a 'persistent gender bias' in which the role of important women leaders was ignored.[11] So, for example, African American worker Lucy Farrow, who was not only a leader at Azusa Street but also was one of the first Pentecostal missionaries to reach Africa (Liberia), or Lucy Leatherman, the first Pentecostal missionary in the Middle East, have largely been written out of the histories. Similarly, Indian reformer and Mukti Mission founder Pandita Ramabai, arguably the most significant woman involved in early Pentecostalism (as much a missionary as any western one), and the revival movement she helped lead, were almost completely ignored from the histories because she did not start a Pentecostal denomination or believe in 'initial evidence' – and perhaps, because the revival she led was not in the western world. Several of the first Pentecostal missionaries from the Azusa Street mission went to Liberia in 1907 and were African Americans (some of whom laid down their lives there), but these too have largely been ignored by historians until Robeck's 2006 work.[12] Many other early Pentecostal leaders in Africa, India and China were similarly obliterated from historiography because their mass movements were later regarded as heterodox.

Postcolonial theory helps us see historiography in better perspective. The skew in Pentecostal historiography is partly because of the exoticization and marginalization of 'the other' that has been prevalent in all western literature, creating Orientalism and colonialist or androcentric stereotypes. These stereotypes were usually unconsciously transferred onto the 'subjects' of the missionary enterprise to create a distorted representation of them.[13] The marginalization of women and national workers is also because most of the main sources used in the writing of these histories (early Pentecostal periodicals, reports of missionaries and missionary letters) were originally written for home consumption and fund-raising. If national workers were mentioned at all, it was usually as anonymous 'native workers' or, at best, they were mentioned by a single name that does not clearly reveal their identity today. Their memory is now extremely difficult or impossible to retrieve. This is not only a problem in Pentecostal mission history, as Brian Stanley has pointed out, since at the beginning of the twentieth century the missionary movement as a whole was overwhelmingly 'indigenous' in the areas of its greatest expansion, even though there was scant acknowledgement of this.[14] Yet because of its emphasis on the empowering ability of the Spirit to equip ordinary believers for missionary service without requiring prior academic qualifications, Pentecostalism was probably more dependent on 'national workers' than any other missions were at the time.

We obviously need to know who and what were responsible for the explosion of Charismatic Christianity from its beginnings until its present prominence in the twenty-first century – and there are glaring gaps in this knowledge. This study is influenced by a postcolonial approach to early Pentecostal history and therefore tries to look at the often unconscious areas of cultural bias in the writings and actions of western missionaries. But the dearth of historical sources on the leaders who were not westerners makes this task very difficult. The historical processes leading to the fundamental changes in global Pentecostal demographics must be charted accurately before it is too late to correct past distortions. In much of the writing of Pentecostal history, however, the 'objects' of western missionary efforts, now the great majority of Pentecostals in the world, remain marginalized. This situation has begun to improve with the welcome appearance in the past two decades of studies relating to the history of Pentecostalism outside the western world, some of which are referred to in this book. Michael Bergunder deals with the issues of historical methodology, and writes of the uneasiness some scholars have with an American-centred history of Pentecostalism that does not seem to do justice to its multifaceted and global nature. He argues for a way out of this dilemma by focusing on the global network of evangelical and Holiness missionaries and their expectations of 'missionary tongues' in an end-time revival as a root cause for the spread of Pentecostalism, which was global and highly migratory from its beginnings.[15]

My study attempts to begin to move in these directions, although the missing information of this early period in the mostly western sources available means that I will not have gone far enough. In addition, most of my sources were written and printed in English. One of my purposes is to challenge presuppositions relating to the origins of Pentecostalism by drawing attention to some significant pioneers in early Pentecostalism outside the western world. Most of these pioneers, like the western Pentecostal missionaries, were not recent converts from so-called 'heathenism' but were already Christians in various 'mission churches' when they became Pentecostals. The Pentecostal missionaries almost invariably started their work within the framework of existing missionary networks, both evangelical and mainline missions. They seldom went to places where there were no Christian missions.[16] This book sometimes separates the so-called 'indigenous' (local) Pentecostals from the foreigners, not to exoticize the former or to suggest that one or the other is more capable, but to clarify a fragmentary historical narrative based on mostly foreign sources and to give more prominence to a neglected area.

The pioneers we know about are only the tip of the iceberg – there were thousands of leaders in Asia, Africa and Latin America during these years whose records have now disappeared or who are mentioned only in passing in the periodicals of the time. Hopefully, some of them will be rediscovered. This book cannot give voice to the subliminal 'subaltern' who can never be represented in an elitist medium of academic discourse.[17] But I hope that the personal excursions sketched here will make visible a few of the stories of the thousands of national workers responsible for the spread of Pentecostalism beyond the western world. These have not hitherto been recognized as pertinent in the historiography of Pentecostalism. Pentecostalism that is made in the USA is only one part of the total picture of many forms of Pentecostalisms, and the hidden treasures of these local histories need to be discovered. This book tries to do this, but because of the particular sources available to me I have not been able always to reconstruct a completely accurate picture of the past. The multitudes of nameless people responsible for the grassroots expansion of the movement have passed into history forgotten and their memory is very difficult to recover. But this may be one of the most important reconstructions needed in Pentecostal historiography.

I freely admit to being a person who writes with bias. Like other researchers, I too will sift and analyse the evidence in order to support my convictions. I have read through thousands of pages of early periodicals, letters and other publications in the years I have been preparing this book. I have concentrated on those events and people that I see as more important to the telling of this story. At the same time, I hope that the result is a fair and balanced analysis. There is abundant evidence in the Pentecostal archives of the progress of Pentecostalism in North America and Western Europe, but this book will concentrate on the so-called 'foreign' missions rather than on 'home' missions. There will be an emphasis on particular regions of the vast continent of Asia (especially China and India) and on certain regions of Africa. Missions in North America, Europe and Australasia receive no attention here and those in Latin America relatively little – my lack of knowledge of Spanish and Portuguese was a distinct disadvantage here. However, this does not pretend to be an exhaustive history; Asia and Africa are where many of the first

Pentecostal missionaries went and these regions also illustrate well the principles of Pentecostal missions globally. The stories, experiences and attitudes of these missionaries and their so-called 'native workers' are representative of the movement as a whole.

This is not a book about Pentecostal denominations either. The reader who expects to find a detailed account of the beginnings of her or his particular expression of Pentecostalism will need to look elsewhere. Although the second decade of the twentieth century was the time of at least three major doctrinal schisms in North American Pentecostalism, the hardening and proliferation of denominational boundaries only really occurred from the 1920s. The first two decades of Pentecostalism were a period of religious ferment, when the experience of Pentecost was much more important than human organizations or particular dogmatic pronouncements. This was the 'ecumenical' period in Pentecostal history. Most Pentecostal missionaries worked independently with whoever would co-operate with them, or they worked within the structures of existing Protestant organizations and faith missions until they were kicked out. Any denominations that existed or were subsequently created were incidental to the fundamental missionary, interdenominational and international nature of early Pentecostalism.

I do not pretend that this book completely corrects the distortion in Pentecostal historiography, but stating the problem at the beginning is necessary in order to cast what follows in its proper context. Some readers may find undue prominence given here to leaders whose role they may consider less significant, but I have done this intentionally out of conviction that they have been ignored or misrepresented in the past. In the process I may have omitted the stories of some significant western pioneers. I will make an attempt to begin seeing the story from the perspective of the recipients of the Pentecostal message as much as possible. I have not always been able to avoid separating 'foreign' missionary from 'native worker' in this process, and I apologize if this inadvertently exoticizes the 'other'. History is not only about the past, but also about the present and the future – and only when we better understand the past will we be able more correctly to evaluate the world around us and even help shape its future.

Documentary Sources

One of the reasons for the distorted picture we have of Pentecostal history is the problem of available documentary sources. Writing the history of early Pentecostalism outside the western world almost entirely depends on letters, reports and periodicals of western Pentecostals and their missionaries. These documents were usually intended for western consumption and loaded to bolster financial and prayer support in North America and Europe. They were also full of assumptions of power and privilege. So, the reports mostly talked about the activities of the missionaries themselves and not those of their so-called 'native workers'. As one of these missionaries herself admitted, these reports were not always forthright about difficulties encountered. She pointed out that missionaries writing home 'hesitate to even mention any of their needs or trials, lest in so doing they should not be properly trusting God, or lest others should think this'. Or, she added, 'perhaps more often, they do not have the slightest desire to allude to these things accepting them as God's appointment, and rejoicing in them'.[18]

So these reports were, at most, fragments of information given in a very different era and context, and so we do not know the whole story and cannot yet retrieve it – this task is still to be done. Furthermore, history cannot be reconstructed from written sources alone, especially when these sources are the only written documents from this period and almost exclusively reflect the 'official' positions of power and privilege that their authors carried. Consequently, this study sometimes tries to read between the lines of the documents, minutes and newsletters in order to discover hints of a wider world than that which they immediately describe. This is certainly a hazardous exercise, for the possibilities of misinterpretation become greater with incomplete information, especially in the case of those who have already died and whose voices have been lost. I underline the importance of retrieving oral traditions here, for we must record for posterity the stories of those still living who remember the past. The early histories of Pentecostalism in several parts of the world are still within living memories and these must be recounted before it is too late. Of course, the further back in time we go, the more difficult it is to recover the histories 'from below', as the sources become scarcer. Some of the reading between the lines and the critique that I attempt here might put some western Pentecostal missionaries in a less favourable light than they have been cast before. It is neither my intention to denigrate the sacrificial efforts of these pioneer missionaries nor to read their reports through the lenses of a very different century. Some of the quotations from their writings given here will be strange and even offensive to twenty-first-century ears, but they must be read within the context of prevalent attitudes and language at that time. These women and men saw themselves as called by God to do what they did and this study does not intend to cast aspersions on their motives, enthusiasm, commitment and spiritual integrity.

That being said, however, there is little doubt that many of the secessions which occurred early in western Pentecostal mission efforts in Africa, China, India and elsewhere were at least partly the result of cultural and social insensitivities on the part of the missionaries, and in some cases there was racism, ethnocentrism and ethical failure. It is true that missionaries may not have been sensitized to these issues in the ways that we are today and equally true that we now have the hindsight of history – although neither sensitization nor hindsight seems to have changed contemporary human prejudice. Nevertheless, the book will portray early Pentecostal missionaries obsessed with a crusading mentality that saw their task of bringing 'light' to 'darkness', who frequently referred in their newsletters to the 'objects' of their mission as 'the heathen', and who were often slow to recognize national leadership when it arose with creative alternatives to western forms of Pentecostalism, one of the key themes of this book.[19] Missionary paternalism, even if it was 'benevolent' paternalism, was widely practised, perhaps universally so. In country after country, white Pentecostals abandoned their egalitarian roots and followed the example of other expatriate missionaries in this regard. They kept tight control of churches and their national founders, and especially of the finances they raised in Western Europe and North America. Most wrote home believing that they were mainly (if not solely) responsible for the progress of the Pentecostal work in the countries to which they had gone. These actions were often prompted by an unconscious imperialist attitude on the part of white missionaries that was convinced of the innate superiority of their own European and Euro-American 'civilization'. The truth was often that the national churches grew in spite of (and not because of) these missionaries, who were actually denying their converts gifts of leadership. But the Holy Spirit was anointing ordinary people to 'spread the fire' to their friends, relatives, neighbours and even to other communities, peoples and nations.

We do not always have to read between the lines of missionary sources, however. Sometimes western Pentecostal missionaries were patronizing and impolite about the people they were 'serving' and on a few occasions their racism was blatant. It is all the more remarkable that some of these racist comments were published in Pentecostal periodicals without disclaimer. In spite of all these weaknesses and failures, the exploits of western missionaries were certainly impressive and we cannot assume that all of them were bigoted racists. We can only greatly admire their sacrificial efforts and (in most cases) their selfless dedication, as many laid down their lives through the ravages of tropical disease and some through martyrdom. They were often very successful in adapting to extremely difficult circumstances; and many showed a servant heart and genuine love for the people they worked with. They achieved much against what was sometimes overwhelming odds. I hope that this book will achieve one of its aims to reveal these strengths as much as the weaknesses without falling back on a narrative of western missionaries. The so-called 'native workers' also had qualities of dedication, courage in the face of stiff opposition and selfless love for the people they were serving and reaching out to. But we cannot ignore the clear evidence that some of the missionaries supposedly responsible for the spread of the Pentecostal gospel throughout the world were by no means exemplary.

The significance of the early Pentecostal periodicals, pamphlets and other literature in spreading the movement's message throughout the world cannot be underestimated. In an important study, Taylor has shown the vital role of these publications and how 'the pioneers of Pentecostalism proved adept at exporting this mass medium'.[20] But these were not only western pioneers. Taylor outlines the profusion of Pentecostal publications and estimates that by 1908 there were at least 34 periodicals, the largest number in circulation being that of *The Apostolic Faith* coming out of the Azusa Street revival in Los Angeles. This, he points out, indicates 'a rapid world-wide penetration of the Pentecostal message'.[21] By 1908 not only were there numerous Pentecostal periodicals in North America, but Alexander Boddy had begun publishing *Confidence* in Sunderland, England, and there were Pentecostal papers in China (Mok Lai Chi's *Pentecostal Truths*), Japan (M. L. Ryan's *Apostolic Light*) and India (Ramabai's *Mukti Prayer Bell* and Max Wood Moorhead's *Cloud of Witnesses*).[22] By March 1909 Elisabeth Sexton was reporting that 'besides the many published in the United States and Canada', Pentecostal papers were being printed in ten other countries.[23]

These periodicals in which missionary reports were regularly printed illustrate the early global spread of Pentecostalism. As Sexton in an editorial of *The Bridegroom's Messenger* put it (quoting Scripture) in December 1908, 'the field is the world', and this paper, just over a year old, was already circulating in 23 countries. It exhorted prayer that the paper would 'carry Pentecostal messages speedily to the utmost parts of the earth'.[24] As illustrative of how effective this medium was in those days, May Kelty in Argentina wrote to Sexton:

> May God bless you in sending out the paper to all parts of the earth. We appreciate the paper very much, and thank you for it. We send each copy, after carefully reading all its contents, to other missionaries in this country who have been seeking the outpouring of the Holy Ghost for a long time, but who have not yet received. Pray for them. Most of them are from the C. and M. A. Mission.[25]

By 1910, *Confidence* reported that it was circulating in over 46 countries.[26] With the exception of *Pentecostal Truths* (published by the Pentecostal Mission in Hong Kong from 1908 at least until 1915 and mostly in Chinese), and *Apostolic Light* published in Tokyo in English, Japanese and Korean (before the use of Korean was banned by the Japanese), these periodicals were published in English in the United States and Britain, mostly monthly. Other early papers were published in various European languages (especially Norwegian, Swedish and German), but I have not been able to read them and am aware of the possibility of missing significant chunks of Pentecostal mission history, especially in Latin America. Because missionary activity was the very essence of the early Pentecostal movement, these periodicals had dedicated pages for reports from the mission field and some made mission reporting their priority. Some like Carrie Judd Montgomery's *Triumphs of Faith* (1881–1949) and Samuel and Addie Otis' *Word and Work* (1879–1940) provide invaluable information on the late nineteenth-century healing and Holiness movements, and the faith mission movement from which some Pentecostal missionaries came and which became a model for others. Because both of these journals turned 'Pentecostal' after 1906 and continued right through this early period, they also offer important and fascinating evidence of how this process happened and how Pentecostal missionary networks emerged.

Other early American periodicals from which I have drawn include the Azusa Street paper *Apostolic Faith* (1906–9), *The Latter Rain Evangel* from the Stone Church in Chicago (1908–39), J. Roswell Flower's periodical *The Pentecost* (1908–10), and E. N. Bell's *Word and Witness* (1912–15). I have also used the periodical that later became the official organ of the Assemblies of God, edited variously by Flower, Bell, J. T. Boddy and Stanley Frodsham, first called *Christian Evangel* (1913–15), renamed *Weekly Evangel* (1915–18), then *Christian Evangel* again (1918–19) and finally *Pentecostal Evangel* (1919 onwards). I have referred to *Trust* (1908–32) from the Elim Faith movement based in Rochester, New York and edited by its leaders the Duncan sisters; *The Upper Room* from an important Pentecostal church in Los Angeles and edited by George Studd (1908–11); and *The Bridegroom's Messenger* from the Atlanta Pentecostal Mission, Georgia (1907–16), edited by Elisabeth Sexton and one of the best sources for Pentecostal missionary information. There are also two British periodicals with extensive missionary materials: Boddy's *Confidence* (1908–26), and Cecil Polhill's *Flames of Fire* (1911–17), a periodical wholly committed to the cause of the Pentecostal Missionary Union (PMU) and a marvellous source for missionary research. The Donald Gee Centre in Mattersey, England also has a most comprehensive collection of original letters, minutes, and official documents of the PMU, which I have drawn on heavily. To a lesser extent I have referred to several other early Pentecostal periodicals from the USA and Britain.

These predominantly western periodicals carried reports written in English by western missionaries – often in remote parts of Asia and Africa – that can hardly be called reliable sources of information on the experiences of the local and national people. The materials contain hidden assumptions about what 'ought' to be happening, and were influenced by the particular movements of which they were an integral part. Nevertheless, these periodicals are still important sources of information and illustration concerning the missionaries, their beliefs, strategies and assumptions, and are used throughout this study. I must also point out that I have been unable to verify the correct spelling of all the names of people and places as given by the foreign missionaries. Many of these names were misspelt by the missionaries; others were corrected and changed in the postcolonial period. When I do not know the contemporary alternatives I have used the spellings current in these colonial times or those used by the missionaries, and apologize for the inevitable errors and confusion – especially in the case of China, where it is most noticeable.

About this Book

One of the aims of this book is to try to balance and make more visible the 'non-western' nature of Pentecostalism in the early twentieth century and to do this without minimizing the international importance of the movement emanating from North America.[27] To achieve this I sometimes concentrate on those activities that fostered local leadership, certain influential local leaders and the expansion of Pentecostalism through local efforts. I hope that such an emphasis will enhance our ability to understand something of what really happened in these pioneering years and help correct any one-sided tendency to exaggerate the role of western missionaries. The book tries to include the contributions of a few local, so-called 'indigenous' missionaries who were often responsible for the expansion of these movements beyond the western world. I focus on the histories, theologies and praxes of various missionaries in the first two decades of the twentieth century and reflect on their impact throughout the world. This was the formative period before the inevitable battle lines of denominations were fully drawn.

In the process of tracing the historical origins of the worldwide spread of Pentecostalism, the book examines those theological, ideological and practical issues that helped form a distinctive mission theology and praxis that contributed towards a renewal of modern Christianity. I try to synthesize the developing mission theology and praxis with its history. I also show how the emerging Pentecostal spirituality related to peoples and their cultures in different parts of the world, but seek to do this honestly from the writings of early Pentecostal missionaries themselves – dealing with both their successes and their failures. The book attempts to portray a global, non-parochial and contextual perspective on early Pentecostal missions. In order to achieve these aims, I conducted extensive archival research in which thousands of pages of periodicals, letters, minutes, and other documents were read. From these sources – many of which were digitalized and marvellously easy to access – I have tried to give an historical narrative that illustrates the principles I have attempted to reconstruct. Finally, I checked my narrative with limited second-ary literature for missing details or contradictory information that needed deconstructing.

This study gives the historical context and narrative of early Pentecostal missions and draws out the emphases that developed in the process of the globalization of the movement. The book is divided into three parts. The first part concerns the historical, theological and social context. The following chapter begins to set the scene by discussing some of the immediate, most important precursors of and models for Pentecostal missions at the end of the nineteenth century. It discusses the roles of the turn-of-century revivals in the evangelical, Holiness and healing movements and of imperialism in the context of Christian missions. It traces the emergence of Charles Parham and his Apostolic Faith movement in Topeka, Kansas, where Pentecostal phe-nomena in 1901 resulted in a distinct, if rather bizarre 'missionary tongues' doctrine that influenced the early Pentecostal missionary thrust. The third chapter narrates the dynamic impetus for American Pentecostal missions beginning in the Azusa Street revival led by William Seymour in Los Angeles from 1906 to 1908. The chapter illustrates the spread of the fires of Pentecost from there to various parts of the world and emphasizes mission flowing from the baptism in the Spirit. The chapter elaborates on early Pentecostal theolo-gies of mission with their emphasis on Spirit baptism and its central relation-ship to the movement of missionaries. It shows how this mission was grounded in the conviction that the Spirit was the motivating power behind all this activity. The chapter traces the belief in 'missionary tongues' giving way to 'unknown tongues' as a sign of Spirit baptism, its impact on missionary service and the inevitable adjustments to language learning. It outlines the significance of the culture of migration and transnationalism in early Pentecostal missions, the motivation for and ideology behind these migrations and the rapid flow of independent missionaries to countries all over the world.

The second part of the book details the spread of Pentecostal missions in three continents until the proliferation of Pentecostal denominations after the First World War. The fourth chapter tells the narrative of Pentecostal missions in India, where the Mukti revival in 1905–7 interacted with other revivals and resulted in the rapid growth of Pentecostal missions and the emergence of Indian leadership. There follows a chapter on China where a proliferation of Pentecostal missions occurred amid difficult circumstances, looking especially at the earliest missionaries, the case of the British Pentecostal Missionary Union operating in Yunnan, the Pentecostal Mission in Hong Kong, and the beginnings of Chinese independent Pentecostal churches. Missions in Japan at this time are also traced. The sixth chapter continues the narrative in Africa and the Middle East, looking particularly at missions in Egypt, West Africa, South Africa and the Congo, together with the role of significant African leaders. This is followed by a consideration of Latin America and the Caribbean and the impact of revival movements there in which Anglo missionaries were seldom involved. This part traces the global spread in the mission networks of radical evangelicalism, with the expanding globalization of the movement as a result of transnational contact. It sketches the beginnings of Pentecostal denominations and missionary paternalism, and its effect upon the emergence of independent national churches. The spread of Pentecostalism in the mission networks is traced, with the expanding globalization of the movement.

The third part of the book deals more comprehensively with Pentecostal mission theories and practices during this period. The eighth chapter considers the priorities of evangelism and healing practices and how these were affected by a premillennial eschatology that posited the soon return of Christ. The effect of this eschatology on the attitudes and pacifism of Pentecostals during the Great War is also traced. The next chapter deals with the religious and socio-political sphere of Pentecostal missions, including attitudes to other religions, the prevailing imperialism, missionary attitudes to culture and politics, and racism and social segregation. The relationship between Pentecostal missionaries and the colonizing powers and their cultural ethics in the light of prevailing views at the time are described. Increasing missionary paternalism and its effect upon Pentecostal missions is discussed. The tenth chapter deals with the subject of the preparation and work of Pentecostal missionaries, the difficulties they encountered and the important role of women in this mobilization, and how Pentecostals bucked the trend towards gender discrimination. It discusses the divisions and sectarianism that increasingly permeated the movement and how effective early Pentecostal missionaries were in translating their message and activities into the context of the local people, raising local leadership, and contextualizing their message. The book closes with some reflections on the lessons learned from early Pentecostalism seen as a missionary movement, a discussion of Charismatic Christianity as a globalized phenomenon as a result of missionary networks, reasons for its widespread contemporary appeal, and the impact of Pentecostalism on the study of global Christianity and religion.

I hope that the reader will enjoy the book as much as I have enjoyed preparing it and that you will catch a glimpse of this stimulating time as you enter into the book's pages. I hope that something of the sheer inspiration of these indomitable and self-sacrificing pioneers of the past will rub off. But the book also aims to be honest and does not gloss over the halos that often wobbled, the manipulation, short-sightedness and pig-headedness that made these missionaries very ordinary, human clay jars carrying the power of the Spirit – but they were also vessels that spread the fires all over the world.

Notes

1 *WE* 174 (27 Jan 1917), p.11.

2 *AF* 2 (Oct 1906), p.1.

3 *WW* 29:4 (Apr 1907), p.113.

4 *AF* 13 (May 1908), p.1.

5 *Conf* 1:1 (Apr 1908), p.5.

6 Barrett, Johnson and Crossing, 'Missiometrics 2006', p.28; and *DPCM*, pp. 286–7, for the higher figure. The lower figure is a conservative estimate (Martin, *Pentecostalism*, p.1).

7 Anderson, *Vision of the Disinherited*; Dayton, *Theological Roots*; Wacker, *Heaven Below*; Jacobsen, *Thinking in the Spirit*; Robeck, *Azusa Street Mission*.

8 Bebbington, *Patterns in History*, pp.5–8.

9 See Anderson, *Introduction to Pentecostalism*, pp.167–84; and Anderson, 'Revising Pentecostal History', pp.157–83.

10 Robeck, *Azusa Street Mission*.

11 Wacker, 'Golden Oldies', p.95.

12 Robeck, *Azusa Street*.

13 King, 'Orientalism and the Study of Religions', pp.286–7.

14 Stanley, 'Twentieth Century World Christianity', pp.71–2.

15 Bergunder, 'Constructing Indian Pentecostalism', pp.177–214.

16 Michael Bergunder, personal communication, 11 Sept 2006.

17 Spivak, 'Can the Subaltern Speak?', pp.24–8.

18 *BM* 131 (15 Apr 1913), p.2.

19 *Conf* 1:2 (May 1908), p.19; 2:5 (May 1909), p.110; Anderson, 'Signs and Blunders', pp.193–210.

20 Taylor, 'Publish and be Blessed', p.15.

21 Taylor, 'Publish and be Blessed', pp.71, 78.

22 *Pent* 1:2 (Sept 1908), p.4.

23 *BM* 33 (1 Mar 1909), p.1.

24 *BM* 27 (1 Dec 1908), p.1.

25 *BM* 66 (15 July 1910), p.4.

26 *Conf* 3:12 (Dec 1910), pp.284–5.

27 I have chosen to use 'North America' to refer to the USA and Canada, and 'America' and 'American' in its current popular usage to refer to the USA. 'The Americas' includes North America, Mexico, Central America and South America. All Spanish-speaking countries (including some Caribbean islands) and Brazil are referred to as 'Latin America'.

2

In All its Pristine Power:
Precursors and Context

On the day of Pentecost the speaking 'with other tongues' and the prophesying was the result of being filled with the Spirit. Here at Ephesus twenty years later, the very same miracle is again witnessed as the visible token and pledge of the other glorious gifts of the Spirit. We may reckon upon it that where the reception of the Holy Spirit and the possibility of being filled with Him are proclaimed and appropriated, the blessed life of the Pentecostal community will be restored in ALL its pristine power.

(Andrew Murray, 1895)[1]

Andrew Murray, Reformed revivalist from South Africa at the turn of the century, penned the above words in 1895, which 14 years later were seized upon by the Pentecostal press as of prophetic significance to their movement. This chapter considers that the revival movements of the late nineteenth and early twentieth centuries in evangelical circles leading to the birth of Pentecostalism were the impetus for an unprecedented missionary thrust that was to continue as a fundamental feature of the early movement (Figure 1). The outpouring of the Holy Spirit empowered believers to preach the gospel to all nations before the coming of Christ. But the Pentecostal revivals did not

Figure 1: The Precursors of Pentecostal Mission

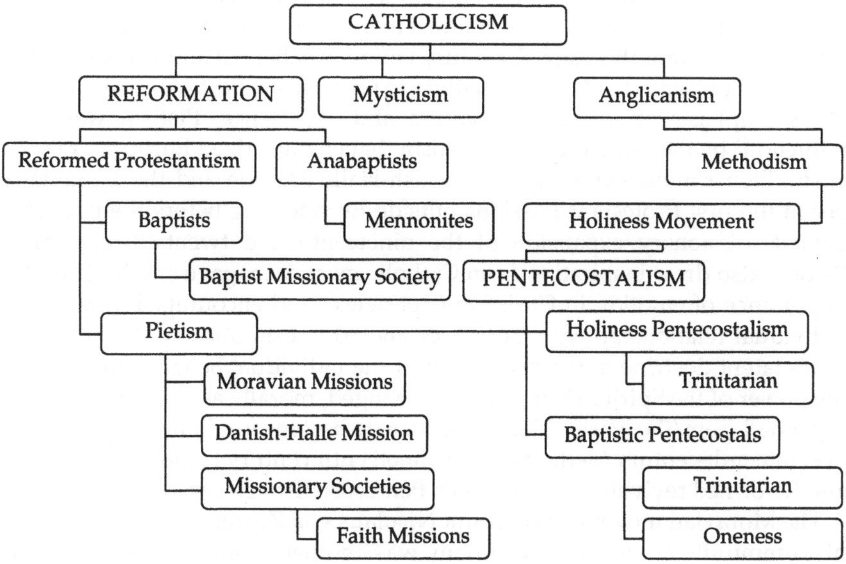

happen in a vacuum. They were conditioned by a movement away from rationalism and secularism, a reaction to modernity that focused on personal spirituality, emotional release and divine intervention in human affairs – even if it used modernity's tools to formulate and justify this reaction. Added to these stimuli was the common perception in these revivals that humanity as a whole, but especially outside the western world, was degraded and sorely in need of the particular Christian message they proclaimed.

These various impulses continued to inspire and motivate early Pentecostal missionaries well into the twentieth century. Pentecostal missions and their missionaries are best understood against the background of the religious and socio-cultural contexts out of which they came. The purpose of this chapter is to identify some of those contexts and precedents, especially as they developed in the nineteenth century, and how they shaped the thinking and praxis of Pentecostalism. Not enough attention has been given to examining how western culture and imperialism influenced and continues to influence the attitudes and practices of its expatriate missionaries. This chapter tries to do this by looking at the important phenomenon of imperialism in the early twentieth century and its enormous and devastating consequences. The ecclesiastical context included Methodism, the Holiness movement, the evangelical revivals and the healing movement. The latter led to the 'missionary tongues' movement in Charles Fox Parham's Apostolic Faith, the immediate forerunner of the missionary movement that proceeded from Los Angeles' Azusa Street revival and considered in the following chapter. But first, an outline of the earliest antecedents must be traced.

Pietist, Methodist and Holiness Antecedents

The Pietist movement that began in seventeenth- and eighteenth-century German Lutheranism emphasized the importance of a personal experience or 'new birth' by the Holy Spirit, in contrast to the rationalism that had overtaken much of Protestant theology. A century before, Anabaptist and Quaker movements had presented radical alternatives to rationalistic Protestantism. In spite of its emphasis on personal devotion and experience, Pietism was also influenced by the rampant individualism that characterized European rationalism. Pietist movements like the Danish-Halle Mission and the Moravians began the first Protestant missions outside Europe long before the unprecedented missionary expansion of the nineteenth and twentieth centuries. Pietism also drew inspiration from Catholic mysticism, gave emphasis to the importance of emotion in Christian experience, and encouraged a personal, individual relationship with God. It promoted a restoration of the Reformation's latent doctrine of the priesthood of the individual believer and sought the power of the Spirit to bring about a changed, morally ascetic Christian life separated from 'the world'. These also were to become fundamental principles of eighteenth-century Methodism, the nineteenth-century Holiness movement and Reformed revivalism, from which Pentecostalism emerged.

The Moravian movement of Count Nicolaus von Zinzendorf (1700–60) and his community at Herrnhut, Germany was another expression of Pietism. In

1727 it was said that the Spirit had been poured out, and a continuous round-the-clock prayer meeting lasted at Herrnhut for a hundred years. One of the convictions of the Moravians was that they were to share their experience of God with as many individuals as possible, and to incorporate these 'saved' individuals into communities that lived together, separated from 'the world' of unbelievers. This had earlier been the practice of some Catholic orders like the Franciscans and became the basis for the 'mission station' model followed by most Protestant missions and continued by Pentecostals. For Moravians, personal obedience to Christ meant obedience to his 'Great Commission' to make disciples of all nations as outlined in Matthew 28.19. To show this obedience, they sent missionaries out to such faraway places as the new colonies of North America, India and South Africa. These missionaries believed that the moral salvation of individuals was the supreme goal of their mission and to this end they traversed the globe.

Pietism profoundly influenced the more immediate precursors of Pentecostalism: Methodism and the nineteenth-century Holiness movement. The latter was based on a particular interpretation of the 'perfect love' teaching of the founder of Methodism, John Wesley (1703–91), and especially on the pneumatology of his contemporary, John Fletcher (1729–85). There was some ambiguity as to what Wesley actually meant by his 'perfect love' doctrine, and this caused some confusion for his later interpreters.[2] But this doctrine of entire sanctification and the possibility of spiritual experiences subsequent to conversion undoubtedly constituted the spark that ignited the Holiness movement and its direct offspring, Pentecostalism. Fletcher, considered Wesley's theologian, taught a distinct experience of 'baptism with the Spirit' giving immediate access to the purifying and personal presence of God. Fletcher differed subtly from Wesley on issues that were later to be important in the shaping of Pentecostal theology, but Pietism influenced both of them. On the boat returning to Europe from Georgia in America, Wesley came in contact with Moravian missionaries who challenged him about his personal experience of Christ, leading him to his Aldersgate conversion experience in 1738. Later, he made a visit to the Herrnhut community to see the revival; and Wesley's new-found revivalism soon spread to his followers. In some early Methodist meetings unusual signs of the Spirit's presence were reported that were to become central features of Pentecostalism, including ecstatic manifestations such as prophecy, speaking in tongues and divine healing. A central emphasis of early Methodism was Wesley's doctrine of a 'second blessing', a crisis experience subsequent to conversion that had a significant influence on Pentecostalism, but only as it was transmitted and reinterpreted through the Holiness movement.[3]

Revival movements with manifestations (including tongues) were happening in different parts of the European world during the nineteenth century, indirectly preparing the ground for the Pentecostal revival of the twentieth century. Edward Irving in the 1830s led what was first a renewal movement within the Presbyterian Church in London and Glasgow where tongues, interpretation, prophecy and healing were common manifestations. After Irving's death the movement became the Catholic Apostolic Church, a name that John Alexander Dowie later found inspirational (see below). Later revivals took

place in Sweden, Germany, Russia and Armenia, and those associated with the
Holiness movement throughout North America and northern Europe. As we
will see, there were also significant revival movements in nineteenth-century
India.

Evangelical Protestantism, especially of the Methodist variety, was the
dominant American subculture in the nineteenth century. Methodism was
the frontier religion *par excellence;* it stressed personal liberty and allowed the
emotional element of popular religion, and it extended its offer of religious
power and autonomy to the dispossessed, subjugated women, African
Americans recently freed from slavery, and the poor. Methodism was also
fundamentally a missionary and migratory religion, and American missionary
bishops like William Taylor (1821–1902) presided over the vigorous expansion
of Methodism throughout the world. With little formal education, the somewhat maverick Taylor entered the Methodist ministry in 1842 and in 1847 was
appointed to California, the year before it was ceded by Mexico to the USA and
two years before the California Gold Rush. There he was known as 'California
Taylor' for his aggressive evangelistic techniques in what was still very much
a frontier region.[4] He opened the first Methodist congregation in San Francisco
and conducted open-air evangelistic meetings. He became an active worker in
the National Association for the Promotion of Holiness founded in 1867, the
most prominent Holiness group at the time.

In 1870 Taylor began his overseas missionary career, arriving in India and
becoming an early advocate of the 'indigenous church', 'three-self' policy (self-
governing, self-supporting and self-propagating churches) developed by
missionary leaders Henry Venn of the British Church Missionary Society
(CMS, evangelical Anglican) and Rufus Anderson of the American Board
(Congregational) – a practice to be adopted early in Pentecostal missions. In
1876 Taylor founded the Methodist Conference of South India and started
work in Australia. He expressed his convictions in a significant 1879 publication, *Pauline Methods of Missionary Work.* After opposition to his independent
methods he went to Chile in 1877, where he founded the Methodist Episcopal
Church – from which the Methodist Pentecostal Church was to emerge over
three decades later. In 1884, Taylor became 'missionary bishop' of Africa,
where he remained until his retirement in 1896, establishing churches in
Liberia, the Congo, Angola, South Africa and Mozambique. Taylor probably
did more to further the global spread of US Methodism than any other person,
and his consequent influence on the spread of early Pentecostal missions
was significant.[5] After his death, the *Christian Witness,* a prominent Holiness
periodical, gave a eulogy in which Taylor was declared to be 'one of the
greatest evangelists the world has ever seen since the days of the Apostle Paul'.
He had been 'true to the experience and doctrine of holiness as taught by John
Wesley' and 'his greatest work was opening the interior of Africa to the
gospel'. It claimed that only 'holiness people' who had 'professed the second
blessing could be found to go with him on this "foolhardy" project' and he was
'a living monument of the blessing that true holiness is to both the church and
the world'.[6] The implication of this high praise was that the 'second blessing'
of holiness was the motivation for Taylor's missionary zeal. Several of the
prominent early Pentecostal leaders and missionaries discussed in this book

such as T. B. Barratt in Europe, Minnie Abrams and Albert Norton in India, the Hoovers in Chile, the Meads in Angola and J. M. L. Harrow and John Perkins in Liberia had been associated with Taylor's various missions across the globe and were deeply influenced by his independent ecclesiology and stress on 'indigenous' churches. This was to have profound repercussions for the shape of Pentecostalism later on.

During the late nineteenth century Methodism was polarized between those in the Holiness movement like Taylor who believed that Wesley's 'Christian perfection' teaching involved a distinct experience of 'sanctification' and those in mainstream Methodism who did not. The Holiness movement was a reaction to liberalism and formalism in established Protestant churches as a whole, and not just the Methodist Church. Its main principles were a biblical literalism – including paradoxically, extensive use of allegory, symbolism and typology; the need for a personal, emotional and individual experience of conversion; and the moral perfection or 'holiness' of the Christian individual. A revival in 1857–8 in the northeast USA fuelled a new expectancy in the Holiness movement, linking the 'second blessing' experience with a worldwide revival – the 'latter rain' that would precede the soon return of Christ. The teachers of premillennialism believed that Christ would come again at any moment to set up a thousand-year rule on earth, but they also promoted the conviction that all those who were not Christians were doomed to eternal damnation, and prayed fervently for the conversion of the 'heathen' world before Christ's imminent return. There was a sharp increase in volunteers for missionary service overseas. Like its Pietist predecessors, the Holiness movement put great emphasis on 'foreign missions' and began to link the experience of the Spirit with the command of Christ to go to the whole world with the gospel.

Developments within the Holiness movement itself and the influence of other revival movements resulted in it becoming less Methodist in orientation in the late nineteenth century, and the term 'Pentecostal' became more prominent. The experience of the Spirit was linked with a search for the 'power' of Pentecost – a new development that was to gain momentum and overtake the earlier emphasis on 'perfection'. Phoebe Palmer, one of the most prominent leaders in the US Holiness movement, began to refer to holiness as 'the full baptism of the Holy Spirit', and Oberlin College president Asa Mahan wrote in 1870 of 'the baptism of the Holy Ghost' with the main consequence being 'power'.[7] By this time, popular evangelical literature was filled with Pentecostal imagery with its twin themes of holiness and power, a literature that has been called 'proto-Pentecostal'.[8] These eschatological, missiological and pneumatological emphases dominated all evangelical publications in the mid-nineteenth century. Towards the end of the century, prominent Holiness teachers began to say that spiritual gifts were connected to the power of the Spirit and should still be operating. Some spoke of Spirit baptism as a 'third blessing' to be sought, separating Spirit baptism from sanctification – but this idea was rejected by most Holiness leaders.

The major churches, which by the latter half of the nineteenth century had become middle-class establishments and rather nervous of the vast numbers of new, enthusiastic converts from the working classes, did not really support these principles, or at least did not emphasize them any longer. Although most of the Holiness associations had sprung up within Methodism, Methodist leaders began to denounce the 'second blessing' teaching with its accompanying emotionalism. The result was that gradually, several separate Holiness churches were created by the end of the century, characterized by revivalism and accompanied by ecstatic phenomena in camp meetings and revival campaigns across North America. One revival in 1896 in a group called the Christian Union in North Carolina was accompanied by healings and, according to some reports, speaking in tongues by 130 people.[9] Church of God (Cleveland) historians link this event with the emergence of their denomination. The Holiness camp meetings and conventions were held regularly all over the country and were often accompanied by ecstatic phenomena, heightening expectation for these to increase as the revival spread around the world. One report of Burning Bush meetings in Grosvenor Dale, Connecticut in 1902 described these phenomena that would rival any neo-Pentecostal 'revival' at the end of the twentieth century. The scene

> beggared description; elderly ladies, with faces radiant, and uplifted to heaven, waving handkerchiefs, cloaks or anything at hand, leaping, shouting, and praising God; young ladies who would grace any drawing room, prostrate under the power, with holy shouts and praises; middle-aged men doubled up like jack knives, holding their sides with holy laughter; fifteen to twenty in the air at a time. No one could preach, for they could not have been heard had they attempted it. Some outsiders left in consternation, while others remained to look on. Others were under tremendous conviction. Beloved, it is the Holy Ghost.[10]

Between 1895 and 1905 over twenty Holiness denominations were set up including the Church of God (1886), the Christian and Missionary Alliance (1887), the Pentecostal Church of the Nazarene (1895), the black-led Church of God in Christ (1896) and the International Apostolic Holiness Union, later Pilgrim Holiness Church and Wesleyan Church (1897) – thus creating a precedent for the further fragmentation that occurred in Pentecostalism. These new denominations were not all of the 'Methodist' variety, as some had arisen in Reformed and Baptist revivalist circles, but they all immediately involved themselves in intensive missions to 'foreign' lands as evidence of their wholehearted commitment to God for the proclamation of the gospel to all nations in the 'last days'. Indeed, foreign missionary service in these groups was seen as the supreme evidence of spirituality and devotion, an ideal that was passed on to the Pentecostal movement.

Evangelical Revivalism and Missionary Fervour

The Methodist-Holiness movement was not the only important influence on Pentecostal missions. American revivalism included a different and more Reformed stream that stressed the role of the emotions in changing lives.[11] The understanding of Wesley's doctrine in American Methodism and the Holiness movement was further shaped by the emphasis on experience in the earlier

Reformed revivalism of Jonathan Edwards and the later 'Oberlin Perfection-ism' of revivalists Charles Finney and Asa Mahan. Because Methodism was the largest denomination in nineteenth-century North America, ideas of sanc-tification as a distinct experience spilled over into Reformed revivalism. Charles Finney (1792–1876), a Congregational minister and the best-known revivalist in the mid-nineteenth century, had an experience in 1821 in his law office which he described as a 'face to face' encounter with Christ and an experience he called 'a mighty baptism of the Holy Spirit'. The Spirit descended on him, as he put it, 'like a wave of electricity, going through and through me. Indeed it seemed to come in waves and waves of liquid love . . . I literally bellowed out the unutterable gushings of my heart.' Finney equated this 'baptism of the Holy Spirit' with an overwhelmingly emotional experience of 'joy and love', and 'present sanctification'. He believed that 'Christian per-fection' or 'entire sanctification' was 'attainable in this life', and here followed the Holiness ideas.[12] He was not a pie-in-the-sky preacher, however, as his message made a deep social impression. He was involved in reform move-ments like the anti-slavery efforts and the 'underground railroad' before the Civil War.[13] But Finney's dependence on the presence of the Spirit throughout his ministry gave his message a profound emotional impact. His revivalist theology was another great influence on the Keswick movement and on the major part of North American Pentecostalism. His spiritual successors, popu-lar evangelists Dwight L. Moody and especially Reuben A. Torrey took his ideas well into the twentieth century. Moody described his own 'experience of God' in which 'God revealed Himself to me, and I had such experience of His love that I had to ask Him to stay His hand'. He clearly distinguished between sanctification and the power of the Spirit, and wrote of a need to have 'the power of the Holy Ghost resting on us for Christian life and service'.[14] Consequently, in these circles the power of the Spirit came to be inextricably linked with 'foreign' missions.

The Keswick Convention, which began annual gatherings in the English Lake District in 1875, recognized two distinct experiences of the 'new birth' and the 'fullness of the Spirit' and represented another major influence on Pentecostalism. Although the 'fullness of the Spirit' was seen in terms of 'holi-ness' or the 'higher Christian life', Keswick was more affected by Reformed teachers like American Presbyterian A. T. Pierson and the South African Dutch Reformed revivalist Andrew Murray, Jr., who taught that sanctification was a possible but progressive experience. Being filled with the fullness of God, he wrote, was 'the highest aim of the Pentecostal blessing' and attainable by the believer who would prepare for it by humility and faith. Although Murray continued to link the 'fullness of the Spirit' with purity and 'overcoming sin', he added the new Keswick emphasis on power for service to others, what he called 'the full blessing of Pentecost'.[15] His expectations regarding the restora-tion of spiritual gifts to the Church were recorded in the quotation at the start of this chapter.

Increasingly in the Holiness and revivalist movements, the phrase 'baptism with the Spirit' was used to indicate the 'second blessing'. By the end of the nineteenth century, Spirit baptism in Keswick and elsewhere was no longer understood primarily in terms of holiness, but as empowering for mission service. Keswick meetings became international events and always featured prominent missionary speakers (including Pandita Ramabai from India), emphasizing the need for the 'higher Christian life' in missionary service.[16] Murray, Pierson and other leaders wrote regular reports to the Christian press on the work of missions. Pierson as editor of *The Missionary Review of the World* was one of the most influential mission motivators in the western world, regarding missions as 'the indispensable proof and fruit of all spiritual life'.[17] In particular, the change of emphasis was taught by Reuben Torrey, Moody's junior associate and successor, who wrote that 'the Baptism with the Holy Spirit' was a definite experience 'distinct from and additional to His regenerating work' and 'always connected with and primarily for the purpose of testimony and service'. Torrey wrote further that Spirit baptism was 'not primarily for the purpose of making us individually holy', and that the power received during Spirit baptism varied according to 'a wide variety of manifestations of that one Baptism with that one and same Spirit'.[18]

Although Torrey endorsed the belief that Spirit baptism would be accompanied by 'manifestations' or gifts of the Spirit, he (like many in evangelical revivalist circles) reacted to the new Pentecostal movement and declared that 'the teaching that speaking with tongues was the inevitable and invariable result of being baptised with the Holy Spirit' was 'utterly unscriptural and anti-scriptural'.[19] Nevertheless, Torrey's influence on the doctrine of Spirit baptism as being distinct from and subsequent to conversion (the central and most distinctive theme of Pentecostal doctrine) was considerable, and his writings were quoted widely (if selectively) by Pentecostals. By the end of the nineteenth century, the idea grew that there would be a great outpouring of the Spirit throughout the world before the second coming of Christ – and it was hoped, at the beginning of the twentieth century – and that those upon whom the Spirit had fallen were to prepare for this by offering themselves for missionary service. Mission was thereby given a new pneumatological and eschatological dimension that was to become the preoccupation of early Pentecostals.[20]

By the turn of the century there were three distinct groups of holiness adherents. First, there was the Wesleyan holiness position typified by Phoebe Palmer, who said that 'entire sanctification' or 'perfect love' was the 'second blessing' or baptism with the Spirit and identified it with moral purity. Second was the Reformed and Keswick position, best expressed by Torrey, who held that the baptism with the Spirit was an enduement with power for service. Torrey would add that there would be evidence of some manifestation of the Spirit – a position with which Pentecostals heartily agreed. Third was the 'third blessing', a radical fringe position, which had both the 'second blessing' of sanctification and a 'third blessing' of 'baptism with fire' – again an enduement with power. The first American Pentecostals were to follow this third position, but equated the 'third blessing' with 'baptism with the Spirit', usually evidenced by speaking in tongues.[21] All these different holiness and evangelical groups made mission service their highest priority. They were the source out of which Pentecostalism gradually surfaced as a distinct movement.

There were other revivals with charismatic phenomena, not directly related to events in North America. In 1902, F. B. Meyer wrote of a revival among

Baptists in Estonia led by Baron Uex Kuell, in which speaking in tongues was frequently encountered together with interpretations about the soon coming of Christ, and in 1905 a similar revival was reported in Sweden.[22] In the first decade of the twentieth century, the Christian and Missionary Alliance (CMA) encouraged revivals among its missionaries where spiritual gifts were often in evidence. The idea of a worldwide revival to precede the 'soon coming King' became a prominent theme in early Pentecostalism and was an important reason for the frantic mission activity that came in the movement's wake, an emphasis traced in the following chapters.

The point is that early North American Pentecostalism received most of its leaders, its missionaries, and many of its members from the strands of these various Holiness and revivalist movements. In particular, non-denominational 'faith missions' like the China Inland Mission, the CMA and the Sudan Interior Mission (among many others) were established from 1865 onwards to give expression to this revivalist emphasis. The mission activities of the Holiness and revivalist movements were linked to their belief that the gospel had to be preached with urgency to every nation on earth before the imminent coming of Christ, and that the 'heathen nations' of the world were in desperate need of their help. Pentecostal mission history is permanently wedded to this premillennial conviction. Mission historian Brian Stanley writes of 'a new and powerful stream of evangelical spirituality' that emerged during the nineteenth century as a result of these various revival and Holiness movements, 'a piety of radical consecration to the ideals of holiness and absolute submission to the will of God', and one that 'lived in conscious anticipation of the immanence of the second coming'.[23] The followers of this radical evangelicalism saw ultimate sacrifice and commitment to the Lord to be found in service in the foreign 'mission fields'. Significantly, the majority of the missionary volunteers (possibly two-thirds) were women. In mission service, women had found a public role abroad for which there was little room at home, either in the churches they were part of or in other forms of public life.

Furthermore, the foreign missionary was seen as an exotic, romantic adventurer, and for the home constituency these missionaries were often their only contact with 'distant shores', the stuff that both popular adventure novels and the reports of intrepid explorers were made of. Following in the wake of David Livingstone and others, the missionaries brought home peculiar and colourful stories of encounters with strange cultures and even stranger, 'demonic' religions. The dramatic martyrdom of John Williams in 1839 in the South Pacific began a tradition of missionary heroism in popular evangelicalism.[24] This was just as true of Pentecostal missionaries, whom Wacker has characterized as 'the true celebrity-heroes of the movement'.[25] Missionaries were somewhat idealized heroes whose reports in the periodicals and their deputizing on 'homeland furloughs' had a profound effect both on their home culture and on evangelical Christianity as a whole. For some it confirmed their prejudices against the so-called 'primitive' and distant lands, but for others there was a more positive result. As Bays and Wacker have put it: 'The missionary culture placed a human face on the alien, making it seem less distant, less foreign.'[26]

As a result of this public interest in the activities of missionaries, evangelical churches placed mission high on their list of priorities and missionaries were given considerable support, both materially and spiritually. This was strengthened by a revivalist theology that linked the power of the Spirit being poured out in the last days with missionary service. Protestant and evangelical 'faith' missions all over the world were affected by it. Leader of the CMA, A. B. Simpson, reported that his organization had been able to send out over three hundred missionaries in the seven years since its founding. He pleaded for a greater number of missionaries and support from the USA.[27] For Simpson, the degradation and poverty he witnessed were a direct result of the religions of the 'Orient'. Only a massive influx of western missionaries could alleviate this desperate situation, was the repeated appeal of these evangelical leaders to their sympathetic audiences. One missionary in India writing 'in the midst of dense heathenism' expressed the conviction of many of these missionaries that they had come from their 'Christian' nations to 'utter darkness' with the light of the gospel: 'our Arch-Enemy raged at this invasion of his territory'.[28]

These appeals certainly worked – for by 1899 it was estimated that there were 11,695 Protestant 'missionaries in foreign lands'. Missionary appeals appearing in periodicals were often based on population statistics that emphasized the great number of missionaries still needed to 'reach' the vast millions of 'heathen', giving estimated numbers of people to each missionary in the hundreds of thousands. China and India received special attention, China alone having more people than the whole of North America, South America and Africa combined and needing the greatest number of missionaries.[29] A graphic example of this use of statistics to recruit missionaries was provided by Scottish pastor Gordon McLeod, whose depiction of 'the crying need of a world without God' was published in 1899:

> The No-Church is the largest on earth. It numbers three fourths of the human race. It is marching on, while I write, a thousand millions strong. A thousand millions! Imagination fairly staggers under such a figure. Suppose this unspeakable army were to file before you at the rate of one a minute: it would be 5844 A.D. when the last man drew up, walking twelve hours a day; in a year, a quarter of a million; and in forty years, ten millions would have passed you, leaving 990 millions yet to come. You would have to stand on that spot 3960 years to see the rear of this prodigious host! All these are now living, and in a few years will be dead, having never heard so much as that there was a Saviour.[30]

The common belief in evangelical circles was that revivals would result in increased missionary activities. This was not just a case of 'from the West to the rest'. Reports of the revivals in India, for example, were accompanied by the news of 'the establishment of home and foreign missionary societies in the Native Church', and these were initiated completely by Indian Christians themselves.[31]

This was the stream of missionary fervour at the beginning of the twentieth century in the midst of which Pentecostalism arose. This new movement was actually an extension of the missionary movement and was to become a major player in the remarkable globalization of evangelical Christianity within a relatively short period. The words from the first issue of the Azusa Street revival newspaper quoted at the beginning of this chapter reveal the essence of the Pentecostal missionary thrust. 'Many are speaking in new tongues', it gushed, 'and some are on their way to the foreign fields, with the gift of the language.' In this way God was 'solving the missionary problem, sending out new-tongued missionaries on the apostolic faith line, without purse or scrip, and the Lord is going before them preparing the way'. The 'missionary problem' was how to get enough missionaries out all over the world in the shortest possible time without any unnecessary delays like theological preparation and language learning.[32] Pentecostals believed they had the short-cut to missionary preparedness. They continued the revivalist emphases of the movements out of which they emerged, convinced that a worldwide revival was preceding the soon coming of Christ.

Early Pentecostal missionaries followed their revivalist compatriots in thinking of 'mission' as 'foreign mission' (mostly cross-cultural, from 'white' to 'other' peoples), and they were mostly untrained and inexperienced. Their only qualification was the baptism in the Spirit and a divine call, their motivation was to evangelize the world before the imminent coming of Christ – and so evangelism was more important than education or 'civilization'. Pentecostal workers from the western world usually saw their mission in terms of from a civilized, Christian 'home' to a Satanic and pagan 'foreign land', where sometimes their own personal difficulties, prejudices (and possible failures) in adapting to a radically different culture, living conditions and religion were projected in their newsletters home. They went out, like many other Christian missionaries before them, with a fundamental conviction that the western world was a Christian realm, that they were sent as light to darkness, and that the ancient cultures and religions of the nations to which they were sent were heathen, pagan and demonic, to be conquered for Christ. This was part of their evangelical conviction that 'heathen idolatry' was a manifestation of rebellion against the true God.[33]

Various revivals occurred within a few years of each other in different parts of the world in the first decade of the twentieth century. These revivals had a decidedly 'Pentecostal' character, with gifts of the Spirit such as healings, tongues, prophecy and other 'miraculous' signs. They were a conscious and deliberate attempt by ordinary people to adapt revivalist Christianity to their own local contexts, thereby giving expression to their desire for a satisfying and relevant religious life. The Azusa Street revival in Los Angeles (1906–8) was one such revival, regarded by most classical Pentecostals as the main centre of origin for early Pentecostalism. In turn, those revivals seen by the Azusa Street revivalists as having special significance for them were those in Wales and India. Frank Bartleman, eyewitness and chronicler of the Azusa Street revival, made an interesting statement some two decades afterwards about the origins of the movement of which he was a part: 'The present worldwide revival was rocked in the cradle of little Wales. It was brought up in India, following; becoming full-grown in Los Angeles later.' By this he meant that Pentecostalism was the outgrowth of two earlier revival movements: the Welsh Revival of 1904–5, a Holy Spirit revival movement that brought several thousands to Christian faith, and the revival in India at Ramabai's Mukti Mission in Kedgaon, near Pune in 1905–7, to be considered in detail later. But

Bartleman also implied that these earlier revivals were less developed or 'full-grown' than the one in Los Angeles. These revivals represented the birth and adolescence of the 'world-wide restoration of the power of God'.[34] As we will see however, the Indian revival was at least as 'full-grown' a Pentecostal revival as that of Azusa Street, and took place before word of the Los Angeles happenings had reached India.[35]

The Welsh Revival (1904–5) was centred mainly among the Welsh-speaking mining community, where there were some 87,000 converts in the four main Nonconformist churches throughout the country. This revival made a far greater impact internationally than did that under Parham in Kansas. During it the Pentecostal presence and power of the Holy Spirit were emphasized, meetings were hours long, spontaneous, seemingly chaotic and emotional, with 'singing in the Spirit' using ancient Welsh chants, simultaneous and loud prayer, revelatory visions and prophecies, all emphasizing the immediacy of God in the services. Revival leader Evan Roberts (1878–1951) taught a personal experience of Holy Spirit baptism to precede any revival. The revival was declared to be the end-time Pentecost of Acts 2, the 'latter rain' promised by biblical prophets that would result in a worldwide outpouring of the Spirit. Elisabeth Sisson, who received Spirit baptism and spoke in tongues while reading an account of the revival in November 1904, believed that the Welsh Revival was the beginning of a worldwide revival in which millions would be converted and 'hundreds of thousands of new missionaries' sent out. She had this revelation 'some months before God's power had broken out in Los Angeles, or we had heard of it in Pandita Ramabai's work, or in the Khassia or Janta Hills'.[36]

Several early British Pentecostal leaders, including George Jeffreys, founder of the Elim. Pentecostal Church, his brother Stephen and Daniel Williams, founder of the Apostolic Church, were converted in the Welsh revival. The first leader of Pentecostalism in Britain, Anglican vicar Alexander Boddy, also visited it and shared a pulpit with Evan Roberts. Although Roberts, influenced by his mentor Jesse Penn-Lewis, later discouraged the use of tongues and although Pentecostalism's emphases were found in the radical and less common manifestations of the revival, early Pentecostal leaders (especially in Britain) drew their inspiration from this revival and saw their movement as growing out of and continuing it. Interestingly, both movements used an abundance of cultural forms to express their experiences and liturgy, the Welsh Revival encouraging a resurgence of the Welsh language, particularly in the singing of hymns and chants.[37] During the Keswick Convention of 1905, the emotionalism of 300 Welsh delegates influenced an unofficial all-night prayer meeting that went, according to an observer, 'out of control'. A. T. Pierson described the meeting and the unfamiliar manifestations of speaking in tongues there as 'disturbing anarchy' and 'a Satanic disturbance'. This appears to be the first twentieth-century appearance of tongues in Britain, prior to those of London and Sunderland.[38]

Pentecostal-like revival movements with prophecy, speaking in tongues, interpretations of tongues, visions, and other manifestations of the Spirit's presence had been known in South India since the revival of 1860–5 under the ministry of the Tamil Christian, John Christian Arulappan. Trained as a CMS evangelist and influenced by the Brethren missionary Anthony Norris Groves, Arulappan lived by faith and worked independently of the missionaries at an agricultural Christian community he founded called Christianpettah. The revival movement started with women and resulted in increased mission activity by Indian Christians.[39] It was followed by another revival initiated by Arulappan's disciples in Travancore (Kerala) in 1874–5, with similar manifestations. T. B. Barratt, the pioneer of Pentecostalism in Europe, discovered that his Indian interpreter Joshua had received Spirit baptism with tongues in 1897, and a missionary mentions it occurring at a girls' orphanage in Gujarat in 1903.[40] The Welsh Revival spread to other parts of the world through Welsh missionaries and in 1905 revivals broke out in the Khassia and Janta hills in north-east India and in Madagascar, both areas where Welsh Presbyterian missionaries were working – but in the latter, also Scandinavian missionaries. According to the reports, these revivals began with local people rather than with missionaries and were accompanied by ecstatic phenomena and miracles of healing.[41]

Hot on the heels of these events was the revival at Pandita Ramabai's Mukti Mission for young widows and orphans in Kedgaon near Pune, commencing in 1905 and lasting two years. This revival made the Mukti Mission a very important centre of international significance for Pentecostalism and will be considered in detail in the fourth chapter. In 1905 western evangelical periodicals reported on both happenings in Wales and India, heightening expectations of a worldwide revival.[42] Elisabeth Sisson wrote of the Welsh revival as the beginnings of a worldwide revival on 'all flesh', the 'latter rain' prophesied by the prophet Joel.[43] Minnie Abrams wrote in 1910 of a whole sequence of interconnected revivals, from Torrey's meetings in Australia in 1903, to the Welsh Revival and the Indian revivals, and from Mukti to Korea, Manchuria and the rest of China. Holiness periodicals, such as J. H. King's *Live Coals* and A. B. Crumpler's *The Holiness Advocate*, reported on the series of revivals in India.[44] Bartleman also documented the influence that reports of the Indian revivals had on their expectations for Los Angeles,[45] and the Azusa Street mouthpiece was to declare only months after their own revival that 'Pentecost has come and is coming in India, and thank God in many other places'.[46]

The 'Korean Pentecost' of 1907–8 commenced at a convention in Pyongyang under the Presbyterian elder Sun Ju Kil and followed an earlier revival that had begun among Methodist missionaries in Wonsan in 1903 – none of which seemed to have had any direct influence on international Pentecostalism at the time, although these events did not escape the notice of the Pentecostal press. These revivals were commonly affected by the North American Holiness movement and revivals elsewhere – especially the one in north-east India.[47] Canadian Methodist missionary Robert Hardie, one of the leaders of the 1903 revival, described his experience as 'baptism of the Holy Spirit'.[48] Missionaries who had visited the revivals in Wales and India visited Korea and inspired the Korean Presbyterians to expect a similar event. The Korean revival, like those in Wales and India, was part of the international Holiness revivals characterized by emotional repentance with loud weeping and simultaneous prayer. Eyewitness William Blair likened the Korean revival to the Day of Pentecost in Acts 2. The 'Korean Pentecost' soon spread throughout the country, Blair recording that 'Christians returned to their homes in the country taking the Pentecostal fire with them'.[49] Hundreds of Korean preachers went out with these revival fires. This was a specifically Korean revival, whose features still characterize both Protestant and Pentecostal churches in Korea today: prayer meetings held daily in the early morning, all-night prayer meetings, vocal simultaneous prayer, Bible study, and an emphasis on evangelism and missions. But beyond these features are other Pentecostal practices like Spirit baptism, healing the sick, miracles and casting out demons.

As was the case in India, national evangelists, especially Sun Ju Kil with his teaching of premillennial dispensationalism and later the Presbyterian pastor Ik Du Kim, famous for his healing and miracle ministry, probably took the revival movement into a more 'Pentecostal' direction than the western missionaries were comfortable with. Although there are no recorded specific instances of speaking in tongues, one report on the revival by a Presbyterian missionary suggested that there might have been. Korean leaders in Pyongyang prayed 'in their world-forgotten language of antiquity', and visiting Chinese Christians 'in their unintelligible monosyllables'.[50] Pentecostal papers also reported on the Korean revival, one comparing the revival to that of Wesley and noting the 'extraordinary manifestation of power', then quoting the interesting speculation that 'it would not be so very wonderful if the Korean revival were to usher in such a religious awakening of the Orient as would transform the great Chinese empire and change the face of the whole missionary situation'.[51] By the end of the twentieth century, this prophecy had been fulfilled, perhaps not exactly as imagined. As late as 1911, reports from Korea about 'the greatest weekly prayer meeting in the world' in Pyongyang with 1,100 in attendance, with one-sixth of all Korean Christians training for the ministry, were being published in the Pentecostal press.[52]

Soon after the Korean revival began, similar revivals broke out in 1908 in Manchuria, North China – like Korea at the time under Japanese occupation – and later in 1909–10 in Shandong in north-east China. These revivals were directly inspired by the events in Korea, as one of the missionary leaders there, Jonathan Goforth, had seen the Korean revival. Goforth visited a Pentecostal church, Elim Tabernacle in Rochester, New York in December 1909 to give a 'stirring account of the recent outpouring of God's Spirit in China'. The congregation was 'greatly encouraged and inspired to lay hold of God in a fresh way, crying to Him for even a mightier power that will sweep the earth and thus hasten the coming of our blessed Lord and Redeemer', said the report. Pentecostal missionaries in North China, including Bernt Berntsen, visited the revival meetings of Goforth there.[53] CIM missionary James Webster reported that a Chinese pastor, after thanking the missionaries for bringing the gospel to China, remarked that 'the Holy Spirit came down from Heaven. You could not send Him to us.' The missionary replied that they could now 'take a back seat' because it would 'not do any longer for us to exercise lordship over God's heritage in China'.[54] The revival movement was thus recognized as the means by which the Spirit was creating an independent Chinese church.

The point was that these various international revival movements were the soil in which a locally contextual Pentecostalism grew and thrived. Two in particular: the revival in an African American mission in downtown Los

Angeles and the one in an Indian mission near Pune, were to have global significance for developing Pentecostalism. We will consider in more detail the impact of these two revival movements on Pentecostal missions in the next two chapters. These various revivals were fires that rapidly spread to other places. The Anglican vicar Alexander Boddy, leader of Pentecostalism in Britain, visited the Pentecostal revival under T. B. Barratt in Christiania (Oslo), Norway in 1907 and wrote that he would not easily forget these four days. He compared it to the time when he had been with Evan Roberts during the Welsh Revival, but said that the scenes in the Torvegadon Mission Room and other places in Norway were 'more supernatural'. Boddy believed that 'very soon we shall witness the same in England'.[55]

So it was that these various revivals created an air of expectancy across the Christian world for a worldwide revival that had never been seen before, that would result in unprecedented missionary activity across the globe.[56] Many believed that 1906 was the beginning of such a revival, but to that we return in the next chapter.

Imperialism and Mission

Although I think that the context for the emergence of Pentecostalism was primarily a religious one and that the socio-political context is often given exaggerated prominence in literature discussing the emergence of religious movements, yet socio-political factors almost always affect the further development and growth of a movement, even in its early stages. Pentecostalism is no exception and this is why understanding its socio-political context is important. We cannot separate the spiritual experiences of Pentecostal missionaries and their converts from the wider context of political, economic and social power. The beginning of the twentieth century was the heyday of modern imperialism, when the nations of Western Europe and the USA governed and exploited the majority of the world's peoples, using the vast natural resources of the rest of the world to sustain their expanding capitalist economies. It has been estimated that European powers together controlled some 85 per cent of the world's surface by 1914. The beginning of the twentieth century was a time when international trade, migration and capital flows were increasing so that Europe and North America could increase wealth and produce industrial goods for profit.[57] As a result of this rampant imperialism, the nineteenth century had seen a single global economy emerge, and the movement of goods, people and money linked the most remote and still pristine parts of the world with the bureaucratic nation-states of Europe and the USA. The development of railway and steamship lines accelerated at the turn of the century, with the result that previously unreachable areas were now accessible to European and American traders, colonizers and, of course, missionaries.

Missionary newsletters enthused about the opening up of the 'heart of Africa' through such ventures as the Uganda Railway and its accompanying telegraph line, which by 1899 had reached 300 miles inland from Mombasa, 'where our missionaries land', wrote one paper.[58] Postal services were greatly improved, all of which proved invaluable for the rapid and unprecedented dissemination of Pentecostal literature. By 1907, letters from missionaries in what were (for westerners) remote corners of the world were often published a month after they were written. China had been forced by the western powers to open up its interior to foreign traders and missionaries by 1860, and the missionaries tacitly accepted this imperialist aggression and availed themselves of its privileges.[59] Africa had been arbitrarily parcelled out between the main Western European colonial powers by the Conference of Berlin in 1884–5, and by the turn of the century these powers were still seeking to establish their hegemony over that continent – although Britain and France between them controlled most of it. British missionary David Livingstone had called Africa the 'open sore of the world' and missionary reports constantly referred to it as the 'Dark Continent' and 'Darkest Africa'.

At the same time, Britain's Queen Victoria had declared herself Empress of India, and Britain, France, the USA and other colonizing nations were establishing treaties with various Asian governments, thus further extending their influence and control over countries they regarded as politically and militarily impotent. This was especially true of the vast nation of China, as western nations vied with each other for dominance there. By 1914 most of the world outside Europe and the two Americas was dominated by a handful of western nations, with a few exceptions like Korea and Taiwan (occupied by the single Asian colonizing power, Japan) and Ethiopia (which had successfully resisted colonization).[60] There was an almost universal belief in the superiority of western culture and civilization. The effect of this was massive and pervaded the thinking of all westerners with little exception. Edward Said describes this as 'a general worldwide pattern of imperial culture' that 'differentiates "us" from "them", almost always with some degree of xenophobia'.[61] The popular imagination was fired by the 'success' of the British Empire in particular, and this imperialist ideology remained a significant influence on western culture throughout the twentieth century – although tempered as it was by two devastating world wars.

Stanley points out that this popular 'humanitarian idealism' conceived of empire as a 'sacred trust', and resulted in the promotion of Christianity hand-in-hand with western education in the colonized territories.[62] Marxist historian Eric Hobsbawm writes of the same connection between imperial policies and popular imagination: 'the idea of superiority to, and domination over, a world of dark skins in remote places was genuinely popular, and thus benefited the politics of imperialism'. The imperial military parades held at home were made all the more resplendent by the presence of colonized peoples in traditional dress, 'the world of what was considered barbarism at the service of civilisation'. This was a time when non-European societies were seen as 'inferior, undesirable, feeble and backward, even infantile'.[63]

The important point for this study is that this rampant colonialism, popular imperialistic ideology and Darwinian socialism was transferred into the ecclesiastical realm and reflected in the attitudes of missionaries, who so often moved in the shadows of the colonizers. Stanley shows that British missionaries were moulded by a public mood that gave a high degree of respect to British imperialism.[64] A missionary of the Africa Evangelistic Mission writing from Nigeria in 1906 expressed a clear example of this, saying that they had 'lived to see these cruel Mohammedan kingdoms fall before British arms, the many pagan tribes come beneath the same civilized rule'. The result was that within less than five years the 'whole vast territory' (of the Western Sudan) had been 'thrown wide open to Christianity and commerce'.[65] It was this confusion between 'Christianity' on the one hand, and 'civilized rule' and 'commerce' on the other, that was a major hindrance for these missionaries, one that prevented them from entering fully into the necessary identification with the people to whom they had gone. In another African context, this was a 'civilizing colonialism' that 'sought to inscribe in "barbarous" Africans the precepts of a largely Protestant, Western modernity . . . and to implant in their minds dreams of a "rational", Christian community of peasant individualists drawn away from what was perceived as heathen abjection in degrading tribal conditions'.[66] This was the ideology that fired the hearts of colonialists and missionaries alike, and the belief lingered long into the twentieth century.

This is not to say that the missionaries were *always* agents and co-conspirators with imperialists, but missionaries from western countries, including Pentecostals, inevitably saw themselves as representing a superior, 'Christian' civilization. They expected and often received much more admiration from the local people than they would ever have received at home – and in any case, they enjoyed the privileges of the colonial rulers, no matter what their social status might have been where they came from. This was especially the case in Africa. Pentecostal missionaries were, like all missionaries, the products of a particular invented tradition, those cultural practices that functioned according to their own accepted rules of behaviour, norms and attitudes regarded as in continuity with the past.[67] So, for example, the British Pentecostal Missionary Union saw its work in China in continuity with the tradition of the China Inland Mission, and adopted similar practices. The writings of the western Pentecostal missionaries and their representatives were loaded with the assumptions drawn from the power and privilege of the society and tradition of which they were part.

However, the theory that missionaries were the religious expression of the colonialists is often based on ideological presuppositions rather than on tangible historical evidence.[68] Although there is only a little in the sources on early Pentecostal missionaries showing any serious critique of colonialism, there were many missionaries who refused to be numbered with the imperialists and who resisted colonialist exploitation to the hilt. Pentecostal missionaries sometimes severely criticized the lifestyles and actions of westerners engaged in commerce and colonial government. The atrocities of the Belgian king Leopold, for example, came in for condemnation by the evangelical press, headlined the 'Congo outrages', and calling him 'the most murderous and merciless of modern times' and even of 'practicing cannibalism on a large scale'.[69] The Pentecostal papers published condemnation of the exploitation and violent abuse of Amerindians in South America, especially the massacres and cruelty being perpetrated by the rubber traders, the Peruvian Amazon Company.[70] But as Hobsbawm has rather cynically put it, 'the success of the Lord was a function of imperialist advance'; and there can surely be little doubt that 'colonial conquest opened the way for effective missionary action'.[71] Missionaries believed that in the providence of God, European nations (especially Britain) had colonized the world in order to bring about its evangelization. Western 'civilization' was seen as 'Christian' civilization; and therefore it was often difficult to separate 'political' from 'Christian' parameters. This was expressed by a Presbyterian missionary in Syria, James Dennis, who wrote in 1908 that missionaries were not only 'ambassadors of Christ, and bearers of His spiritual gifts to men', but were also agents in 'the material blessings of a higher civilization'.[72]

Missionary explorers such as Livingstone also believed that the missionary movement promoted European commercial interests,[73] and they certainly went hand in hand. Missionary leaders such as John R. Mott recognized this. He is recorded as saying, with almost hidden assumptions of ethnocentricity, 'The Sway of Protestant Nations extends over three eighths of the population of Asia and Oceanica [sic]'. He went on to assert that Africa was 'largely under the direct rule of Christian powers' and that as a result of the 'treaties and relationships' between the 'great Protestant nations and nearly all the remainder of the non-Christian world' the 'missionary forces' would be ensured 'the largest freedom of access and all reasonable protection'.[74] Mott was later to temper these views with a more informed approach expressed in 1914, when on the eve of the First World War he warned his Student Volunteer Movement for Foreign Missions of 'the corrupt influences of so-called western civilization ... eating like gangrene into the less highly organized peoples of the world'.[75] But the event that had convinced many of the new evangelical missionaries already indoctrinated with western feelings of superiority that African leadership had failed was the assumed mismanagement and subsequent dismantling of the first African Bishop Samuel Crowther's Niger Mission in the 1880s. This came to a climax when young English clerics challenged the authority of and reprimanded the elderly bishop.[76] All the established missions (Protestant and Catholic) throughout the world had a largely white clergy by 1914, and this situation was to remain at least until the middle of the century. The fundamental conviction that the Protestant missionary enterprise was a campaign against idolatry led in turn to attitudes and actions on the part of its missionaries from the West that can only be described as ethnocentric, bigoted, and at times racist.

Of course, while this period was the heyday of imperialism and missionary paternalism, there was a corresponding rising tide of an anti-colonial nationalism, particularly in India and Africa. Associated with this was increasing opposition to the presence of foreign missionaries, who were seen as accomplices in this intolerable interference in national life. Nationalism was to gain momentum as the twentieth century progressed and culminated in the movements to independence after 1945. But at the beginning of the twentieth century, the seeds of nationalism and independence were already being felt in both the civil and the ecclesiastical spheres, largely through the influence of the western education introduced by missionaries.[77] One of the manifestations of this nationalistic resistance was the rise of independent churches, some of which were already well established by the time Pentecostal missionaries appeared on the scene, especially in Africa.[78] The Pentecostals sometimes absorbed these churches into their own organizations, providing a radical alternative to their independent Christianity, which until that time had been modelled largely on European Protestantism. The independent churches were to imbibe elements of this new Pentecostal spirituality into their particular local expressions of Christianity, and there were many resonances with their traditional spirituality. Several instances of these are treated in the following chapters. But the external socio-political forces had a profound influence on the progress or otherwise of western Pentecostal missions and there was nothing they could do to change that. It is not in the interests of historical accuracy to attempt to separate Pentecostal missionaries from this social and political context.

The Healing Movement

Pentecostalism was in direct continuity with the divine healing movement at the end of the nineteenth century. Gifts of healing are listed among the charismata in the Pauline letters and healing through faith has been practised at different times in the history of the church. Miracles of healing were attributed especially to the activities of Catholic saints and mystics in the Middle Ages. Reformation churches tended to believe that healings were either part of Catholic 'superstition' or Anabaptist 'heresy' and had now ceased. These negative convictions were strengthened by northern European rationalism in the eighteenth and nineteenth centuries. However, such radical groups as Anabaptists and Quakers made claims of healings, John Wesley the founder of Methodism reported occasional miracles of healing in his journal, and healing through prayer was part of the tradition of Pietism.

The healing movement was one of the most important influences on early Pentecostalism and another expression of the popular beliefs on the fringe of Christianity out of which it emerged. In all the divisions that were later to erupt in Pentecostalism, divine healing remained perhaps the only constant on which they all agreed, at least in most of its details. Like the earlier advocates of divine healing, even though they suffered from severe illnesses and many of their missionaries died from tropical diseases, Pentecostals remained unshaken in their conviction that physical divine healing had been restored to the church in the worldwide revival of the last days and was both an indispensable ingredient of their message and the means by which the nations would be brought to faith in Christ. The Pentecostal emphasis on evangelism was not only to 'save souls'; it was also the proclamation of the 'full gospel'. Christ not only came into the world to save people from sin (and 'heathenism') and was the 'Soon Coming King', but he was also Sanctifier, Healer and Baptizer with the Spirit. Pentecostals believed that 'signs and wonders' would follow their preaching in fulfilment of Christ's 'Great Commission'. These themes so filled the work of the missionaries that their converts expected the same to accompany their proclamation. Pentecostals believe that the coming of the Spirit brings an ability to do 'signs and wonders' in the name of Jesus Christ to accompany and authenticate the gospel message. The role of 'signs and wonders', particularly that of healing and miracles, is prominent in Pentecostal mission praxis. It is first necessary to trace the background to these beliefs in the healing movement on the fringes of nineteenth-century evangelicalism.

The nineteenth century brought healing into sharper focus as it became more acceptable within mainline Protestantism. One of the particular reasons for this was the ministry in continental Europe of Johann Christoph Blumhardt (1805–80), of a Pietist background, who for 30 years operated a healing centre in Bad Boll, Germany. His reputation as a healer and exorcist and his Christological emphasis 'Jesus is Victor' were known internationally. Significantly, Blumhardt (like the later Pentecostals) linked the healing ministry of Christ with the power of the Spirit. In Männedorf, Switzerland, Dorothea Trudel (1813–62) and her successor Samuel Zeller (1834–1912) operated a similar centre called Elim for healing through prayer. The fame of Blumhardt and Trudel began to reach the English-speaking world in the second half of the century.

Charles Cullis, an Episcopalian physician in Boston, Massachusetts and a major figure in the Holiness movement, visited Männedorf in 1873 and returned to the USA to pray for the sick in healing conventions, where he linked forgiveness of sin to healing from sickness. Cullis influenced CMA leader A. B. Simpson, who began a healing home in 1884 and wrote about healing provided in the atonement of Christ. Simpson coined the phrase 'Fourfold Gospel' that remained an important concept in Pentecostalism – with 'divine healing' as an essential part, together with regeneration, holiness and the premillennial second coming of Christ. The 'Fourfold Gospel' was popularized in the slogan 'Jesus Christ: Saviour, Healer, Baptizer and Soon Coming King' (with modifications adding 'Sanctifier' and 'Baptizer with the Spirit'). Simpson's CMA missionaries were to play a major role in early Pentecostalism. He was at first sympathetic to the new movement and many of its leaders were associated with his organization. The 'Fourfold Gospel' was emphasized by several Holiness groups at this time. A New England camp meeting in 1902, for example, showed this trend in the advertisement for the event, in which the 'truths and experiences of regeneration and sanctification' were to be 'kept most prominently and emphatically in the forefront while the kindred truths and experiences of divine healing and the personal coming of the Lord' were to be 'given their proper and proportionate emphasis'.[79]

Other figures in the divine healing movement in North America included Boston Baptist minister and associate of Cullis, A. J. Gordon, and Presbyterian W. E. Boardman, who moved to England and set up a faith healing home, Bethshan, in London.[80] Some leaders in the healing movement like Dowie (see below) taught that divine healing was possible without medical assistance while others rejected the 'use of means' (medical science) altogether and although this was not the view of the majority, it was also a feature of early Pentecostalism. Divine healing had become a prominent teaching in the Holiness movement and Reformed revivalism by the beginning of the twentieth century and was taught by such well-known Keswick speakers as Andrew Murray and A. T. Pierson.[81] Murray, Pierson and Simpson all published extensively on divine healing and together formed a theological foundation for it in the late nineteenth century. This emphasis was continued with greater intensity by the Pentecostals, who saw it as an essential part of their message to proclaim throughout the world.

The presence of healing gifts sometimes broke down barriers of gender and race discrimination. One of the earliest healing ministries in North America was that of the African American woman Elizabeth Mix. She prayed for healing from an incurable disease of the Episcopalian woman (later Salvation Army member, CMA leader and finally Pentecostal), Carrie Judd, later Montgomery (1858–1946), and had a formative influence on her healing ministry that Montgomery always acknowledged. For her part, Montgomery taught that healing was part of the gospel of Christ and began her *Triumphs of Faith* monthly periodical in 1881, which continued for almost seven decades until after her death in 1946. The banner during the first four years of this paper declared it was 'devoted to faith-healing, and to the promotion of Christian holiness'. Many, if not most of the articles were on healing and written by women, and some leading ministers in the healing movement (especially Simpson) were featured in different issues. The first issue contained a short article by Elizabeth Mix on the continuation of the gifts of the Spirit, and subsequent issues continued to publish Mix's teachings. Montgomery's early views of physical healing in the atonement were clear, included the rejection of medicine, and remained her conviction for the rest of her life. These views were to typify those of Pentecostals through much of the twentieth century. She wrote, 'Christ bore our sicknesses as well as our sins, and if we may reckon ourselves free from the one, why not from the other? And if, after prayer for physical healing, we reckon the work as already accomplished in our bodies we shall not fear to *act out* that faith, and to make physical exertions which will justify our professed belief in the healing.'[82]

Maria Woodworth-Etter (1844–1924) was a tent evangelist who travelled around the USA in radical evangelical circles, and before the advent of Aimee Semple McPherson at the end of her life, the most popular featured speaker in early American Pentecostalism. She added a message of healing to her evangelistic ministry after 1885, and her meetings were characterized by people 'slain in the Spirit' – another feature of early Pentecostalism – when people would fall to the ground as if unconscious. Montgomery was greatly influenced by Woodworth-Etter. She first wrote in 1890 about a 'wonderful revival work' in Oakland, California 'under a Mrs. Woodworth from Ohio'. Her contacts had told her that 'the power of God was so greatly displayed in these meetings, as to cause many to lose their strength and fall, apparently lifeless, to the ground'. She investigated these meetings herself and was so impressed that she cancelled her own meetings in order to go to these, attended by two to three thousand people. She reported that she had heard 'one of the most solid Gospel sermons to which we have ever listened, delivered in great power of the Holy Ghost'. The result was that 'multitudes of sinners are converted, believers are filled with the Holy Ghost, and the sick are often marvellously healed'.[83] According to Woodworth-Etter's account, speaking in tongues occurred in her tent meetings on several occasions prior to the commencement of Pentecostalism – like Montgomery, she later joined the Pentecostal movement.[84]

John Alexander Dowie (1847–1907) was a prominent and radical healer at the close of the nineteenth century. He was alienated from those associated with the Holiness movement because of his sensationalism, outspoken criticisms and tendency to work in isolation and exclusivism. Born and educated in Scotland and at first a Congregational minister then an independent healing evangelist in Australia, he emmigrated to the USA in 1888 and initiated the Divine Healing Association in 1890. He followed this by founding the Christian (Catholic) Apostolic Church in 1895 as his following grew. The name of this new movement signified that Dowie was in the tradition of the Scottish reformed revivalist Edward Irving, and it is Dowie who forms the link between Irving and Pentecostalism.[85] He set up the first of several healing homes in Chicago and began publishing a periodical, *Leaves of Healing*, that was sent all over the world with testimonies of healing from Dowie's meetings in Zion Tabernacle, the spacious auditorium he had built. In 1900 he set up a city called Zion as a 'theocracy' north of Chicago, Illinois, which grew in five years to about eight thousand residents, with some 200,000 members in his church worldwide.[86]

Many early Pentecostal leaders were undoubtedly influenced by Dowie's views, which were revolutionary ideas at the turn of the century in North America. Dowie with his Reformed roots was somewhat in the Keswick tradition, with a 'Full Gospel' that included 'Salvation, Healing and Holy Living'. Healing for Dowie was part of the atonement, and like some Pentecostals, Dowie's followers shunned medicine, medical doctors and pork. His stress on holiness had a strong social dimension, modelled by the creation of the city of Zion. In 1903 while on a tour in Australia he castigated King Edward VII of Britain for his vices, and in *Leaves of Healing* denounced Britain's colonial treatment of Africans. 'His Voice', the paper declared, 'has ever been raised fearlessly and effectively in behalf of Ethiopia and her people in all parts of the world.'[87] His 'theocracy' sought to be a classless, pacifistic society, was committed to racial and gender equality, sent missionaries overseas, encouraged interracial marriages and supported the disadvantaged. His was a realized eschatology, however, as from 1901 Dowie placed himself in the centre and announced that he was the 'Messenger of the Covenant' prophesied by Malachi, and 'Elijah the Restorer'. In 1904 he declared himself 'First Apostle' of a new end-times church, renamed the Christian Catholic Apostolic Church in Zion. In 1905 Zion City went bankrupt and Dowie suffered a stroke and died in disgrace within two years.

The Zion City community now continued under several factions and Pentecostal preachers like Charles Parham moved in to gather in the spoils. Several early Pentecostal leaders such as healing evangelists F. F. Bosworth and John G. Lake, William Hamner Piper (influential pastor of the Stone Church, Chicago), Marie Burgess Brown (pioneer of Pentecostalism in New York), South African P. L. le Roux, British Pentecostal and leading pacifist Arthur Booth-Clibborn (son-in-law of William Booth), and Gerrit Polman (founder of Dutch Pentecostalism), were all part of Dowie's Zion movement. Alexander Boddy visited Zion City in 1912 and preached in a Pentecostal church there. Dowie made an impact on global Pentecostal mission through his followers who became significant Pentecostal leaders. His radical eschatology included a strong missionary orientation and an emphasis on healing. Dowie's end-time restorationism and his acceptance of people from all walks of life became prominent motifs in Pentecostalism.[88] His Zionist movement was one of the most important formative influences on the growth of both

Pentecostalism and of 'Spirit' African independent churches in southern Africa, where the largest denomination today is called the Zion Christian Church. Millions of 'Zionists' attend large celebrations at African 'Zion Cities', where healing, prophecy and speaking in tongues are often the main activities.

Another influential revivalist and healer at the turn of the twentieth century was Frank Sandford (1862–1948), a former Baptist pastor in Maine who came to an experience of sanctification through the Holiness movement and a belief in divine healing through contact with A. B. Simpson. In 1894 he received an experience of Spirit baptism that he described as an enduement of power. He founded the 'Holy Ghost and Us Bible School' in 1895, where several future Pentecostal leaders were trained. Here, speaking in tongues as known foreign languages was believed to be a sign of the imminent return of Christ and the means by which the world would be evangelized – an idea that Pentecostals would pursue with vigour. Sandford published his first periodical called *Tongues of Fire*, established a large community called Shiloh (a name that Dowie used for his auditorium) whose residents had to give over all their possessions to the community, and purchased ships for the evangelization of the world. Like Dowie, he believed that the end time would be brought nearer by divine/human co-operation; and he motivated his followers into world evangelization through 'signs, wonders, and mighty deeds'. But in 1901 he too called himself 'Elijah the Restorer' and 'First Apostle', six months after Dowie's declaration. Sandford lacked Dowie's ethnic inclusiveness and pacifism, adding emphases on the imminent premillennial return of Christ, 'spiritual warfare' (a form of intercessory prayer) and Anglo-Israelism, the racist theory that the White Anglo-Saxon Protestant nations (especially Britain and the United States) were descended from the 'lost tribes' of Israel. Sandford also later advocated circumcision, observance of Saturday as the Sabbath, and abstinence from pork. 'Israel' was to be a blessing to all nations, which re-inforced his missionary zeal. Although opposed to Pentecostalism, his main impact was the formative influence he had upon Charles Parham, who imbibed many of his teachings, especially that of 'missionary tongues'. Sandford died in relative obscurity.[89]

It was not only in the western world that divine healing was being practised in the nineteenth century. Hsi Shengmo (1836–96), an independent pastor of the China Inland Mission (CMI) in Shansi province in China operated opium refuges in which his own Chinese medicines were used for the treatment of opium addiction, and he was greatly used in casting out demons and healing the sick through prayer. Hsi was no slave to foreign forms of Christianity, criticized by one acquaintance for his 'tendency to exalt things Chinese' and 'not a little under-estimation of the foreign missionary'.[90] Unfortunately, our information on this Chinese Christian healer is miniscule. But it may be that Hsi was one example of other preachers in China and elsewhere in the Majority World for whom divine healing and deliverance from demons was an essential part of Christian ministry in the late nineteenth century. It has to be said, however, that divine healing was rarely part of the Protestant missionary establishment's practice as a whole, and that it was only with the advent of the Pentecostals in the twentieth century that this practice became more wide-spread.

Charles Parham and 'Missionary Tongues'

Many, but by no means all 'classical' Pentecostals (and certainly those first associated with the Azusa Street revival) hold a belief that the baptism in the Spirit is invariably accompanied by the 'initial evidence' of speaking in tongues. The person credited with discovering the doctrine of 'initial evidence' is Charles Fox Parham (1873–1929), but as we will see, his teaching of 'missionary tongues' did not endure in later Pentecostalism. Parham was an independent Kansas healing evangelist who resigned from the Methodist Church in 1895, experienced healing from the consequences of rheumatic fever and began his own healing ministry thereafter. He moved to Topeka, Kansas in 1898 where he opened a healing home and began publishing *The Apostolic Faith* in 1899. There are indications that this periodical was influenced by that of Dowie in Chicago. *The Apostolic Faith* propounded Parham's views on healing in the atonement of Christ (accompanied by abundant testimonies by people claiming healing), premillennialism with the belief in a worldwide revival (the 'latter rain') to precede the imminent coming of Christ, and a 'third blessing' beyond conversion and 'entire sanctification' called 'baptism with the Spirit'.

There is evidence that Parham came to believe in 'missionary tongues' in 1899 through the testimony of one of Frank Sandford's disciples. In February 1900 he met some of Sandford's followers from Shiloh and Sandford himself came to Topeka in June that year. Parham was so impressed that he decided to accompany Sandford to Shiloh and enrol in his Bible school. He accepted Sandford's views, including his Anglo-Israelism and the possibility of foreign tongues given by Spirit baptism to facilitate world evangelization – doctrines that remained with Parham for the rest of his life.[91] The idea of 'missionary tongues' was not new, nor unique to Parham and Sandford. Bartleman recorded the following quotation from A. B. Simpson:

> We are to witness before the Lord's return real missionary 'tongues' like those of Pentecost, through which the heathen world shall hear in their own language 'the wonderful works of God', and this perhaps on a scale of whose vastness we have scarcely dreamed, thousands of missionaries going forth in one last mighty crusade from a united body of believers at home to bear swift witness of the crucified and coming Lord to all nations.[92]

En route to Maine, Parham visited Dowie's Zion City and Simpson's Bible and Missionary Training Institute, among other places. After six weeks of attending Sandford's lectures, hearing speaking in tongues for the first time, and accompanying Sandford on a preaching trip to Canada, Parham returned to Topeka convinced that God had called him to enter a new phase of ministry. He opened Bethel Gospel School in a newly leased building known as Stone's Folly and enrolled 34 students in a short-term school to train for world evangelization, where the only textbook was the Bible. Before leaving on a three-day preaching trip, Parham gave the students the assignment to discover in the book of Acts 'some evidence' of the baptism with the Spirit. He convinced them that they had yet to receive the full outpouring of a second Pentecost, and he called them to seek this with fasting and prayer. They reached the conclusion that the biblical evidence of Spirit baptism was speaking in tongues, which they told Parham on his return. New Year's Eve 1900 was set aside for praying for this experience. A 'watch-night' service was held with great expectation. Throughout New Year's Day of 1901 they prayed and waited until finally at 11p.m., Agnes Ozman asked Parham to lay hands on her to receive the gift of the Spirit. She was the first to speak in tongues, described later by Parham as 'speaking in the Chinese language', and followed by others, including Parham 'in the Swedish tongue' three days later.[93] Although this revival attracted the sceptical curiosity of the local press, for two years there was little acceptance of it. Leading Holiness and healing periodicals, including Montgomery's *Triumphs of Faith* and Otis' *Word and Work* were either unaware of it or did not consider it of any significance.

After the death of the Parhams' son and their move to Kansas City, Parham preached at Holiness missions in Kansas and Missouri in 1903–4, where there were again experiences of tongues and healings. By 1905, several thousand people were said to have received Spirit baptism in this new movement known as the 'Apostolic Faith'. Parham's theology (unlike that of Dowie or Sandford) was in the 'Third Blessing' framework. He formulated the 'evidential tongues' doctrine that became the hallmark of white American Classical Pentecostalism – but unlike them, his theology insisted on the belief that tongues were authentic languages *(xenolalia* or *xenoglossa)* given for the proclamation of the gospel in the end times. These tongues were the second Pentecost that would usher in the end, achieve world evangelization within a short period, and seal the Bride of Christ, the Church. This was the doctrine that was proclaimed by William Seymour at Azusa Street, motivating scores of early Pentecostal people to go out immediately as missionaries and begin to speak in the tongues of the nations to whom they had been called. It is no accident that Parham's biographer, James Goff, subtitles his book 'Charles F. Parham and the *Missionary Origins* of Pentecostalism'. For Goff, the essence of early Pentecostalism is contained in Parham's 'intense millenarian-missions emphasis' and his belief that tongue-speaking was 'specifically xenoglossa'. He wrote that 'this new gift from God signalled the dawn of a missionary explosion' because now through these 'missionary tongues' 'almost anyone could now be christened a missionary'.[94]

We must acknowledge Parham's role in this all-important early motivation for frantic missionary migrations in early Pentecostalism. We must also agree with Goff's thesis of the missionary origins of Pentecostalism – this was primarily and fundamentally a missionary movement from its beginnings to the present day. But it is also necessary to see Parham's role in the light of earlier precedents – especially that of Sandford, Dowie and the healing movement – and to ask how effective he was in actualizing the outflow of these missionaries. He was, as Blumhofer has pointed out, more interested in tongues-speech as an experience of a deeper spirituality, although his wife later said that he aimed to train 'Apostolic Faith' missionaries in Topeka 'to go to the ends of the earth'.[95] Indications are that he did not succeed in taking the missionary potential of his doctrine beyond an 'initial evidence' theory and that his Anglo-Israelism may have contributed to his lack of enthusiasm for 'foreign' missions. After his break with Seymour, his differentiating between 'true' and 'false' tongues in fact stopped any flow of missionaries from his movement altogether. This left Azusa Street and other centres of Pentecostalism to spearhead the American missionary advance.

Although Goff considers Parham to be the founding father of Pentecostalism, he was ultimately rejected from this status by almost the entire North American Pentecostal movement. Thomas Junk, missionary in Shandong, China, rejected his leadership claims in 1909 and E. N. Bell, former Baptist pastor associated with Parham and later first Chairman of the Assemblies of God, wrote a repudiation of Parham in October 1912. He warned 'all Pentecostal and Apostolic Faith people of the churches of God' to 'take notice and be not misled by his claims'.[96] Parham's doctrine of xenoglossa for the proclamation of the gospel was quite different from the doctrine of evidential unknown tongues that later emerged in classical Pentecostalism, although as we will see in later chapters, belief in xenoglossa was widespread in their early years and never repudiated.[97] Some of Parham's other beliefs like Anglo-Israelism, 'soul sleep' and the 'annihilation of the wicked' doctrines were also at variance with generally accepted Pentecostal doctrine.

Unlike his predecessors Dowie and Sandford, Parham did not actively engage in world evangelization. His efforts did not constitute the driving force that resulted in Pentecostalism being quickly transformed into an international missionary movement. That role was filled by his one-time disciple, William Seymour. After his failure to gain control of either Zion City or the Asuza Street revival in 1906 and his arrest in an unproven homosexual scandal in 1907, Parham lost most of his supporters. He spent the last two decades of his life in relative obscurity in Baxter Springs, Kansas, from where he led his Apostolic Faith. He continued to embrace Anglo-Israelism and became increasingly racist in his views, supporting racial segregation. He also had the ignominy of speaking to gatherings of the Ku Klux Klan, who he thought had 'high ideals for the betterment of mankind'.[98] Most Pentecostals in North America distanced themselves from him, especially his claiming to be the sixth angel of the book of Revelation. But despite his many failures, there can be no doubt that it was probably Parham more than anyone else who was responsible for the theological shift in emphasis in early American Pentecostalism to tongues as the 'evidence' of Spirit baptism, given for the evangelization of the nations.

This chapter has sketched a great deal of history that is discussed in more detail elsewhere and to which the interested reader is referred. Pentecostal missions have had many revivalist influences and other impulses, from Pietism to Methodism and the evangelical and Holiness movements, the globalizing forces of imperialism, to the nineteenth-century healing movement with its maverick healers Dowie, Sandford and Parham – the latter with his Apostolic Faith movement and teaching of 'missionary tongues'. These are the various forces from which a new missionary movement of the Spirit emerged in the early twentieth century. The following chapter will trace its more immediate historical and theological context.

Notes

1 Quoted in *UR* 1:1 (June 1909), p.8.
2 Cox, *Fire from Heaven*, p.91.
3 Dayton, *Theological Roots*, pp.44–5, 49–50.
4 *THW*, p.219.
5 Bundy, 'William Taylor', pp.172–6.
6 Reproduced in *WW* 24:6 (June 1902), p.179.
7 Dayton, *Theological Roots*, pp.74, 88–9; Faupel, *Everlasting Gospel*, pp.73–5.
8 Taylor, 'Publish and be Blessed', pp.20–2.
9 Tomlinson, 'Brief History', p.8.
10 *WW* 25:1 (Jan 1903), pp.402–3.
11 Lederle, *Treasures Old and New*, p.15.
12 Rosell and Dupuis, *Original Memoirs*, pp.16–19, 288–90.
13 Rosell and Dupuis, *Original Memoirs*, pp.272, 298; Robert, *Occupy Until I Come*, pp.2–3.
14 *TF* 12:3 (Mar 1892), pp.68–9.
15 Murray, *Full Blessing*, pp.22–3, 26–7, 95–6.
16 Robert, *Occupy Until I Come*, pp.256, 264.
17 *WW* 23:8 (Aug 1901), p.237.
18 Torrey, *The Holy Spirit*, pp.112, 117, 119, 122.
19 Torrey, *The Holy Spirit*, p.123.
20 Faupel, *Everlasting Gospel*, pp.84–7; Dayton, *Theological Roots*, pp.95–100, 103; Robert, *Occupy Until I Come*, p.259.
21 Anderson, *Vision of the Disinherited*, pp.28–46.
22 *WW* 29:1 (Jan 1907), pp.20–1; *TF* 27:6 (June 1907), pp.128–9.
23 Stanley, *Bible and Flag*, p.82.
24 Austin, '"Hotbed of Missions"', p.137; Stanley, *Bible and Flag*, p.78.
25 Wacker, *Heaven Below*, p.160.
26 Bays and Wacker, 'Introduction', p.8.
27 *TF* 16:1 (Jan 1896), pp.1–2.
28 *TF* 26:4 (Apr 1906), p.82.
29 *WW* 21:1 (May 1899), p.83; 21:6 (Oct 1899), p.181.
30 *WW* 21:3 (July 1899), p.18, pp.20–1.
31 *WW* 28:4 (Apr 1906), p.117.
32 *AF* 1 (Sept 1906), p.1; 3 (Nov 1906), p.2.
33 Stanley, *Bible and Flag*, p.64; Hastings, 'Clash of Nationalism', pp.15–21.
34 Bartleman, *Azusa Street*, pp.19, 90.
35 McGee, '"Latter Rain" Falling', p.650.
36 *WW* 32:2 (Feb 1910), pp.40–1; *BM* 94 (15 Sept 1911), p.1.
37 *Conf* 3:8 (Aug 1910), p.193; Evans, *Welsh Revival*, pp.190–6; Robert, *Occupy Until I Come*, p.260; *DPCM*, pp.1187–8.
38 Robert, *Occupy Until I Come*, pp.261–2; cf. Hudson, 'Strange Words', pp.53–7.
39 For the information on Arulappan, I am indebted to Paul Joshua, PhD candidate at the University of Birmingham, 2006.
40 Burgess, 'Pentecostalism in India', p.85; Barratt, *When the Fire Fell*, p.1.
41 Nongsiej, 'Revival Movement', p.1.
42 *TF* 25:11 (Nov 1905), pp.251–3.
43 *TF* 26:3 (Mar 1906), pp.57–60.
44 *Live Coals* 3:48 (18 Oct 1905), p.1; 4:21 (23 May 1906), p.1; *Holiness Advocate* 6:3

(15 May 1906), p.8; *WW* 32:5 (May 1910), pp.138–40.

45 Bartleman, *Azusa Street*, p.35; McGee, 'Latter Rain', pp.649, 653–9.

46 *AF* 3 (Nov 1906), p.1.

47 *LRE* 11:5 (Feb 1919), p.20.

48 Quoted in Park, 'Korean Pentecost', p. 192.

49 Blair and Hunt, *Korean Pentecost*, pp.71, 75.

50 Quoted in Park, 'Korean Pentecost', p. 199; Lee, 'Holy Spirit Movement', pp.80–90.

51 *BM* 7 (1 Feb 1908), p.1.

52 *WW* 33:1 (Jan 1911), p.27.

53 *Trust* 8:12 (Feb 1910), p.2; *UR* 1:3 (Aug 1909), p.5.

54 *TF* 29:8 (Aug 1909), p.181.

55 *AF* 6 (Feb–Mar 1907), p.1.

56 McGee, '"Latter Rain" Falling', p.650.

57 Said, *Culture and Imperialism*, p.6; *THW*, p.254.

58 *WW* 21:1 (May 1899), p.20.

59 Taylor, 'Publish and be Blessed', pp.47–8; Stanley, *Bible and Flag*, p.136; Said, *Culture and Imperialism*, p.4.

60 Hobsbawm, *Age of Empire*, pp.56–62.

61 Said, *Culture and Imperialism*, pp.xii–xiii.

62 Stanley, *Bible and Flag*, pp.46, 52.

63 Hobsbawm, *Age of Empire*, pp.70–1, 79.

64 Stanley, *Bible and Flag*, p.46.

65 *WW* 28:8 (Sept 1906), p.245.

66 de Kock, *Civilising Barbarians*, p.2.

67 Hobsbawm, 'Introduction: Inventing Traditions', pp.1–2.

68 Stanley, *Bible and Flag*, pp.29–30.

69 *WW* 29:1 (Jan 1907), p.19.

70 *LRE* 5:2 (Nov 1912), pp.6–7.

71 Hobsbawm, *Age of Empire*, p.71.

72 Quoted in McGee, *This Gospel*, p.23.

73 Stanley, *Bible and Flag*, pp.70, 81.

74 *WW* 28:9 (Nov 1906), p.278.

75 Quoted in McGee, *This Gospel*, p.25.

76 Sanneh, *Translating the Message*, pp.132, 139–40; Noll, 'Evangelical Identity', pp.44–5.

77 Stanley, *Bible and Flag*, pp.64–5, 80–1, 133–4.

78 Anderson, *African Reformation*, pp.45–64.

79 *WW* 24:7 (July 1902), p.210; Alexander, *Pentecostal Healing*, pp.16–23.

80 *TF* 2:11 (Nov 1882), pp.164–6.

81 Dayton, *Theological Roots*, pp.119–29; Kydd, *Healing through the Centuries*, pp.33–45, 142–53; Robert, *Occupy Until I Come*, p.264; Alexander, *Pentecostal Healing*, pp.23–4.

82 *TF* 1:1 (Jan 1881), pp.1, 3–5; Alexander, *Pentecostal Healing*, pp.24–7, 151–60.

83 *TF* 10:1 (Jan 1890), pp.21–2.

84 Woodworth-Etter, *Signs and Wonders*, pp.58, 105, 135, 141, 471–2.

85 Faupel, *Everlasting Gospel*, pp.121–7, 132–5; *DPCM*, pp. 803–4; Alexander, *Pentecostal Healing*, pp.58–63.

86 Letter, J. A. Dowie to A. A. Boddy, 12 June 1903, reproduced in *Conf* 6:2 (Feb 1913), p.38.

87 *Leaves of Healing* 15:25 (8 Oct 1904), p.853.

88 Faupel, *Everlasting Gospel*, pp.121, 123, 127, 132–5; Goff, *Fields White*, p.110; *DPCM*, pp.586–7.

89 Goff, *Fields White*, pp.57–60; Faupel, *Everlasting Gospel*, pp.149–50, 157–8; *DPCM*, pp.1037–8.

90 Taylor, *Pastor Hsi*, pp.164–5, 191.

91 Goff, *Fields White*, pp.50–1, 57–60, 73–4.

92 Bartleman, *Azusa Streeet*, pp.65–6.

93 Charles F. Parham, 'The Latter Rain', in Kay and Dyer, *Pentecostal and Charismatic*, p.12.

94 Goff, *Fields White*, p.15.

95 Blumhofer, *Restoring the Faith*, p.52; Wacker, *Heaven Below*, p.263.

96 *WWit* (20 Oct 1912), p.3.

97 Wacker, *Heaven Below*, pp.44–51.

98 Faupel, *Everlasting Gospel*, pp.158–80, 185; Goff, *Fields White*, p.157; Anderson, *Vision*, pp. 87, 190.

3

Burning its Way into Every Nation:
The Missionary Spirit

Pentecost has stirred our hearts on behalf of the heathen. Their cries have been heard, and out from Pentecostal centers everywhere comes a hearty response, a real offering up of their lives for the Gospel; and missionaries are hastening away to the ends of the earth with the true Bread of Life for hungry souls.

Beloved, this work is laid on us. This mighty baptism of the Holy Ghost is too great a fire to be bound by a narrow range, it must burn its way into every nation. We must hasten the work that God has given us to do before He comes.

(*The Bridegroom's Messenger*, 1910) [1]

The Holy Spirit, as this quotation put it, had entered the hearts of Pentecostals to cause them to rapidly migrate, 'hastening away to the ends of the earth'. The baptism in the Spirit could not be limited to one place or nation, but such great fire would 'burn its way into every nation'. There were at least four factors creating impetus for the international movement of hundreds of independent Pentecostal migrants in the early twentieth century. First, this was a time when the vast migration of peoples was unprecedented in extent, facilitated by the new steamship and railway networks that had made travelling vast distances possible. Second, as we will see later, the premillennial eschatology of these Pentecostals posited the urgent task of world evangelism at the end of time before the imminent return of Christ. These eschatological expectations motivated them in their task and filled the earliest reports of their activities.

Third, the focus of this chapter is that they had a firm belief in their experience of Spirit baptism by which they had been given 'foreign languages' to preach their gospel to the nations of the world. Pentecostalism, in common with other Christian revivalist movements at the time, held that their ecstatic manifestations were evidence of the end-time outpouring of the Spirit given to evangelize the world within the shortest possible time. Pentecostals would seek to identify which particular language they had been given (usually through some member of the assembly who would be 'familiar' with a foreign language), and then they would make arrangements to go to that country as soon as possible. Following the earlier ideas of Parham and Seymour, the first Pentecostals almost universally believed that when they spoke in tongues, they had spoken in known languages by which they would preach the gospel to the ends of the earth in the last days. There would be no time for the indeterminable delays of language learning. Early Pentecostal publications were filled with these missionary expectations, often referring to their tongues as the 'gift of languages'. We return to this below.

Fourth, these missionaries often met up with other, more experienced missionaries once in the field, especially when they discovered that God had not given them the ability to speak any language that people could understand. Missionary networks like those of the CMA were very significant in the spread of Pentecostal ideas throughout the world and especially in China and India. *The Bridegroom's Messenger* reported the astonishing news in December 1908 that in India, 60 missionaries had received Spirit baptism and 15 missionary societies had 'witnesses to Pentecost' in 28 stations throughout the country.[2] All this had happened in the space of only one year. But before discussing the implications of this any further we will need to return to the events of 1906. We start in the USA not because this has precedence in the sequence or significance of formative events in the emergence of Pentecostal missions, but because the subsequent regional chapters are better understood in the light of the Azusa Street revival.

William Seymour and the Azusa Street Revival

The first issue of the Azusa Street newspaper *Apostolic Faith*, in its first paragraph, virtually bristled with the excitement of what had happened. Clearly, this new 'Apostolic Faith' saw itself as a missionary movement whose main task was to 'spread this wonderful gospel' to 'all points of the compass'. There was a direct link between the Azusa Street revival and the Welsh revival. Key to this connection was Los Angeles pastor Joseph Smale (1867–1926), an English Baptist. Bartleman referred to him as 'God's Moses' who had led God's people to the brink of the 'Promised Land' but had failed to enter in himself – which task was left to Seymour.[3] Smale visited the Welsh revival in 1905 and returned to his First Baptist Church with a series of meetings in which his church members were stirred to make public confessions. The church records reveal that Smale conducted daily services on the revival immediately after his return, in which there were 'many manifestations of the Spirit'. On one occasion Smale was unable to deliver his planned talk because 'the Spirit led the meeting and no chance was given him'. Instead, 'The Spirit had come on the membership in a remarkable way'.[4] *The Los Angeles Times* reported that Smale had 'caught the Pentecostal fire' and indications were that Smale's church was 'on the eve of a great revival'.[5] Bartleman then corresponded with Evan Roberts, asking for prayer for such a revival in Los Angeles.[6] By the end of 1905, revival expectations were at an all-time high among these radical evangelicals in Los Angeles – a direct result of the reports of the Welsh revival.

Smale was asked to resign from the Baptist Church because of the manifestations in his congregation and together with his supporters he started the First New Testament Church in September 1905, a church dedicated to 'evangelical preaching and Pentecostal life and service'. Although he taught Spirit baptism and encouraged speaking in tongues, deliverance from demons and the exercise of other spiritual gifts, Smale was opposed to the teaching that tongues was 'initial evidence' of Spirit baptism, which was his main difference with Azusa Street and Seymour. Nevertheless, Smale was generally supportive of the Azusa Street revival and saw this as a sign of the imminent return of Christ. He also acted as a mediator between the Azusa Street mission and other churches in Los Angeles.[7] The *Los Angeles Times* mentioned the gift of tongues ('unintelligible jargon') at Smale's church, through which believers 'would become missionaries to heathen lands'.[8] Bartleman was involved there for about a year before joining the Azusa Street mission and according to him, Smale himself visited Azusa Street to offer his members more freedom in spiritual gifts if they returned.[9] One of those who attended Smale's church was Jenny Moore, later married to William Seymour. Smale's meetings in the Burbank Hall were so crowded that they looked for a larger gathering place, services lasted all day well into the night and attracted the attention and ridicule of the local press as much as Azusa Street did.[10] Missionary statesman A. T. Pierson saw the revival in Smale's church positively as the result of the Welsh revival's impact on Smale. He reported that not only did the Los Angeles revival result in 'the prostration of caste barriers' as 'high and low, fashionable and outcast, white and black forgot their differences in the unity of the Spirit', but it was also the source of the formation of a new 'mission band . . . to follow as the Lord leads', two missionaries already having been sent to China.[11]

But the Azusa Street revival (1906–9) in central Los Angeles was the fire that spread to make it the best known of the earliest centres of Pentecostalism in North America and that which immediately sent out missionaries to other places. The revival began in a relatively poor, working-class neighbourhood, in an interracial and intercultural church led by the African American preacher William Joseph Seymour (1870–1922), a Holiness preacher and the son of freed slaves. Seymour heard Parham preaching in Houston, Texas in 1905 and was allowed to listen to his lectures at his short-term Bible school there for about a month, through a half-opened door – in keeping with the segregation of the southern states. Seymour was persuaded by Parham's views on the baptism in the Spirit and was then invited by the preacher Julia Hutchins to pastor a small African American Holiness church in Los Angeles in April 1906 – but his sermon saying that tongues was a sign of Spirit baptism caused Hutchins to lock the church building against him. Members of this church, soon joined by the evangelist Lucy Farrow from Houston and others (including, eventually Hutchins herself), continued meeting with Seymour in prayer in Richard and Ruth Asberry's house in North Bonnie Brae Street, where the Pentecostal revival began. At the house where Seymour was staying, his host Edward Lee asked the preacher and Farrow to lay hands on him on 9 April, after which he fell to the floor as if unconscious and began speaking in tongues. Later that evening and over the next three days, seven others including Seymour and his future wife Jennie Moore received the same experience. Farrow seems to have been a central figure in the beginning of this revival and at least one author has suggested that she, rather than Seymour, was the leading personality there.[12] For three days and nights the house was filled with people praying and rejoicing, continuously and loudly. A few whites joined this group of African Americans and the house became too small for the rapidly increasing numbers.

Within a week the new movement had rented and moved into an old wooden building used for storage at 312 Azusa Street, a former African Methodist Episcopal Church building, where the Apostolic Faith Mission began. Daily meetings commenced at about ten in the morning and usually lasted until late at night, completely spontaneous and emotional, without planned programmes or speakers. Singing in tongues and people falling to the ground 'under the power' or 'slain in the Spirit' were common phenomena. By mid-July, five to seven hundred people were in regular attendance.[13] This revival in a run-down part of the city was instrumental in turning what was until then a fairly localized and insignificant new Christian sect into an international movement.[14] Early Pentecostals, like Wesley, saw the world as their parish, the space into which they were to expand.[15] They were convinced they would overcome all obstacles through the power of the Spirit and thereby defeat the enemy Satan and conquer his territory, the 'world'. *The Apostolic Faith*, the revival's mouthpiece, wrote in its first issue in September 1906 that the 'power of God' now had Los Angeles 'agitated as never before'. As a result of the coming of Pentecost with 'the Bible evidences' many were being converted, sanctified and filled with the Spirit, 'speaking in tongues as they did on the day of Pentecost'. The daily scenes in Azusa Street and in other parts of the city were 'beyond description'. It declared that 'the real revival has only started, as God has been working with His children mostly, getting them through to Pentecost, and laying the foundation for a mighty wave of salvation among the unconverted'. These Spirit-baptized saints were now 'daily going out to all points of the compass to spread this wonderful gospel'.[16] This was the transnational, universal orientation that was an essential part of Pentecostalism from its beginnings.

The new mission also saw itself as an ecumenical movement, albeit one that had 'the truth' in distinction to the denominations that did not. 'Jesus was too large for the synagogue', it declared. 'He preached outside because there was not room for him inside. This Pentecostal movement is too large to be confined in any denomination or sect. It works outside, drawing all together in one bond of love, one church, one body of Christ.'[17] For this reason, early Pentecostal missionaries worked with whoever was willing to accept them – of whatever denomination or mission organization. The racial integration in the Azusa Street meetings was also unique at that time and people from ethnic minorities discovered 'the sense of dignity and community denied them in the larger urban culture'.[18] *The Apostolic Faith* exalted in this inclusiveness, newly discovered in the freedom of the Spirit. The paper stated that this was indeed proof that 'Pentecost has come to Los Angeles' and was the main cause for the popularity of the Azusa Street revival among so many different ethnic and social groups:

> We prayed that the Pentecost might come to the city of Los Angeles. We wanted it to start in the First Methodist Church, but God did not start it there. I bless God that it did not start in any church in this city, but out in the barn, so that we might all come and take part in it. If it had started in a fine church, poor colored people and Spanish people would not have got it, but praise God it started here. God Almighty says He will pour out of His Spirit upon all flesh. This is just what is happening here. I want to warn every Methodist in Los Angeles to keep your hands off this work. Tell the people wherever you go that Pentecost has come to Los Angeles. . . .

It is noticeable how free all nationalities feel. If a Mexican or German cannot speak English, he gets up and speaks in his own tongue and feels quite at home for the Spirit interprets through the face and people say amen. No instrument that God can use is rejected on account of color or dress or lack of education. This is why God has so built up the work.[19]

So, the mission saw its interracial and intercultural nature as one of the reasons for its success, which also facilitated Pentecostalism's remarkable expansion across the globe. The core leadership team was fully integrated, with blacks and whites being responsible for various aspects of the work – more than half were women. Seymour at the helm was described as a meek and gracious man of prayer, even allowing his critics to speak to his congregation and advertising the meetings of his rivals.[20] Such was the impression that he made on people that healing evangelist John G. Lake, Pentecostal missionary to South Africa, meeting him in 1907, commented that Seymour had 'more of God in his life than any man I had ever met'.[21] Seymour was certainly spiritual father to thousands of early Pentecostals.

The Spread of the Apostolic Faith

The American evangelical press began to report on the happenings in Los Angeles, something they had not done on the Topeka events. From Oakland, California, Montgomery's *Triumphs of Faith* did so with cautious support in December 1906, quoting from Bartleman's account in another periodical, *The Way of Faith*.[22] The Massachusetts-based *Word and Work* reported on the revival in the Mukti Mission nine months before it first reported on the Los Angeles revival (in February 1907). The latter issue also carried a report on the Pentecostal revival that had commenced in November 1906 in the Queen Street Mission, Toronto, Canada under Ellen and James Hebden. Seemingly unrelated to the Los Angeles events, this revival had an equal emphasis on speaking in tongues.[23] In this paper, the Mukti, Los Angeles and Toronto revivals were given equal treatment. But significantly, the periodical saw Los Angeles as the place where the 'Apostolic Faith' movement began. For the next two years, the revival in Azusa Street was further promoted by Seymour's periodical *The Apostolic Faith*, which reached an international circulation of 50,000 at its peak in 1908, the largest of any Pentecostal periodical printed at the time.

The purpose of this new 'Apostolic Faith' was clear: to stand for 'the restoration of Apostolic faith, power and practice, Christian unity, the evangelization of the whole world preparatory to the Lord's return, and for all of the unfolding will and word of God'. The followers of this new movement were convinced that they had 'the simple but effective Scriptural Plan for evangelizing the world'.[24] The going out from Azusa Street was immediate, in ever-widening circles. People affected by the revival started new Pentecostal centres in the Los Angeles area, so that by 1912 there were at least 12 in that city. *The Apostolic Faith* stated that what was happening in Azusa Street was also occurring 'at Missions and Churches in other parts of the city' and that the 'real revival' had only just started.[25] Hundreds of visitors from all over North America and soon from other continents came to see what was happening and to be baptized in the Spirit. Many of these began Pentecostal centres in various US and Canadian cities and eventually further abroad. *The Apostolic Faith* reported receiving letters from all over the world requesting prayers for Spirit baptism and healing.[26] Hostile press reports helped further publicize the revival.[27] After the showdown in October 1906 when Parham was rejected as leader by Seymour and his followers after he tried to stop the manifestations of the revival, Parham remained bitterly opposed to them for the rest of his life. But the revival continued unabated for two years. By November 1906 in a paragraph titled 'Spreading the Full Gospel', *The Apostolic Faith* reported that 16 'Spirit filled' workers had recently gone out to nine different American cities, some of whom (including Thomas Junk, Edward McCauley and Tom Hezmalhalch) were to later move out to 'foreign' fields. The paper suggested that there was some co-ordination of these early efforts: 'We wish to keep track of the workers in the field and be united together in prayer for each other and the work in the different fields.'[28] Missionaries soon were heading for India and China, Europe, Palestine and Africa, and on their way to embarking from the east they visited several cities and started new fires there.

Most Western European Pentecostal churches have their origins in the revival associated with Thomas Ball Barratt (1862–1940) in Christiania (Oslo), Norway. Barratt was a pastor in the Methodist Episcopal Church of Norway who visited the USA in 1906 to raise funds (unsuccessfully) for his City Mission to the poor of Oslo. In New York he read the first edition of *The Apostolic Faith* from Azusa Street, and began writing to Los Angeles. Barratt was baptized in the Spirit through the ministry of (among others) Lucy Leatherman, who met him at the Alliance House in New York. He sailed back to Norway via Liverpool together with the party of Azusa Street missionaries to Africa, including Samuel and Ardelle Mead on their way back to Angola and Lucy Farrow on her way to Liberia. Farrow's special gifts were noticeable – she had, in the words of Howard Goss (who had observed her ministry in Houston, Texas), 'an unusual ability to lay hands on people for the reception of the Holy Spirit'.[29]

Barratt was now a zealous Pentecostal destined to become the founder and prime motivator of Pentecostalism in Europe, giving oversight to the establishment of Pentecostal centres in many parts of this continent. His new teachings were unacceptable to his bishops and he was eventually forced to leave the Methodist Church and found what is now the largest non-Lutheran denomination in Norway, a fellowship of independent churches known as Pinsebevegelsen (Pentecostal Revival). Starting with a small group of believers, the revival in Barratt's independent Filadelfia Church in Oslo caused an explosion in numbers and was a place of pilgrimage for people from other European centres – including Pentecostal pioneers Alexander Boddy from England, Jonathan Paul from Germany and Lewi Pethrus from Sweden. Large crowds attended Barratt's meetings all over Europe. He sent missionaries to Sweden and Germany, and went himself to the Middle East and India in 1908. He wrote to the Hoovers in Chile, encouraging them and others wherever he went to establish self-governing, self-supporting and self-propagating

Pentecostal churches. By 1910, Norwegian Pentecostal missionaries had already gone to India, China, South Africa and South America.[30]

Some other well-known early Pentecostal preachers made extended world tours, including Frank Bartleman, Alexander Boddy and Daniel Awrey, who toured the Pentecostal work in Japan, China and India 'giving Bible readings'.[31] At the beginning of 1910 Daniel and Ella Awrey were in Canton and Hong Kong, where they set up a mission. Daniel died in Africa in 1913.[32] Within three years of the beginning of the revival in 1906, Apostolic Faith missionaries who had received their experience of Spirit baptism at Azusa Street were found in at least three African and six Asian countries.

Although the international initiative in American Pentecostalism had passed to Seymour, after two years his leadership role was frustrated through racism, power struggles and doctrinal bickering. Several competing white missions in Los Angeles drew away members from Azusa Street. One of the most acrimonious divisions took place in 1911, when Chicago preacher William Durham, who had received Spirit baptism at Azusa Street in 1907, came to Los Angeles to try to take over the mission. Seymour was away east on a preaching trip at the time, until he returned and locked the church against Durham. Glenn Cook, Seymour's business manager and later Oneness pioneer, left with Durham and they started a rival congregation in the same vicinity. Bartleman also supported Durham in his new mission, remarking that God had been locked out of the 'old cradle of power', which was now 'deserted'. Alexander Boddy visited the mission in 1912 and found a small gathering there.[33] Despite this early opposition and bitter division, at least 26 different American denominations trace their Pentecostal origins to Azusa Street, including the two largest: the Church of God in Christ and the Assemblies of God. In a real sense, the Azusa Street revival marks the beginning of classical Pentecostalism as a national and eventually an international movement.

Some scholars have referred to the 'myth' or 'legend' of Azusa Street that has overlooked the importance of other centres and have either suggested or implied that its role was not as central as has been generally accepted today.[34] There were indeed other important early North American centres of Pentecostalism independent of Azusa Street, in particular the Hebdens' Queen Street Mission in Toronto (a Pentecostal centre from 1906), and Levi Lupton's Missionary Faith Home in Alliance, Ohio, which had become Pentecostal by December 1906 through the ministry of Ivey Campbell, herself baptized in the Spirit at Azusa Street. The January 1907 issue of *The Apostolic Faith* reported on the Home in Alliance as having 'received the Pentecost' and that it was now 'a center of power' to which people were going for their 'Pentecost'.[35] In addition to these were several prominent centres that commenced or became Pentecostal during 1907 (most of which were founded and led by women) and were particularly significant in the promotion of Pentecostal missions, including the Glad Tidings Tabernacle in New York City founded by Marie Burgess (later married to Irish Pentecostal Robert Brown), which commenced initially under Parham's direction; the Elim Tabernacle in Rochester, New York, founded by Elizabeth Baker and her four sisters; the Beulah Heights Assembly in North Bergen, New Jersey, founded by Virginia Moss; the Bethel Pentecostal Assembly in Newark, New Jersey, led by Minnie T. Draper and others; and William Hamner Piper's Stone Church in Chicago – an interracial church with African American members and roots in Dowie's Zion movement. Baker's, Moss's and Draper's organizations included Bible training schools for missionaries and ministers. The Azusa Street revivalists also acknowledged earlier, 'other Pentecostal saints' such as those in New England, Minnesota and Manitoba.[36] They never saw themselves as the first cause or headquarters of Pentecostalism – rather, they were one part of a widespread outpouring of 'Pentecost' that they believed would reach the whole world. As *The Apostolic Faith* put it, 'Azusa Mission is not the head of this movement; we are a body of missions with Christ as the Head'.[37]

By 1907 most of the evangelical Christian world had heard of the events in Los Angeles and at Mukti and were taking sides either for or against the manifestations taking place there. In particular, speaking in tongues became a dividing issue, with well-known preachers like A. T. Pierson, Jessie Penn-Lewis and Campbell Morgan railing against it, while others like A. B. Simpson, Pandita Ramabai, Carrie Judd Montgomery, William H. Piper and some of the Holiness periodicals accepted that speaking in tongues was one of the gifts of the Spirit needed in the contemporary church, but that to insist on speaking in tongues as 'necessary evidence' of Spirit baptism was unscriptural.[38] The Azusa Street Mission and some of the early Pentecostals, especially in the USA, had adopted this dogmatic position first enunciated by Parham. But dogmatic differences relating to 'necessary evidence' aside, speaking in 'missionary tongues' was undoubtedly the primary reason for a sudden surge of missionary activity among Pentecostals from 1906 onwards. The first Pentecostal missionaries left the Los Angeles revival for Africa and Asia almost immediately after they had received their Spirit baptism. Azusa Street was also a place of pilgrimage for returning missionaries, as word spread about the revival there. Bartleman recollects that 'it seemed that everybody had to go to Azusa'. He recorded that 'missionaries were gathered there from Africa, India, and the islands of the sea . . . an irresistible drawing to Los Angeles'.[39] The following chapters trace the stories of these missionaries in the few years following the beginning of this revival.

In the first issue of Azusa Street's *The Apostolic Faith* (September 1906), the expectations of early American Pentecostals were clear. They fully expected through Spirit baptism to be able to speak 'all the languages of the world' in order to preach the gospel 'into all the world'.[40] The rather haphazard sending 'by the Spirit' resulted in several Azusa Street missionaries itinerating from place to place, and even from country to country. Many of these various missionaries did not stay long in one place, but had itinerating ministries. One of the earliest and most remarkable was Lucy Leatherman, a wealthy doctor's widow and former student at A. B. Simpson's Missionary Training School in Nyack, New York. She had received Spirit baptism at Azusa Street, where she believed she had spoken Arabic and was called to go to Palestinian Arabs. She travelled from country to country sending back reports to several Pentecostal papers. She was among the first group of missionaries reported as having left Los Angeles for Jerusalem via the east coast in August 1906. Among the languages this group believed they were able to speak through Spirit baptism were Turkish and Arabic, but there were no reports of them being understood by their hearers.

Furthermore (and as the following chapters show), the spread of global Pentecostalism was as much through the networks of the evangelical 'faith missions' like the CMA and the CIM as it was through the initiatives of missionaries from Azusa Street. In particular, the revival within the CMA during these early years was directly responsible for many of its missionaries becoming Pentecostal, especially after the organization became more outspokenly against Pentecostal 'initial evidence' teaching. But what cannot be denied is that for three years, Seymour's Apostolic Faith Mission was the most prominent and significant centre of Pentecostalism on the continent. It was recognized as the birthplace of Pentecostalism by most of its later missionaries, and it was also an important sending centre for many of the first Pentecostal missionaries, as the following chapters demonstrate. Bartleman believed that Los Angeles was the new Jerusalem for the global expansion of the 'restoration of the power of God'.[41] Tragically, although William Seymour died in 1922, the same year as Pandita Ramabai died, neither his death nor his significance was given as much coverage in the Pentecostal press as that of Ramabai. He was all but forgotten and would only receive due recognition much later in the twentieth century. Yet as this book shows, the movement he initiated in Los Angeles was a very significant instrument in spreading the Pentecostal full gospel all over the world.

In its first years, the rapidly spreading fires of Pentecost through migrant missionaries was quite remarkable. In September 1908, the second issue of J. Roswell Flower's *The Pentecost* listed in its 'Apostolic Faith Directory' seven American missionaries: in South Africa (Lake, Lehman and Hezmalhalch), India (Berg), Ceylon (Post), China (Berntsen) and Japan (Ryan). These were heads of teams in these countries, and the periodical explained that they were 'sent out by God, without any salary or dependence upon man. They rely solely upon God for their existence.' Prayers were sought for them, so that the Spirit would be poured out on them 'in mighty power'. Their chief purpose was clearly to be individual and spiritual: 'in the salvation of many heathen souls for His name's sake'.[42] In December 1908, A. S. Copley listed in the same 'Apostolic Faith Directory' Hezmalhalch, Lehman, Lake, Elliott and Schneiderman in South Africa; Miller in Kisimu, Kenya; Berg, Post and Norton in India; Berntsen in China, Ryan in Japan, and Leatherman in Palestine. In addition to these were listed J. M. L. Harrow in Cape Palmas, Liberia, and Robert Atchison in Osaka, Japan – 14 in all.[43] In September 1909, when the last Directory was published, to these names were added the Brelsfords in Egypt; Dick Mahaffey at the Boys' Christian Home in Dhond, India; Thomas Junk in Shandong, China; and Moomau and Phillips in Shanghai.[44] The Pentecostal fires were spreading rapidly.

The migrants who carried the Pentecostal message all over the globe were mostly poor, untrained and unprepared for what awaited them; but some left comfortable middle-class homes for lives of relative deprivation to spread their newfound faith. Most of them fully intended to go permanently to the places they believed they were called to, and many did not return. Andrew Johnson wrote to Azusa Street in August 1906 on his way to Palestine, but he stopped in Sweden before ending up in China some five years later. He represented many when he wrote, 'I would like to say good-bye to you before I leave this land, it may be never to return in this life.'[45] Anna Deane Cole from Birmingham, Alabama arrived with the Daniel Awreys in Hong Kong in 1910 to work with her aunt Anna Deane in a children's school. She remained there for 52 years, writing: 'I would not go to America if I had my passage paid. I am here until God says move on.'[46] Miss C. B. Herron, a missionary from the Rochester Bible Training School in New York state who left for India in 1913, said similarly, 'I am going out expecting never to return, for since, as we trust, the coming of the Lord is near, my work is for India, and I shall not return, except by a clear word from Him.'[47]

This was the indomitable spirit in which some of these missionaries departed from their homelands. There was also an underlying fierce individualism and independence that often came with their experience of Spirit baptism. Sometimes it empowered ordinary, oppressed and disadvantaged people to resist the status quo and those who were an institutional part of it. Andrew Urshan told of the first Pentecostal martyr in Persia, a 15-year-old Russian girl named Sophia, whose parents were Orthodox and who was killed by a young boy with a rifle on her way to an evening meeting in 1915. She stood up against her parents, her priest, and the accepted conventions of that time and place. Urshan wrote that her parents had known that she had been at their meetings and had accused him of hypnotizing her. They sent for the Russian priest who threw holy water on her but 'she just lifted up her hands and praised the Lord'. The priest then began 'to rebuke the devil, but she looked into his face and told him to get right with God and that he needed to pray for himself'. Urshan concluded: 'She was filled with the glory of God and became a wonderful missionary in that place and the Lord blessed because of her faithfulness.'[48] Spirit baptism had made this girl independent and anti-establishment and her newfound individualism had led to her death.

Many missionaries did not return to their homelands and died in the field. Although he disappears from the records, Thomas Junk, another Azusa Street missionary was probably one of these, whose measure of commitment to China was poignantly expressed in a letter he wrote in 1910. A Christian had asked him to return to the USA 'and tell personally of the work and the need here if he, the brother, paid the expenses'. He replied, 'No, dear brother, no, I cannot afford to waste the time and money that way. My work is here till Jesus comes or I am called home. I never shall see the home land again till I see it from the clouds.'[49] Some missionaries went out 'by faith' without any income, sometimes referred to as 'on the faith line', going out with very little and 'trusting God' to supply the necessary finances usually through home contacts and periodical support. In return, the missionaries provided long and regular newsletters that were reproduced in order to raise funds back in the homeland. The disasters that befell the Batman family (who all died in Liberia) and the team that went with M. L. Ryan to Japan without financial support are now legendary. But as we will see, many Pentecostal missionaries were poorly funded and some had to depend on the local people for their bare necessities.

Pentecostal leaders had to pull in the reigns on overly excited and poorly prepared Pentecostal missionaries who became both a burden and an embarrassment to the fledgling movement. Alexander Boddy published a 'kindly suggestion' to those 'friends in distant lands' who felt they were called to Britain, asking them not to embark on the journey there 'unless the Lord has invited through some of His children' who would be 'in a position to receive them'.[50] John G. Lake wrote an exasperated letter home in 1909 about sending missionaries to South Africa without funds, as one young American had arrived in Cape Town without the necessary minimum of $100 and a guarantee of support. To get him through to Johannesburg had cost them 'a great deal of trouble and expense', Lake complained.[51] Minnie Abrams addressed the financial difficulties faced by 'faith missionaries' by reference to her own experiences with Ramabai, and she appealed for better support for Pentecostal missionaries, who had left on the ships from their homelands 'with such joy and gladness in the midst of shouts and hallelujahs'. But once reaching their destination, she charged, these missionaries had 'literally been starved in foreign lands' and some had had 'to live on roots or anything they could get, because those hallelujahs did not sink down into the heart'.[52] We will return to this subject later.

These early Pentecostal missionaries went out to live 'on the faith line', to bring 'light' into 'darkness', and in some cases they had no fixed plans for their arrival and certainly none for their return, for they were led to their destinations by the Spirit, and the Spirit would show them what to do when they got there. As one of these missionaries, May Law, put it, speaking of her team in Hong Kong: 'Three young women, and one of mature years, left their homes of wealth, and comfort . . . and their beautiful native State of Washington, for dark S. China.'[53] Two of these three young women died there from tropical diseases in the next four years, and this was the tragic fate of many of these unprepared missionaries who would refuse to take medicines, because to do so would show a lack of faith in divine healing. Some of them went to these faraway places leaving behind their wives and children (in a few cases) and sometimes they took their families with them only for them to perish from smallpox or malaria soon after arriving there. The sacrifices made by these missionaries were in some cases quite extreme. G. S. Brelsford gave an account of their departure for Egypt that was not atypical. They left their children behind 'with tears streaming down our faces', and a week later sailed for Egypt. They tried to provide for the children 'as well as we could . . . divided what was on hand, and went third-class over to Egypt, but I cannot recommend that way of traveling.'[54]

In fact, most of these missionaries travelled 'third-class'. The Brelsfords arrived in Alexandria with $2 in their pockets and were only able to continue with the help of two Egyptian Christians until a $20 donation from home arrived afterwards. Such was the plight of many of these faith missionaries. Many were independent, without financial or organizational backing and related only in a loose way to small Pentecostal congregations in their home country. After all, the Spirit had set them free from human ecclesiastical institutions. As Nettie Moomau in Shanghai put it, 'Jesus is doing much more for us than any board could do and we are happy to know that we are free creatures in Him.'[55] Arthur Booth-Clibborn expressed the common Pentecostal resistance to organization and institutionalization when he wrote about keeping the 'unity of the Spirit' 'in the bond of peace'. He declared, 'Man-made bonds have hitherto failed. Were this revival to be organised or centralised, it would quickly go wrong, because carnal unity soon becomes a dead uniformity.' Human organization led to idolatry, he said: 'Man cannot be trusted to take things into his own hands. He quickly makes a thing, an idol. His carnal "unions" can be the union of many small weaknesses to make a large one.'[56]

However free they were or thought they were, these Pentecostal migrants needed to remain in regular contact with their home countries and sending churches for their very survival. Letters went back and forth between missionaries and home churches, the latter producing periodicals often issued free of charge to these missionaries, keeping them abreast with the developing movement both at home and around the world. Often the only link with any form of organization was through these periodicals, which served the threefold function as home bases for missionaries, the means of disseminating information about them, and for raising funds for their support. Many of the periodicals saw the promotion of Pentecostal missions to be one of the main reasons for their existence. William Piper in Chicago expressed one of the main purposes of *The Latter Rain Evangel* in an editorial in 1910 'to use the columns of our paper to stir up the missionary spirit among God's children'. Piper went on, 'God is opening up the heathen world as never before. In many places the heathen themselves are reaching out their hands and saying, "Come over and help us", and the home church must awaken to her privileges. Beloved, let us be laborers together.'[57] Similarly in the same year, Elisabeth Sexton of Atlanta in *The Bridegroom's Messenger* wrote in another editorial, 'The work of all Pentecostal missionaries is ours. They represent us wherever they go.' She expressed clearly the role of her periodical, that both 'our prayers and our substance must go with them'. The paper would send money and would 'be glad to receive your offerings, and to forward to Pentecostal missionaries in any field'.[58] These periodicals were also important vehicles for internationalizing and creating norms for Pentecostal beliefs and values. They were perceived by the missionaries as being the primary sources of both their own identity and that of their converts. Later, missionary training schools and Bible colleges were established that further helped normalize a global Pentecostal identity. The revivals in the nineteenth and early twentieth century had the effect of creating an air of expectancy that the whole world would be reached for Christ in as short a time as possible and that supernatural gifts of the Spirit like tongues, healing and prophecy were being restored to the Church in order to facilitate this. This was the driving force behind the first Pentecostal missions, and the Azusa Street revival was a vital part of this.

Speaking the Languages of the Nations

We have seen that early American Pentecostals were convinced that they had been given 'missionary tongues' through Spirit baptism and that when they reached their destinations they would be able to speak miraculously to the local people without having to undergo the arduous task of language learning.

By 1906, the year of the Azusa Street revival, the first Pentecostals almost universally believed that by this means they would preach the gospel 'abroad' to the ends of the earth in the last days. But apart from some instances when it was claimed this had actually happened, most admitted that they were unable to speak in any languages and a minority returned to the USA disillusioned.

Early Pentecostal publications, especially Azusa Street's *The Apostolic Faith*, were filled with these optimistic missionary expectations. As the first issue of *The Apostolic Faith* put it, although they could not count the numbers of people 'saved, and sanctified, and baptized with the Holy Ghost, and healed of all manner of sicknesses', there were many speaking in tongues, some of whom were 'on their way to the foreign fields, with the gift of the language'. They were determined to continue 'to get more of the power of God'. It went on: 'God is solving the missionary problem, sending out new-tongued missionaries on the apostolic faith line, without purse or scrip, and the Lord is going before them preparing the way.'[59] This passage illustrates vividly how this new movement saw its mission to the world. The 'foreign fields' would be easily reached with the newfound 'gift of the language'. A shortage of missionaries would be a thing of the past. The 'new-tongued missionaries on the apostolic faith line' would immediately go to the nations with the gospel of Jesus Christ. Thus, God was 'solving the missionary problem' by sending out missionaries who could, through the power of the Spirit, supernaturally speak the languages of the nations. This was what the early Apostolic Faith missionaries sincerely believed.

But even when the 'languages' did not appear, it was the fundamental experience of Spirit baptism that motivated them to mission. The gift of tongues was often referred to as the 'gift of languages'. *The Apostolic Faith* revealed that the expectations of early North American Pentecostals were very clear. The 'gift of languages' had been given to fulfil the commission 'Go ye into all the world and preach the gospel to every creature'. As a result, 'the Lord has given languages to the unlearned Greek, Latin, Hebrew, French, German, Italian, Chinese, Japanese, Zulu and languages of Africa, Hindu [sic] and Bengali and dialects of India, Chippewa and other languages of the Indians, Esquimaux, the deaf mute language and, in fact the Holy Ghost speaks all the languages of the world through His children.'[60] When 'the Holy Ghost fell on a preacher' at Azusa Street he was able to speak 'Zulu and many tongues more fluently than English'.[61] In keeping with common practice of Pentecostals at that time, this unnamed preacher probably turned up in South Africa to work among the Zulu. A missionary from Africa, possibly Ardelle Mead, recognized some of the languages spoken at Azusa Street as being 'dialects of Africa', confirming her need to return there with these new linguists. The Meads' own accounts of xenolalia and their return from Angola within a few months cast serious doubts on their abilities to make such an identification.

But there was no shortage of the reports of missionary tongues. One young woman 'had the gift of the Chinese tongue', and a 'rough Indian' [sic] from Mexico heard his language being spoken.[62] Such accounts abound on every page: Russian, Italian, Arabic and Turkish were some of the languages given as confirmation of the recipients' mission calling. The paper also reported that when Alfred and Lillian Garr received the Spirit, they had 'received the gift of tongues, especially the language of India and dialects', they had both been able to speak in Bengali, and Lillian Garr had spoken in Tibetan and Chinese.[63] The Spirit had apparently not revealed at the time that there were well over a thousand Indian languages, but the undaunted missionaries went off to Kolkata fully expecting to speak Bengali on their arrival. They did not and they could not, but unlike many others who returned home disappointed and disillusioned, they stayed for some time and went on to Hong Kong – although they never tried to study Chinese. Speaking the tongues of the nations was, the Azusa Street paper declared, the 'divine plan for missionaries' that they would receive before they arrived in the 'foreign field' and be 'a sign to the heathen that the message is of God'. This 'gift of languages' could not be learned 'like the native tongues, but the Lord takes control of the organs of speech at will'. It was, the paper concluded 'emphatically, God's message'.[64]

The next issue of The Apostolic Faith continued this theme. Julia Hutchins received the gift of speaking 'Uganda' (there is no such language) but went to Liberia. A young girl received 'the language of Africa', a preacher's wife began to speak French, a missionary to Palestine testified to speaking 'eleven or twelve languages', and a young woman spoke a 'dialect in Africa' with a 'perfect accent' as well as 'two Chinese dialects'.[65] But before the following issue could be published, an event of momentous significance occurred at Azusa Street. Charles Parham attempted to 'control' this revival and was disgusted particularly by the interracial fellowship and the 'Africanisms' he saw there. He termed this 'hypnotism' and a 'freak imitation of Pentecost'. 'Horrible, awful shame!' he cried. Years later, Parham referred to Azusa Street as making him 'sick at my stomach . . . to see white people imitating unintelligent, crude negroism of the Southland, and laying it on the Holy Ghost'.[66] He was rejected as leader, was never reconciled with William Seymour, and went into obscurity and eventual disgrace.[67] The leadership of the movement passed to Seymour and took on international dimensions.

It appears that this break also signalled the impending but slow erosion of Pentecostal confidence in Parham's doctrine of xenolalia. The following issues of The Apostolic Faith in 1906 and 1907 still mention xenolalia in five instances: a Swedish woman 'given the gift of the English language with the understanding of the words', the testimonies of Ardelle Mead receiving 'an African dialect', Lucy Leatherman speaking in Arabic, Henry McLain reported to have been imprisoned for his faith and to have spoken 'the Mexican language' to the men with him in a chain gang, and a 12-year-old girl who 'preaches and signs in the Indian language'.[68] The 'identification' of these various languages was so vague as to cast serious doubts on their veracity, as even a missionary of a few years' experience in Africa, India or China would have known that many different languages were spoken there – but those who 'identified' them did not.

The Apostolic Faith in December 1906 again linked the baptism in the Spirit with the ability to 'speak in the languages of the nations'. Spirit baptism not only 'makes you a witness unto the uttermost parts of the earth', it declared, but it also 'gives you power to speak in the languages of the nations'. T. B. Barratt, Pentecostal apostle to Europe, writes here that he 'must have spoken seven or eight languages . . . one foreign tongue after another' when he received Spirit baptism in New York. George Batman, African American missionary, writing en route to his impending death in Liberia, believed he could 'speak in six foreign tongues given me at God's command'. This issue mentioned a woman speaking 'many languages, one of them being that of the Kalamath Indians' and another woman speaking in Hindustani; George Berg, missionary to India, testified that the languages at the revival were 'real languages' including languages of British India, another person was mentioned speaking in Kru and Italian, another woman spoke Chinese and Japanese, and others African dialects. The January 1907 issue reported that a mother had been given the Hawaiian language and the next issue of *The Apostolic Faith* carried a report from Liberia that one of the missionaries from Los Angeles (probably Lucy Farrow) 'had been able to speak to the people in the cru [sic] tongue'. The paper continued to give testimonies of people who spoke 'the languages of the nations' and there are reports of people speaking Syriac, Armenian, Chinese, Korean, English (in Norway), Italian, Hebrew, 'High German', Japanese, Spanish and Latin, among others.[69] There was no shortage of such testimonies to xenolalia in the Azusa Street revival.

One wonders how the identification of some of these 'languages' was arrived at. Perhaps it was the sound that gave the particular clue. A quick analysis might reveal that Chinese is the most frequent language 'spoken' in these reports, but a closing paragraph in *The Apostolic Faith*, quoting from 'Banner of Truth' yields a darker hint at what might be behind some of these evaluations. It said that there were 50,000 languages in the world, some of which sounded 'like jabber'. The 'Eskimo' language could 'hardly be distinguished from a dog bark', it observed, but the Lord let 'smart people talk in these jabber-like languages', while a child would 'talk in the most beautiful Latin or Greek, just to confound professors and learned people'.[70] The sheer ignorance displayed in these words is obvious. Nevertheless, there are indications that by the end of 1907, Seymour and his workers at *The Apostolic Faith* were gradually giving up on 'missionary tongues' and that this belief was being replaced by one in 'unknown tongues', the almost universal belief of Pentecostals today.

The first reports from Pentecostal missionaries in the field begin to be published in the April 1907 issue of *The Apostolic Faith*, from Liberia, Calcutta and Hawaii. One missionary in Dhond, India wrote of her experiences on board ship being able to speak no less than four Asian languages: Japanese, Tagalog, Chinese and Hindustani – but she noted sadly that she had been unable to speak Marathi, the language of her chosen field.[71] A report by Tom Hezmalhalch, later missionary to South Africa, of a man hearing someone speaking in 'Marathi' indicates that the idea of 'missionary tongues' was still prevalent but noticeably less frequently mentioned. A letter from India gave a first-hand account of the Mukti revival, where the seasoned missionary Albert Norton wrote of hearing about the revival 'about six months ago' (about September 1906) and described 'illiterate Marathi women and girls' speaking idiomatic English. Significantly, in this issue of *The Apostolic Faith* much more reference was made to 'unknown tongues' and tongues which were interpreted than in previous issues. There was a report from Florence Crawford about people speaking in 'the African tongue' and Italian in meetings in Oakland, California and one from Spokane, Washington where a businessman was reported to have spoken in 'Holland-Dutch, Chinese and other languages'.[72] The next issue carried several testimonies of xenoglossa and gave a report from Minneapolis of a woman who spoke successively in Polish, 'Bohemian', Chinese, Italian and Norwegian.[73] A pastor testified of his experience in a CMA convention in 1907 where he spoke and sang in 'pure Tamil', confirmed by a listening missionary from South India.[74]

The missionary reports also abounded with hints of the frustrations these missionaries felt because they could not communicate in the languages of the people. Some resorted to spending time with other missionaries and bringing them into the experience of Spirit baptism, which often became their main occupation. Alfred and Lillian Garr wrote in *The Apostolic Faith* in 1907 that 'reaching the missionaries' was like 'laying the axe at the root of the tree, for they know all the customs of India and also the languages'. Through their own bitter experience, the Garrs had changed their tune. 'The only way the nations can be reached', they declared, 'is by getting the missionaries baptized with the Holy Ghost.'[75] Nevertheless, as late as July 1910 Elisabeth Sexton published a vigorous defence of xenolalia in *The Bridegroom's Messenger*, giving examples of its occurrence from all over the world.[76]

Those more sceptical about the fantastic claims that were being made, such as Alexander Boddy in Sunderland, England, cautioned great care with regard to so-called 'missionary tongues'. In a 1911 article in his paper *Confidence* he wrote that those who felt that they had 'a call to the Foreign Mission Field because they believe that they speak in Chinese, Indian, or African languages, etc.' should 'be very careful not to go before God' and 'before leaving home they should take steps to verify the fact that they really have a complete language in which at all times they can preach the Gospel'. Boddy said that he felt justified in saying that 'from among the very many who have gone abroad after the Pentecostal blessing we have not yet received one letter stating that they have this miraculous gift in any useful fullness'.[77] He had initiated this debate almost three years earlier in 1908, by publishing letters from the first Pentecostal missionaries to South China, T. J. McIntosh and A. G. Garr, discussing the issue that had already caused some considerable controversy and made mockery of Pentecostals in the eyes of other missionaries. This debate seemed to be occasioned by an attack by a missionary in Macao, who had apparently investigated the claims of the Garrs and the McIntoshes and stated that 'at no time has there been any *known* tongue spoken, all has been an *unknown* utterance'.[78] Boddy firmly stated his position, which would become the accepted tradition of Pentecostalism for the rest of the century. He referred to articles that had appeared in religious papers referring to 'the disappointment of those who had gone from their homes to distant lands after receiving their "Pentecost", and hoping to speak fluently the language of the natives'. He stated that many of these people had not at the time realized that the gift of tongues was 'not the gift of any known language in its entirety'. Boddy was 'sure that God honoured their zeal' and had 'permitted them to be a blessing though not as they expected'. He said that the Lord had given some of them language interpreters and they had all 'reached English speaking people with their Pentecostal message, while missionaries with whom they came in contact were encouraged to seek the Baptism of the Holy Ghost'.[79]

The two missionaries to China responded to Boddy in a rather ambiguous fashion, as clearly they did not want to lose face. McIntosh wrote that he had 'not come in contact with anybody that is able to preach to natives in their own tongue, so that they could understand'; but declared that he had himself on two occasions spoken in tongues that people could understand. Garr also claimed to have spoken in Indian languages in Los Angeles in 1906, but that his 'languages changed'. Now he admitted that he knew 'no one having received a language so as to be able to converse intelligently, or to preach in the same with the understanding, in the Pentecostal Movement'. He had also been unable to speak Bengali in Calcutta and explained his change of view on the issue of tongues as foreign languages:

> Whether or not I was speaking an Indian language in Los Angelos [sic] does not shake my faith or even cause me anxiety. I know that God was talking through me, and what it was He knew all about it, and that was quite enough for me . . . I am delighted with all God has done for me on this line. I supposed He would let us talk to the natives of India in their own tongue, but He did not, and as far as I can see, will not use that means by which to convert the heathen, but will employ the gifts – such as wonderful signs of healing and other powers, that the heathen can see for themselves and know that there is no cheat to the performance . . . So far I have not seen any one who is able to preach to the natives in their own tongue with the languages given with the Holy Ghost. Here in Hong Kong, we preached the word to the Chinese through an interpreter, and God has saved some, and there are about twenty-five or thirty that were baptised with the Spirit of God and spoke in other tongues, seen visions, and received interpretations, etc.[80]

The Garrs had lived together with other workers in their mission but did not learn Chinese or any other language during the time they spent in Asia – although Lillian apparently tried to. During their second term in India they expressed a desire to get a 'working knowledge' of Hindustani in order to be able to preach, but they never did and returned to Hong Kong after nine months.[81] Perhaps the lack of a language and their personal tragedies were the main reasons that they finally returned to the USA. A. G. Garr told a convention in Chicago in 1914:

> One of the big trials you run into, especially if you go among the raw heathen, is that when you talk to them they cannot understand you. You have the fire and you have the message, but they cannot understand you. So the first thing you will get awfully discouraged at the thought of having to settle down to the grind of studying the language, and it takes quite awhile, but if you have a real call you are going to stay.[82]

He did not.

Despite all these setbacks for missionary tongues, Boddy penned the prevalent optimism of Pentecostal leaders when he described the 'Hall-Marks' of

Pentecostal baptism in August 1909. The fifth 'Hall-Mark' was what he called the 'Missionary Test'. He wrote that although missionaries had been disappointed when they found out that 'they could not preach in the language of the people, and in spite of mistakes made chiefly through their zeal', God had blessed and 'now more than ever the Pentecostal Movement is truly a Missionary Movement'. This 'increasing band' of Pentecostal missionaries had 'more training now' and were 'going out ... to preach Christ and Him crucified to the heathen people, often in very hard places, amidst terrible difficulties'.[83] Nevertheless, Boddy and other Pentecostal believers seemed to cherish the thought that there would be occasions when the 'tongues of the nations' would be spoken and the belief in missionary tongues lingered on. Even as late as 1913, Congo missionary Alma Doering claimed to have heard a tongues speaker in the last Sunderland convention speaking in a language of Central Africa with which she was familiar.[84] Another incident in 1913 was related in which an American missionary was preaching to a Xhosa congregation in South Africa without an interpreter. An African preacher who did not understand English rose to 'interpret' for the American, who was convinced that the Spirit had given him the understanding and miraculous ability to translate exactly what was being preached, although we will never know what actually happened.[85] Carrie Judd Montgomery gave her own experience of speaking and singing in Chinese dialects (apparently confirmed by a Friends missionary in China), and of a woman speaking 'the Basuto language' in an Upper Room meeting in Los Angeles in 1910.[86]

One of the more dramatic and well known of the accounts of missionary tongues concerned a Pentecostal missionary in China. A CMA missionary in Shanghai reported an incident in 1909 in which Pentecostal pioneers George and Sophia Hansen were heard speaking Mandarin miraculously during a street meeting, resulting in the conversion of a Chinese student. A letter signed by 14 Chinese people confirming that Sophia Hansen had spoken Chinese on a regular basis without having learned it (apparently in response to severe criticism they had received) was published in *The Upper Room*, and a testimony from her to that effect appeared in at least three different periodicals during the next seven years.[87] By 1916 she was still claiming to have this gift:

> After we had been here six months the Lord first led me out to speak to the Chinese in their own tongue. Sunday, July 26, 1908, I was moved by the Holy Ghost to start outside our own home. Wonderful! Wonderful! Many listened with tears in their eyes as I spoke to them on that chapter where Jesus wept over Jerusalem. A Chinese believer there who knew a little English, understood and told us what I said. I was afterwards led to go from street to street and from house to house and speak to them, and Jehovah was with me and held back the powers of darkness, so if any one mocked they either had to give up and listen or go. To God be all the glory! The language has remained ever since; some have denied it, yet it is true. It can be used at any time, but to preach the Gospel only; I can not read nor write the Chinese language.[88]

Wacker thinks that Hansen was the only 'first-generation pentecostal who claimed a permanent gift of missionary tongues'.[89] Although many misunder-standings arose from the belief in missionary tongues, the primary motivation behind this was the conviction that the Spirit had been given to enable the nations of the earth to be reached with the gospel. From the beginning, the movement placed an emphasis on evangelism and missions. As *The Apostolic Faith* declared, it was 'the baptism with the Holy Ghost which is the endue-ment of power, that will make you a witness to the uttermost parts of the earth'.[90] People went to Azusa Street from Europe and went back with the 'baptism', and Pentecostal missionaries were sent out all over the world, according to one estimation reaching over 25 nations in two years.[91] Frank Macchia points out that although 'the mistaken notion of tongues as divinely given human languages as an evangelistic tool was abandoned, the vision of dynamic empowerment for the global witness of the people of God . . . remains fundamental to a Pentecostal understanding of tongues'.[92] Consequently, the failure of the belief in the 'languages of the nations' given at Spirit baptism did not mean that all was lost. There have been isolated but continuing reports of xenolalia throughout Pentecostalism's history.

But the tide was changing. G. B. Cashwell was one of the first to make a dis-tinction between the 'unknown tongues' given at Spirit baptism and the 'gift of tongues' through which 'we will have divers kinds of languages and will speak and be understood'.[93] Thomas Junk in China expressed the increasing pragmatism of Pentecostal missionaries in the field when he wrote, 'Although He [God] hasn't given the language outright, He has wonderfully blessed us in the learning of it.'[94] Berntsen also wrote from China that some missionaries in Beijing had returned home because they 'did not get the language' and the emphasis had shifted in his mission to language learning.[95] In fact, these same language-less Pentecostals depended on 'native workers' who had acquired English and often other languages. They were certainly better linguists than the western missionaries were. Their mission schools focused on teaching English to national people, especially children, in order to communicate their message. In many cases, the nationals acquired a foreign language much quicker than the foreign missionaries did. Alice Wood in Argentina was another example of the new pragmatism, writing in 1910 that they were learn-ing Spanish, 'obliged to go slowly and exercise much patience at first', and that new missionaries could come and learn the language at her station 'unless the Spirit imparts the gift'.[96] Charles Leonard in Cairo, Egypt wrote that he had 'been digging away at the Arabic'. Although Pentecostals still believed 'in the soon coming of the Lord', he went on, and they had 'some very good inter-preters, yet we feel it a duty to study prayerfully the language, to render more efficient service till He come'. He continued, 'God sent the manna from heaven, but the people had to work to gather it. So we are working and praying that in some measure we may have a knowledge of this very difficult language.'[97]

Most early Pentecostal missionaries took this more pragmatic approach. James Harvey from India had a perceptive reason for the failure of Pente-costals to speak in missionary tongues. He said that although the Lord had 'at different times anointed people for a little while to give a message in different languages'; he had not 'given them the language as a gift'. He believed there was a 'good reason' for this, because these new missionaries did 'not understand the customs of the people, and would be doing peculiar things if they went out to preach at once'. He observed that the time spent in language study would help them become acquainted with these customs.[98] By 1917 the newly formed Missionary Conference of the Assemblies of God submitted a series of resolutions for missionaries that were approved by the General Council, including one that insisted on 'two full years of language study, if necessary, before taking up the active work'. These language courses with examinations should be arranged by Advisory Committees of senior missionaries on each field.[99] American Pentecostal missionary ideas on the languages of the nations had come a long way in ten years.

The Role of the Spirit in Mission

The quotation at the start of this chapter illustrates the emphasis that early Pentecostals placed on missions as a result of the experience of Spirit baptism. The promise of Acts 1.8 was that when the Holy Spirit was received people would become witnesses to the 'uttermost parts of the earth'. This was not an option; it was the only way that the Great Commission could be fulfilled and it had to be sought in haste before it was too late and Jesus had returned. As Indianapolis Pentecostal leader and first General Secretary of the Assemblies of God, J. Roswell Flower put it in 1908: 'When the Holy Spirit comes into our hearts, the missionary spirit comes in with it; they are inseparable.' He went on to write that 'carrying the gospel to hungry souls in this and other lands is but a natural result'.[100] Cecil Polhill, director of the Pentecostal Missionary Union (PMU), expressed the conviction in the same year that for any revival to endure it must have 'the true Missionary Spirit'. The Welsh revival 'went back' because it had lacked this, but the 'Pentecostal Blessing', he declared, 'must go right through the world' and was 'the very best thing in the world for the Mission Field'. The gift of the Spirit was a 'Missionary Gift'. The PMU had been founded on the conviction that 'every true Pentecost means missionary service to the ends of the earth'.[101] Alexander Boddy wrote in similar vein that a true 'Pentecost' meant 'a growth of the Missionary Spirit', that 'the indwelling Christ is an indwelling Missionary' who had sent Pentecostals to go, and when they obeyed 'He goes with us in the power of the Holy Ghost to preach a great and a full Salvation for Body, Soul, and Spirit'.[102] There are many examples of this mission emphasis in early periodicals. Gerrit Polman, leader of the Dutch Pentecostal movement wrote, 'The Holy Spirit is a Missionary Spirit and therefore must every baptized Christian be a missionary at home or abroad.'[103]

The theological link between Spirit baptism and missions has always been made in the Pentecostal movement. It is very important to understand the significance of this, because just as Spirit baptism is Pentecostalism's central, most distinctive doctrine, so mission is Pentecostalism's central, most important activity. Minnie Abrams explained that Spirit baptism should 'make us world-wide' and 'enlarge us'. Jesus Christ had said 'that repentance and remission of sins should be preached in His Name to all nations, beginning at Jerusalem', which was 'the program that He laid out for us'. Christ had said that 'He would endue us with power from on high that we might be able to do it'.[104] Abrams was probably the first to give a detailed exposition of Spirit baptism (within a Holiness framework) linking spiritual gifts with missions. Pentecostals were given gifts of the Spirit in order to engage in service to others. This was their mission to the world. As she put it, the 'full Pentecostal baptism of the Holy Ghost' had not been received unless someone had received both the fruit of the Spirit and the gifts of the Spirit as outlined in 1 Corinthians 12. These gifts alone 'enabled the early church to spread the knowledge of the gospel, and establish the Christian church so rapidly'.[105] This fundamental and inseparable link between Spirit baptism, spiritual gifts and missions remained the central plank of the whole structure of Pentecostalism in its first decade. Polhill stated that every missionary needed the baptism of the Spirit with the accompanying spiritual gifts for the task. There had to be 'a distinct seeking of the baptism for service for every missionary, and equally a clear receiving or manifestation, probably the speaking in tongues, accompanying which will be some distinct spiritual gift or gifts to each one'. Only in this way, said Polhill, would 'the Gospel be presented to every creature in the shortest possible time'.[106]

Reflecting on the expansion of Chilean Pentecostalism after two decades in 1930, Willis Hoover wrote that it was 'the missionary spirit' that moved Pentecostals to go to places where the Pentecostal experience was not known. For this some were prepared to migrate to other towns, work at their trade, and 'sow the Word of the Lord'.[107] Some became pastors as a result – to this day Chilean Pentecostalism prefers tried-and-proven leaders who have shown their gifting in ministry to merely theologically trained ones. For early Pentecostals, the baptism in the Spirit was both the primary motivation for and only essential prerequisite for missions. C. W. Doney, on the way to Egypt in 1913, testified in the Stone Church to his Spirit baptism six years earlier as if this experience had been dependent on his agreeing (in a two-way conversation with the Lord) to go out in obedience to any place that the Lord directed. When he declared his willingness to go from his heart, the result was 'down came the blessed Holy Ghost'. This was how God was 'raising up missionaries to go to the regions beyond to carry the Gospel', he concluded.[108]

Spirit baptism was regarded as the supreme preparation needed for engagement in mission in the 'regions beyond'. For early Pentecostal missionaries this meant evangelizing the world before the coming of Christ. Although they did engage in all sorts of philanthropic activities, they had their empowerment by the Spirit to 'go into all the world' as their primary aim. In those days, Spirit baptism was no quick-fix solution to the troubles of humanity. Early Pentecostals spent days, sometimes weeks and even years, waiting in prayer for the 'promise of the Father'. Coupled with the overwhelming desire for power was a conviction that the only way to receive it was through prolonged, constant and persistent prayer, sometimes called 'tarrying' or 'waiting' upon God. There was no other way. As Will Norton in India put it:

> Pentecostal preparation is the only preparation that will meet the need of this peculiarly dark and trying hour. It is a preparation found while on the knees. It means a personal and complete surrender to the will of God. It means a putting away of sin as has not been known since the days of the

apostles. It means a return to the Word of God, and a preaching of that Word in simplicity and deep earnestness. It means the adoption, in the life, of Jesus' method of winning souls.[109]

Pentecostals placed primary emphasis on being 'sent by the Spirit' and depended more on what was described as the Spirit's leading than on formal structures. People called 'missionaries' did that job because the Spirit had directed them to do it, often through some spiritual revelation like a prophecy, a dream or a vision, and even through an audible voice perceived to be that of God. *The Apostolic Faith* declared that Spirit baptism was 'not a work of grace but a gift of power' making the recipient 'a witness unto the uttermost parts of the earth' with 'power to speak in the languages of the nations'.[110] Even though the perceived ability to speak the languages of the nations failed (in most cases), Pentecostal missionaries got on with the job in a hurry, believing that the time was short and the second coming of Christ was near. Reflection about the task was not as important as action in evangelism.[111] The Pentecostal movement from its commencement was a missionary movement made possible by the Spirit's empowerment.[112] It was this fundamental belief in the enabling power of the Spirit that motivated, inspired and sustained the mission of early Pentecostals. Although their missions may be described correctly as pneumatocentric in emphasis, this must not be construed as an over-emphasis on the Spirit to the exclusion of Christ. Most Pentecostals throughout the world have a decidedly Christocentric emphasis in their proclamation and witness. The Spirit bears witness to the presence of Christ in the life of the missionary and the message proclaimed by the power of the Spirit is of the crucified and resurrected Jesus Christ who sends gifts of ministry to humanity. Christian Schoonmaker, CMA and later Pentecostal missionary in India, described his experience illustrating the relationship between Spirit baptism and a high Christology that was characteristic of these early Pentecostals. This was a pneumatological Christology:

> I was deeply conscious that the Holy Spirit had entered into His temple, and was in full control at that moment, because He spoke forth in words His own thoughts through my mouth. The sufferings of Jesus on Calvary were at the same time brought before my soul's vision: He was making real in me what He had purchased on the Cross for me, my union with Him in His death and also my union with Him in His resurrection. Since Christ immersed me in the blessed Spirit I have realised as I never did before what Galatians 2:29 means. As the days come and go, identification with Christ in death and in resurrection unfolds more and more. Greater love for prayer and the study of the Word have sprung up and I find as I pursue these desires with constant watchfulness that my spiritual being is nourished and kept filled with God's love.[113]

Even though the belief in the divine gift of foreign tongues was almost entirely replaced with a belief in 'unknown tongues', the experience of Spirit baptism remained their central point of departure, for they had been thus enabled for the task of going all over the world. The belief in 'missionary tongues' was overshadowed (at least in American Pentecostal circles) by a dominant belief in 'Bible evidence', later called 'initial evidence' and 'initial physical evidence'. Early on, it was declared that 'the bible gives the speaking in tongues by the Spirit of God as the reason, evidence, or proof to those who saw and heard that the persons thus speaking were baptized with the Holy Ghost'.[114] As we have seen, however, belief in xenolalia was not altogether a thing of the past, as occasional reports appeared in the Pentecostal press of tongues as a sign to unbelievers. The doctrine of 'initial evidence' was also challenged in the Pentecostal papers by Pastor Paul in Germany and became a divisive issue in the Pentecostal churches in the USA.[115] Albert Norton, an experienced Pentecostal missionary, had doubts on the doctrine as late as 1920, writing about two of the Indian preachers who had received Spirit baptism. He thought that one of them had received the baptism but had not received 'the gift of tongues'.[116]

Putting aside these doctrinal disputes for the moment, the fact is that from Azusa Street and other centres (including those in other continents), 'Apostolic Faith', Spirit-filled missionaries were sent out to places as far away and diverse as China, India, Japan, Argentina, Brazil, all over Europe, Palestine, Egypt, Somaliland, Liberia, Angola and South Africa – all within two years.[117] This was no mean achievement and the beginning of what is arguably the most significant global expansion of a Christian movement in the entire history of Christianity. The primary motivation for this was that these Pentecostals believed they had received the Missionary Spirit who had empowered them to go to the nations. Everything else we read in what follows must be seen in this light. This chapter has outlined the important role of Seymour and the Azusa Street revival in the thrusting out of American missionaries who believed they could speak the languages of the nations and how these missionaries adjusted when they discovered they could not. Although the belief in 'missionary tongues' had originated with Parham, it took a new revival movement to put these teachings into practical effect and create a missionary migration movement of extraordinary proportions, whose primary motivation was the baptism of the Spirit and whose stated intention was to reach every nation on earth within the shortest possible time. The second part of this book shows how they and others went about this.

Notes

1 *BM* 69 (1 Sept 1910), p.1.
2 *BM* 27 (1 Dec 1908), p.2.
3 Bartleman, *Azusa Street*, p.62.
4 First Baptist Church, Los Angeles, Records, Volume IX (1905), 29 May, 31 May. I am indebted to Timothy Welch, PhD researcher at the University of Birmingham, 2006, for documents on Smale. See also Robeck, *Azusa Street*, pp.58–60.
5 'Pastor Smale Stirs 'Em Up', *Los Angeles Times* (8 June 1905), p.2.3; Bartleman, *Azusa Street*, p.13.
6 Bartleman, *Azusa Street*, p.15.

7 First New Testament Church, *Weekly Bulletin* (8–15 July 1906), pp.1–3; Robeck, *Azusa Street*, pp.83–6.

8 'Rolling on Floor in Smale's Church', *Los Angeles Times* (14 July 1906), 2.1; '"Holy Roller" Mad', *Los Angeles Times* (17 July 1906), 2.14.

9 Bartleman, *Azusa Street*, pp.19–42, 54.

10 'Queer "Gift" Given Many', *Los Angeles Times* (23 July 1906), 1.5

11 *Missionary Review of the World* (July 1906), pp.482–3.

12 Wacker, *Heaven Below*, p.159.

13 Faupel, *Everlasting Gospel*, pp.194–7, 200–2; Robeck, *Azusa Street*, pp.60–9, 81–2.

14 Faupel, *Everlasting Gospel*, pp.182–6, 208–9, 212–16.

15 *AF* 1 (Sept 1906), p.1.

16 *AF* 1 (Sept 1906), p.1.

17 *AF* 1 (Sept 1906), p.1.

18 Anderson, *Vision of the Disinherited*, p.69.

19 *AF* 3 (Nov 1906), p.1.

20 *DPCM*, pp.344–50, 1053–8.

21 Lake, *Adventures in God*, p.19.

22 *TF* 26:12 (Dec 1906), pp.247–53.

23 *WW* 28:5 (May 1906), p.145; 29:2 (Feb 1907), pp.51–2, 54–5.

24 *WW* 29:4 (Apr 1907), p.117

25 *AF* 1 (Sept 1906), p.1.

26 *AF* 4 (Dec 1906), p.1.

27 Faupel, *Everlasting Gospel*, pp.202–5, 208.

28 *AF* 3 (Nov 1906), p.1.

29 *WE* 129 (4 Mar 1916), p.4.

30 *AF* 4 (Dec 1906), p.3; Bundy, 'Thomas Ball Barratt', pp.19–40; Bundy, 'Historical and Theological Analysis', pp.66–92.

31 *Conf* 2:5 (May 1909), p.115; *BM* 78 (15 Jan 1911), p.1; 81 (1 Mar 1911), p.1.

32 *Pent* 2:4 (Mar 1910), p.3; Bartleman, *Azusa Street*, p.83.

33 Bartleman, *Azusa Street*, p.151; *Conf* 5:10 (Oct 1912), pp.233–4.

34 Creech, 'Visions of Glory', pp.405–24; Blumhofer, *Restoring the Faith*, pp.71–84; Wacker, *Heaven Below*, p.6.

35 *AF* 5 (Jan 1907), p.4; Robeck, *Azusa Street*, pp.228–9.

36 *AF* 4 (Dec 1906), p.3; McGee, *This Gospel*, pp.53–67.

37 *AF* 8 (May 1907), p.3.

38 *Live Coals* 5:6 (13 Feb 1907), p.2.

39 Bartleman, *Azusa Street*, p.53.

40 *AF* 1 (Sept 1906), p.1.

41 Bartleman, *Azusa Street*, p.90.

42 *Pent* 1:2 (Sept 1908), p.8.

43 *Pent* 1:4 (Dec 1908), p.16.

44 *Pent* 1:10 (Sept 1909), p.8.

45 *AF* 2 (Oct 1906), p.3.

46 *BM* 56 (15 Feb 1910), p.1; 59 (1 Apr 1910), p.4; 108 (15 Apr 1912), p.1; personal communication, Daniel Woods, 14 Apr 2004.

47 *Trust* 12:8 (Oct 1913), p.2.

48 *LRE* 8:11 (Aug 1916), p.2.

49 *BM* 59 (1 Apr 1910), p.2.

50 *Conf* 1:6 (Sept 1908), p.11.

51 *Pent* 1:7 (June 1909), p.3.

52 *LRE* 2:6 (Mar 1910), p.17.

53 Law, *Pentecostal Mission*, p.2.

54 *LRE* 3:2 (Nov 1910), p.10.

55 *Pent* 1:7 (July 1909), p.5.

56 *Conf* 3:6 (Jun 1910), p.145.

57 *LRE* 2:11 (Aug 1910), p.15.

58 *BM* 64 (15 June 1910), p.1.

59 *AF* 1 (Sept 1906), p.1; 3 (Nov 1906), p.2.

60 *AF* 1 (Sept 1906), p.1.

61 *AF* 1 (Sept 1906), p.2.

62 *AF* 1 (Sept 1906), p.3.

63 *AF* 1 (Sept 1906), p.4; 2 (Oct 1906), p.2.

64 *AF* 1 (Sept 1906), p.1.

65 *AF* 2 (Oct 1906), pp.1–3.

66 Anderson, *Vision*, p.190.

67 Faupel, *Everlasting Gospel*, pp.182–6, 208–9.

68 *AF* (Nov 1906), pp.2, 3, 4.

69 *AF* 4 (Dec 1906), pp.1, 3, 4; 5 (Jan 1907), p.1; 6 (Feb–Mar 1907), pp.1, 3, 4.

70 *AF* 7 (Apr 1907), p.4.

71 *BM* 9 (1 Mar 1908), p.3; *TF* 29:1 (Jan 1909), pp. 11–12.

72 *AF* 7 (Apr 1907), pp.1, 2, 3, 4.

73 *AF* 8 (May 1907) pp.1, 3

74 *Word and Work* 32:1 (Jan 1910), p.13.

75 *AF* 9 (June–Sept 1907), p.1.

76 *BM* 66 (15 July 1910), p.1.

77 *Conf* 4:1 (Jan 1911), p.8.

78 Quoted in Robeck, *Azusa Street*, p.246.

79 *Conf* 1:2 (May 1908), p.21.

80 *Conf* 1:2 (May 1908), pp.21–2.

81 *BM* 14 (15 May 1908), p.1; 51 (1 Dec 1909), p.2; 52 (15 Dec 1909), p.2; 55 (1 Feb 1910), p. 4; 58 (15 Mar 1910), p.2; 61 (1 May 1910), p.2; 62 (15 May 1910), p.2; 64 (15 June 1910), p.2; *Conf* 3:5 (May 1910), pp.113–14; 3:11 (Nov 1910), p.251; Wacker, *Heaven Below*, pp.49–50.

82 *LRE* 6:10 (July 1914), p.18.

83 *Conf* 2:8 (Aug 1909), p.181.

84 *Conf* 6:7 (July 1913), p.143; *LRE* 5:10 (July 1913), p.15.

85 *LRE* 5:5 (Feb 1913), p.14; *BM* 129 (15 Mar 1913), p.4.

86 *TF* 30:11 (Nov 1910), pp.253–5; *WW* 32:12 (Dec 1910), p.372.

87 *Pent* 1:9 (Aug 1909), p.2; *UR* 2:1 (Aug 1910), p.6; *BM* 70 (15 Sept 1910), p.2; 86 (15 May 1911), p.3; *LRE* 3:11 (Aug 1911), p.13.

88 *TF* 36:6 (June 1916), pp.141–2; *WE* 148 (15 July 1916), p.11.

89 Wacker, *Heaven Below*, p.46.

90 *AF* 6 (Feb–Mar 1907), p.1.

91 Faupel, *Everlasting Gospel*, pp.212–16; Robeck, 'Pentecostal Origins', pp.176–7.

92 Macchia, 'Struggle for Global Witness', p.17.

93 *BM* 8 (15 Feb 1908), p.1.

94 *BM* 26 (15 Nov 1908), p.4; *BM* 32 (15 Feb 1909), p.1.

95 *BM* 51 (1 Dec 1909), p.3.

96 *BM* 62 (15 May 1910), p.4.

97 *WW* 36:1 (Jan 1914), p.24.

98 *LRE* 9:5 (Feb 1917), pp.17–18.

99 *WE* 210 (13 Oct 1917), p.3.

100 Quoted by McGee, 'Pentecostals and their Various Strategies', p.206.

101 *Conf* 2:1 (Jan 1909), p.15; 2:6 (June 1909), p.129; 3:8 (Aug 1910), p.198.

102 *Conf* 3:8 (Aug 1910), p.199.

103 *WE* 211 (20 Oct 1917), p.13.

104 *LRE* 3:8 (May 1911), p.8.

105 *WW* 33:8 (Aug 1911), p.244.

106 *FF* 12 (July 1913), p.3.

107 Hoover, *History*, p.124.

108 *LRE* 5:12 (Sept 1913), p.6.

109 *TF* 36:9 (Sept 1916), p.202.

110 *AF* 4 (Dec 1906), p.1.

111 Dempster, Klaus and Petersen, *Called and Empowered*, p.201.

112 Penney, *Missionary Emphasis*, pp.11, 15; McGavran, 'What makes Pentecostal', p.122; Wagner, *Look Out!* p.29.

113 *WW* 31:2 (Feb 1909), 31.

114 *Pent* 1:3 (Nov 1908), p.5.

115 *Conf* 3:10 (Oct 1910), p.233.

116 *WW* 42:5 (May 1920), p.28.

117 Faupel, *Everlasting Gospel*, pp.182–6, 208–9, 212–16.

Part Two

Spread in Three Continents

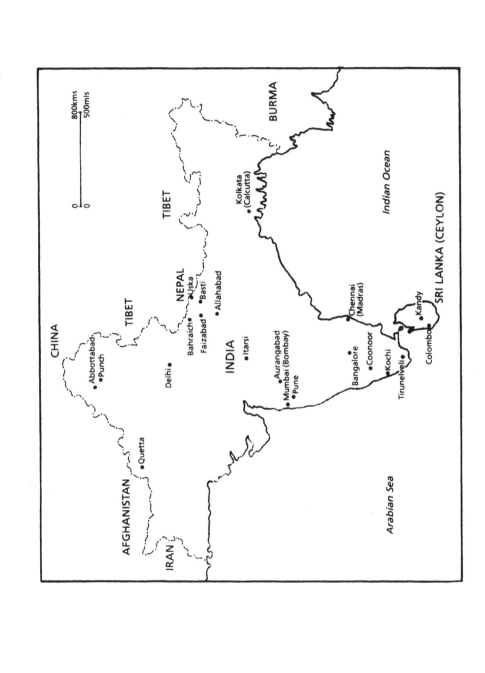

4

To Suit their Nature and Feelings: Indian Beginnings

Let the revival come to Indians so as to suit their nature and feelings, [as] God has made them. He knows their nature, and He will work out His purpose in them in a way which may not conform with the ways of Western people and their lifelong training. Let the English and other Western Missionaries begin to study the Indian nature, I mean the religious inclinations, the emotional side of the Indian mind. Let them not try to conduct revival meetings and devotional exercises altogether in Western ways and conform with Western etiquette. If our Western teachers and foreignised Indian leaders want the work of God to be carried on among us in their own way, they are sure to stop or spoil it.

(Pandita Ramabai, 1905)[1]

Britain regarded India, with a population of over three hundred million by the end of the nineteenth century and vast natural resources, as the jewel in her imperial crown. All her relationships with other European powers and other colonies were dependent on and subservient to the primary purpose of Britain maintaining firm sovereignty over India. Even Britain's participation in the 'scramble for Africa' was conditioned by her desire that trade routes to India should not be endangered. The imperial Indian army was the backbone of British military might, protecting British interests for a century. India and Sri Lanka's resources, especially raw materials like rubber, tea and cotton, were exported to supply British industries and then sold back to Indian traders at exorbitant prices. Britain subverted and almost destroyed India's lucrative textile trade, so that India had to import British textiles in order to meet its own demands. British prosperity increasingly became India's poverty during the nineteenth century. British control was not easily achieved however, as determined Indian resistance to colonial oppression and racism included the violent Indian Mutiny in north and central India in 1857. As a result, direct British rule was imposed in place of the East India Company.

Not all India was ruled by Britain however, for over a third of the subcontinent consisted of semi-autonomous states and territories administered by Indian rulers, and at least until the 1930s there were five small French enclaves and a larger Portuguese one at Goa. The creation of the Indian National Congress in 1885 was the first subcontinent-wide political party, which increasingly challenged British rule. This organization successfully resisted British plans to partition Bengal (1905–11) and by the end of the Great War was demanding home rule. By 1920 Mahatma Gandhi had launched his non-violent mass resistance that led ultimately to the independence of India in 1947. But there was also religious and cultural resistance. The 'Indian

Renaissance' manifested itself in various ways both in fomenting resistance to colonialism and in Hindu movements like the Brahmo Samaj, founded by Ram Mahan Roy in the 1820s to promote the restoration of Hindu monotheism.[2] For some Indians in the early twentieth century, Christian missionaries were agents of the empire imposing their religion in order to ensure subjection to their rule. For some others, however, especially women suffering under a harsh patriarchal social system, the unscheduled 'tribal' peoples and the pariah 'untouchable' classes, the Dalits, the egalitarian principles of Christianity provided certain relief.

Pentecostal missionaries from the West came to a subcontinent in turmoil, with a deep resentment of the imperialistic policies that had impoverished its peoples. Evangelical societies of the 'faith mission' type were increasing and independent Pentecostal missionaries used these contacts. India, like China, was regarded by evangelicals as a land of unparalleled opportunities. As far as they were concerned, this was a country whose people were receptive to the gospel as never before. One missionary report put it:

> The removal of long standing obstacles, the eagerness of the people to hear, the growing friendliness of all classes, the deepening sense of the inadequacy of the old religions to meet their spiritual needs, and the, as yet dim, but sure, convictions that in Christ their soul hunger can find satisfaction – all these constitute an opportunity the like of which has never been witnessed before. The splendid spiritual harvests of past years are harbingers of still greater to come.[3]

I have been unable to enter into the lives of the Indian pioneers who spread Pentecostalism in villages and cities all over the subcontinent, because of the emphasis in the sources on 'their' foreign missionaries. But here and there we get a glimpse – even in these rather chaotic beginnings – from scattered reports. In India, expatriate missionaries depended almost entirely on Indian evangelists and Bible women for communicating effectively and for the growth of their work. These Indian workers are sometimes referred to in their reports, probably more than in any other 'mission field'.

Will Norton, born in India and son of a missionary, believed that Pentecostals had no time to lose. They had the solution for the salvation of the lost millions of India, whose 'awful need of help' could be met through the power of the Spirit. Preparing themselves in prayer for 'Pentecostal power' was 'right now needed for world witnessing'. He said that there were 'millions of people now in India' who had 'never once heard the Name of Jesus, a heaven to go to or a hell to be warned of'. Thousands of these people were 'dying daily without Christ'.[4] The problem in India was not receptivity, according to these circles, but the great shortage of missionary volunteers. Pentecostals were urged to join an 'aggressive campaign' to reach the 'depressed classes'. The caste system was one of the greatest challenges for western missionaries. Pentecostals joined in its general condemnation by Christian missionaries, pointing to the benefits of the message that proclaims unity and equality of all in Christ.[5] The 'Pariah' (Dalit) caste was considered the most open to Christian advances and missionaries were urged to penetrate into their villages.[6] But the story of the beginnings of Pentecostalism in India must begin at the other end of the stratified Indian social system, with a Christian Brahmin woman and the revival movement she led.

Pandita Ramabai and the Mukti Revival

Pandita Sarasvati Ramabai (1858–1922), that most famous Indian woman, Christian, reformer, Bible translator and social activist – and in particular the revival movement in her mission – had an important role in the emergence of Pentecostalism worldwide. Ramabai is both significant in the origins of Pentecostalism and in the acceptance of its phenomena among some in the wider Christian community. The importance of her revival movement is born out by the prominence given to it in reports in the emerging Pentecostal press, both in India and especially in Britain and North America. Ramabai was a converted Brahmin who had earlier rejected Hindu social propriety and married out of her caste. She was widowed with her baby daughter Manoramabai after less than two years' marriage. She became a Christian during her almost three-year stay in England, where she studied education at the Cheltenham Ladies' College and was baptized in the Church of England in 1883. She also spent time studying Greek and Hebrew with Canon Cooke, to whom she in turn taught Sanskrit.[7]

From England she travelled to the USA, where she spent two-and-a-half years (1886–8) studying education systems in Philadelphia and later publicizing her planned mission in India by travelling across the USA, for which she also received pledges of financial support. She published a book in 1887 outlining the plight of Indian women titled *The High-Caste Hindu Woman*, pleading for the creation of educational institutions for Indian women and setting out her own vision to create one.[8] As a result, a 'Ramabai Association' was founded in the USA to pledge financial support for her school for the next ten years.[9] During this time she also wrote a book in her mother tongue Marathi on her observations of life in the USA, in which she contrasted the free democracy there with the colonial oppression of Britain, and gave her preference for voluntary denominations over state churches like the Church of England. Her rejection of British colonialism remained with her all her life – like most educated Indians, she believed in Indian nationalism, stimulated by the British rulers' repression and arrogance towards Indian social structures that had resulted in determined Indian resistance. She favourably commented on women's rights in American society, although not without fair criticism of shortcomings there.[10] She was a dedicated ecumenist before the word was coined in the twentieth century, deploring the divisions within Christianity and pleading for a united Indian church.[11]

She returned to India in 1889 and started a home for widows near Bombay (now Mumbai) that moved to Pune after a year. In 1895 she established a mission on a farm she had bought at Kedgaon near Pune, and her work shifted from a religiously 'neutral' charity to an overtly evangelical Christian organization. As a result, she lost the support of Hindu parents and the resignation of her committee ensued.[12] This mission was given the name 'Mukti' ('salvation') and its main purpose was to provide a refuge for destitute girls and young women, particularly those who had been the victims of child marriages and had become widows, and those rescued from starvation in famine areas. It had 48 girls and young women in 1896, but during that year 300 girls were rescued from famine in Madhya Pradesh and by 1900 there were almost 2,000 residents there.[13] This faith mission was well known internationally by 1905, the year the revival started. For some years the mission struggled to make ends meet and funds only came in to cover bare necessities.[14] But Ramabai believed that Hindu women could only find complete freedom by converting to Christianity and her Mission aimed to do this and provide a total environment for its large community trained in income-generating skills. Her overtly evangelistic aims brought her into conflict with the Hindu majority. But by 1907 the Mission had expanded to include a rescue mission, a hospital, an oil-press, a blacksmith forge, a printing press, a complete school that provided college entrance, a school for the blind, and training departments in teaching, nursing, weaving, tailoring, bread and butter making, tinning, laundering, masonry, carpentry and farming. In 1907 the blurb on the back of the newsletter, *Mukti Prayer-Bell* (most of which was written by Ramabai herself) said that the Mission was a 'purely undenominational, evangelical, Christian Mission, designed to reach and help high-caste Hindu widows, deserted wives and orphans from all parts of India', who would receive 'a thorough training for some years' after which they would 'go out as teachers or Bible women to work in different Missions'.[15]

Ramabai and her daughter Manoramabai made further visits to the USA and Britain,[16] and she had a team of 70, including 25 volunteer workers from overseas. One of these was Minnie Abrams, a 'deaconess missionary' in the Methodist Church since 1887 who joined Ramabai as an independent faith missionary in 1898 and took care of the mission during Ramabai's trip that year to the USA.[17] Abrams was a very significant contact person between Ramabai and the emerging global Pentecostal network. Although Mukti was partially supported by various western sources, Ramabai provided food for her Mission from its 230-acre farm and sent financial support to other missions in India, Korea and China on a regular basis. In 1904 she began her translation of the Bible into Marathi from Hebrew and Greek, a process that took her 18 years (almost to the end of her life) and a most remarkable, if somewhat anachronistic achievement. Of course she would have benefited from the tools of modern exegesis and the professionalism that usually characterizes team translation efforts today. It also seems that she intended her translation to replace the existing Marathi translation with its terminological leanings to Sanskrit Hinduism, a practice the rather narrow fundamentalism of her later years found unacceptable. Her own stated intention was for the Marathi Bible to be 'simpler that it may be better understood by common men and women', and 'to rid the Bible . . . of certain words which express idolatrous ideas'.[18] Ramabai also arranged for a musician to set her translation of the Psalms to Indian chant tunes, in order to change the over-westernized Indian Christian liturgies that she so disliked. She died in 1922, less than a year after her daughter's death.[19]

Much of the Christian half of Ramabai's life resonated with Pentecostal images and experiences. The earlier experiences were expressed in terms already in vogue in evangelical circles at the time. In about 1894 she had a definite experience described by her niece as 'the blessing of the Holy Spirit', when she was filled with joy and peace. Ramabai herself did not refer to this as 'baptism in' or being 'filled with' the Spirit, but wrote: 'I found it a great blessing to realise the personal presence of the Holy Spirit in me, and to be guided and taught by Him.'[20] It was later reported that she saw her need to be 'filled with the Spirit' and she professed to 'enter on a new experience of God's power to save, bless and use'.[21] From this time onwards she identified increasingly with the radical evangelicals, the Keswick, 'higher Christian life' and Holiness movements, and D. L. Moody and many revivalist networks began to promote her work in their publications. Ramabai attended and addressed the Keswick convention in England in 1898, where she asked for prayer for an outpouring of the Spirit on Indian Christians and pleaded for '1,000 Holy Ghost missionaries'.[22]

After hearing of the Welsh revival and a revival conducted by R. A. Torrey in Australia, she dispatched Manoramabai and Minnie Abrams there in 1904 to observe what was needed, and they returned with the conviction that prayer and 'pouring out your life' were required for revival.[23] As a result of their visit, in January 1905 Ramabai instituted a special early-morning daily prayer meeting, when 70 women would meet and pray, in her own words 'for the true conversion of all the Indian Christians including ourselves, and for a special outpouring of the Holy Spirit on all Christians of every land'. The number at this daily prayer meeting gradually increased to 500. In July 1905, as she wrote two years later, 'the Lord graciously sent a Holy Ghost revival among us, and also in many schools and churches in this country'.[24] Some of the biographical accounts of Ramabai do not mention the Mukti revival at all for ideological reasons,[25] while others and Ramabai herself only elaborate a little on it. But the revival lasted for a year and a half and resulted in 1,100 baptisms at the school, confessions of sins and repentances, prolonged prayer meetings and the witnessing of some 700 of these young women in teams into the surrounding areas, about 100 going out daily, sometimes for as long as a month at a time. Ramabai formed what she called a 'Bible school' of 200 young women to pray in groups called 'Praying Bands' and to be trained in witnessing to their faith. These Praying Bands spread the revival wherever they went and some remarkable healings were reported.[26] Ramabai was also convinced in the second coming of Christ to take away the church, though lacking the more elaborate theories and sense of imminence that characterized the ideas of some contemporary premillennialists.[27]

The revival was reported in the western evangelical and Pentecostal press soon after it occurred, one editor stating how it would spread. Ramabai was on a missionary tour through the Mahratta country, had had meetings at Pune at different centres for Indian churches, and had with her 'a band of Spirit-filled women to bear their testimony'. The paper fully expected 'the "fire" to spread more rapidly from the Mukti center, because Pandita Ramabai is able to move about among the Indian churches and take with her a band of Spirit-filled witnesses'.[28] These various reports give a clearer understanding of the significance of this revival to the new movement there and abroad. References to the revival are plentiful and clearly situate it within the emerging Pentecostal movement.

The Apostolic Faith had major articles on it, including one by Albert Norton, a former Methodist missionary of over 30 years' experience working near and in co-operation with the Mukti Mission, two from Max Wood Moorhead's Cloud of Witnesses published in India and extracts from Ramabai's own periodical, the Mukti Prayer-Bell. All these attest to the importance placed on this revival by the Azusa Street Mission. The revival and the work of the Mukti Mission was reported on in Confidence, The Pentecost and The Latter Rain Evangel, in the latter case continuing from 1909 to 1913. The first report of the revival in India entitled 'Pentecost in India' was carried in the third issue of The Apostolic Faith in Los Angeles, an excerpt from India Alliance, a paper of the CMA:

> News comes from India that the baptism with the Holy Ghost and gift of tongues is being received there by natives who are simply taught of God. The India Alliance says, 'Some of the gifts which have been scarcely heard of in the church for many centuries, are now being given by the Holy Ghost to simple, unlearned members of the body of Christ, and communities are being stirred and transformed by the wonderful grace of God. Healing, the gift of tongues, visions, and dreams, discernment of spirits, the power to prophecy and to pray the prayer of faith, all have a place in the present revival.' Hallelujah! God is sending the Pentecost to India. He is no respecter of persons.[29]

Although this report refers to several gifts of the Spirit occurring in the wider context of community transformation, it states that speaking in tongues occurred in the Bombay area before news of Azusa Street had reached India,[30] and the first missionaries to India from Azusa Street, Albert and Lillian Garr, only reached Calcutta (Kolkata) a month after the report.[31]

The first direct report from Mukti came from Albert Norton (c. 1850–1923), a senior Pentecostal missionary in India who wrote regularly in most Pente-costal papers. He had been there since 1872 as a graduate Methodist minister under William Taylor. He was committed especially to orphanage work and famine relief. His mission at Dhond in the Pune district commenced in 1900 after Ramabai invited him to come there, and two of his sons helped him in this work. The Dhond mission worked in tandem with Mukti Mission and took over all the boys previously housed at Mukti. Norton was an early observer of the revival in Mukti that began in 1905 and was clearly sympathetic with the spiritual gifts that had erupted there. At one time the Dhond mission was caring for 600 boys who were orphans and famine victims.[32] His letter dated 21 March was published in the April 1907 issue of The Apostolic Faith. Norton said that in about September 1906 they had heard of the gift of tongues being received by 'Christian believers in different places and countries'. He had visited Mukti Mission a week earlier, where in a prayer meeting he had seen an uneducated Indian girl whom he knew to be 'utterly unable to speak or under-stand English' praying in English 'idiomatically, distinctly and fluently'. At the same time others were speaking in English and some speaking in tongues ('not gibberish', he hastened to add), but 'it closely resembled the speaking of foreign languages' which he did not understand. On the previous weekend he had again visited the Mission where he described 'some 24 different persons had received the gift of tongues'. He suggested that those girls who had spoken in English (and not in some other Indian language) had done so because 'it is in mercy to us poor missionaries from Europe and America, who as a class seem to be doubting Thomases in regard to the gifts and working of the Spirit, and are not receiving the power of the Holy Spirit, as we ought'. Norton concluded that this was 'abundant evidence that God was working in a wonderful way' and that 'those speaking in tongues gave evidence that their souls were flooded with blessing from God'. He wrote that they were 'waiting on God for the bestowment of all the Spirit's gifts which He has for us' and asked for prayers to this end.[33] A Pentecostal revival was reported to have broken out in Dhond among the boys in Norton's school in April 1908 and Norton was a convinced Pentecostal thereafter, later listed with George Berg and A. H. Post in *The Pentecost* as Pentecostal missionaries supported in India.

In September 1907 *The Apostolic Faith* published a letter from the Garrs, who mentioned that Ramabai and her daughter had been 'tarrying' for the Spirit, who had come to them, a number of her teachers, and 300 'native girls'. This issue ran another report on the revival titled 'Manifestations of the Spirit in India' taken from a 'published report from the Mission at Mukti'. It refers to frequent scenes of various phenomena experienced in the revivals in 'Assam and India', including trembling, shaking, loud crying and confessions, unconsciousness in ecstasy or prayer, sudden falling to the ground twisting and writhing during exorcisms, and 'joy unspeakable' manifested by singing, clapping, shouting praises and dancing. Speaking in tongues is not mentioned in this report, but it warns against those who would 'suppress these manifestations' and thereby grieve the Holy Spirit and stop the work. The writer was Minnie Abrams, whose admonition is significant:

> We do not need to worry over these manifestations, nor seek to suppress them . . . we have seen over and over again during the past fifteen months, that where Christian workers have suppressed these manifestations, the Holy Spirit has been grieved, the work has stopped, and no fruit of holy lives has resulted . . . The writer testifies that she has in the silence of the midnight hour, alone in her room without a sound in the house, been shaken from her innermost being, until her whole body was convulsed, and filled with joy and consciousness that the Holy Spirit had taken possession of every part of her being. No one had greater prejudice against religious excitement than she, but every time she put her hands upon the work at Mukti to suppress joy or strong conviction, or reproved persons being strongly wrought upon in prayer, the work of revival stopped, and she had to confess her fault before it went on again. We have learned that God's ways are past finding out, as far above ours as the heavens are above the earth.[34]

In the *Mukti Prayer-Bell* of September 1907 Abrams also has an account of the revival, which she said began two years earlier, but that they felt that they 'had not yet received a mighty Pentecost'. In February 1907 one of the Praying

Bands and a Swedish missionary Miss Stroberg received 'an outpouring of the Holy Spirit' in which they sang and spoke in tongues and this soon was spread in the main Mission. She wrote that the 'praise and intercession in unknown tongues are full of power', but added significantly that the manifestations which she called 'demonstrations' – including shaking, rolling on the floor, clapping, jumping, groaning and crying – were 'not as great as in the revival of 1905'. In Abrams' account prominence is given to speaking in 'unknown tongues'. She also gave an outline of the 'creed' of the Mukti Mission and *inter alia*, said that the 'baptism of the Holy Ghost, giving power for service, is given with the gifts of the Spirit as recorded in 1 Cor. 12.4–11' and that these doctrines are 'accepted and taught by all of the Mukti staff of workers'.[35]

Max Wood Moorhead, a Presbyterian missionary who became Pentecostal through the ministry of the Garrs in Calcutta, published a series of pamphlets called *Cloud of Witnesses to Pentecost in India*, from which an extract in *The Apostolic Faith* (September 1907) appeared, titled 'Pentecost in Mukti, India'. After a general account of the work going on in the Mission, he made this interesting observation:

> Both Pandita Ramabai and Miss Abrams were deeply impressed by the truth contained in the reports which came from Los Angeles concerning Pentecost, and believing that God was willing to send like Pentecostal blessings to Mukti which up to that time had not been received, after the manner described in Acts 2, they exhorted all the Christian boys and girls to begin to tarry for the promised baptism of the Holy Ghost. In taking this step, Pandita Ramabai fully acknowledged all that God had bestowed through His Spirit in the past; but she discerned there was the deeper fullness of the outpouring of the Holy Ghost accompanied with the gift of tongues which had not yet been received. Before Christmas 1906, the seekers assembled in the Church daily at 6 o'clock in the morning for a time of waiting on God.

Moorhead thought that Pentecostal manifestations at Mukti were only received at Christmas 1906 after they had heard of the events in Los Angeles. That is partly correct, as widespread tongues speaking at Mukti probably followed the visit of Maud Orlebar there after her own Spirit baptism in Calcutta. A group of 20 girls had visited another mission station where Moorhead reported that all 20, with two missionary women, 'received the Pentecostal baptism of the Holy Ghost and all were speaking in new tongues'. This spread to others at Mukti (perhaps hundreds), and Moorhead commented that Mukti is now 'the glad scene of a continuous Pentecost' with speaking in tongues, interpretation, prophecy and healing (including in the Mission hospital) taking place regularly. The report concluded that the Mukti people were 'believing for the restoration to the Church of all the lost gifts of the Spirit'.[36] Moorhead became the origin of the mistaken assumption that the Pentecostal revival in India was a direct consequence of the Azusa Street revival. His source for the chronology of events and his linking the tongues at Mukti with the Los Angeles revival is uncertain, as he seems to have used indirect reports. Undoubtedly, his own introduction to Pentecost through the

Garrs in Calcutta in January 1907 influenced his suppositions, expressed in a 1913 article, 'How Pentecost came to Calcutta' and later reproduced by Stanley Frodsham. But there were several occasions of tongues speaking in different parts of India in the months before the Azusa Street revival was heard of there. Two months after a visit by a Praying Band from Mukti to an Anglican mission station in Aurangabad in April 1906 (the month the Los Angeles revival began), tongues were evident among those who had been present – in June in Manmad and in July 1906 in Bombay. Abrams later recorded that this was the first speaking in tongues to be made public in India.[37] It was this revival movement that was reported by Norton in *The Apostolic Faith* as occurring in September 1906. Furthermore, the April 1907 issue recorded the first letter from Lillian Garr in India in which she clearly did not think that they had been the first to bring the Pentecostal experience there, writing, 'We found India ripe for [Pentecost], in fact the revival had already broken out among the natives, and some were speaking in tongues.'[38]

It is unlikely that Los Angeles had any influence on what happened at Mukti, even if Ramabai and Abrams had heard of the American revival before that, which is also unlikely. Abrams' own account of revivals in various parts of the world specifically links the Mukti revival with those in Wales and north-west India, sees the Korean and Manchurian revivals as issuing from these same sources, and the Los Angeles and European Pentecostal revivals as connected but separate movements.[39] Since meeting with the Garrs in Calcutta and receiving Spirit baptism there in March 1908 after two months of 'tarrying', Moorhead had become a convinced exponent of the 'initial evidence' teaching – one that alienated him from those with a more inclusive yet sympathetic view of tongues like Ramabai, Abrams and William Hamner Piper in Chicago.[40] Although the Garrs did visit Mukti at Ramabai's invitation, a later report reveals that before they got there a repetition of 'Pentecost' had happened in which 'all the nine gifts of the Spirit were in manifestation'.[41] Moorhead also considered Calcutta to be the birthplace of Pentecostalism in India because this was where the 'initial evidence' teaching had first been taught – even though only some 13 or 14 had spoken in tongues there, compared to possibly hundreds in the Bombay and Pune areas.[42] He mentions Mukti once more in *The Apostolic Faith*, briefly stating that the revival was continuing in May 1908.[43] But the actual origins of Pentecostalism in India have been obscured through this assumption of a Los Angeles 'Jerusalem'.[44] Another report came from a professional journalist William Ellis in January 1908. At Mukti he witnessed what he wrote was 'utterly without parallel in all my wide experience', a 'Baptism with fire' and pouring out of 'the gift of tongues' whereby 'ignorant Hindoo girls speak in Sanskrit, Hebrew, Greek, English and other languages as yet unidentified'. He described in detail the ecstatic manifestations he saw at a prayer meeting of young women, including speaking in 'unknown tongues' and he interviewed both the leader of this meeting and Ramabai herself.[45] It is best to see both the Mukti and the Azusa Street revivals (as well as the 1909 Chilean revival) as formative events contributing towards the emergence of Pentecostalism.

The reflections of Ramabai herself on these events portray her as a sympathetic and involved participant in a Pentecostal revival. She is quoted as saying that she had regarded the manifestations during the Mukti revival 'with much concern for some time', but that she 'did not try to interfere with God's work in any way'.[46] The January 1908 issue of *The Apostolic Faith* carried a report directly from the *Mukti Prayer-Bell*,[47] selectively cut from a longer article by Ramabai whom the editors of *The Apostolic Faith* did not mention by name. In its original form this is one of the most revealing passages because it demonstrates the thoughts of Ramabai on this fledgling Pentecostal movement, which she wisely but firmly defended. Writing in September 1907, Ramabai said that 'earlier this year, the Lord began to give us a fresh spiritual uplift, another and greater outpouring of the Holy Spirit'. She then discussed the fact that some of the young women in her Praying Band were speaking in tongues, for which she 'praised God for doing something new for us'. She wrote that God had given her an explanation (quoting the 'tongues' passages in Isaiah 28 and 1 Corinthians 14) and that she would not try to stop the work of the Spirit. Ramabai wrote that she was 'not aware that anything like the present Holy Ghost revival, has ever visited India before the year 1905', and that many had 'stumbled' over the manifestations and criticized the revival. 'Mountains have been made out of mole hills', she wrote, and were 'greatly exaggerated' reports. Ramabai did not think that the 'tongue movement' was 'of the devil, or is confined to a few hysterical women' (as A. T. Pierson had charged), but was 'convinced more and more' that those given the gift of tongues had been 'greatly helped to lead better lives' and were more effective in prayer and evangelism as a result.[48] Pierson had described the tongues at Mukti as leading to 'indecencies' committed by 'hysterical women'; and after mentioning this searing criticism of Indian Christians by a 'great preacher',[49] Ramabai had this tongue-in-cheek comment about western criticisms of the revival:

> Why should not the Holy Spirit have liberty to work among Indian Christian people, as He has among Christians of other countries? And why should everything that does not reach the high standard of English and American civilization, be taken as coming from the devil? I do not understand . . . I see that God is doing great things for us and among us . . . What has happened here, during this revival, is not an imitation of anybody. Had these people who have come under the power of the Holy Ghost been mere imitators, they would certainly have shown their inclination toward that way before the revival began . . . We do not find many such hypocrites among them.[50]

Her underlying nationalism and desire for an authentically Indian church moved on by the Spirit in an Indian way is revealed. She went on to write about the gift of tongues, which she said was 'certainly one of the signs of the baptism of the Holy Spirit' and for which there was 'scriptural ground' – but Ramabai did not find 'scripture warrant' for the belief that 'speaking in tongues is the only and necessary sign of baptism of the Holy Spirit'. The gifts of healing, tongues, prophecy and other gifts were 'not to be discarded' but encouraged.[51] She ended this ten-page exhortation by witnessing to the physical manifestations happening to both 'the most ignorant of our people' and 'the most refined and highly educated English men and women', and stated: 'I, for one, do not dare to put them down as a few ignorant and "hysterical women". I wish that all of us could get this wonderful and divine hysteria . . .' After quoting the words of Christ, 'How much more shall your Heavenly Father give the Holy Spirit to them that ask Him', Ramabai concluded: 'We have been asking our Heavenly Father to give us the Holy Spirit and not evil spirits. He has answered our prayer. We praise Him, we bless Him, we magnify His Holy Name, and we thank Him with all our heart.'[52] The significance of this passage is that Ramabai defends the Indian Pentecostal manifestations, including tongues, against the prevailing criticisms of prominent western evangelical leaders. She repeats this defence and her sympathetic view of tongues in her interview with the journalist Ellis.[53]

A couple of months later, Ramabai again expressed her own thoughts on the revival published in the local Christian press. Her 'Stray Thoughts on the Revival' repeated her conviction that she should not interfere with the work of the Holy Spirit in the revival by laying down laws. Her article gave a clear indication of what Ramabai thought its effects were: the means by which the Holy Spirit was creating a contextual form of Indian Christianity. This revival was to proceed according to the will of the Spirit, who knew perfectly well how to work in harmony with the Indian psyche to 'suit their nature and feelings', and would be hindered by 'foreignised' western ideas of decorum.[54] These ideas were shaped by Ramabai's background in philosophical Brahmanism and her resistance to all forms of imperialism. Other biographers of Ramabai mention the features of this revival: ecstasy, singing to familiar Indian tunes, praying aloud simultaneously, and speaking in tongues. Ramabai was completely at home with these Pentecostal phenomena, and although we do not know whether she herself experienced the more ecstatic manifestations, we do know that her daughter Manoramabai had spoken in tongues.[55]

T. B. Barratt arrived in Bombay in 1908 for what was to include a two-month stay at the missionary retreat station at Coonoor and the CMA had supported him.[56] There he prayed for many CMA missionaries for Spirit baptism and met up with other missionaries like Post.[57] Barratt himself reported that he had been invited and financed in January 1908 by Anthony H. Groves, a tea planter in the Nilgiri hills in South India and son of Brethren missionary and revivalist Anthony Norris Groves. Barratt had also received encouraging letters from Moorhead and Maud Orlebar. He travelled from Europe via Syria and met Lucy Leatherman in Lebanon. On arrival in Bombay he was met by Moorhead and held meetings mainly with CMA missionaries. His journey to Coonoor was primarily to visit missionaries during their three-month recess to the hills in the hot season, and to help alleviate the 'bitterness' created by the Garrs' recent visit to Coonoor.[58] We don't know exactly what the nature of the controversy around the Garrs was, but it may have had something to do with their insistence on tongues as necessary evidence of Spirit baptism – a view which Barratt did not share. Barratt reproduced a letter of support from Minnie Abrams to gainsay what he called those 'evil-minded persons' who had said 'that the revival at Mukti had nothing to do with the Pentecostal revival'.[59] He wrote that there were 13 mission organizations spread over five Indian provinces in which there were 'fire-baptized witnesses' and later, before he left India in August 1908, he had visited Mukti, spoken to 1,200 young women in an assembly there, and was awestruck by the simultaneous praying he had heard among them. After they had dispersed to classes, some remained 'lying prostrate on the floor, praying and speaking in tongues'.[60]

The annual conventions in the Stone Church in 1909 and 1910 featured Minnie Abrams as speaker during her last furlough at her home in nearby Wisconsin; and her six addresses were published in the periodical.[61] In one, she gave a detailed account of the second revival at Mukti (1907), where she described the prayer meetings and how important the gifts of the Spirit were in that revival. She said that 'a mighty spirit of prayer' had come upon their people, who pleaded earnestly 'for salvation and the out-pouring of the Spirit upon the children of God, and upon the heathen'. The result of this was that 'God poured out upon us a mighty wave of speaking in other tongues, and a mighty wave of interpretation; He used the Spirit of prophecy in witnessing to the heathen, and He sent us out on several occasions a hundred at a time.'[62] Abrams' report abounds with Pentecostal imagery and situates the Mukti revival squarely within the parameters of early Pentecostalism. She also appealed for experienced women to go with her to Mukti, because she felt that the young Indian women could not evangelize without 'the protection of older women'. Because there were no older Indian women among the Mukti workers, she wrote, 'we have to look to foreign lands for women who have the experience and grace and have the power to witness, who will go out with these hundreds of native women to enable them to preach the Gospel to their own country people'.[63]

In January 1909 Carrie and George Montgomery began their six-month tour of Pentecostal and CMA missions in South China and India. George's report from two days at Mukti mentioned that four to five hundred of the 1,500 girls at Mukti had 'been baptized with the Spirit and speak with new tongues'. 'None can doubt', he wrote, 'that the Latter Rain as a great flood has been poured out at Mukti', and that 'all the workers there are baptized with the Spirit and speak in tongues'. Visitors from other parts of India and all over the world were visiting there.[64] During her furlough in 1909–10, Minnie Abrams spoke at major Pentecostal conventions on behalf of Ramabai, not only at Piper's Stone Church, but also at Montgomery's mission in Oakland, Elim Tabernacle in Rochester, New York, a large missionary camp meeting run by Lupton and his associates in Homestead, Pennsylvania, and Copley's Christian Assembly in Kansas City.[65] Both Mukti and Dhond missions continued to be main centres for Pentecostal mission, so that Norton referred to Dhond in 1911 as 'one of the mother colonies for Pentecostal work in India'.[66] The appeals of the seasoned Christian workers Ramabai and Norton to the West were often directed towards the millions of poor Indians suffering the effects of drought and famine. This continued to be a priority in Pentecostal missions. During these years droughts resulting in devastating famine were regular occurrences. Manoramabai and the three Norton families in particular kept the Pentecostal periodicals well informed of the desperate physical needs in India.

Minnie Abrams wrote to Alexander Boddy in England thanking him for sending *Confidence* and remarked, 'the Pentecostal Fire is spreading in India, though slowly'.[67] Boddy reported on the famine in India in 1908 presenting 'great opportunities and great difficulties to the brave band of workers at

Mukti', and that 'the outpouring of the Holy Spirit with the gift of Tongues on hundreds of these young widows' had reduced the financial support for the Mission – presumably because of evangelical opponents of the Pentecostal movement. Boddy announced that *Confidence* would act as a conduit for finances to support Mukti, and other Pentecostal papers in North America did the same.[68] Abrams outlined her views on Spirit baptism in an article titled 'The Scriptural Evidence of Pentecost' and wrote of the 'outpouring of the Holy Ghost' on the CMA that had 'greatly strengthened our hands at Mukti', and gave clear indication that Mukti operated as the main centre in India for the spread of Pentecostalism – much as Los Angeles did in the USA or Oslo did in Europe. At Mukti they were having visitors from all over India and Sri Lanka who had received Spirit baptism there or in other centres like Bombay. Abrams made this report to the English newspaper *Confidence:*

> It gives me great joy to testify concerning the grace of God, which I have seen manifest in my brothers and sisters in India who have received the Pentecostal blessing with tongues and other gifts of the Spirit. At Mukti we have had visitors from Calcutta, Coonoor, Bulsai, and Colombo who have received this Baptism of the Holy Ghost and Fire, and our people have visited those in Bombay who have thus been Spirit-baptized, and we, at Mukti, believe that all these together with us have been baptized into one baptism.[69]

The Mukti revival can be seen as one of international significance as far as the origins of Pentecostalism are concerned. Its importance for the Pentecostal missionary movement, not only in India but also much further abroad, cannot be underestimated. Abrams also wrote that she would accompany Manoramabai in an impending trip to England. The November 1908 *Confidence* reported on Ramabai's fiftieth birthday celebration at Mukti and reprinted her testimony, together with a report of a serious physical attack from a mob on three Pentecostal women missionaries in Pandharpur with a Mukti team of 86 young women. One missionary, Miss Steel, was beaten and left for dead but recovered later from her serious injuries.[70] But the work continued to grow. Ramabai herself wrote of a 'deeper work in the hearts and lives of many of the children who were blessed in the revival', asking for prayer that 'the Holy Ghost revival may be continued among us until the glorious appearing of our Lord Jesus Christ'.[71]

William Piper's monthly periodical *The Latter Rain Evangel* is a valuable source of information on Mukti and the later work of Minnie Abrams. The periodical first published two addresses by Rachel Nalder, Ramabai's North American representative, in which she introduced readers to the testimony of Ramabai, Mukti and the revival, and the desperate plight of child widows in India. The paper in turn pledged to act as a centre for financial support for Ramabai.[72] Thereafter, regular reports were given on what funds had been sent to the Mission and Nalder's two addresses were published as separate tracts to support the work at Mukti.[73] For the next two years, most of the finances raised at the Stone Church for 'foreign missions' were sent to Mukti. Not only did this early centre of American Pentecostalism refer to the Mukti Mission as a

'Pentecostal mission',[74] but the paper abounded with expressions of support for the work Ramabai was doing, seeing her mission as an extension in India of the worldwide movement of which they were part.

Although the Mukti revival may not have resulted directly in the formation of Pentecostal churches and Ramabai was apparently to bequeath her mission to the CMA,[75] the revival had at least four far-reaching consequences. First, it is clear that Bartleman, Seymour, and the writers of *The Apostolic Faith* saw the Indian revival as a precedent to the one in which they were involved, a sort of prototype, earlier Pentecostal revival that they thought had become 'full-grown' in Los Angeles. It is more likely that these were simultaneous rather than sequential events in a general period of revival in the evangelical world accompanying the turn of the century.

Second, women played a more prominent role in the Indian revival than in the American one – although by this I do not want to minimize the very significant role of women leaders in both the Azusa Street revival and the early missionary movement that issued from it. But the fact that Ramabai was an Indian woman who resisted both patriarchal oppression in India and western domination in Christianity and was attracted to what a recent biographer calls 'the gender-egalitarian impulse of Christianity' was even more significant.[76] Or as Abrams put it, Ramabai was 'demonstrating to her countrymen that women have powers and capabilities which they have not permitted them to cultivate'.[77] The Mukti Pentecostal revival was pre-eminently a revival among women and led by women, motivating and empowering those who had really been marginalized and cast out by society. As Ellis remarked at the time, he was reminded of 'the prominent place which young girls in praying bands – timid, untutored Hindoo maidens, reared to believe in the complete subjection of women – have had in this revival'. He thought that this was 'a feature altogether amazing to men who know India'.[78] This was another case of Pentecostalism's early social activism, empowering the marginalized and oppressed for service and bestowing dignity on women. In this the Mukti revival and Ramabai herself were pioneers within global Christianity and without precedent. The revival movement was to result in an unparalleled missionary outreach of Indian Christians into surrounding areas and further abroad. As one periodical observed, Ramabai's Praying Bands of young women were going 'in every direction to scatter the fire that has filled their own souls' and the result was that 'many parts of India are hearing of the true and living God'.[79]

Third, both Ramabai in her ministry and the revival she led demonstrate an openness to other Christians, an ecumenicity and inclusiveness that stand in stark contrast to the rigid exclusivism of subsequent Pentecostal movements. This was undoubtedly one result of the pluralistic context of India and Ramabai's indebtedness to her own cultural and religious training in Brahmin philosophy and national consciousness, despite her later Christian fundamentalism.

And fourth was its impact on Latin American Pentecostalism. Abrams contacted her friend and former Bible school classmate in Valparaiso, Chile, May Louise Hoover with a report of the revival in Mukti contained in a booklet she wrote in 1906 titled *The Baptism of the Holy Ghost and Fire*. In its second edition later that year, the booklet included a discussion of the restoration of speaking in tongues (the first written Pentecostal theology of Spirit baptism), and 30,000 copies were circulated widely. As a result of Abrams' booklet and her subsequent correspondence with the Hoovers, the Methodist churches in Valparaiso and Santiago were stirred to expect and pray for a similar revival, which began in 1909. Willis Hoover became leader of the new Chilean Methodist Pentecostal Church. It is important to note that Chilean Pentecostalism has its roots in the Mukti revival and was specifically a Methodist revival that did not promote a doctrine of 'initial evidence'. An alternative to the 'initial evidence' form of Pentecostalism was developing globally and Mukti was its earliest expression.[80]

The various revival movements in Mukti, Valparaiso and Los Angeles were all part of a series of events that resulted in the emergence of global Pentecostalism. The Mukti revival can legitimately be regarded with Azusa Street as one of the most important early formative centres of Pentecostalism.[81] This is one of the most important caveats to be recognized in the debate on Pentecostal origins.

The Apostolic Faith in North India

Alfred G. (1874–1944) and Lillian Garr (1878–1916), pastors of a branch of the Burning Bush in Los Angeles, a white Holiness congregation that merged with Azusa Street for services early in the revival, were among the first Azusa Street missionaries to leave Los Angeles. Baptized in the Spirit at Azusa Street and reported to have received 'the gift of tongues, especially the language of India and dialects', the Garrs were both supposedly able to speak Bengali – and in the case of Lillian, also Tibetan and Chinese. They left Los Angeles in July 1906 via Chicago and Danville, Virginia, where they held a series of meetings in the Burning Bush church they had pastored the previous year.[82] From there they went to India, arriving in Calcutta in December 1906 with an African American nanny Maria Gardner and a baby daughter Virginia. Because of a shortage of funds they rented cheap accommodation. Although disillusioned with their lack of any divinely given language abilities, they persevered. In January 1907 they were invited to testify about the Azusa Street revival and hold nightly meetings in William Carey's old Baptist church in Bow Bazaar. The invitation was made by its Pastor Hook, and shortly afterwards a British military captain donated enough money to the impoverished Garrs to sustain them during their entire time in India. They continued meetings in a house in Creek Row rented by Max Wood Moorhead, at the time Presbyterian secretary of the YMCA in Sri Lanka. Lillian Garr wrote her first report to Azusa Street in March 1907, saying that 13 or 14 missionaries and other workers had received Spirit baptism, among whom were Moorhead and Maud Orlebar, a CMA missionary in Bombay. Moorhead seemed to have immediately left (or was asked to leave) his mission to become an independent Pentecostal missionary. More than six years later, he reported that from Calcutta 'the fire spread to nearly all the provinces of the Empire' through the missionaries returning to their stations.[83]

The Garrs continued to work in the Indian subcontinent amid controversy because of their dogmatic stance on Spirit baptism. They moved to Bombay in March 1907 and visited Mukti Mission and the missionary retreat station in the hills at Coonoor. By September they were in Colombo, Sri Lanka, where it appears they might have influenced Dias Wanigasekera to become Pentecostal (see below).[84] They were on their way to Hong Kong. The focus of their ministry was now on reaching missionaries with their message, as this was, as they put it, tantamount to 'laying the axe at the root of the tree', because these missionaries (unlike the Garrs) knew the customs and languages of India. 'The only way the nations can be reached', they declared, 'is by getting the mission-aries baptized with the Holy Ghost.'[85] This became a strategy for many expatriate Pentecostals in foreign countries who could not speak local languages and resulted in a rapidly developing network of interconnected missionaries who spread the Pentecostal message throughout the world with astonishing rapidity. Most of these came from evangelical faith missions like the CMA and the CIM, but sometimes missionaries from older denomina-tional missions were affected. The Garrs returned to India for nine months in 1909–10 to help Maud Orlebar in Bombay, they visited Albert Norton's work in Dhond and worked in Shorat Chuckerbutty's orphanage and school in Allahabad, where a revival was taking place, before returning to Hong Kong.

The founder of this mission in Allahabad, Chuckerbutty was a Bengali and Brahmin with an MA degree – unusual for Indian women at that time. She became a Pentecostal in early 1910 with co-worker Dorothea Chandra and her centre became another place for the spread of Pentecostalism. Daily services were held there when many were reported converted and baptized in the Spirit, including three very significant missionaries: general secretary of the YWCA Agnes Hill, Eva Groat (a Pentecostal missionary in India for many years) and the English missionary Alice Luce of the CMS (later Assemblies of God (AG) missionary to Mexicans in the USA), their testimonies appearing in Pentecostal periodicals. Chuckerbutty moved her centre to Nanpara in the northern Bahraich district in 1911 and organized a Pentecostal convention there in which more missionaries and other Christian workers received Spirit baptism.[86] Lillian Garr wrote of Chuckerbutty and Chandra that 'it is beautiful to see how true these two Indian sisters are to this blessed Truth. There is absolutely no compromise on their part and yet they are kept filled with a tender love to all who oppose.'[87] Agnes Hill spoke at the Stone Church in Chicago in 1912, where she described this as a place where a 'great many' received Spirit baptism. She made the interesting observation that the time had come 'when those from Christian nations going to that country can receive spiritual blessings from the Indians'. There was 'no monopoly of the grace of God', she continued, and she was so pleased that 'God baptized Sister Chuckerbutty first'. Both Alice Luce and she had gone to Chuckerbutty's centre 'and received the baptism in the Holy Spirit through the prayers of an Indian woman, glory to God for the great sisterhood there is!'[88] Cecil Polhill visited Allahabad in 1914 and Chuckerbutty was back there.[89] Moorhead reported that by the end of 1908 not only were the orphanages at Mukti and Dhond centres of Pentecostalism, but four other CMA orphanages in the Bombay Presidency were centres 'where the Holy Ghost has come in blessed reality'. In these places there were 'hundreds' of Indian young people who had had the Pentecostal baptism, he reported.

Faizabad, Bahraich and Basti near Nepal became the main centres of Pentecostalism in the North. Dick Mahaffey wrote from Faizabad that he with the Masseys and Joseph Cumine (an Indian worker) were preparing to move to the Basti district, north-east of Faizabad. They expected to live initially in tents during the cold season but to get more comfortable accommodation before the hot season and to move into Nepal when doors opened. Moorhead reported on a three-week Pentecostal conference attended by missionaries and workers from Mukti and elsewhere throughout India.[90] The missionaries wrote glowing reports about this first 'All India Pentecostal Conference' in October 1909 held in William Carey's church in Calcutta. The thirty or so delegates were mostly foreign workers, but the effect on the missionaries was apparent. A Bengali Christian worker, Gracelove Bonarjee, received Spirit baptism during these meetings. Reports spoke of the Spirit 'moving upon the assembly', 'days of heaven upon earth' with intense simultaneous prayer and praises, and remarkable healings and deliverances from demons.[91] During the conference a delegation from the Wynberg Girls' School in Mussoorie received Spirit baptism and the principal, Miss G. E. Browne and four other teachers (out of a total of eight) were summarily dismissed when the revival spread to the pupils.[92] Another consignment of four American missionaries arrived in India the same month with Mary Norton and they were distributed to various co-operating missions. Kathleen Miller wrote at the end of 1909 that 'in all parts of India' there were 'witnesses to this glorious outpouring of the Spirit' and that 'hundreds of Indian Christians also' were 'rejoicing in the Baptism of the Spirit according to Acts 2.4'.[93]

Pentecostal missionary work continued unabated after the first 'All India' conference and missionaries from the West kept arriving. During 1910 there was significant expansion to different parts of North India. By the middle of the year, Moorhead, working with Norton's mission, reported that there were seven places where Pentecostal centres had opened, apart from 'seekers' all over the Punjab and North-West India. A second, larger 'Pentecostal Conference' was held in Faizabad in 1910, again attended by some 40 Pentecostal missionaries, but with some significant Indian and Sri Lankan leaders, including Misses Chuckerbutty and Chandra from Allahabad and Dias Wanigasekera from Colombo – the latter receiving Spirit baptism after more than three years as a 'seeker', the first Sri Lankan Pentecostal leader. Robert Massey and Albert Norton were the main speakers at these two conferences. The Basti district bordering Nepal remained a priority with these missionaries; and the Masseys, Mahaffeys and Abrams all began setting up stations there in 1911. In 1911 a third conference was held in Faizabad and the main speakers were Abrams, Norton and Agnes Hill of the YWCA. This was the last time Abrams would speak in a public meeting, and Mary Norton died soon after this conference. Ironically a year before her death, Abrams spoke there about her hope that Christians would be able to overcome death, just as they had begun to defeat pain and disease. In October 1912 the fourth All India Pentecostal Conference was held in Bahraich. During that year Abrams contracted malaria during one of her preaching trips. She never really recovered and died that December at the age of 53. She left behind two stations at Uska Bazaar under Edith Baugh (who also died there of smallpox in 1920) and Basti under Lillie Doll, with teams of Indian and American women assisting them.

A Brahmin couple, a Dr and Mrs Kumode Goswami (a medical doctor), were converted in Faizabad and joined the Pentecostal mission during the conference in 1910, giving up medical practice (presumably on the advice of the missionaries) and going with the Masseys and two Indian couples from Norton's mission to their new mission at Basti. Soon afterwards they moved with Mrs Holder to Basti and then to the border of Nepal, where Kumode Goswami made forays into Nepal to distribute Gospels almost every day. The matron of the boys' home in Bahraich was Sacodabal, another zealous Pentecostal worker mentioned often in missionary letters. On preaching trips to villages around Bahraich, she was usually in charge of the team, which sometimes included foreign missionaries. In 1916 there were reports of a fresh revival occurring in the girls' home at the mission in Bahraich. Four Indian workers went to live in Nepal in 1911, but they were unnamed. Moorhead sent in the testimony of an 'Indian missionary' to Spirit baptism that was published, but this person too remained anonymous. An Indian evangelist from Madura in South India, John Manoah, wrote in 1912 to *The Bridegroom's Messenger* of his work with the assistance of two Australian Pentecostal missionaries, and another worker in Gorkhpur, Samuel Morar, was working with a Sister McCarty from Indianapolis.[94] Another Pentecostal evangelist was Phailbus, son of a Muslim judge, who together with his wife had converted and had charge of a mission in Mansehra in North India in 1917.[95] An American AG missionary wrote of two Indian missionaries 'of high caste' who were sent to Mesopotamia (Iraq) in 1917, but we know neither their names nor their fate.[96]

There was even an early Pentecostal mission in Punch, part of Kashmir not under British India at the time, where two Anglo-Indian women, Edith Kirschner and L. A. Baker had worked since 1910 in very difficult circumstances. They lived for over three years in a mud house without transportation or adequate financial support. Despite the opposition of the rajah and being forbidden to engage in public preaching, they ran a girls' school and itinerated in surrounding mountain villages by foot, mainly reaching out to women in house visitation. By 1913 they had received funds to purchase ponies. From 1914 Edith Kirschner worked alone, but in 1916 an Indian evangelist Niskerson and his wife arrived to join her. Kirschner had her first baptisms, four Muslim young men who endured persecution and physical violence. She was admitted to hospital in Calcutta (her home) in 1917, and among other things was suffering from malnutrition. A remarkable Pentecostal revival took place in 1919–20 in a Friends (Quaker) mission in Itarsi, 400 miles north-east of Bombay. This was led by Indians, the most prominent being Khushi Lal, a full-time worker, Jaganath and Pyare Lal, both young men, and Har Chand, a school teacher. In this revival tongues, interpretation, deliverance from evil spirits and the confessing of sins were prominent. It spread from Itarsi to several other Quaker missions.[97]

Albert Norton married again, but his second wife Nellie also died in India. He became ill in 1920 and funds were collected for him to return to the USA for a rest but characteristically he replied that their 'kind appeal' had reached him, he was 'much touched', but did 'not feel that the Lord would have me take a furlough'. He continued, 'My two darling wives, Mary Kelly and Nellie Andrews, fell on the firing line here in pioneer warfare in dark India, and if I have to meet death I would like to lie as near as possible by their side, and the side of my two missionary sons, Eben and Bert.' He again thanked them for their kindness and suggested that any money sent for his furlough be used for famine relief in India, his life's passion.[98] Albert Norton died in India less than three years later. He left behind two sons leading Pentecostal missions in India: John, who moved from Orai in the north to take over his father's work at Dhond, and Will, now in Benares.[99] Two of Ramabai's most senior foreign helpers had gone.

Moorhead observed the significance of an increasing number of experienced missionaries joining the Pentecostal movement in India. After describing how the delegates to the 1911 conference had gathered from all over India (and added that one Burmese 'seeker' was there), he wrote how 'beautiful' it was that 'the Lord is detaching experienced Pentecostal missionaries from the conservative societies who are not in sympathy'. Because these missionaries were sometimes skilled in more than one 'Oriental' language, they could be a great help to new missionaries who still had to acquire a language. Furthermore, he wrote that their discipline and experience made them qualified for 'pioneer work'.[100] The Pentecostal work in India continued to grow apace, so that in 1913 a report stated that some 200 foreign missionaries and 20,000 Indian Christians had received Spirit baptism and had spoken in tongues.[101]

Ill health continued to dog the Masseys and in 1913 they returned to Georgia permanently, leaving their station in the hands of James Harvey, a British soldier who had become a Pentecostal in India and joined the mission.[102] Harvey married Esther Bragg, an American missionary; they joined the AG in 1916, and established a mission with an orphanage, home for widows, and training school for boys. James Harvey died unexpectedly in 1922 but his wife continued to oversee the mission until her retirement and return to the USA in 1961.[103] In Baluchistan (part of present-day Pakistan), a Pentecostal mission was run by Arthur and Minnie Slocum, a physician from the Elim Tabernacle in Rochester, New York. In 1917 they related an interesting incident of revival meetings held in a rented Methodist Episcopal manse in Quetta, when they were given immediate notice by the church to vacate the house because of 'the most outrageous noises' and 'scandalous behaviour' that would 'reflect on the excellent name, and reputation of the church'.[104] Instead of the 'right hand of fellowship', Pentecostals were beginning to get the left foot from other missions, and were becoming increasingly defensive and isolated as a result.

Maud Orlebar was a CMA missionary in her mid-sixties who had been in Bombay since 1892 and was among those in Calcutta at the meetings of the Garrs. In 1908 she opened a 'Pentecostal home' with 15 rooms called Beulah, where the 'principal object' would be 'tarrying' for Spirit baptism and spreading 'the full Pentecostal Baptism in the Holy Spirit in the Church in India'. Orlebar was soon joined in her work by various missionaries.[105] This home also operated as an orientation station for newly arriving Pentecostal missionaries in India, and departing and itinerating missionaries stayed there at regular intervals. It was a Pentecostal mission centre for regular services too, and people from the outcaste (Dalit) societies as well as tribals from surrounding villages were welcomed there. Orlebar described them as 'the very lowest of all low caste people, utterly despised by all and everybody' and she proceeded to rent a room for services, a school for children and a refuge for women. She wrote of the two 'splendid native workers' assisting her in her mission in Bombay involved in preaching and teaching for five hours every evening, and of an Indian preacher Gumut Row, who began a Marathi Pentecostal periodical in 1910 – the first Pentecostal paper in an Indian language. Beulah Home was an important centre for the spread of Pentecostalism and remained so for some time after Orlebar's death in December 1910, after which Annie Murray, a blind woman from Toronto, first took charge.

Murray was assisted by various British PMU missionaries, especially Constance Skarratt and Margaret Clark, who had been in India since 1888 and had become a Pentecostal while on furlough. Murray reported in 1910 that missionaries from 11 different mission societies had visited the home seeking Spirit baptism.[106] In 1912 Moorhead assisted in the work at Beulah, which he described as a place 'filled with the presence and power of God, and the Spirit of Love'. Beulah also operated as a training centre for Indian evangelists and Bible women and an hour's daily Bible exposition given by Murray with interpretation from English into Marathi was attended by both Indian workers and guests.[107] Later, Annie Murray wrote of a work starting in the Aurangabad district among poor people, where many were becoming Pentecostal believers through the work of four Indian preachers who had read a copy of the Marathi newspaper and had gone to Beulah in Bombay to receive Spirit baptism. She wrote that these unnamed and poor preachers had at their own expense preached the gospel within a radius of 80 miles around their homes. Two had sold water-buffaloes to buy ponies to travel to distant villages, and Murray said the result was 'a great awakening' and 'a wide-spread work of God'. Clark and Skarratt and an Indian Bible woman went there and rented a large house in Jalna for their mission. They worked with three evangelists, one of whom was getting financial support, as was the Bible woman.[108]

When Murray died in December 1911 Margaret Clark took charge of Beulah, moving in 1913 for financial reasons to smaller premises, from where she and Skarratt carried out successful evangelistic work under the name of the Apostolic Faith Mission, with several Indian workers. Activities included regular services, street preaching and daily meetings in workmen's flats, women's workrooms and the Poor Asylum of Bombay.[109] This mission now depended on its Indian workers even more. One that Clark named is Sumantrao, 'a successful, Spirit-filled evangelist, preaching a full gospel with power in four languages'.[110] Four years later it was reported, 'Much of the work in Bombay is being done by the Indians themselves and there are signs of a real revival'.[111] Skarratt later moved to Pune and was working there in 1917.[112] At a convention in Chicago in 1914, Mary Chapman, a veteran missionary soon to return to Madras (and later to Kerala) as the first missionary sent by the AG, told of the significance of the Pentecostal mission in Bombay under Clark. But she gave as much credit for the success of this mission to the work of Indian workers, an unnamed one in particular who had received Spirit baptism and had 'preached to large crowds in four different languages, an able, eloquent man'. She said that was 'the way Pentecost was started in Bombay'. In Madras, Chapman was to work with another Indian preacher, Benjamin Jacob.[113]

There were many other missionaries in India who had received Spirit baptism within a year of the events of 1907. Blanche Hamilton, a CMA missionary in Gujarat, wrote in 1908 that 'nearly all the missionaries are baptized here, and have the gift of tongues also'.[114] One of these was Christian Schoonmaker, a CMA missionary who received Spirit baptism in Calcutta in the Garr meetings in December 1907, and who spent a year touring various mission stations in India sharing his experience of Spirit baptism and praying for missionaries to receive the Spirit. He also worked with Orlebar in Bombay and began learning Gujarati. Like many Pentecostals, he refused vaccinations, and died of small-pox in 1919. His wife Violet and five of their six children were missionaries in India for several decades.[115]

Pentecostalism in South India

George and Mary Berg, Brethren missionaries in India for five years before going on furlough to southern California, were baptized in the Spirit at Azusa Street in September 1906, after George thought he heard someone next to him speaking Hindustani – a language with which he was probably not familiar. They went back to India in February 1908 to become, if Berg's reports are to be believed, among the most successful early expatriate Pentecostal missionaries in India. After extensive travelling visiting various missions, they worked in Adheri, near Bombay, where Berg wrote of an open door among 'native Christian preachers and workers'. These were clearly Brethren preachers – Berg used his Brethren contacts and kept his Brethren principles, referring to his meeting places as 'gospel halls' and emphasizing the ministry of the laity. He mentioned that Indian preachers (23 on one occasion) came to his house once a week for prayer and Bible study, and that on Sundays and during the week he went to the city to preach in 'two or three different places'. Later he spent time in Telugu, and wrote from the Coonoor retreat centre about his desire to work among the 'jungle tribes of South India', before he moved to Bangalore. He worked in the Madras (Chennai) area with other missions who apparently received his message warmly, including the Church of Scotland, the Church Missionary Society (CMS), the Methodists and the Salvation Army.[116] He was probably present at T. B. Barratt's meetings in Coonoor in 1908. An Indian preacher C. P. Abraham is mentioned as one of the leaders in Adonia, South India in 1909–10, and appeals are made for support (which was forthcoming) to build a home, place of worship, missionary home, and for Pentecostal workers to assist him.

Berg was based in Cleveland near Bangalore in 1910, appealing for funds to commence a mission among the jungle tribal people in the Nilgiri Hills and to build a Bible school to train Indian leaders. He also went to the Syrian Christians in Kerala, reporting one meeting there of 1,500 people. By this time Berg was operating with a team of six Indian preachers he had personally trained – including two preachers from the 'jungle tribes', two working in Madras, and two with him in Bangalore. He planned a printing press to make Christian literature available in Indian languages. He itinerated between Bangalore, Madras, Bombay, the Malabar coast (Kerala), and Sri Lanka, reporting conversions, healings and exorcisms. He held a convention for Indian preachers seeking Spirit baptism in January 1911 because they were not able to afford the long trip to Faizabad. He worked in Travancore (Kerala) and in Colombo, Sri Lanka with Charles Hettiaratchy until he returned to his native Switzerland, Germany, Holland and the USA in 1911, leaving his wife and family in India. While in the USA he spoke at various Pentecostal conventions and churches and pleaded for funds to support 25 Indian workers for the jungle tribes in the mountains, a fishing settlement near Madras, and among the Syrians in Kerala.

In an address he gave at the Atlanta Pentecostal Mission in 1911, Berg promoted his ministry as one of signs and wonders. Healing in particular was the evangelistic eye-opener that he used to win people for Christ, he said, yet he also established self-supporting schools for children and spent time in training Indian preachers. Wherever he went on his many itinerating trips throughout South India people flocked to be prayed for healing, and Berg reported several remarkable healings. He returned to India that October and had 20 Indian workers on the field by the beginning of 1912 working from six stations. His meetings in Kerala were especially noteworthy, Berg reporting crowds of over 3,000 attending and many being healed.[117] Berg described one such meeting in 1912 in graphic detail.[118] In these places there were 'hundreds' of Indian young people who had had the Pentecostal baptism, he reported. In the light of subsequent events, the accuracy of these reports (especially the numbers) is open to considerable question. That year Berg and his associate J. L. Bahr moved their headquarters from Bangalore to Kandy, Sri Lanka, where he worked for a short while with Dias Wanigasekera, an early Singhalese Pentecostal leader (see below), intending to make this his base for South India.

By the end of 1912 Berg reported that he was supporting 17 Indian workers (14 men and 3 women) and 5 foreigners in his mission in South India, and that there were altogether 70 people to be cared for. Berg had used his several Brethren contacts in Kerala to spread the Pentecostal message there. Among the earliest Indian leaders were Robert Cumine (an Anglo-Indian named as Berg's 'colporteur'), Paruttupara Ummachan (whose work in Thuyavur near Adur and another in Kottarakara, Kerala may have been the first Indian-initiated Pentecostal congregations in 1910), Umman Mammen and Pandalam Mattai – who were all preachers trained by Berg. Berg mentioned that 'Oomen' (Umman Mammen) prayed for a poor widow's dead cow to be raised from the dead in a village in Travancore. This well-known Indian leader wrote in 1913 as A. M. O. Mammen from Adur and mentioned that he was a Syrian Christian, son of a CMS archdeacon and a CMS medical evangelist before he became a Pentecostal, after which he resigned his position. By late 1919 Mammen was still working in Travancore, running a congregation and reporting conversions, remarkable healings and Spirit baptisms.[119] Berg commented that such Indian workers were emerging with great faith in the power of God.

He wrote of 11 Indian workers baptized in the Spirit in 1912, and enthused about this 'band of native workers' in South India who would 'stand the tests of these last evil days' and would 'not flinch'.[120] In one letter Berg named 22 of his workers in India, including Charles Cumin in the Nilgiri mountains as a travelling evangelist and a pastor there (later part of Cook's travelling team), N. Samson, and other workers who were only given single names: Ruthnam, Jesudason, James and John. In Tirunelveli, Jesudas and Benjamin were working and in Travancore, the workers included Umman Mammen, Ninan, Daniel, Matthew and John Thomas. Thomas wrote a long letter describing his Spirit baptism (after seeking it for a year) and the work among outcastes and the poor near Adur in Travancore.

During one of her husband's frequent away trips in India in January 1913, Mary Berg had to flee with her four children from their house through heavy rain and a landslide, then moving to 'an ugly native built house'. Berg began to hint at leaving India because of poor health and in May 1913 went to the USA to settle his family there. He returned to a new station in Ootakamund in the Nilgiri hills in October that year with Robert and Anna Cook, whom he had met at a conference in Los Angeles and two other women workers, but his family never joined him and he returned to the USA in late 1914.[121] A combination of factors led to him leaving India permanently: he was of German descent in a British colony, his funds from Germany had dried up and his family had remained in the USA.[122] But Berg left under a cloud – the most serious allegations were made about his exaggerated reports and that his 'own personal life has been very reprehensible'.[123] The details of what happened have now disappeared, but it appears that moral lapse was behind these opaque references.

Meanwhile, the Cooks set up base first in Bangalore and then moved to the Tirunelveli district, where they reported crowds of people coming, with remarkable healings and exorcisms. An Indian believer had given them an acre of land on which they erected a chapel. After clashing with Berg, they were working separately by early 1914 with eight Indian preachers assisting them, some of whom had previously worked with Berg. In effect they had taken over Berg's work in South India. The Cooks and their teams preferred to travel third class rather than use coaches reserved for Europeans – probably as much out of necessity as conviction and because they used the opportunity to preach and sing to a captive Indian audience. The Cooks also used the American funds they raised to recruit and support their Indian workers, but the Great War brought increasing financial pressures on the Cooks. His family of four lived in one room of an Indian house in the Koilpati village, eating local food entirely, but they moved back to the safe garrison of Bangalore before taking furlough in 1915. Charles (Robert) Cumine described an evangelistic tour in the Tirunelveli district. Cumine took charge of the mission when the Cooks went on furlough, went on a tour of Kerala with Cook in 1916–17, and was still the main Indian leader with Cook in 1920. In the 1916 tour it was reported that Paruttapara Ummachen in Thuvayur, Umman Mammen and Pandalam Mattai were missionaries in Kerala with thriving works.

Pentecostalism in Kerala was already progressing with little expatriate supervision. N. John Joseph was an independent evangelist in Madras (later

Lakkadi, Malabar) who worked with Cook and wrote reports outlining a busy itinerating ministry. Arullappen Jacob was another, based in Koilpati in Tirunelveli district. John Joseph mentioned two other Indians working with him, a woman named E. I. Sara and a man V. C. Lukoo. In the 1920s more Indian evangelists and leaders, especially from Brethren or Holiness backgrounds, became Pentecostal. Several Indian preachers associated with Cook were instrumental in starting independent Pentecostal churches, including K. E. Abraham, who joined Cook in 1923, was ordained by Paul of the Ceylon Pentecostal Mission in 1930, and founded the Indian Pentecostal Church of God in 1934, now one of the two largest Pentecostal denominations in India.[124] Anna Cook died of typhoid in 1917 and Cook married Bertha Fox the following year, a missionary who had worked near Bangalore with a Mukti Mission worker, Mary Bai Aiman.[125] The Cooks were listed as AG missionaries living in Dodballapur, Mysore in 1920 and they moved to Kerala in 1922, being based in Chengannur, Travancore in 1927. The Cooks left the AG in 1929 and eventually affiliated with the Church of God, remaining in India until 1949.[126] They were missionaries who really engaged with Indian Pentecostals, but were also involved in various subsequent secessions.

The Legacy of Mukti

Although the Garrs, the Bergs and the Cooks played significant roles in the emergence of Pentecostalism in India, we cannot discuss this subject without primary reference to the Mukti Mission – undoubtedly the most important centre during the first decade of Pentecostal missions. The Garrs were transient missionaries in India, and the Bergs and the Cooks with their key Indian workers were responsible for the expansion of Pentecostalism in South India. Further north, the three main centres of Pentecostalism were Pune, Bombay and the province of Uttar Pradesh bordering Nepal, the heartland of Hinduism. The legacy for Indian Pentecostalism of the Mukti revival continued well into the twentieth century through Indian leaders trained there and through missionaries like Albert Norton and Minnie Abrams who had been associated with Mukti. The western Pentecostal press continued to publish reports on the activities of Mukti, seeing it fully part of the worldwide Pentecostal revival.

From the time that Ramabai started working on her Bible translation, her daughter Manoramabai was the main correspondent with the Pentecostal press. The Praying Bands of young women trained in evangelism went out all over India, often sleeping in tents and usually under the supervision of an older woman missionary. Workers from Mukti were sent out to accompany Pentecostal preachers throughout India and Mukti was often the first port of call for Pentecostal missionaries and global itinerating preachers. There was a sense in which Ramabai provided legitimation for foreign Pentecostal workers. Among Mukti's many foreign visitors were such Pentecostal luminaries as A. G. and Lillian Garr, Carrie Judd and George Montgomery, J. H. King, Daniel Awrey, A. H. Post, Lucy Leatherman, T. B. Barratt and many others. New Pentecostal missionaries to India were usually channelled either to Mukti or to Albert and Mary Norton's co-operating mission in nearby

Dhond and later, to their stations in North India in Faizabad and Bahraich, run by their son Will. In December 1908 ten new American Pentecostal missionaries came to Norton's mission from Lupton's training centre in Ohio. Norton began new boys' homes in Faizabad and Bahraich in Uttar Pradesh. He and other missionaries at Dhond had not yet received Spirit baptism and were 'tarrying' for it until they received it in March 1909.[127] Missionary letters from Mukti and Dhond during 1908 were preoccupied with the ravaging famine that had scourged that part of India, and efforts were concentrated on raising money in western Pentecostal churches for famine victims.[128]

Leading American Pentecostal periodicals and organizations, including those of Carrie Judd Montgomery, William Hamner Piper, Elizabeth Baker and Levi Lupton regarded Mukti as the main mission to support worldwide both in finance and in personnel.[129] In particular, Piper's Stone Church in Chicago in *The Latter Rain Evangel* and the British Pentecostal periodical *Confidence* in Sunderland published frequent reports from Mukti and letters and addresses by Ramabai, Manoramabai, Norton and Minnie Abrams. Alexander Boddy, Anglican vicar in Sunderland, leader of the Pentecostal movement in Britain and editor of *Confidence*, mentioned Ramabai in the first issue as emphasizing love 'being the great result of "Pentecost"'. *The Bridegroom's Messenger*, the early Pentecostal periodical from the Atlanta Pentecostal Mission, Georgia, also published regular reports from Mukti and Dhond, sending support there.

Moorhead wrote from Bombay that many Indians were becoming Pentecostals and that these 'ignorant, lowly Indians' were becoming 'channels of blessing to their own people', including a young man of 19 who had been healed of tuberculosis and was 'instrumental in winning souls to Jesus'.[130] Albert Norton in Dhond, India, wrote of young Indian men and women who had been rescued from famine seven years previously and were now 'filled with the Holy Spirit, and being greatly used in the extension of Christ's kingdom'.[131] Both Norton and Ramabai made one of their chief objectives the training of Indian Christian workers. It must be remembered that the revival that sparked off the Pentecostal movement in Mukti in 1905 was an Indian movement among women, with the participation and observation of a small number of expatriate missionaries. This remained the main source for trained Indians to work in Pentecostal missions for at least a decade. In 1910 there were 125 young women training in the Mukti Bible school to become Christian workers.[132]

At a convention in Rochester, New York, a missionary said that what 'most deeply impressed her from the beginning of her work in India was the 'extreme *unimportance* of the missionary' when she discovered 'the Spirit laying hold of the girls themselves, in her school, as He had done in the work of Ramabai, so that teachers and leaders sat down and God by the Spirit wrought with those young native girls so wondrously'.[133] Norton describes the young men at his mission who had all married young women from Ramabai's mission, and writes that 'a good number of the ablest and most heaven-blest workers for Christ in India, were once famine orphans' (from Mukti and Dhond). Will Norton in Bahraich wrote of young men from Dhond who were now there in North India and of invaluable help to the mission, touring daily from village to village preaching and distributing Scripture portions.[134] One of them, Vihala Shankar, left with his wife for Gujarat in 1910 to preach to his own people in an area that had never heard the Christian message. Norton wrote from Dhond that trained young men had gone to other provinces to 'spread the fire'. Two of these, Kubera and Ghisi, worked in the Bahraich district on the border of Nepal, and Will Norton described 'two of our Christian boys' who were arrested in a Nepali town and kept in custody for two days. On being brought before the magistrates they were able to speak about their faith to people who had never heard of Christianity and wanted to know more. The two Christian missionaries returned enthusiastically to Bahraich because they had been given the 'freedom of the town' to return and sell gospels there as often as they liked, which they did several times.[135] Abrams also mentioned four Indian workers by name when she started the new mission at Uska Bazaar in Basti district. Three of them were 'educated, trained and converted at Mukti' and included Chatur and Dukheabai Wazoji, and John Paul, with their fami- lies. Abrams considered them two of the best young men from Mukti, who had given up employment at another mission in order to work at a lesser salary in her mission. They were joined by Nannu, also from Mukti, and Korea, from Dhond.

In fact, all the Indians who worked with Abrams, the Will Nortons, Masseys and Moorhead in North India and on the borders of Nepal were from Mukti or Dhond.[136] In 1918 Albert Norton wrote of his work at Dhond over the previous 17 years. More than 800 'famine orphans or deserted boys' had been received in the Boys' Christian Home at Dhond and a 'goodly number' of these had become 'preachers and witnesses for Christ in different parts of India'. They had 'done much to circulate the word of God in some of the principal lan- guages of India', he added.[137] His son Will Norton in 1920 referred to the revival that began in Dhond in 1907 and wrote that all those 'competent to become Christian workers' were still 'workers in the Master's Vineyard' and had proven themselves to be trustworthy, fearless in physical dangers and faithful in the midst of persecution.[138] We cannot underestimate the enormous impact these Indian workers and especially the Mukti and Dhond missions had on the spread of Pentecostalism throughout India. There were other centres like that. At the Zenana Training Home in Pune where Soonderbai Powar was principal, young Indian women were trained to become Bible women supported by Pentecostal churches. Soonderbai founded the Home in 1900 and had 125 girls in her school when the revival from Mukti spread there in 1905. She corresponded with Pentecostal papers for at least the next eight years.

In early 1910 Abrams, on extended furlough in the USA through ill health, received word from Ramabai that there was not enough room for the extra six women missionaries she planned to take to Mukti. This decision was an initial disappointment but as a result Abrams felt that God was leading her to set up a new mission under Ramabai in a 'wholly unevangelized' area of North India on her return in October. Two of the new women stayed at Mukti and Abrams with the four others went to Bahraich, 20 miles from Nepal, where they lived temporarily in the Nortons' house until they moved to Faizabad, again to live in the Nortons' house. Five Indian women from Mukti joined them in this work. Lillian Denney had reported on the 'deepening and spreading' work there, where people had 'come out of raw heathenism and go on with God'. Mary Courtney, soon to be married to the Nortons' son Will, wrote from Bahraich of the teams of Indians who were constantly itinerating and of the missionaries who had gone to the Nepal border. Abrams' team of ten women worked from two properties in Basti and Uska Bazaar – a plan that was to lead to hardship and because of her poor health on arrival, ultimately to Abrams' death in December 1912 after several months of blackwater fever.[139] A letter written by Abrams at the beginning of that year outlined the difficulties that she and other missionaries faced:

> I live in a ten by twelve-foot mud shanty, thatched, so have to live very simply and keep my 'office' department in a 'nutshell'. Miss Edith Baugh is with me. We eat, cook, sleep and work in that room. Now we have a tiny ten by six room for a kitchen, which greatly helps us. Groups of women and children gather in our little room to hear the gospel and the songs; they bring their sick to be prayed for. It is all very precious and the Lord supplies His life, 'morning by morning'.[140]

Abrams' mission was based on the Mukti model – to rescue widows, orphans and famine victims – and Ramabai prepared to send a band of Indian young women to assist them when they had sufficient housing. The mission was put under Norton's oversight and the majority of Pentecostal workers in Uttar Pradesh were Indian women from Mukti or men from Norton's mission in Dhond. Two of the unnamed Indian men – Abrams called them 'Mr Norton's boys' – went into Nepal to preach and sell Scripture portions in Nepalese, the first Pentecostal missionaries in this country. They were arrested and jailed but later released and returned to India. Mary Courtney Norton, Mrs McCarty, and a converted Brahmin couple, Kubera and Ghisi, then travelled into Nepal by wagon to see what prospects there were for a mission in a country that refused entry to Christian missionaries.[141]

After the death of Pandita Ramabai in 1922, a year after her daughter Manoramabai died from heart failure, the overseas Pentecostal press continued to reflect on her life and work. The official organ of the American Assemblies of God, *The Pentecostal Evangel* published an article on the revival after hearing of her death, a touching tribute from their veteran missionary Albert Norton a month later, a letter from Ramabai's designated successor Lissa Hastie, Ellis' report of his visit to Mukti in 1908 (republished in 1916 and 1924), and a front-page republication in 1946 of Ramabai's recollections of the revival.[142] As far as Pentecostals were concerned, Ramabai and the Mukti revival were an essential part of their heritage. With the passing of Ramabai and Manoramabai went an era, but their legacy lives on today.

The First Sri Lankan Pentecostals

The early history of Pentecostalism in Sri Lanka has been shrouded in mystery and confusion. The same involvement of local workers that was true of India was also the case with the Pentecostal work in Sri Lanka. The most significant early Sinhalese leader was D. E. Dias Wanigasekera, a former CMS pastor and associate of Berg who lost his job for advocating Pentecostal teaching. He attended the conference in Calcutta in 1909 but only received Spirit baptism at the Faizabad conference a year later. He worked in villages preaching and distributing Scripture portions with an American assistant who arrived in 1910, Bartholomew Dean, and Wanigasekera kept in regular contact with American sponsors. After his Spirit baptism he began to pray for others for this experience and established Pentecostal churches. In 1911 two English missionaries joined them. Dias led these young missionaries, who lived with him in his house. After Dean's marriage to one of the new missionaries, the other one, Harper, became Dias's itinerating assistant. One particular trip was made to the Buddhist festival at Anuradapura, where Dias described their work of Scripture distribution among the crowds and preaching in the surrounding villages and praying for healing of several people, including a Buddhist priest. The first person baptized in the Spirit in Sri Lanka (in Dias's 'Praise Cottage') was Matthew Karumeratne. Dias hosted J. H. King during his visit in 1911, a tour that met with much opposition from CMS workers. Dias met any Pentecostal missionaries calling in Sri Lanka and arranged for Berg and Bahr to move to Sri Lanka in 1912.[143] Wanigasekera must have had some difficult experiences with some of these missionaries, especially those who did not learn the languages, for they could 'practically do very little', and were 'quite helpless', 'used by the enemy' in their 'ignorance to do much harm to the cause of Christ'. Without a commitment to language learning on the parts of expatriate missionaries, 'the work suffers seriously, and money is misspent'.[144] He may have been referring to Berg. In 1914 Wanigasekera sought and obtained credentials as a missionary in the newly established Assemblies of God, but we do not hear of him thereafter.[145]

Another prominent Sri Lankan evangelist, Charles Hettiaratchy, received Spirit baptism on his own through reading about the revival in Los Angeles, visited the USA in 1910, wrote articles published in Pentecostal papers, and featured as a speaker in conferences at Glad Tidings in New York and the Stone Church in Chicago. From there he spent some time in England, speaking at Boddy's Sunderland Convention before returning to Colombo via Genoa, Italy, travelling together with outgoing PMU missionaries. He worked with Berg in his meetings in Kerala and accompanied him on his trip to Switzerland, Germany and the USA in 1911. He also hosted an Anglican clergyman from England, Clement W. Dickinson, in December 1911, who went there with the intention of setting up a Pentecostal missionary home in Kandy – but Dickinson went from there to Assam.[146]

A third early Sri Lankan Pentecostal leader was Alwin de Alwis (d. 1967), who was preparing for the coming of American missionary W. D. Grier to Colombo in 1913. De Alwis was an early convert, receiving Spirit baptism in 1912, possibly as a result of Berg or Bahr's ministry in Sri Lanka. Bergunder thinks that he might have been born in 1901 (which is unlikely) and that he was formerly a Baptist. The Griers also worked with Wanigasekera, but de Alwis was their main co-worker and took charge of their work in Peradeniya in 1915. Amazingly, the Griers told their supporters that all the Pentecostals had left the island by the time they arrived in 1913 – perhaps they meant foreign missionaries. They left Sri Lanka themselves in 1917.[147] It is indicative of how important the careful reconstruction of early Pentecostal history is that some have suggested that Pentecostalism in Sri Lanka began with the Danish actress Anna Lewini and Walter Clifford, a former British soldier in India, who arrived in Colombo in 1919 and 1923 respectively. From their work evolved the Assemblies of God and the independent Ceylon Pentecostal Mission of Alwin de Alwis and Ramankutty Paul, founded in 1921. It is also suggested that the de Alwis family became Pentecostals as a result of Clifford's healing services, whereas de Alwis had already been a Pentecostal for at least ten years.[148] There is also record of a Sri Lankan Baptist, J. J. B. de Silva, who became Pentecostal, started an independent congregation in these early years, and assisted Anna Lewini.[149] In fact, Pentecostal missions were active in Sri Lanka for more than a decade before Lewini and Clifford, and its pioneers were Sri Lankans. Out of the Ceylon Pentecostal Mission came the inspiration for a whole series of independent Pentecostal secessions.[150]

South Asian Pentecostal history is complex and any assessment of it must first recognize that sources relating to the earliest years are limited and sporadic. This chapter has attempted to give evidence of that complexity as Pentecostal missionaries from outside came into India and interacted with existing missionaries and their Indian and Sri Lankan converts. But at best, this is a fragment of the complete picture. The whole story has yet to be told. At the heart of it, however, is the work of Pandita Ramabai and her Mukti Mission, the reverberations of which are still with us today.

Notes

1 *Bombay Guardian and Banner of Asia* (7 Nov 1905), p.9.
2 *THW*, p.234–5.
3 Quoted by Cecil Polhill in *FF* 16 (Mar 1913), p.4.
4 *TF* 36:9 (Sept 1916), p.202.
5 *LRE* 5:7 (Apr 1913), p.17.
6 *FF* 9 (Jan 1913), p.3.
7 Adhav, *Pandita Ramabai*, p.147.
8 Kosambi, *Pandita Ramabai*, pp.129–80; Blumhofer, '"From India's Coral Strand"', pp.152–70.
9 Fuller, *Triumph of an Indian Widow*, p.29; Blumhofer, '"From India's Coral Strand"', pp.160–1.
10 Kosambi, *Pandita Ramabai*, pp.181–244.
11 Adhav, *Pandita Ramabai*, pp.114–15.
12 Kosambi, *Pandita Ramabai*, pp.9–12; Fuller, *Triumph of an Indian Widow*, pp.30–5. I use modern place names like Pune (Poona) here, but colonial ones in the case of familiar cities like Bombay, Madras and Calcutta.
13 Mair, *Bungalows in Heaven*, pp.87–8.
14 Dongre and Patterson, *Pandita Ramabai*, pp.18–19; Kosambi, *Pandita Ramabai*, p.16; *LRE* 2:6 (Mar 1910), pp.13–18.
15 *Mukti Prayer-Bell* (Sept 1907), pp.21–2; Kosambi, *Pandita Ramabai*, p.12.
16 Fuller, *Triumph of an Indian Widow*, pp.51–2.

17 McGee, 'Minnie F. Abrams', p.91; Blumhofer, '"From India's Coral Strand"', p.165; *BM* 126 (1 Feb 1913), p.1.

18 Adhav, *Pandita Ramabai*, pp.201–2.

19 Dongre and Patterson, *Pandita Ramabai*, pp.27–8; Kosambi, *Pandita Ramabai*, pp.12–13.

20 Dongre and Patterson, *Pandita Ramabai*, pp.18, 24, 72–3; Fuller, *Triumph of an Indian Widow*, p.41.

21 Quoted in Blumhofer, '"From India's Coral Strand"', p.164.

22 Blumhofer, '"From India's Coral Strand"', p.167; Adhav, *Pandita Ramabai*, p.216.

23 *LRE* 1:10 (July 1910), p.8; McGee, 'Minnie F. Abrams', p.93.

24 Dongre and Patterson, *Pandita Ramabai*, p.78; Kosambi, *Pandita Ramabai*, p.320; *LRE* 1:10 (July 1910), p.11.

25 Kosambi, *Pandita Ramabai*; Fuller, *Triumph of an Indian Widow*.

26 *WW* 28:4 (Apr 1906), p.16; *Trust* 9:8 (Oct 1910), pp.12 and 13.

27 Dongre and Patterson, *Pandita Ramabai*, pp.30–1, 79–81, 88–9; Kosambi, *Pandita Ramabai*, pp.321–2.

28 *TF* 25:11 (Nov 1905), p.253.

29 *AF* 1:3 (Nov 1906), p.1; cf. McGee, 'Minnie F. Abrams', p.97. The original *India Alliance* article was not available to me, but it would be important to make a comparison with this edited version.

30 McGee, 'Latter Rain', pp.654–6.

31 McGee, 'Calcutta Revival', pp.123, 126.

32 *WW* 32:12 (Dec 1910), p.363.

33 *AF* 1:7 (Apr 1907), p.2; later reprinted in *TF* 28:1 (Jan 1908), pp.14–16.

34 *AF* 9 (June–Sept 1907), pp.1, 4; c.f. *WW* 33:8 (Aug 1911), p.247.

35 *Mukti Prayer-Bell* (Sept 1907), pp.17–21; also reproduced in Adhav, *Pandita Ramabai*, pp.225–9.

36 *AF* 10 (Sept 1907), p.4.

37 *LRE* 6:3 (Dec 1913), pp.22–3; McGee, 'Latter Rain', p.655; McGee, 'Minnie F. Abrams', pp.96–7; Frodsham, *With Signs Following*, pp.173–84.

38 *AF* 7 (Apr 1907), p.1.

39 *WW* 32:4 (Apr 1910), pp.138–41.

40 McGee, 'Latter Rain', p.662; McGee, 'Minnie F. Abrams', p.99; *LRE* 1:1 (Oct 1908), p.18; *TF* 28:9 (Sept 1908), pp.203–5.

41 *PE* 442–3 (19 Apr 1924), pp.8–9.

42 McGee, 'Calcutta Revival', p.135.

43 *AF* 1:13 (May 1908), p.1.

44 McGee, 'Minnie F. Abrams', p.101.

45 *Chicago Daily News*, p.14 Jan 1908; reproduced in *PE* 543 (29 Apr 1922), p.7.

46 Mair, *Bungalows in Heaven*, p.76.

47 *AF* 1:12 (Jan 1908), p.1.

48 *Mukti Prayer-Bell* (Sept 1907), pp.3, 4, 6, 8; also quoted in Adhav, *Pandita Ramabai*, pp.218–23.

49 McGee, 'Latter Rain', pp.660–1; McGee, 'Calcutta Revival', pp.131–2; Robert, *Occupy Until I Come*, p.263.

50 *Mukti Prayer-Bell* (Sept 1907), p.10.

51 *Mukti Prayer-Bell* (Sept 1907), pp.10–11.

52 *Mukti Prayer-Bell* (Sept 1907), pp.12–13.

53 *PE* 543 (29 Apr 1922), pp.7–8.

54 *Bombay Guardian and Banner of Asia* (7 Nov 1905), p. 9.

55 Mair, *Bungalows in Heaven*, p.76; *Trust* 9:8 (Oct 1910), p.16; *Conf* 5:6 (June 1912), p.142.

56 *Conf* 1:1 (Apr 1908), p.17; 1:2 (May 1908), p.13.

57 *Pent* 1:5 (Jan–Feb 1909), p.10.

58 *BM* 25 (1 Nov 1908), p.1; Barratt, *When the Fire Fell*, pp.157–8.

59 Barratt, *When the Fire Fell*, p.160; *Conf* 1:3 (June 1908), p.25.

60 Barratt, *When the Fire Fell*, p.167; *Conf* 1:6 (Sept 1908), p.16.

61 *LRE* 1:9 (June 1909), pp.10–13; 1:10 (July 1909), pp.6–13; 1:12 (Sept 1909), pp.3–9; 2:6 (Mar 1910), pp.13–18; 2:7 (Apr 1910), pp.12–15; 2:11 (Aug 1910), pp.6–12.

62 *LRE* 1:10 (July 1909), p.11.

63 *LRE* 1:10 (July 1909), p.13.

64 *UR* 1:1 (June 1909), p.6; *WW* 31:8 (Aug 1909), p.169.

65 *TF* 29:12 (Dec 1909), p.288; *Pent* 2:4 (March 1910), p.4; *BM* 68 (15 Aug 1910), p.2.

66 *BM* 77 (1 Jan 1911), p.4.

67 *Conf* 1:3 (June 1908), p.28.

68 *Conf* 1:3 (June 1908), p.2; 1:6 (Sept 1908), p.10.

69 *Conf* 1:6 (Sept 1908), p.14.

70 *Conf* 1:8 (Nov 1908), pp.19–21.

71 *Pent* 1:7 (June 1909), p.9.

72 *LRE* 1:2 (Nov 1908), pp.7–12, 14; 1:4 (Jan 1909), pp.13–17.

73 *LRE* 1:8 (May 1909), p.12.

74 *LRE* 2:6 (Mar 1910), p.13.

75 Fuller, *Triumph of an Indian Widow*, pp.4–5.

76 Kosambi, *Pandita Ramabai*, p.18.

77 *TF* 31:1 (Jan 1911), p.5.

78 *PE* 543 (19 Apr 1924), p.9.

79 *WW* 28:5 (May 1906), p.145.

80 *Pent* 2:11–12 (Nov–Dec 1910), p.9; *LRE* 3:7 (Apr 1911), p.19; *BM* 126 (1 Feb 1913), p.1.

81 McGee, 'Latter Rain', pp.651, 656–7, 664.

82 *AF* 1 (Sept 1906), p.4; 2 (Oct 1906), p.2; Thompson and Gordon, *Alfred Garr*, pp.71–6.

83 *AF* 7 (Apr 1907), p.1; *LRE* 6:3 (Dec 1913), p.23.

84 *WW* 29:6 (June 1907), p.184; Robeck, *Azusa Street*, pp.250–2; Thompson and Gordon, *Alfred Garr*, pp.81–9; *DPCM*, p.248.

85 *AF* 9 (June–Sept 1907), p.1.

86 *BM* 57 (1 Mar 1910), p.1; 61 (1 May 1910), p.4; 62 (15 May 1910), p.3; 77 (1 Jan 1911), p.4; 80 (15 Feb 1911), pp.2–3; 141 (1 Oct 1913), p.1; *Conf* 3:5 (May 1910), pp.113–14; *UR* 1:10 (May 1910), p.5; 2:5 (May 1911), p.6; *LRE* 9:7 (Apr 1917), p.18.

87 *BM* 66 (15 July 1910), p.3.

88 *LRE* 5:4 (Jan 1913), p.11.

89 *Conf* 7:3 (Mar 1914), p.60.

90 *Conf* 3:2 (Feb 1910), pp.68–9; *BM* 45 (1 Sept 1909), p.2.

91 *BM* 52 (15 Dec 1909), p.2; 54 (15 Jan 1910), p.3; 56 (15 Feb 1910), pp.3–4; 57 (1 Mar 1910), p.4; *WW* 32:3 (Mar 1910), pp.90–2.

92 *BM* 57 (1 Mar 1910), p.1; 58 (15 Mar 1910), p.4; 59 (1 Apr 1910), p.1; 61 (1 May 1910), p.4.

93 *Conf* 2:12 (Dec 1909), p.272.

94 *BM* 51 (1 Dec 1909), p.2; 76 (15 Dec 1910), pp.1, 4; 77 (1 Jan 1911), p.1; 84 (15

Apr 1911), p.4; 100 (15 Dec 1911), pp.1, 3–4; 108 (15 Apr 1912), p.2; 127 (15 Feb 1913), p.1; 129 (15 Mar 1913), p.2; *Pent* 2:2 (Jan 1910), p.8; 2:4 (Mar 1910), p.8; *WW* 32:11 (Nov 1910), p.348; *WWit* 8:10 (20 Dec 1912), p.4; *TF* 36:8 (Aug 1916), pp.186–7.

95 *LRE* 9:6 (Mar 1917), p.16.

96 *WE* 199 (21 July 1917), p.11.

97 *LRE* 13:2 (Nov 1920), pp.5–9.

98 *LRE* 13:5 (Feb 1921), p.9.

99 *WW* 42:5 (May 1920), p.28.

100 *BM* 98 (15 Nov 1911), pp.1–2; 99 (1 Dec 1911), p.3.

101 *BM* 130 (1 Apr 1913), p.4; 135 (15 June 1913), p.2; *LRE* 5:12 (Sept 1913), p.21; 6:1 (Oct 1913), p.16; 6:3 (Dec 1913), p.10; 7:6 (Mar 1915), pp.13–14; *WE* 208 (29 Sept 1917), p.13.

102 *UR* 1:6 (Jan 1910), p.7; 2:4 (Jan 1911), p.5; *Pent* 2:4 (Mar 1910), p.1; *BM* 57 (1 Mar 1910), p.4; 60 (15 Apr 1910), p.2; 62 (15 May 1910), p.2; 72 (15 Oct 1910), p.1; 75 (1 Dec 1910), p.2; 81 (1 Mar 1911), p.4; 83 (1 Apr 1911), p.2; 86 (15 May 1911), p.1; 93 (1 Sept 1911), pp.1–2; 119 (15 Oct 1912), p.1; 122 (1 Dec 1912), p.1; 136 (1 July 1913), p.1; *WW* 32:3 (Mar 1910), pp.92–3; 32:12 (Dec 1910), p.382; 36:7 (July 1914), p.217; *LRE* 5:4 (Jan 1913), p.15.

103 *LRE* 9:7 (Apr 1917), pp.6–8; *DPCM*, p.692.

104 *Trust* 16:5 (July 1917), p.23.

105 *Conf* 1:8 (Nov 1908), p.18; 3:2 (Feb 1910), p.43; *BM* 67 (1 Aug 1910), p.1; *LRE* 6:1 (Oct 1913), p.16.

106 *UR* 2:2 (Sept–Oct 1910), p.6; 2:5 (May 1911), p.6; *BM* 72 (15 Oct 1910), p.1; 80 (15 Feb 1911), p.1; 108 (15 Apr 1912), p.3; *Conf* 5:2 (Feb 1912), p.48.

107 *TF* 29:1 (Jan 1909), p.19; *Trust* 11:7 (Sept 1912), p.18.

108 *Conf* 3:2 (Feb 1910), p.43; 4:4 (Apr 1911), pp.94–5; 4:6 (June 1911), p.143; *BM* 71 (1 Oct 1910), p.4; 85 (1 May 1911), p.1; 139 (1 Sept 1913), p.3; *Trust* 9:8 (Oct 1910), p.19; 10:3 (May 1911), p.16; 10:12 (Feb 1912), p.16; *LRE* 3:10 (July 1911), p.17; *FF* 2 (Nov 1911), p.5.

109 *Conf* 3:8 (Aug 1910), p.199; 6:3 (Mar 1913), p.62; 6:7 (July 1913), p. 147; 7:1 (Jan 1914), p.15; *FF* 10 (Feb 1913), p.5; 14 (Oct 1913), p.5; *LRE* 6:3 (Dec 1913), p.2.

110 *BM* 146 (15 Dec 1913), p.2.

111 *LRE* 9:8 (May 1917), p.13.

112 *FF* (Dec 1917), p.9.

113 *LRE* 6:9 (June 1914), p.9; Bergunder, *Die südindische Pfingstbewegung*, p.37.

114 *BM* 17 (1 July 1908), p.2.

115 *WW* 31:2 (Feb 1909), p.31; *UR* 2:2 (Sept–Oct 1910), p.6; *BM* 73 (1 Nov 1910), p.2; *LRE* 11:8 (May 1919), pp.15–16; McGee, *This Gospel*, p.100; 'Constitution and By-Laws', 1939, p.182; *DPCM*, p.1043.

116 *BM* 13 (1 May 1908), p.2; *Pent* 1:4 (Dec 1908), pp.2–3; 1:9 (Aug 1909), p.5; *UR* 1:5 (Oct–Nov 1909), p.7; *LRE* 2:7 (Apr 1910), p.15; Bergunder, *Die südindische Pfingstbewegung*, p.29.

117 *Pent* 2:5 (Apr 1910), p.6; *Conf* 3:4 (Apr 1910), p.92; 5:3 (Mar 1912), p.68; 5:4 (Apr 1912), p.90; *WW* 32:4 (Apr 1910), p.120; 32:12 (Dec 1910), p.380; 34:5 (May 1912), p.124; *LRE* 2:11 (Aug 1910), p.12; 3:3 (Dec 1910), p.10; 3:12 (Sept 1911), pp.2–8; 4:7 (Apr 1912), p.22; 4:12 (Sept 1912), p.22; *BM* 71 (1 Oct 1910), p.2; 77 (1 Jan 1911), p.1; 92 (15 Aug 1911), p.3; 93 (1 Sept 1911), p.4; 100 (15 Dec 1911), p.2.

118 *LRE* 4:9 (May 1912), pp.9–10.

119 *WW* 42:3 (Mar 1920), p.32; Bergunder, 'Constructing Indian Pentecostalism', p.192; Bergunder, *Die südindische Pfingstbewegung*, p.29.

120 *BM* 125 (15 Jan 1913), p.3; *WWit* 10:8 (Aug 1914), p.4.

121 *LRE* 5:1 (Oct 1912), p.12; 5:8 (May 1913), p 14; *BM* 119 (15 Oct 1912), pp.2, 3; 125 (15 Jan 1913), p.3; 130 (1 Apr 1913), p.3; *Trust* 11:10 (Dec 1912), p.18; *Conf* 6:3 (Mar 1913), p.60.

122 *WWit* 9:12 (Dec 1913), p.1; *WW* 36:1 (Jan 1914), p.25; 36:9 (Sept 1914), p.275; 36:10 (Oct 1914), p.316; 37:1 (Jan 1915), pp.23, 29; *LRE* 6:11 (Aug 1914), p.17.

123 *TF* 35:1 (Jan 1915), p.23.

124 *Conf* 6:1 (Jan 1913), p.20; *BM* 125 (15 Jan 1913), p.3; 135 (15 June 1913), p.2; 138 (15 Aug 1913), p.2; 145 (1 Dec 1913), p.1; *WW* 36:6 (June 1914), p.187; 36:10 (Oct 1914), p.316; 36:11 (Nov 1914), pp.349–50; 42:1 (Jan 1920), pp.14, 20; 42:6 (June 1920), p.13; *CE* 56 (29 Aug 1914), p.4; *WWit* 12:5 (May 1915), p.6; Bergunder, 'Constructing Indian Pentecostalism', p.192; Bergunder, *Die südindische Pfingstbewegung*, pp.31–3; Hedlund, 'Indigenous Pentecostalism', pp.216–17.

125 Bergunder, *Die südindische Pfingstbewegung*, p.28.

126 *Trust* 12:8 (Oct 1913), p.11; *WWit* 9:9 (Sept 1913), p.4; 12:5 (May 1915), p.6; *WE* 93 (5 June 1915), p.4; 216 (24 Nov 1917), p.12; 'Combined Minutes', 1920, p.67; 'Constitution and By-Laws', 1927, p.114; Bergunder, 'Constructing Indian Pentecostalism', p.192; Bergunder, *Die südindische Pfingstbewegung*, pp.50–1.

127 *BM* 30 (15 Jan 1909), p.1; 31 (1 Feb 1909), p.2; 36 (15 Apr 1909), p.1.

128 *WW* 30:6 (June 1908), p.185.

129 *TF* 27:2 (Feb 1907), p.27; *BM* 73 (1 Nov 1910), p.2; 108 (15 Apr 1912), p.1; *LRE* 9:7 (Apr 1917), p.16.

130 *AF* 13 (May 1908), p.1.

131 *BM* 5 (1 Jan 1908), p.2.

132 *WW* 32:4 (Apr 1910), p.122.

133 *Trust* 10:4–5 (June and July 1911), p.15.

134 *BM* 18 (15 July 1908), p.1; *Trust* 10:5 (May 1911), p.18.

135 *BM* 59 (1 Apr 1910), p.2; 77 (1 Jan 1911), p.4; 80 (15 Feb 1911), p.1; *Trust* 10:3 (Mar 1911), p.92.

136 *LRE* 3:11 (Aug 1911), pp.15–16; *BM* 104 (15 Feb 1912), p.3; 131 (15 Apr 1913), p.4.

137 *Trust* 17:6 (Aug 1918), p.15.

138 *Trust* 19:3 (May 1920), p.15.

139 *Pent* 2:3 (Feb 1910), p.4; *BM* 56 (15 Feb 1910), p.1; 78 (15 Jan 1911), p.3; 82 (15 Mar 1911), p.4; 86 (15 May 1911), p.4; 125 (15 Jan 1913), p.2; *LRE* 2:11 (Aug 1910), p.11; *TF* 32:4 (Apr 1912), p.81.

140 *WW* 34:2 (Feb 1912), p.62.

141 *BM* 57 (1 Mar 1910), p.4; 78 (15 Jan 1911), p.4; *LRE* 2:11 (Aug 1910), 6; 3:1 (Oct 1910), p.11; 3:4 (Jan 1911), pp.12–13; 5:2 (Nov 1912), p.12; *Trust* 9:8 (Oct 1910), pp.2, 15; *TF* 30:10 (Oct 1910), p.225; *WW* 32:11 (Nov 1910), p.349; *Pent* 2:11–12 (Nov–Dec 1910), p.14.

142 *WE* 145 (24 June 1916), pp.4–6; *PE* 442–3 (29 Apr 1922), p.7; 446–7 (27 May 1922), p.9; 468–9 (28 Oct 1922), p.13; 543 (19 Apr 1924), pp.8–9; 1669 (4 May 1946), pp.1, 12–13.

143 *Trust* 8:12 (Feb 1910), p. 19; *BM* 54 (15 Jan 1910), p.3; 61 (1 May 1910), p.4; 63 (1 June 1910), p.2; 67 (1 Aug 1910), p.4; 74 (15 Nov 1910), pp.1, 3; 75 (1 Dec 1910), p.4; 81 (1 Mar 1911), p.4; 85 (1 May 1911), p.4; 88 (15 June 1911), p.4; 89 (1 July 1911), p.3; 92 (15 Aug 1911), p.1; 95 (1 Oct 1911), p.4; 96 (15 Oct 1911), p.2; 134 (1 June 1913), p.3; *LRE* 4:1 (Oct 1911), p.21.

144 *BM* 132 (1 May 1913), p.3.

145 *CE* 61 (3 Oct 1914), p.4.

146 *TF* 30:3 (Mar 1910), pp.66–8; *WW* 32:2 (Feb 1910), pp.39, 55; 33:5 (May 1911), p.156; *LRE* 2:7 (Apr 1910), p.7; 2:8 (May 1910), pp.9–13; 3:2 (Nov 1910), pp.2–7; 4:2 (Nov 1911), p.16–17; 4:3 (Dec 1911), pp.6–10; *BM* 64 (15 June 1910), p.1; 103 (1 Feb 1912), pp.2, 3; 106 (15 Mar 1912), p.3; *Conf* 3:10 (Oct 1910), p.248; 5:1 (Jan 1912), p.18; 12:3 (July–Sept 1919), p.49.

147 *WE* 145 (24 June 1916), p.11; 186 (21 Apr 1917), p.12.

148 *WWit* 9:1 (Jan 1913), p.2; 9:11 (Nov 1913), p.4; 9:12 (Dec 1913), p.1; 10:4 (Apr 1914), p.4; 12:5 (May 1915), p.7; *BM* 144 (15 Nov 1913), p.1; *CE* 70 (12 Dec 1914), p.4; *WE* 91 (22 May 1915), p.4; Somaratna, *Origins of the Pentecostal Mission*, pp.12–23, 27–32, 41, 45–7.

149 *DPCM*, p.248.

150 Bergunder, *Die südindische Pfingstbewegung*, p.32.

5

Opening Doors of Nations:
China and East Asia

The doors of the nations are open to us today as never before, which makes our responsibility greater than it has ever been. China, India, Africa, Japan, South America and many islands of the sea are groaning under the curse of heathendom, and reaching out their hands for help.

(*Latter Rain Evangel*, 1910)[1]

At the beginning of the twentieth century China was ruled by a dynastic emperor in a system of government that had lasted for over two millennia. But this was soon to collapse before the forces of modernity and globalization. European interference and foreign incursions into China threatened her sovereignty and were resisted by various methods, including religious ones. One of the most violent anti-foreign revolts was the Boxer Rebellion of 1900, when it was estimated that at least 16,000 Christians were killed, including many expatriate missionaries. The rebellion was easily put down by an international force and the Chinese imperial government was humiliated – one of the events that helped hasten its end. Pentecostal missionaries went to China in the wake of these awful events. China was in the throes of fundamental changes that were to culminate in the Communist revolution. The nation was seeking to shed its feudal past by overthrowing its ruling emperor and set up a modern republic that could meet the West on its own terms. The 1911 Revolution resulted in the overthrow of the Manchu emperor and the setting up of a republic. There was some admiration for the USA in these republican circles – their missionaries were generally made welcome and their educational and philanthropic activities eagerly sought after. Sun Yat-Sen founded a revolutionary nationalist republican organization in 1905 that was at first a secret society until 1912 when the Nationalist Party emerged.

But from this year, China also began a period of violent anarchy, when feuding factions and warlords created a chaotic and unstable country where law and order disintegrated, leading to the Communist revolution in 1949. Within weeks of becoming China's first republican president in 1912, Sun Yat-Sen was replaced by the former imperial general Yuan Shih-kai. When Yuan died in 1916, generals in various provinces gained increasing power and fought each other for influence. In this vulnerable situation three imperial powers in particular, Britain to the west in Tibet, Russia to the north in Mongolia and Japan to the east in Manchuria and Korea began to vie for further power and exerted greater pressures on a weak and unstable Chinese government. In the Yunnan and Schechwan provinces in the east, warlords presided over anarchic conditions, and only the Treaty Ports along the coast and on the Yangtze River

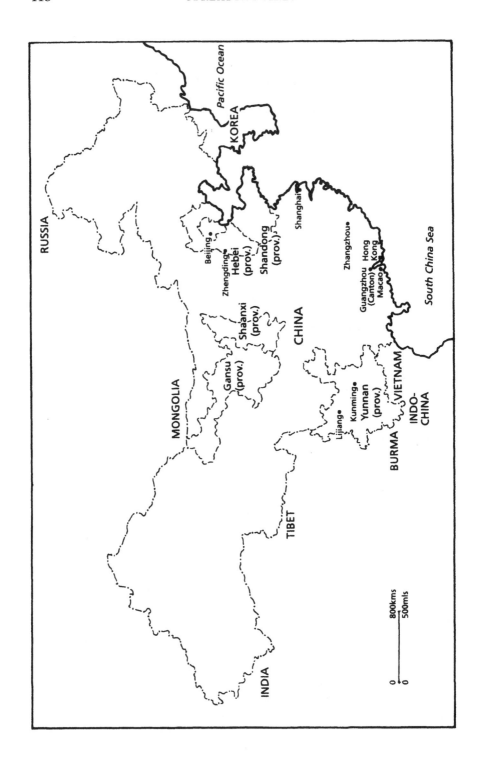

were relatively safe places for foreigners – these ports were European protectorates where westerners could trade and open missions free of Chinese
jurisdiction. Although the new republican government was not in favour of
continuing these privileges, they continued well beyond the 1911 Revolution.[2]

None of the tumultuous events fazed the Pentecostal missionaries who
began to arrive on China's coast in 1907. China was a favourite destination for
them; it was regarded as the most important place for missionaries to go to,
having a quarter of the estimated world population at the time with very few
Protestant Christians, despite a century of missions. The radical evangelical
'faith missions', especially the China Inland Mission and the Christian and
Missionary Alliance had the greatest influence on the activities and policies
of the Pentecostals, as many of their missionaries came from these organizations. Pentecostal periodicals made regular pleas for more missionaries to
China, declaring that a million Chinese souls were passing into eternity every
month and the onerous responsibility was that 'to us God has committed
the destinies of the human race'.[3] China was seen as the 'land of Sinim' from
which the prophet Isaiah prophesied that people would come to join God's
people.[4]

This was a land of great need but also of unparalleled opportunities, where
the interior had opened up to western interests as never before and the way
was open for missionaries to flood in. Constant appeals were made on the basis
of estimated population statistics and the relatively small number of missionaries. During the first two decades of the twentieth century many new and
independent missionaries arrived from the West, of which Pentecostals were
only part. But this period also saw the establishment of Chinese independent
churches, particularly because of the desire to be independent from paternalistic foreign dominance in leadership and financial control, but also because of
the 'three-self' policies adopted by most Protestant missions but seldom imple-
mented. Many of these independent groups were Pentecostal and influenced
by foreign Pentecostal missionaries.[5] The first Apostolic Faith missionaries to
South China arrived in 1907. This was also the year of the national missionary
conference in Shanghai, attended by all existing Protestant missions at the time
but very few Chinese. These missions all operated under smoothly running
comity arrangements respected by all, restricting each mission to defined
areas.[6] The scene was set for dramatic change, as most Pentecostals did not
have the word 'comity' in their vocabulary. This chapter sets out to describe
some of these changes.

The Apostolic Faith in South China

Alfred and Lillian Garr and their African American helper Maria Gardner,
were among the first missionaries from Azusa Street. They continued their
journey from India, where they had pioneered work (outlined earlier) via Sri
Lanka, and after an invitation by missionaries in Hong Kong, arrived there in
October 1907. They were followed three days later by two women from Seattle
who had travelled with Martin Ryan's party of missionaries to Japan, May

Law and Rose Pittman, who on arrival had neither plans nor accommodation. They went to the American consul to be directed to the American Board (Congregational) Mission where the first Pentecostal services were held and where the Garrs joined them. These four missionaries were augmented in October 1908 by Cora Fritsch and Bertha Milligan, who had both spent a year with Ryan's team in Japan. Fritsch, only 18 when she arrived in Japan, was to spend four years in South China before she died of malaria, and she and Milligan were later to work in Canton (Guangzhou), where Milligan was still working in 1920.[7] The meetings in the American Board Mission were interpreted by a capable Chinese schoolteacher, Mok Lai Chi, to whom we return later. In this mission, *The Apostolic Faith* reported, 'a glorious revival' broke out,[8] and later, that 'a good many of the Chinese' had 'received their Pentecost and are singing, praying, and praising in new tongues'. It went on, 'The burden of it all is that Jesus is coming soon and we must prepare to meet Him. The best part is to see these dear Chinese Christians yielding fully to God and being filled with the blessed Holy Spirit.'[9]

By January 1908 all the converts were Chinese. The new Pentecostal believers were encouraged by fellowship with the McIntoshes from Macao, who visited them regularly.[10] Law and Pittman both contracted smallpox and were quarantined in an offshore boat, but recovered. Between four and seven hundred people attended the first meetings, but opposition from the missionaries mounted, they were ejected from the American Board building, and they moved to the much smaller venue of Mok Lai Chi's school. A hostile missionary critic charged 'the authoritative Garr' with pronouncing anathemas on him and other 'faithful missionaries of Hongkong'.[11] This appears to have been a habit that did not exactly endear Garr to other missionaries. A Shanghai missionary periodical said that Hong Kong had been disturbed by the 'Pentecostal church', a sect whose aim seemed 'rather to pervert Christian Chinese than to convert the heathen'.[12]

Within six months about a hundred people in South China had become Pentecostal. In Hong Kong, some 30 people met regularly at Mok's Morrison English School. During this time, as Garr later related, their financial needs were met by a Chinese woman. A photograph of the Pentecostal Mission taken early in 1908 shows the Garrs, Gardner, Law, Pittman and Mok with a group of 40 Chinese adults and children.[13] In a letter to G. B. Cashwell, Garr wrote that although they would love to remain in China 'until Jesus comes', they now believed 'that God is going to take us to the states [sic] in a few months'.[14] These were hard times. Lillian Garr gave birth to a stillborn child and in March 1908 their invaluable assistant Maria Gardner and three-year-old daughter Virginia died of smallpox within a day of each other. After these tragic events they spent two months with Ryan in Japan and returned to America, where they itinerated for over a year on behalf of the Chinese church. The aristocratic Alexander Boddy met the Garrs at a camp meeting near Toronto in June 1909 and described them as 'Southerners, of a refined type . . . good-looking, well-made young people, fit to move in any society'. Lillian Garr, he wrote, was 'about six feet high' and both she and her husband had voices that 'would carry a great distance in the open-air'. The Garrs also met Robert and Aimee Semple (later McPherson) and probably influenced them in their decision to go to Hong Kong as missionaries in 1910, where Semple died of malaria soon after arrival and Aimee returned to the USA.[15]

The Garrs were back in Hong Kong in October 1909 to open a missionary home. They left for India three months later, and returned to Hong Kong for another year during which time their son was born. Their philosophy was simple: Garr explained that they did not expect to spend long in Hong Kong because the Lord had 'put Evangelistic work' on them and they would leave whenever work was established. He added that 'we are seeing the fruit of our labour already' and significantly, that Mok was 'the head of the work here'.[16] The Garrs left permanently for the USA in December 1911 to engage in church planting and healing evangelism until the premature death of Lillian in 1916.[17]

The Garrs were not the first Pentecostals to reach China, but were preceded by two months by Thomas J. and Annie McIntosh. They had been baptized in the Spirit in early 1907 through the ministry of G. B. Cashwell, the latter having received Spirit baptism at Azusa Street. McIntosh believed that he had been given the Chinese language in his tongues experience and after a revelation and a visit to Azusa Street he set sail with his wife and daughter for the Portuguese colony of Macao, arriving in August. McIntosh's letter to Cashwell the day after his arrival mentioned a welcome meeting in which 25 missionaries and 'five or six Chinamen' were present. Two weeks later the missionaries were resisting McIntosh's teaching but despite this, greater numbers of Chinese were attending the services.[18] A report in September 'from missionaries in Macao, China' mentioned that some of the Chinese Christians had received Spirit baptism and were speaking in tongues.[19] Four months later, Cashwell reported that 70 had received Spirit baptism 30 days after McIntosh arrived in Macao.[20] Like the Garrs, McIntosh also reached out to other missionaries. He wrote that Pentecost had come to the South China CMA mission in Wuzhou through two missionaries who had attended meetings in Macao. Numbers of Chinese had also 'received their Pentecost' there, he recorded; and this was also reported by the missionaries themselves in a CMA newsletter.[21] At that stage, the CMA welcomed such manifestations of spiritual power. The Azusa Street newspaper reported that among the CMA missionaries in Macao and Wuzhou, a number of Chinese Christians were baptized in the Spirit. The CMA annual report for 1907 reflected on the need for revival in China, 'a mighty outpouring of the Holy Spirit' that would 'awaken her out of this fearful sleep of death' and would 'mean the bestowal of the old Pentecostal power and gifts promised so long ago, but lost for all these centuries'. Then it described what had happened in Wuzhou in September 1907:

The Spirit fell in a quiet Saturday night meeting and, without there having been any special exhortation or request in prayer on this line, a number 'began to speak with other tongues'. It was an entirely new experience, but a blessed one to many, both foreign and native brethren and sisters, old and young. The features and manifestations of these meetings were very similar to those of which we have read in various parts of the world. It seems as though the Holy Spirit is falling on the children of God simultaneously in all parts of the world, often without the intervention of a human leader.[22]

By all accounts, the McIntoshes (unlike the Garrs) were simple and uneducated people. One missionary critic of these 'curious fanatics' charging that
McIntosh's ignorance was so great that he could only read 'simple English',
although he was 'cast in a gentler mold than the authoritative Garr'.[23]

McIntosh usually never spent longer than a few months in each place,
itinerating widely in the vicinities of Macao and Canton. He reported that
within a month some 70 people in Macao, Canton and Wuzhou had received
Spirit baptism, including 14 missionaries. The McIntoshes received increasing
criticism, particularly because they were young and inexperienced and had
not been able to speak Chinese, despite their original claims to do so.[24] The
Spirit gave McIntosh the names of places before he went there. The result of
this was to send him to Palestine, as *The Apostolic Faith* recorded that 'many
souls in China' had received Spirit baptism through the work of the
McIntoshes at Macao and other places. The Lord had told him 'to "go to
Macao" before he knew there was any such place but he looked it up on the
map and found it'.[25] McIntosh himself said that Palestine 'was given me
just like Macao, China'.[26] After nine months in China, McIntosh was opposed
publicly by a CMA missionary and left for Palestine in May 1908. Much of the
passage there was paid for by compassionate Chinese people and CMA
missionaries.[27] From Jerusalem the McIntoshes returned to the USA but
returned to Hong Kong in December 1909 with a party of eight Pentecostal
missionaries to work with the Garrs. The Garrs left for Bombay shortly after
and left the McIntoshes in charge of their mission home.[28]

During his extended world tour of Pentecostal missions, Joseph H. King of
the Fire-Baptized Holiness Church – soon to be presiding bishop of the Pentecostal Holiness Church – with a team of eight Americans visited Shanghai to be
with Apostolic Faith missionaries Moomau and Phillips, and then moved on to
Hong Kong in October 1910. He was met by McIntosh and taken to a welcom-
ing meal where there were 15 American Pentecostal missionaries.[29] More were
yet to come. In December 1910 McIntosh persuaded a large group of missionaries, including May Law and the visitor King, to go 27 miles from Canton to
Sainam, apparently because this was a city with no resident missionary and
a population of 'about a million' within a radius of five miles – probably an
exaggeration. He said that he doubted the wisdom of having all the Pentecostal workers concentrated in Hong Kong, as there were 'already a goodly
number here and others are coming'. He thought it a much better plan to begin
establishing mission stations throughout China, and much cheaper both for
accommodation and for language learning. The Sainam mission was to
become a main centre for Pentecostalism in the region. May Law was there for
many years, operating a children's school from 1912.[30] King left for India in
January 1911 after four months in the region. The McIntoshes soon moved
back to the USA via Palestine in 1911 where Thomas wrote of his desire to open
a rescue home for Jewish beggars, leaving Homer Faulkner (who married Cora
Fritsch) in charge of the Sainam mission. By 1913 McIntosh had disappeared
from the Pentecostal scene when he was excommunicated from the PHC for
'apostasy'.[31]

Annie Kirby (Annie McIntosh's aunt) and Mabel Evans arrived to assist the
McIntoshes in Macao in January 1908, but on the departure of the McIntoshes

in May they moved to Canton with an experienced missionary, Fannie Winn. She spoke Chinese, and they worked with Chinese leaders there.[32] To be sure, some of these missionaries 'living by faith' were on a shoe-string and simply could not afford to go home, even for furlough. Once in Canton, Kirby, Evans and Winn established work with a Chinese leader called 'Brother Ho'. Then they moved two miles across the city to stay with his sister and a wealthy Chinese Christian woman, Ho Si Tai, who fitted out a chapel for them in the house they rented from her. They spent most of their time in evangelistic work, two street meetings and two services in the chapel daily. Kirby and Evans drew the crowds by singing with a portable organ, and Winn then preached in Chinese. This was a method used frequently by western evangelical missionaries at the time, but because most of the Pentecostals could not yet speak Chinese, they depended on Chinese assistants for the preaching. Within a year, these three American women had returned to the USA.[33]

Carrie and George Montgomery's tour of South China and India in 1909 was mainly to visit CMA missions and although they had relatively little contact with the independent Pentecostal missionaries, their meetings in the CMA must have confirmed the newfound Pentecostal experience of the missionaries. After arriving in Hong Kong, they proceeded up river to Wuzhou, where they visited two 'Bible schools' (one for 'boys' and one for 'girls'), where students were trained as Bible teachers. Once or twice on this brief journey in both China and India, Carrie Montgomery referred to 'native workers' who had particularly impressed her. There must have been hundreds of these workers assisting the foreign missionaries and making a great impact on local people. Montgomery commented that 'no one could doubt what God is doing in the earth in these last wonderful days if they could see these beautiful, transformed, Spirit-filled lives, both among the missionaries and the natives, as we have seen them'.[34] In Wuzhou they met a remarkable but unnamed Chinese woman who was one of the teachers in the girls' school, and she and many of the girls had 'received their Pentecostal baptism'. According to the missionaries, through the 'great spirituality' of this Chinese woman many girls in the school had become 'so deeply spiritual'.[35] The Montgomerys then visited Canton, where they 'found great prejudice against the Pentecostal movement' because there had been 'so much wildfire and fanaticism'.[36] Possibly, this prejudice was occasioned by the visits of McIntosh to that city. At this stage the Montgomerys were still leaders in the CMA, which took a moderate line to spiritual gifts and did not teach 'initial evidence' as the missionaries generating from Azusa Street did, causing tension that would flare up later. The Montgomerys returned to Hong Kong and made a brief visit to Macao before leaving for India.

More missionaries arrived to stay at the mission home in Hong Kong and reported on the ongoing work there, including open-air meetings featuring mainly Chinese workers and a 'Bible woman' working for the Mission named as Poon Yun Choe.[37] The Pentecostal Mission in Sainam was led by Homer Faulkner assisted by May Law, Mattie Ledbetter, Addell Harrison and her daughter Golden, George and Margaret Kelley (former Free Baptist missionaries), and a Chinese worker, Wai Meng. There they operated a boys' school and an orphanage, stating that this was an independent, interdenominational and 'thoroughly Pentecostal' mission. Soon these workers had began three new missions, passing through a succession of workers. By 1913 George Kelley was leading the Sainam mission, Addell Harrison running the orphanage, and May Law assisted by Olive Mau starting a boys' school in another city, Fatshan. That year saw a severe typhoon in the district, the resulting floods almost destroyed the Sainam buildings and an estimated 100,000 people were drowned. The following year equally devastating floods struck Canton and vicinity, the worst in memory. As a result of the repeated damage done to the orphanage, in 1915 Harrison moved the orphanage to Macao and opened a blind school there, but she was soon afterwards to move to Hong Kong.[38] By 1917 the Kelleys were still in Sainam and were the senior missionaries in the area, running a two- to three-year training school for Chinese preachers and in affiliation with the AG.[39] Their mission (and all missions) were greatly affected by the civil war and lawlessness that prevailed in 1920 in South China.[40]

Canton was another important centre for early Pentecostalism in China. Ho Maan Leung and his wife, the people in whose house the McIntoshes had first preached, ran a regular Pentecostal meeting-place there. Anna Deane, a former school principal from New York, attended the meetings in the Ho home, writing that 'a large number of heathen' were hearing the gospel message every night. Ho was also described by Paul Bettex as the one who had helped them 'more than any other man in China', a 'blessed brother . . . never tired of praying'. Another preacher, Lo Heung Lun, was pastor of 'Salvation Church' in Canton, described as an 'independent native Baptist church', a 'quite independent and a very humble man', supported by a medical dispensary next to the church that his father had built. Bertha Dixon described Lo as having 'the distinguishing marks of a deep life with the Lord . . . one of the noblest and gentlest of men, and very sensitive to the movings of the Holy Spirit'. His church had become a significant Pentecostal centre in Canton since Lo's Spirit baptism in 1908. The Dixons stayed in the rooms over his chapel, but within a year their two children, aged four and two, died, and they left.

Lo's elder sister Ho Si Tai was a Bible woman of mature years who had been matron of a Methodist girls' boarding school – until she lost her job after receiving Spirit baptism. Ho Si Tai was an ardent preacher in Canton with a large home which she had opened to the first Pentecostal missionaries there. Lillian Garr described her preaching in a church service she attended late in 1909 and mentioned a Chinese nursing sister in Hong Kong who had left her job to go into Pentecostal ministry.[41] Ho Si Tai had used her house as a preaching place too with a chapel in which nightly services were held, Deane reporting that the chapel was filled with an attentive audience at every service. She commented that God was greatly using this woman and had raised her up as a leader. Bettex described her as having 'a rich, deep anointing of God' and 'a well-rounded, mature and uncompromising Pentecostal witness'. She was President of the Monthly Meeting of Christian Chinese Women in 1912, an ecumenical organization, and many people came into Pentecostal experience through her mission. So there were three independent Pentecostal churches in Canton in 1910 all run by extremely capable Chinese leaders with little foreign help. According to Paul Bettex from Azusa Street and a former missionary in Chile, the Pentecostal work in Canton was represented by these three Chinese congregations. A 60-year-old woman, Wong Tai Koo, was an 'indefatigable' itinerant preacher there who 'tramps, preaches and prays without ceasing, going out without scrip or purse, and bringing souls to Jesus', and 'Brother Sin', a young Bible Society colporteur had been employed as the missionaries' language helper and preacher.[42]

In 1910, Nellie Clark married Paul Bettex, and they worked together with several women missionaries in the Canton Pentecostal Mission, holding three services a day, including daily prayer and Bible study for between 15 and 20 Chinese workers. They estimated reaching between two to three hundred people a day and five to six hundred at Sunday services. The Bettexes published a paper called *Canton Pentecost*, until their lives were tragically cut short, Nellie from a brain haemorrhage in 1912 and Paul from an attack by robbers in 1916. Soon after the death of Nellie, the American women moved back to Hong Kong and Bettex remained in Canton alone with 15 Chinese workers. He continued to hold services in the city and itinerated in surrounding villages.[43] He lauded the praises of his Chinese workers, who were 'really preachers, efficient soulwinners' in an attempt to raise more funds for their support. In 1914 he handed over the work to Mrs Johnson, although no reason was given for his sudden withdrawal. But just before his disappearance and mysterious death in 1916, a letter finds him still working with 17 Chinese evangelists in what appears to have been a self-supporting work in Canton. Bettex was receiving income from a Chinese general for superintending a large housing estate. By 1920 the congregation Ho Si Tai helped establish was still going and she had handed over her property to the AG under George Kelley.[44]

Mok Lai Chi and the Hong Kong Pentecostal Mission

Not much is known about the Chinese schoolteacher in Hong Kong who edited the first Pentecostal newspaper outside the western world for at least nine years. But some information on this remarkable early Chinese leader Mok Lai Chi (Mo Lizhi, 1868–1926) remains. Mok was born into a Christian family, attended an English school in Hong Kong as a teenager (and excelled), and went into government service as a translator in 1886. According to government records, he was the best of four candidates in an English and Chinese translation test for the post of clerk at the Observatory.[45] After some time living a profligate life 'at large in the world', as he put it, he repented and in 1892 began a school for English and shorthand. He remained in government service for a little longer, as he was Chinese clerk and interpreter for the Registrar General in 1893.[46] He was also deacon in the American Board church, superintendent of the Sunday School and secretary for the local YMCA, where he had done evangelistic work among the 'coolies' (dock workers). He met the Garrs and interpreted for them in their nightly services at the American Board Mission. According to her son, the first Chinese person baptized in the Spirit in these services was Wong Chit Kee, later wife of the superintendent of the Pentecostal Mission in Hong Kong until 1958.[47] Mok was Spirit baptized in November 1907, stating: 'The Spirit spoke through me in the Mandarin dialect, the Hakka dialect, and an African tongue.' His wife, Alice Lena Mok followed a few days later. Mok led the departure from the American Board. Without him there would have been no Chinese Pentecostals in Hong Kong, and he led the Pentecostal mission that ensued.[48]

Mok's four-page broadsheet was called *Pentecostal Truths* and contained articles mostly in Chinese with up to a page in English.[49] Many of the Chinese articles were translations of teachings published elsewhere but Mok also wrote articles in Chinese himself. Six thousand copies of the paper in 1909, which increased to eight thousand in 1915, were printed and freely distributed throughout China and overseas. Although originally a monthly paper, during the Great War years only three issues were published, it seems due to a short-age of donations towards the paper.[50] Mok began the paper in January 1908 with the encouragement of T. J. McIntosh. It made front-page news in *The Apostolic Faith* in May 1908, which reported that a hundred in South China had received Spirit baptism and had started a Chinese paper called *Pentecostal Truths*, which was 'being scattered in China and Japan'. This was, the report assured its readers, 'a blessed paper and one can feel the power in it even though unable to read it'.[51]

In the same issue a report from McIntosh told how the paper started. He said that 'the Lord laid it on my heart to get out a paper in the Chinese language'. He 'put it before my Chinese brethren and they prayed over it and God put it at once on their hearts, and they began to translate pieces into Chinese'. God has given the Pentecostal missionaries 'a Chinese brother who has received the baptism of the Holy Ghost and is a good printer' (probably Mok), and the paper was 'already being scattered among the millions of China'. He asked for 'offerings to help the dear Chinese brethren, who are poor in this world's goods, get out their paper and circulate this Gospel'. These should be sent to 'Brother Mok Lai Chi, 5 Laddes St., Hong Kong, China'.[52] This paper was therefore a Chinese initiative from the start and Mok was in charge of its publication. Mok's own description of its commencement, written from 'The Apostolic Faith Mission, Hong Kong, China' confirmed McIntosh's account and showed Mok's role:

> One day, Brother McIntosh told me that the Lord had spoken to him about starting a free paper, giving the name of 'Pentecostal Truths', and asked me to pray about it. When I prayed the Lord spoke to me, commanding me to take charge of it. I said, 'Lord, I am not a writer', but the Lord reminded me of what Moses said on Mount Horeb, and promised that He would make my brothers to help me. So in January, 1908, 'Pentecostal Truths' made its first appearance . . . It is a free paper . . . It reaches, as many other Pentecostal papers do, many hungry souls, both in China and foreign countries. Besides the paper, we are publishing free tracts.[53]

Mok wrote that he started the paper 'without any fund and without any help whatever',[54] and its purpose was 'especially for proclaiming the truth of the baptism of the Holy Spirit to inspire the downcast Church'. Its content would be kept 'simple but understandable to make sure that women and children can know and gain the heavenly blessings'.[55] By 1914 the paper seemed to have shifted somewhat to a particular emphasis on 'the fact of Jesus' imminent coming', and Mok exhorted his readers to 'keep this paper to avoid regret'; as when Christ soon appeared in the sky the paper would stop and Mok's work be finished.[56]

Mok was one of several leaders in the Apostolic Faith Mission at 56 Connaught Road, Hong Kong in 1909, the mission associated with Alfred and Lillian Garr.[57] The Garrs had had a hand in persuading Mok to become Pentecostal, but on their arrival in Hong Kong he already had a reputation as an influential Christian leader and respected director of a private school, the Morrison English School.[58] In 1909, when the Garrs were back in America they spoke about their visit to Hong Kong at a conference, and said that Mok was among the first of their Chinese contacts to receive Spirit baptism. He immediately became their interpreter, and Lillian Garr added with unintended pun, 'the subject gained immensely when he interpreted'. On a later occasion, Mok interpreted for the Garrs during their evangelistic mission to Wanchai, Alfred Garr reporting: 'God has so blessed us with having Bro. Mok to interpret, and also made him a preacher to the heathen.'[59] Cora Fritsch wrote of Mok in a letter to her parents in January 1909, soon after she arrived in Hong Kong. He is 'the pastor' of the 'dear band of [Chinese] baptised souls here' and 'surely a chosen child of God, so devoted and consecrated to God. He gives all his time to the gospel work. Printing a paper as well as preaching and teaching school.'[60] Four days later she wrote to her brother that Mok took full charge of the services in the mission. In a letter to her father she describes Mok as a 'highly educated Chinese' who 'speaks and writes English almost as well as if he had been educated in America'.[61] Anna Deane also referred to Mok as the pastor of 'our church' and that the church was governed entirely by the Chinese, Mok and the deacons.[62]

Daniel Awrey from rural Oklahoma ('very quaint in his Americanisms from the far West', the English paper *Confidence* added) was on a 'journey round the world'. He had visited India and Hong Kong, and *Confidence* recorded that he had reported 'a strong, little company of Chinese brothers and sisters at Hong Kong, with whom he companied for some weeks'. He never had had 'more enthusiastic lovers of God's Word to speak to'. His commendation of his interpreter, Mok, was that he was 'all on fire with Pentecostal zeal', he had been 'a Government Interpreter', and he 'interprets addresses splendidly'.[63] Awrey departed again from the USA with his family, and after preaching visits in Honolulu and Shanghai, they arrived in Hong Kong again by 1910 and commenced a Bible school soon afterwards with twelve students. A year later Awrey had opened another Bible school in Canton with the Dixons, who had arrived there in January 1910.[64]

The Pentecostal Mission services at Connaught Road were held in the 'upper room' of a large house, the 'Pentecostal Missionary Home' where the Garrs and other missionaries lived.[65] But this building was far from where the 'heathen' lived and too small for Mok's large family. So by April 1909 Mok had opened a new 'mission hall to the heathen' in Wanchai in the 'slums of the town', filled with an attentive crowd of over 150 for nightly services. Four Chinese workers and at least some of the women missionaries helped him in this work and were 'living by faith'. He reported on nightly conversions, with 'idol-worshippers' coming to kneel at the altar, and that 'cases of beri-beri,

fever, sores, consumption, diarrhoea, dysentery, and other diseases have
been miraculously healed by our Lord Jesus through the prayers of our little
apostolic company'. He closed the school he had been running for the past 17
years in order to give himself to full-time Christian ministry, as he put it, 'no
more a schoolmaster, but God's own evangelist walking by faith'.[66] Cora
Fritsch wrote in her personal letters that this new mission was in the poor
part of the city.[67] Teams of Chinese workers went out into the surrounding
countryside taking copies of *Pentecostal Truths* and packs of tracts for the
'heathen' with them; a team of four women went to the villages on the main-
land and another two went further into the interior.[68] At the end of 1909 Mok
wrote about the first two Chinese missionaries being sent to Hebei province in
northern China.[69] All this seems to have been co-ordinated by Mok's mission.
Alfred Garr wrote of Mok as 'an able man in the work of God' who had been
greatly persecuted for his faith. 'In reality', he went on, 'Bro. Mok is the head of
the work here, and God is blessing him in the Scriptures, and blessing the work
of his hands.'[70] Mok himself wrote to George Studd at the Upper Room in Los
Angeles thanking him for financial support and writing of the attractive offer
to visit the USA, commenting, 'yet I would not leave my post unless God so
leads'.[71]

By February 1910 Mok was looking for a building near the Chinese residen-
tial areas of Hong Kong, as Connaught Street was in the business district. A
month later, he had moved to a much larger rented building at 69 Caine Road
where he lived with his family. There were enough rooms for Anna Deane's
English school with 63 women enrolled, another kindergarten school for 73
children (these two schools did not charge fees), and rooms for counselling
'seekers to come and tarry for their baptism'.[72] This became the Hong Kong
Pentecostal Mission. By June there were 135 Chinese girls and women in the
school and Deane had an unnamed Chinese woman assistant.[73] Deane herself
wrote that the church was governed by the Chinese and that Mok was its
pastor with 'all Chinese deacons'.[74] Bertha Dixon wrote that Mok was 'a wise,
careful leader under God – a man full of faith and of the Holy Ghost'.[75] Mok
visited villages near Hong Kong on a regular basis to preach to what he called
'heathen villagers', and he networked with several Chinese preachers, including some of considerable means. Anna Deane and Nellie Clark, a former LMS
missionary, were associated with Mok in 1910, also reporting the three
Pentecostal centres in Canton and living in Ho Si Tai's house. Clark refers to
her as a 'leader in the battle', but 'kept blessedly free from all desire to control'.
Another Chinese woman worker is named by Clark as Wong Tai Ku, who is
'constantly sent by the Lord on country errands'.[76]

A long letter Mok wrote to the *The Bridegroom's Messenger* in July 1910
reveals that Mok was already beginning to be disturbed by divisions creeping
into American Pentecostalism. He wanted to be sure that future American
workers would not be causing divisions in China. He stated that the Chinese
Pentecostals agreed with the Holiness Pentecostal position of the periodical
and that 'in addition, we observe foot washing'. He went on to declare his
belief that it was the Chinese themselves who should evangelize China but
that they needed teachers to train them in a Bible School, and English teachers
to help Anna Deane – other missionaries had turned down the offer to be

involved in her school.[77] Later that year Mok wrote another letter criticizing those missionaries who lived in luxurious houses with several servants, a lifestyle 'higher than some of the leading European merchants', he added. This was not the case with Pentecostal missionaries and Mok suggested what would be a suitable sum to support them, including 'native missionaries'. He dispelled the rumour that the Chinese ate less than foreigners and said that Chinese workers needed more adequate support.[78]

PHC leader Joseph H. King on a world tour in 1910 spent a month in Hong Kong, preaching every night with Mok interpreting. King spent his first night at 'the mission of Rev. Mok Lai Chi far up the mountain side' and described this Chinese leader with 'the air of a quiet, statue-like educated Chinaman, and his influence was strong and extensive among the Chinese'.[79] King also revealed that Mok's wife was American-born Chinese (which he thought made Mok more favourable towards American missions) and that Mok was leading this mission. During this visit, King spent over a month staying in the Mok family home at the Caine Road mission, where he 'enjoyed the visit immensely' and 'everything needful was done for [his] comfort'.[80] The outreach in the Wanchai mission continued and Mok's 16-year-old son Robert testified of his own Spirit baptism there in February 1910. A letter from the Garrs in May 1911 did not mention Mok and the editors suggested that the mission at Caine Road was under the Garrs' leadership, 'now the only Pentecostal work in Hong Kong'.[81] The truth was that the Garrs and Mok were working together and that the nature of the Garrs' itinerant ministry outside Hong Kong (and by their own admission) meant that Mok was actually in charge of the mission. Bartleman visited this mission in December 1910 and confirmed this, saying that Garr and Mok were together 'in charge' of the home and school there. When the Garrs returned they rented a large house next to the Mission. Mok himself was directing affairs and receiving overseas donations to distribute to the workers there. He mentioned three Chinese working with him, one called Brother Leung, who spent a month at a time in the interior distributing tracts and hundreds of copies of *Pentecostal Truths*.[82]

By 1913 the Hong Kong Pentecostal Mission was situated at 2 Bridges Road in the central district and seems to have become an independent Chinese church. Some kind of break between Mok and the Chinese leaders on the one hand and the American missionaries on the other occurred, for in September 1912 Anna Deane was writing from the 'American Pentecostal Mission' at a different address in Hong Kong and discussing their need for a Chinese pastor to assist them. She and her niece Anna Deane Cole, now affiliated with the PHC, opened a day school for boys and girls and a night school for men, did evangelistic work among the sampan boat people and were associated with Homer Faulkner, a Chinese pastor Ng Sui Shan and a worker named as Ko Sz Nai. Anna Deane died in China in 1918 and her niece returned temporarily to the USA, sent out again by the PHC in 1920.[83] In 1913 David Barth reported working with Mok in his school holding services that were well attended. The latest report of Mok's work in the overseas press was published in E. N. Bell's *Word and Witness* in November 1913, where Mok wrote of a convention in August 1912 and ongoing conversions, baptisms and Spirit baptisms. There is no mention of foreign missionaries – in fact Mok makes a point of saying that all ten Sunday school teachers were 'natives'. The Mission continued its daily activities, including a Chinese Bible class five times a week for training workers (with 20 students); a Sunday school with 130 children 'mostly from heathen families' with ten Chinese teachers; an English school which Mok had resumed to support his family of eight children (two adopted) and two 'native workers' – and the newspaper, for which Mok was having difficulties raising funds.[84]

There was much activity at Mok's Pentecostal Mission in Hong Kong during the Great War reported in his paper, although the distribution of the paper, especially to overseas readers, was severely hampered. A Sunday school was held there every Sunday for two hours, followed by a three- or four-hour afternoon service and a two-hour evening service, which could be longer. A Bible class continued to be held every weekday evening and a Communion service once a month. It seems that Mok was still responsible for all these services, and the paper announced that 'all brothers and sisters, insiders and outsiders of Christianity, are all welcomed'. It appears that this congregation met most of the costs of printing and postage for *Pentecostal Truths* but donations towards these costs from readers were also encouraged. In November 1914 Mok had a family of ten, and wrote that his income did not meet his needs. He mentions other workers: Brother Leung Iu Wa and Sister Tsang Kam 'our native missionaries', and Connie Wan and Edith Ko in the mission school. In the previous four months, 21 people had been baptized at the mission of whom 11 had 'received the gift of the Holy Spirit'.[85] These figures indicate that the Mission was experiencing steady growth. In 1915 May Law was still promoting *Pentecostal Truths* as a most effective evangelistic tool, which she said 'ought to be in the hands of every Chinese boy in America'.[86] By 1917 Mok reported that he was still running a weekday school that enabled him to support his family, and two 'Pentecostal girls schools'.[87] The periodical may have stopped production soon after 1917, as no later copies are known, although at least one donation was made to Mok's mission from the USA as late as 1918.[88] By July 1921, Mok was found presenting a 'very voluminous petition' to the Secretary for Chinese Affairs on behalf of 10,468 tenants (representing a substantial part of the population) against spiralling rents levied by Chinese landlords. Now 53, Mok was still running the Pentecostal Mission and was recognized as a community leader, being referred to as 'Mr Mok Lai Chi, representing Chinese tenants of the Colony'. The tenants he represented were also petitioning for proper legal representation on the Council.[89]

This is the last we hear of Mok, but his Pentecostal Mission still exists today with two churches in Hong Kong and one in San Francisco. According to its present leader, the Mission has relied on part-time workers and leaders since its foundation, it does not take up collections, and members spend an hour praying while kneeling in services. After Mok became terminally ill in 1923, leadership of the Mission passed to his long-time co-worker Sung Teng Man, a civil servant and father of S. H. Sung, a businessman who took over as superintendent of the Mission after his father's death in 1958 and has led it ever since. The Pentecostal Mission opened two branch churches in China near Macao in 1916 and 1924, a branch in Kowloon in 1928, and one in Canton in 1934.[90]

The leader of the first Pentecostal church in China and obviously a very influential Pentecostal pioneer has been left out of the popular histories and his contribution forgotten – despite the fact that he led the first Chinese Pentecostal church, published the first Chinese Pentecostal periodical *Pentecostal Truths*, and conducted outreach and planted churches not only in Hong Kong but also in areas surrounding Canton and Macao. One published letter from a pastor in a village near Swatow in South China, Lam Ko, shows the pervasive influence of Mok and his paper in the spread of Pentecostal ideas throughout the region.

> Upon receipt of two copies of 'Pentecostal Truths' sent me by Mr. Mok Lai Chi from Hongkong, I was inspired. So commencing on the 29th of the 11th moon (21 December 1910) we began meeting every evening in the chapel. We prayed in one accord for the gift of the Holy Spirit. I conducted the meeting every evening. On Sunday I read the Word exhorting the congregation to seek earnestly. I also read to them the news contained in 'Pentecostal Truths' about the outpouring of the Holy Spirit in many lands, thus provoking to their faith. On the tenth evening, the power fell. While I was praying, confessing my sins, my whole body shook. My wife trembled more than I did, and wept, so bitterly that she could not pray aloud. My little daughter, twelve years of age, shook from head to foot, crying and confessing her sins. Elder Woo Chi Shi wept aloud too, confessing his negligence, coldness, worldliness and promised God that he would act faithfully in future as an elder. Mr. Cheung Yeung Tsing who takes care of the chapel also shed tears and confessed his sins. The rest made confessions too and prayed for salvation. This time God heard our prayer and poured out His Spirit to help us. We were very joyful. We bless God for His great grace.[91]

There were probably many other unrecorded instances of this type of response to the spreading fires held in independent Chinese Christian gatherings. Mok himself wrote that the paper had reached 'many Chinese in different parts of China' and that it 'preaches to thousands of Chinese in their own homes'.[92] There is evidence that Mok's influence extended way beyond South China into North China, and the largest indigenous Pentecostal church in China, the True Jesus Church traces its beginnings to his influence.[93]

The Pentecostal Missionary Union and West China

As there were no organized Pentecostal denominations during the first decade of Pentecostal missions, some attempts were made to co-ordinate the activities of the various missionaries. One of the more successful was the Pentecostal Missionary Union for Great Britain and Ireland (PMU), constituted by Cecil Polhill, Alexander Boddy and others in Boddy's vicarage in Sunderland in January 1909. Although this organization was relatively small and somewhat unique, it represents Pentecostalism in its formative stage and is therefore a good case study for understanding the inner dynamics of Pentecostal missions. Polhill was the driving force behind the PMU both ideologically, administratively and financially. He attempted to create a 'Pentecostal' mission society exactly after the model of the society he belonged to, the China Inland Mission (CIM), and to some extent he was a benevolent despot. The PMU was followed by a short-lived organization of the same name in the USA under Levi Lupton, formed at a camp meeting in Alliance, Ohio in June 1909 at Boddy's urging and folding after revelations of Lupton's marital infidelity the following year. A London solicitor, T. H. Mundell became 'Honorary Secretary' of the British PMU and handled the administration and correspondence with missionaries in the field.

Polhill, wealthy owner of Howbury Hall in Rennold, Bedfordshire, had been one of the 'Cambridge Seven' group of young men who had gone to China as evangelical missionaries in the 1880s. Straight after his marriage in 1888 he went with his wife to work with the CIM in Sining in Gansu, 30 miles from the northern Tibetan border. Nearly 20 years later he returned to England after his father's death to manage his estate and look after his own wife who had become an invalid – soon after their return she died. On a visit to the USA in 1907 Polhill received Spirit baptism in the Upper Room in Los Angeles and became Pentecostal, meeting up with Boddy on his return to England.[94] A considerable amount of Polhill's personal finances went into supporting the Missionary Training Schools that were established and the PMU missionaries sent out from February 1909 – most of whom went to western China. The early PMU co-operated with the CIM, followed CIM policies and used Polhill's CIM contacts in China whenever possible. It has been estimated that a total of almost £11,000 (a considerable sum in those days) was donated by Polhill to the PMU.

Thirty-six of the sixty PMU missionaries went to China, twelve to India, nine to Africa, and three to South America. Thirty-six of the missionaries were women and twenty-four men.[95] Most came from various scattered churches in Britain associated with the emerging Pentecostal movement, but some were from Anglican and other churches, some from Ireland and from Gerrit Polman's Pentecostal church in Amsterdam. The latter continued to send in financial contributions for the PMU missionaries, as did other Pentecostal assemblies in Britain and Ireland, and (until the war) a church in Breslau, Germany.[96] The PMU Council, and especially Polhill and Mundell, were rather austere and authoritarian by today's standards, keeping tight but mostly benevolent control of the organization, its missionaries and its candidates.

The first meeting of the PMU Council published the resolution that its English candidates would go to a house purchased by Polhill in London for a 'Bible School' for a 'course of some months study' and that another school would be set up in Scotland. No salaries were guaranteed and candidates were either to support themselves or get the help of their local 'Pentecostal Centre'. Polhill would lead the first 'contingent of Pentecostal Missionaries' to western China and Tibet in September 1910 and settle them with a superintendent (yet to be identified), after which he would return to England. The Council decided that all PMU missionaries would at first work in the same district 'within reach of one another'.[97] By July 1909 the PMU Training Home in London was in full swing with A. M. Niblock as principal. By November eleven men were attending classes – the propriety of the day did not allow women and men to train together – but the intention was to open a similar training centre for women, which was realized in January 1910.[98] Seven left the PMU Training Homes for China in September 1910, including John Beruldsen, his two sisters Christina and Thyra from Edinburgh, and four young men: Percy Bristow, Frank Trevitt, Amos Williams and John McGillivray. The party travelled with the Sri Lankan Pentecostal leader Charles Hettiarachy from Genoa to Colombo, where they spent a day at his home. They arrived in Hong Kong that October and travelled on the next day to Shanghai. In Hong Kong the four men visited the Pentecostal Mission, where they described a meeting of about thirty Chinese and eight American missionaries (J. H. King's party) on their knees in prayer led by Mok Lai Chi. In Shanghai they were met by CIM workers, but they also visited a Pentecostal mission in Haining Street where they said they found four Canadians and about a hundred Chinese. This was probably George and Sophia Hansen's mission – the Hansens were in Shanghai at least until 1921. From Shanghai the Beruldsens went to the Scandinavian Alliance mission of Mr and Mrs Söderbom in Suan-hwa-fu, Hebei, in the north (the same mission with which the Berntsens were working), while the four men went to the independent mission of Mr and Mrs Stanley Smith (another of the 'Cambridge Seven') in Shanxi for language learning. In a short time the Smiths had received Spirit baptism. Eventually Trevitt and Williams went to the Tibetan borders in the west, Bristow married Thyra Beruldsen and worked in North China at least until 1920 (eventually endorsed by the American Assemblies of God), and McGillivray left the PMU and worked with Stanley Smith.[99] The Beruldsen sisters began a girls' school and John Beruldsen started a new station and was to spend 35 years in North China. The mission in Suan-Hwa-fu became independent of the Scandinavian Alliance in 1913, and operated a school for children and a street chapel.[100]

These missionaries immediately immersed themselves in language learning with the assistance of other missionaries. The men travelled to a CMA mission in Gansu province on the borders of Tibet to begin learning Tibetan with the help of veteran CMA missionaries William Christie and William Simpson. During May 1912 a convention at the CMA station resulted in 20 missionaries and Chinese workers, including the Simpson family and members of the Christie family receiving Spirit baptism. Polhill travelled independently to China in 1910 and among other activities, mainly in CIM circles, he spent some time with his friend Stanley Smith and his wife, who were also former associates of the famed Pastor Hsi. He stayed with the Smiths at their station and reported a 'ready response' to the Pentecostal message.[101] The Smiths remained friends of the PMU until ten years later they were promoting an unacceptable doctrine (to Pentecostals) of 'ultimate reconciliation', affecting John McGillivray.[102] Polhill made another visit to PMU missionaries in India and China in 1914, holding a convention in Kunming in co-operation with the CIM.[103]

The four new missionaries soon upset the PMU Council with an announcement of their prior engagements to four Scottish young ladies (before they had left England), without seeking the required permission. The Council took swift disciplinary action and forbade them to marry 'within at least 4 years from the 1st January 1911'. The reasons given for this decision were that the PMU was 'in its infancy' and that other 'Missionary bodies' adopted this four-year

restriction.[104] One of the most interesting of these young headstrong missionaries was Frank Trevitt, a mechanic from Birmingham. He had received Spirit
baptism and healing from tuberculosis (the disease from which he was to die
seven years later) at Emmanuel Hall in Bournemouth.[105] He and his Welsh
companion Amos Williams protested vigorously at the decision of the
Council, writing to Mundell that they wondered 'if there hasn't been a mistake
made as to the 4 years of waiting' and that 'here a man has very little influence
over the natives if un-married', backed by pleas to Scriptures, circumstances
and culture.[106] Their desperate petitions fell on deaf ears although their
fiancées, Maggie and Lizzie Millie from Stirling entered the Women's Training
Home in London. Trevitt seemed to have been a flamboyant but difficult
character, not easy to get along with and frequently involved in controversy.
He earned the ire of his organization not only on the issue of his intended
marriage, but also in his relationships with other missionaries, clashing at
different times with his companion Williams, CMA missionary Christie, CIM
missionary Smith and senior Dutch PMU missionary Kok. The latter wrote a
letter to the Council in 1913 pleading that they should not send Trevitt, who
had been 'causing trouble in different circles', to work with them at Lijiang –
although Williams would be welcome. Kok wrote that it was 'impossible for
me to agree with him, or to work with him in a district as this, where mutual
trust and harmony is essential for God's blessing and the people's confidence'.
As a result of Trevitt's obstinate behaviour the Council resolved to further
delay the sending out of the Millie sisters.[107] They were eventually sent in
April 1914 and told to wait 12 months before marrying. Trevitt and Williams
itinerated around China against the wishes of the PMU Council, who on at
least one occasion ordered them to return to their station. The Trevitt and
Williams couples were married in Hong Kong in 1915 and tragically, within
months of this long-awaited event both husbands died – Williams suddenly of
smallpox and Trevitt of tuberculosis after a year of intense suffering. Their
widows Maggie Trevitt and Lizzie Williams continued to serve in south-west
China for another ten years.[108] The PMU (probably Polhill himself) gave their
sometimes wayward son a moving tribute, summing up what Trevitt and
many like him were all about:

> Certainly, if to no one else, the Baptism into the Holy Ghost, with signs
> following, made all the difference in the world to Frank Trevitt. Seven years
> were added to the life of the worn, emaciated consumptive given less than
> six months to live; glorious, strenuous years; tested, difficult times, includ-
> ing the ups and downs of life on the Chinese border, with two languages to
> cope with for the young mechanic, and with the strain of revolution and the
> white wolf perils. Well done, Frank Trevitt – we believe he has earned the
> Master's 'Well done'. You did bravely, Friend. Enthusiastic to a point, some-
> times beyond discretion, it is an undoubted fact that the Lord signally used
> this dear Brother, both in the Homeland, and during his stay in China. There
> was a fire, a life, an enthusiasm, a faith about him that carried things
> through, and secured victory. Many owe healings to him under God, many
> baptisms in the Holy Ghost. He was faithful, too; no looking back, thank
> God; even to the last, with him, it was 'Tibetward'.[109]

The diminutive Arie Kok was among the most prolific writers in the PMU and one of their most organized missionaries. He was among the first Pentecostals in Amsterdam and first editor of the Dutch periodical *Spade Regen*. He left with his wife Elsje for China in March 1910 after a few months in the PMU Training Home and began language learning first with the McLeans in Shandong and then in 1912 moved to Yunnan-fu (Kunming).[110] This was the headquarters for the PMU work in West China, the capital city of Yunnan province and a missionary centre. By 1914 there were five different societies there with 21 missionaries, ten of whom were Pentecostals from seven different western countries.[111] Activities at the PMU work at Kunming were buzzing by 1912. Kok wrote that over 200 Miaos (a large ethnic minority) had been baptized and that their nightly meetings in the YMCA hall were crowded with people seeking conversion and healing. 'Without any doubt' he went on, 'now is the day for China's salvation. O, how one feels sad for the millions that can not be touched! The hundreds of unopened cities!' The 'unreached cities' and the Tibetan and mountain peoples were Kok's passion. He went on to describe the co-operation between the various missionaries of ten different nationalities in the city and the openness of these missionaries to the Pentecostal message. After two years in Kunming, in 1913 the Koks relocated to Lijiang, some three weeks' journey further north-west into the mountains and one of the last cities with Chinese merchants on the route to Tibet. In the surrounding villages there were various tribal peoples and Tibetans and Kok declared that 'the whole district is practically untouched'. The city of Lijiang was 'much laid upon our hearts', and he requested they be sent there together with another Dutch worker, Elize Scharten and an English worker, Elizabeth Biggs.[112]

After four years, the PMU had established two churches with five trained evangelists, and a 'half Tibetan evangelist speaking Chinese, Tibetan and Nashi [sic], is baptized in the Spirit' and was supported by 'a hard-working servant girl in England'.[113] Another Dutch missionary, Pieter Klaver joined the mission in 1914, a former Salvation Army officer in Amsterdam like his leaders the Polmans (and the Polmans' mentors the Booth-Clibborns). The PMU Council, quintessentially English, decided that having only Dutch missionaries at one station was threatening their identity. Through their secretary Mundell they wrote to Klaver in 1916 that the Council thought it 'most desirable that there should also be an Englishman in the work at Likiang'. Because Klaver and Kok were both Dutch the Council did not want to give an impression that 'the Mission belonged to that country' (the Netherlands) and as they were 'of course . . . very international in these days it is desirable to avoid any possible question as to our work', although Mundell hastened to add that they had 'the utmost confidence and regard for you and our dear Brother Kok'.[114] Perhaps it was the possible identification of the Dutch with the Germans during these war years (even though the Netherlands remained neutral) that led to this extraordinary decision. Finding an English missionary willing to move to Lijiang was to prove difficult however, and Klaver moved there on his own in 1917 to join the Koks.[115]

Another prolific correspondent was Ethel Cook, who arrived in China with Fanny Jenner (later Mrs William Boyd) in 1914. These two women were among the best educated of the PMU missionaries, Cook the daughter of a company director and 'confidential clerk' in her father's firm and Jenner a certified teacher in London. On account of their previous education and both being over 30 when accepted (unusual for the PMU), neither spent long at the Training Home.[116] During the war years the PMU found it increasingly difficult financially to support its policy to expand into Tibetan territory, Kok writing a long letter to Polhill and the Council explaining his considerable difficulties and debts with building and travelling expenses.[117] The Koks requested furlough after nine years in the field and asked the Council to make a decision over the urgent need of education for their children. They apparently received no satisfactory answers, which led to their resignation, and thereafter Kok worked as a translator for the Dutch legation in Beijing (Peking).[118] The Klavers now led this station and Elize Scharten remained with them. Criticism of Dutch missionary methods and English ethnocentrism led the PMU to keep trying to send an English missionary there. After much reluctance and circumstantial delays, the newly married James and Jessie Andrews were sent to Lijiang to replace the Klavers in 1925 against the Klavers' wishes, leading to their resignation.[119] Although Andrews remained in China until 1945, he was not initially popular with the other PMU missionaries. Increasing tension between the English and the Dutch culminated in the withdrawal of the Dutch from co-operation with the PMU in 1925.

The PMU relied on older missionaries to direct their first missionaries. The first given this responsibility were Hector and Sigrid McLean, Canadian CIM missionaries working in China since 1901 (mainly in Yunnan) and baptized in the Spirit at Azusa Street in 1909. On their return to China in January 1910 they worked independently, first with Moomau in Shanghai, then north in Chefoo on the coast of Shandong province. There (among other things) they held 'tarrying meetings' for CIM workers to receive Spirit baptism and visited Wei-Hsien, where a new Pentecostal work had started. In 1912 they moved back to Kunming and their house became the first base for the new PMU missionaries. They arranged with Cecil Polhill (whom they knew in their mutual CIM days) that they would keep an eye on the inexperienced PMU missionaries.[120] Sigrid McLean did much itinerating in remote parts of Yunnan alone with a Chinese worker, with her husband and child remaining at Kunming. Ethel Cook, after spending a week itinerating with her had nothing but praise for her work and popularity with the Chinese. Cook's letters praised the effectiveness of Sigrid McLean's ministry and described her travelling many miles to visit outstations of the mission, often walking over mountainous terrain.[121] The McLeans requested to be relieved of their supervisory role however, and after a furlough continued as independent missionaries in Yunnan, moving away from Kunming to a remote area where there were no missionaries. A long report given by Sigrid in 1917 told of her ministry in healing the sick and of her own personal healing. Grace Agar spent some time with the McLeans in ministry and wrote that it was 'a refreshing privilege to be in their loving home once more'.[122] Sigrid returned to visit the PMU stations again in 1920, when her ministry was 'much appreciated'. The McLeans remained in China and then were the first Pentecostal missionaries over the border in Burma. They returned to Canada in 1927, 26 years after they first came to China.[123]

The McLeans were followed by the first field superintendents, Allan and

Carrie Swift, experienced Pentecostal ministers with a CMA background who joined the PMU and went to China in 1914. They had been associated with Marie and Robert Brown's Glad Tidings Hall in New York City and Bethel Pentecostal Assembly in Newark, which they had led for the previous three years. Allan Swift, another Canadian, had received two and a half years' training in the CMA in Nyack, New York. They lost a child to smallpox in the first few months after their arrival.[124] They too resigned the position in 1920 to begin a Bible school for Chinese leaders, and they continued as 'associate members'.[125] They were succeeded by William Boyd, a PMU-trained worker from Ireland and the last of the PMU superintendents, to lead the missionaries until their merger with the British Assemblies of God in 1925 (and to remain in Yunnan until the late 1940s). By 1922, the PMU had a total of 12 stations in Yunnan with rented properties.[126]

The PMU, in common with most missionary societies, was adversely affected by the Great War, as the passage of personnel and funds was restricted. Mundell commented that many of the missionary societies were 'feeling the effects of this terrible war and especially the foreign missionaries, many of whom are finding difficulties in getting their monies forwarded to them and there is of course a great falling off in the monies contributed towards the Societies owing to the special strain upon the people in England at this time'.[127] With the withdrawal of Chinese soldiers to the war front and the general instability in the Chinese interior, brigands and robbers in the countryside increased, and missionaries found it safer to remain within walled cities. Ethel Cook wrote that 'the Province is quite overrun with robbers'.[128]

By 1916 the Men's Training Home in London was closed because there were no longer any students. The Military Service Act that year had called up all men between 18 and 41 years of age, and some of the Pentecostals, being pacifists, were sent to labour camps.[129] The increasing financial difficulties in the PMU and the seeming administrative inability to respond adequately to missionary needs were creating strains on the field: the mission in India was closed down and resignations from missionaries in China escalated, including that of the Koks, the Swifts and the Klavers. Swift's letter of resignation in 1918 was because 'Council does not satisfactorily deal with business letters'; the Koks left in 1919 because they had 'lost confidence in the management of the PMU'; and in 1924 the Klavers resigned because of disagreements over their future appointment.[130] After the War the financial situation began to improve and an immediate 50 per cent increase in missionary allowances was agreed on.[131]

From all the documents relating to the PMU, there is scant information on the 'native evangelists' and 'Bible women' always in the background, but upon whom these expatriates depended so much for support. Without them their mission was in vain, for they alone were capable of setting the Pentecostal message relevantly in the context of the local people. Sometimes the names of the Chinese (and tribal) preachers were revealed, most often just referred to as 'natives' and 'native workers' but occasionally by name. So in 1916 for example, in various PMU missionary reports from Kunming and Lijiang the names of Chu, Hsie, Ien Hsien Sen, Zan Hsien Sen, Chi-Hsin-Choh, Len-in-cho, Shi-t'in-chon, Ko-ta-ko, Tseng, Ho, Hsuan, Ch'en, Mrs Chang were mentioned – a total of 13 (there were 16 missionaries this year in Yunnan).[132] Alfred Lewer said that at Kunming there were ten Chinese evangelists, three colporteurs supported by the Bible Society and one Bible woman.[133] Mr Mingteh was a Tibetan evangelist at Lijiang, Mr Lu (Chinese), Mr Ho (Nahsi) and Mr Hsuan (Tibetan) evangelists trained for three years at Lijiang, and Mr Chang and Hong Hsien Seng were Chinese evangelists at Kunming in 1917.[134] In 1919 Allan Swift gave the names of ten Chinese workers (with some curt annotations) in a letter to the PMU Secretary: Mr Luh, Mr Pen, Mr Suen, Mr Hsu, Sr., Mr and Mrs Leng, Mr Keo ('once a coolie, but doing his best'), Mr Iao ('blind but on fire for souls'), Mr Hsu ('the only one really trained in the Word'), Mrs Chu ('a Bible woman supported by the friends in Leeds'), and Mr Hu, who 'gives nearly all his time to helping me in the business' (office).[135]

The PMU agreed and enshrined in Clause 10 of its 'Principles' that 'native helpers should on the recommendation of the missionary in charge, be recognized as missionary workers and as such be supported by the Mission Funds'.[136] Swift had pursued this, requesting that more funds be made available, because 'we cannot get along without these [Chinese] men'. The PMU had been working under a 'long outstanding deficiency', even though Polhill had given the missionaries to understand 'that Native helpers supported by the Council, would be considered Employees of the Mission, just as any missionary is now regarded'.[137] Eighteen months later Fanny Boyd reported that many of the workers had left (the reasons not given) and that Mr Luh and Mrs Chu were the only ones left – although she mentioned several voluntary workers by name, including a 79–year-old Mrs Lieu 'who went on an 8 day trip to six villages with gospels' – though the blind evangelist Mr Iao is mentioned by Cook as still working later.[138] One PMU missionary threatened to resign, complaining of 'the slackness of the people in the Homeland in supporting Native Workers for itinerating purposes'.[139]

Throughout China the strategy of Pentecostal missionaries was to spread their beliefs about Spirit baptism among as many people as possible, and apart from the Chinese themselves, the foreign missionaries of the evangelical faith missions became primary targets. As late as 1915, PMU missionaries in Yunnan were having special prayer meetings for Spirit baptism for CMA missionaries from Annam (Vietnam) who had retreated there to escape the worst of the hot season.[140] When Pentecostal phenomena broke out in a CMA convention in Taozhou, Gansu in 1912, Otilia and William W. Simpson (1869–1961), he a missionary in China from 1892 to 1949, became Pentecostal after five years of seeking. During a two-week period they passed on their Pentecostal experience to many CMA churches in south-western Gansu and their testimony was published in the CMA's *Alliance Weekly*.[141] Clearly the CMA in their Tibetan Border district was greatly affected by the Pentecostal revival and the presence of the PMU missionaries. Their annual report at the end of 1912 was very positive about all that was happening – probably because the authors were the Simpsons.

We praise the Lord that He is working with us and confirming His Word with these same mighty signs as of old. Many cases of instantaneous and remarkable healings have occurred. After prayer and the laying on of hands in the name of Jesus the scale that had grown over an eye dropped off, a man was healed of the bite of a mad dog, and a child that had been given up to die was restored fully. Cases too numerous to mention have occurred in the Girls' School. More than thirty have received the Holy Spirit accompanied by speaking in tongues and prophesying.[142]

Soon after his own Spirit baptism, Simpson prayed for the same experience for Chinese workers and wrote that there was as a result 'such an increase of earnestness, faith and power that it is bound to favourably affect the spiritual life of the churches'. He went on, 'The pastors, teachers and evangelists are much more enthusiastic and fervent in their labours, and conversions are more frequent and thorough than formerly. The hopes of all are fixed on the coming of the Lord Jesus.'[143] Simpson's relations within the CMA soured and he applied to join the PMU. The PMU Council expressed support for his 'faithfulness' to the Pentecostal position and asked that they may be 'led aright when dealing with this matter'.[144] Simpson's letter to them described the support he was getting from CMA Chinese churches. His mission committee had 'just plainly ordered us off the Field, but the Churches have petitioned the Board to retain us'. He wrote that the Board had been 'compelled to take a stand either for or against the Pentecostal teaching'. He continued:

If they uphold me they will have to remove the opposers from the field and permit the work to be entirely Pentecostal, and if they go against me the great body of the Churches, all the really spiritual ones, will join me in an independent Pentecostal work. Also Mr Kaufman and Mrs D. V. Ekvall stand with me in this matter.[145]

He was forced to resign from the CMA in 1914 'because they required us to subscribe to unscriptural teaching about the Baptism in Holy Spirit', he wrote.[146]

Simpson was controversial in his dealings with his former mission and the CIM. He travelled about their stations praying for missionaries and Chinese pastors to be baptized with the Spirit, later claiming to have visited all the mission stations of the CMA and that 'nearly all' the Chinese leaders had received Spirit baptism 'according to Acts 2'. 'Pentecost' had come 'in every station', he declared.[147] In Shanghai, Simpson visited the Door of Hope rescue mission for prostitutes where Pentecostal pioneer Nettie Moomau had had meetings. Some of the leaders there said they would resign if their workers became Pentecostal – although most of the leaders and workers had had the Pentecostal experience since Moomau's time. Simpson wrote that several Chinese workers in Gansu (including three pastors) would leave the CMA and he asked Polhill if the PMU could take on the entire work.[148] The PMU realized the sensitivity of this and did not do so, and by 1915 Simpson was courting the new American AG.

In a printed circular distributed to various missionaries, Simpson wrote that he hoped 'to carry the Pentecostal Baptism and the faith once for all delivered to the saints all over Northern and Central China, to every part of Mandarin speaking China where Pentecost has not fallen before I get there'. He said this 'stupendous task' would 'arouse all the pent up wrath of the Laodicians' – meaning evangelical 'lukewarm' missionaries. This circular predictably stirred up a hornet's nest and in January 1915 CIM director D. E. Hoste wrote to Polhill to complain about Simpson's 'propaganda'. Simpson had named prominent Pentecostals Polhill, Trevitt, Boddy and Berntsen as character references, among others. Hoste asked Polhill to consider 'in some public way disavowing Mr. Simpson's mention of you as his referee', warning that he would 'unavoidably be regarded as his sponsor' if he did not do so.[149] Polhill had a serious dilemma, as he was a member of the CIM Board. Several other missionaries in China had already left the CIM and the CMA to become Pentecostals. Polhill did not exactly do as Hoste had requested and he defended Simpson rather than rebuff him. He published a formal statement in July 1915 'to let his position be known, especially in view of difficulties that have arisen on the Field'. He said he would have 'no sympathy with any propaganda' if Pentecostal missionaries entered smaller towns (not capital cities) in China occupied by the CIM, unless invited by CIM missionaries. He believed that PMU missionaries and particularly Simpson had followed this policy 'in each case'. Polhill would take no responsibility for non-PMU missionaries other than Simpson, 'so long as our dear brother carries out these conditions', and would deplore any Pentecostal missionary who did not. Polhill also needed to distance himself from the recent anti-Pentecostal stance of the CIM, saying that he 'was not a party to and has not any sympathy with his colleagues in the CIM in the Minutes recently passed . . . forbidding waiting meetings in any CIM station and declaring that the CIM now looks upon the whole "Pentecostal" or "Tongues" movement with disfavour'.[150] Polhill was referring to a CIM statement that had accused Pentecostals of doctrinal error, of holding meetings 'characterized by disorder', and of manifestations that in some cases 'had led to mental derangement and maniacal ravings'.[151]

The opposition by established missions was now firmly in place. Simpson returned to the USA in 1915 and for two years led the newly established Bethel Bible School in Newark, New Jersey. He returned to China in 1918 after the death of his wife and made his base in Minzhou, Gansu province in north-west China. He travelled throughout China and was one of the best-known Pentecostal missionaries. His letters brimmed with confidence in the progress of his work. One example of this is from 1919, when he wrote of two Chinese preachers in charge of the main Pentecostal congregation in Minzhou and 'the great explosion of the work in the country places'. They needed to employ three more evangelists from those he had been training in the 'Bible school' to care for the 'hundreds of believers' in the villages outside Minzhou.[152] By January 1920 he reported that there were ten 'Assemblies' with about 300 'Spirit-baptized saints spread over three counties', and there were 24 students in his Bible school. Two Chinese preachers, Wei Chen-mo and Feng Tsi-hsin had started a new congregation to the south of Minzhou.[153] Other early full-time preachers in Simpson's mission were Chow Feng Ling, pastor of a congregation in Taozhou (Simpson's former CMA mission base), Meng Mingshi at Minzhou, and Mei Paochen at a congregation in Titao. These preachers came from other churches, because Simpson stated that they had been Christians for between 12 and 16 years. Wei and Meng had received Spirit baptism the same year as Simpson and were probably from the CMA. Later in 1920 Simpson reported 400 baptized in the Spirit and a total of 1,000 people connected with the AG in the province of Gansu. He was committed to raising up and encouraging Spirit-filled Chinese leaders, which became his life's work. He married Martha (another missionary) in 1925 and remained working in China until the Communist takeover in 1949, when he returned to the USA at the age of 80. Much of his itinerant preaching and teaching all over China was done on foot, and he assisted in the training of Chinese ministers, especially at the Truth Bible Institute in Beijing.[154]

Pentecostals in North and East China

Scandinavian Alliance missionaries in Shandong since 1904, Norwegians Bernt and Magna Berntsen received Spirit baptism at Azusa Street in 1907. In early 1908 they returned with a team of 13 missionaries and their ten children (mostly from a Norwegian Pentecostal church in Los Angeles) to spread Pentecostalism in Cheng Ting Fu (now Zhengding), some 200 miles southwest of Beijing in Hebei province. They held regular meetings and cared for the poor and orphans, feeding 50 to 100 'beggars' every day for seven months. They lived in community in one house, learned Chinese and made evangelistic forays to surrounding villages, distributing Christian tracts. The Hansen and Roy Hess families later moved from this mission to Shanghai to work there, the latter eventually joining the CMA mission in Wuzhou. Canadian nationals George and Sophia Hansen had seven children, of which three died in China. The Berntsens and their team had co-operation and encouragement in the work from neighbouring CIM, American Board, and Presbyterian missions. Four of the missionary children died in the first year, two from the Berntsen family. The mission expanded with some missionaries leaving and others coming to fill their places from Norway and Canada, and by 1909 a second mission station had been opened further north in Baoding. In 1910 Berntsen went on a tour of Norway and the USA (leaving his family in China), and wrote that he had recruited 12 Norwegian missionaries to accompany him back to China. He reported a new awakening in his orphanage in 1912, when confessions of sins, prolonged prayer meetings, and young people receiving Spirit baptism and having revelatory visions were reported. There were three outstations and six Chinese evangelists associated with this mission in 1914.[155] The Berntsens had 33 orphan children to care for by 1910 and they founded a Chinese periodical called *Popular Gospel Truth* in 1914, remaining in Zhengding at least until 1916. Berntsen stated his intention 'to stay in China until Jesus comes'. This periodical called the church under which it operated the Faith Union, an important influence in the founding of the True Jesus Church, one of the largest independent Pentecostal churches in China.[156] A missionary working in this area, Horace Houlding, wrote about a 'pastor Chang' working with him in Tai Ming-Fu, 'a man filled with faith and the Holy Ghost'. Chang is mentioned several times as a leader in this mission over a period of at least three years, but we have no knowledge of his life or ministry.[157]

Thomas and Helen Junk, he an early German convert at Azusa Street, had joined Florence Crawford's team in Oakland, California, and were later holding meetings in Seattle, then in Honolulu en route to Caoxian, Shandong province, in July 1908. There they discovered poverty of such dimensions that they were determined to do something tangible. Junk wrote of 'self-righteous' missionaries who lived 'in fine houses with every comfort, but allow no Chinese around them but their servants'.[158] After he had discovered that he could not speak Chinese 'by the Spirit' he began to learn the language, estimating that this would take him two years. After less than six months, Helen Junk died and Thomas continued alone. An elderly Chinese preacher, Lee Wang, worked with Junk at his mission and appears to have done most of the preaching to increasingly large crowds. They operated a home where children were rescued from starvation and by October 1910 it had 55 residents of which 25 were children. Junk took personal care of them himself and taught them skills like carpentry, tailoring, weaving, milling, cooking and housekeeping. The number of children rose in the next year to 43, and Junk held services three times a day.[159] Fascinating and sometimes heart-rending letters from Junk demonstrate his unusual ability to identify with and love the people, to 'be a Chinaman', as he put it, and not conform to common 'missionary' behaviour. His letters sometimes contain searing criticisms, writing of the disadvantages of several missionaries 'flocking' together (in mission homes), 'having what they call a good time together, but caring very little for the Chinese'.[160] He also reported remarkable healings and casting out demons, including the raising of a Mennonite missionary from his deathbed.

Junk began ministry in prisons three times a week, where he described the most awful and dehumanizing, life-threatening conditions meted out to men whose crimes were sometimes very petty. In one of his reports in 1910 he wrote that he had visited 52 different towns and villages preaching, and all but seven of these places had never heard the Christian message. By this time he was regularly spending two to five days a week in village itinerating. He received a visit from Berntsen that greatly encouraged him in his work. Most of the funds he received from abroad he used to help other children and a number of destitute adults, taking them into his home, and employing three teachers for them. He bought a donkey and a millstone in order to grind flour for increasing numbers of people needing food in the home. He told of his despair over two baby girls who had been left out in the cold to die, brought to him because he loved children, but too late to save. He wrote of why he was loved by the people so much, because 'I look upon them as my brothers and sisters, and those of my household share everything with me. Love begets love.'[161] Junk wrote of extreme difficulties caused by famine, cholera epidemic and floods in 1910–11 and a letter written in March 1911 finds him taking in a blind baby boy into his home to sleep in the only space he had in his own bedroom. He wrote of the severe cholera plague and that his mission had no sanitary conditions, but characteristically added 'but the Lord is with us' and his faith in the power of God to heal two who had caught the disease. By this time he had 43 children in his home and reported that the three services a day were overcrowded.[162] By 1912 his name had disappeared from the lists of missionaries, there were no further letters from him and we do not know what ultimately happened – but he probably died in China.

Antoinette (Nettie) Moomau (1872–1937), a Presbyterian missionary in Shanghai since 1899, was trained in Moody Bible Institute in Chicago. Originally from Iowa, she went to Azusa Street during furlough in 1906 and spent several weeks 'tarrying' there until she received Spirit baptism. She returned to Shanghai as an Apostolic Faith missionary in 1908 and soon reported several influential Chinese Christians becoming Pentecostals. Beginning five weeks of meetings in the Door of Hope rescue mission for prostitutes, she and her assistant Leola Phillips were later given a six-roomed house furnished by Chinese Christians from which to work – her letter also hinting at how little they had in possessions or support, but that what provision they had they received from the Chinese. A photograph taken in about 1910 shows the Apostolic Faith Mission in Shanghai led by Moomau with about 30 adults, and another taken in 1928 with over 100. Moomau wrote of miraculous healings and miracles among Chinese believers. Phillips died of smallpox in 1910 but Moomau was joined by other missionaries. Among the early converts was Mrs Soong, who was said to be mother-in-law of the first president of China, Sun Yat-Sen. Another Mrs Soong, a wealthy woman in whose home Moomau stayed, is described in 1913 as the wife of one of Sun Yat-Sen's old friends and fellow revolutionary. The first Chinese Pentecostals in Shanghai were Brother and Sister Chang, he a well-paid bookkeeper who gave up his job to go into full-time ministry at Suzhou, 50 miles from Shanghai. Moomau stayed with them in 1913. Another 'Apostolic Faith' mission was opened in Ningpo in 1913 by the Nichols and Hofer families and began with an orphanage. Another Pentecostal mission was started in Nanjing by the Chinese preacher Joshua Yang from Shanghai, which by 1916 had over 200 people attending. Nettie Moomau almost disappears from the pages of Pentecostal periodicals after 1914, but in 1917 one report from an AG Shanghai missionary said that her two missions in Shanghai and Suzhou were 'blessed' and that she travelled with 'native workers' to different parts of China. In all, she would spend 38 years in the Shanghai district until her death in 1937.[163]

The Door of Hope mission in Shanghai continued to be a Pentecostal centre, one missionary writing in 1912 that five out of nine 'native helpers' had received the 'Latter Rain Baptism'. This mission had been founded in 1901 as an independent faith mission to rescue girls from Shanghai's notorious prostitution district. The mission was led first by Cornelia Bonnell and then after her death in 1916 by Ethel Abercrombie. After the visit of Moomau in 1908, Abercrombie and many of the workers received Spirit baptism and the mission was frequently visited by Pentecostal preachers. By 1916 3,000 girls had passed through the home and the work was continuing to grow in 1920, with a budget of $2,000 being met every month (outside of government subsidy for charity work).[164] Several other Pentecostal missionaries came to work in Shanghai, including Harland and Beatrice Lawler, who arrived there in 1911 and were part of Ryan's original party to Japan and began an orphanage and two other missions. One was in Sing-Chih, 25 miles from Nanjing and under a Brother Yang. By the end of 1912 there were four Pentecostal missions in

Shanghai.[165] During 1913 the missionaries were affected by the civil war ravaging China at the time, Shanghai coming under heavy bombardment from Southern forces.[166] After his resignation from the CMA in 1914 W. W. Simpson was in Shanghai for a while and helped open a new work in Nanjing where Chinese preacher Nathan C. S. Ma and his wife were working, a year later running a girls' school. Simpson continued to visit mission stations, once reporting that six out of nine Norwegian missionaries had been Spirit baptized and another was 'seeking', so that 'the entire mission is practically Pentecostal'. One of the missionary couples Simpson recruited was Leslie and Ava Anglin, Free Baptists who in the period following their Pentecostal conversion established a community called the House of Onesiphorus, with workshops, schools and an orphanage, eventually affiliating with the AG.[167]

In 1915 Harold and Margaret Hansen and Idalia McGuire began a mission in the West City of Peking (Beijing), where they rented a large compound and carried out various activities under the AG (the Hansens were still listed there in 1939). There is evidence that an Apostolic Faith Mission was already in Beijing as early as 1910 under an Elder Peterson.[168] There were even Pentecostal missionaries working in Inner Mongolia by 1917. Thomas and Louise Hindle went there as Pentecostal missionaries from the Hebden Mission in Toronto, Canada in 1909 and were still listed as AG missionaries there in 1939.[169]

Chinese Independent Pentecostal Churches

The Chinese independent churches (particularly of a Pentecostal kind) were founded in the early twentieth century and by 1930 were a significant section of the Christian population, a phenomenon that has escaped the attention of most scholars.[170] But as in Africa, the evidence in China that Pentecostalism converged with and strongly influenced the phenomenon of independency is incontrovertible. Pentecostalism in its emphasis on the supernatural was in sync with Chinese folk religion; its offer of spiritual power to everyone regardless of status or achievements; and its deep suspicion of hierarchical and rationalistic Christianity, encouraged the development of new, anti-western independent churches. Resentment against western interference in Chinese affairs and patriotism increased during the 1920s, which was when most of these churches began. Pentecostal missionaries were unwittingly drawn into this process. Simpson was in contact with Chinese independent churches in Manchuria and made pleas for more missionaries to come to China to work with them; Pentecostal missionaries frequently interacted with Chinese independent churches in this period. Their policy of creating self-supporting Chinese churches assisted in developing independency. One missionary writing from Taiyuan in Shanxi wrote of a strong Pentecostal church he visited in Sinzhou, 50 miles north, which was started in 1914 and run completely by Chinese leaders with four full-time workers.[171] As Deng Zhaoming has pointed out, independent Chinese Pentecostalism had both foreign and domestic influences in its formation. Pentecostal missionaries from the West brought their teachings of divine healing (although not a new idea for some

Chinese Christians) and speaking in tongues. At the same time there was a strong anti-western and nationalistic feeling in China at the beginning of the twentieth century, causing many newly emerging Chinese Christian groups to distance themselves from western missionaries.[172] The two largest Chinese Pentecostal denominations to arise during this period were the True Jesus Church (TJC) and the Jesus Family, both of which came under these two influences.

Paul Wei, a former member of the LMS, founded the International Assembly of the True Jesus Church (TJC) in 1914 in Beijing, at first called the 'Restored True Jesus Church of All Nations'. He had been healed through the laying on of hands of Elder Xin Shengmin in 1912, and shortly afterwards had received the Spirit and baptized himself in a river. After Wei died in 1919, Zhang Lingsheng, a former Presbyterian deacon from Weixian, Shandong, succeeded him. Zhang had received Spirit baptism through an Apostolic Faith missionary in Shanghai in 1909 (this might have been either Moomau or the Hansens) and had been baptized by immersion by Elder Peterson of the Apostolic Faith Mission in Beijing in 1910. In 1916 Zhang had a revelation about keeping Saturday as the Sabbath which he apparently shared with Peterson, who was persuaded by him. It appears that Zhang had afterwards met other American Pentecostal missionaries who had convinced him about Oneness teaching and after his joining the TJC in 1918 the church became both Sabbatarian and Oneness, with a militant millennialist and anti-foreign orientation. Barnabas Zhang, also a Presbyterian from Weixian, was converted to Pentecostalism in 1912 through the preaching of Zhang Lingshen. He joined the TJC with Zhang Lingshen and Wei ordained him in early 1919. The TJC set up its headquarters in Nanjing in 1926 and was a radically anti-foreign independent church that owed much of its early growth to the efforts of three preachers led by Barnabas Zhang, who travelled the length and breadth of China on foot, reporting many signs and miracles, establishing churches and baptizing thousands in the name of Jesus. Barnabas Zhang was later involved in a schism and excommunicated in 1931. By 1929, the TJC was found throughout China, Taiwan, Singapore, Malaysia and Hong Kong, its main attractions being deliverance from demons and opium addiction, and the healing of the sick. By 1948 it had 700 congregations in every province in China and was one of the largest denominations in China.[173]

The second prominent, although smaller Chinese Pentecostal church is the Jesus Family, founded by Jing Dianying at Mazhuang, Shandong in 1927, a communitarian and Trinitarian Christian group forbidding private ownership. After Jing's contact with the Pentecostal (AG) community in Tai'an, Shandong under the Anglins, the Jesus Family was formed and steadily increased in numbers. Members live simply, work hard and contribute to the community after the pattern of the early Church. Jing and others established a savings society in 1921, a co-operative store attempting to meet the needs of the socially marginalized, followed by a silk-reeling co-operative by 1926. Those who joined the community had to renounce the world and their allegiance to natural families, committing themselves totally to the community. Jing sent out believers to set up other Family homes throughout China.[174]

China was the largest of the early fields for Pentecostal missions. It has been estimated that there could have been as many as 150 expatriate Pentecostal missionaries there by 1915, and the emergence of the AG in 1914 and the affiliation of the majority of these missionaries with them meant that by 1920 they were by far the largest of the Pentecostal bodies in China.[175] But even more significant was the fact that by that time there were already strong nationalist forces forming churches totally independent from western missions and developing a Pentecostal spirituality that was distinctively Chinese. These Chinese churches already formed the majority of Pentecostals by the time the expatriate missionaries were forced to leave China in 1949. Questions concerning how these churches differ from western-founded Pentecostals and the extent of conscious or unconscious adaptation to the Chinese context require much more research.

Missions in Japan, Korea and the Pacific

Pentecostals put considerable effort into the evangelization of Japan, usually with meagre results. Martin L. Ryan was another of the earliest missionaries associated with Azusa Street. He first appeared in November 1906 as a 'holiness evangelist' and editor of *Light* (soon changed to *Apostolic Light*) in Salem, Oregon who had received Spirit baptism at Azusa Street. His letters from Salem reveal a zealous worker for Pentecost, holding regular meetings in which remarkable healings were reported. By January 1907 his offices had moved to Portland, Oregon, and by March he was working in Spokane, Washington.[176] By the end of 1907, he was leading a party of 14 'Apostolic Light' missionaries (four married couples, five single women and one single man) from Spokane and Seattle to Japan and China, and his periodical was thereafter published in Japan.[177] Twelve of these missionaries went with him to Japan, and two (May Law and Rose Pittman) went directly to Hong Kong, arriving there soon after the Garrs. Ryan went to Yokohama and set up a preaching house, with schools for teaching the Bible in two places. Japanese people and missionaries were attracted to the meetings, including William and Mary Taylor, who became Pentecostals and later joined the PMU.[178] But Ryan found life as a missionary in Japan tough from the start. He wrote that the younger generation were losing faith in 'idol worship', but were also rejecting 'anything that is miraculous or supernatural'; whereas the older generation were 'seldom turned' from their beliefs. China, he thought, was 'a much better field'.[179]

Ryan corresponded regularly and excerpts from his *Apostolic Light* were reproduced. By August 1908 he reported 'several healed, but no one baptized with the Holy Ghost', and he encountered opposition from other missionaries.[180] Later he reported the first Spirit baptism, a Japanese student Mr Ito who had 'received his Pentecost' and that 'others were earnestly seeking'. Ryan even purchased a small boat for evangelistic and literature work in the bay and called it 'Pentecost'. The missionary team moved from the fishing village where they were based to Tokyo itself and worked among students of English there with a school and mission with the co-operation of the YMCA, from where they operated an office. There, several Japanese students were converted but most were 'earnestly enquiring the way of life', and Ryan reported the presence of Chinese and Korean students there. As indication of the great difficulties Ryan's team experienced, there were now only four – 'all the rest having left Japan', wrote Ryan – and Ryan had been unable to produce his *Apostolic Light* through shortage of funds.[181] Later, although Ryan's reports indicated a number of individual Japanese receiving Spirit baptism, there are revealing hints about 'the kind of Christianity that leaves its missionaries to struggle along meagrely, if not almost altogether unaided' and the 'unconcern' that would lead more Japanese to 'go down in sin and darkness forever'.[182] One of Ryan's letters to his supporters yields no hint of his increasing difficulties, but consists entirely of quotations from Pauline letters. One of his last activities in Japan was to distribute food by means of a rented police boat in Honjo during the floods of August 1910, and he wrote appealing for funds to establish a 'relief station'.[183] It seems that the funds did not arrive. Ryan's mission may have ended in failure, but perhaps his most lasting achievement was his team's influence on other Christians, especially their Japanese converts and a few foreigners who were open to their teaching. Ryan was the last of his group to leave Japan in 1910, but new Pentecostal missionaries had begun to arrive.[184] Four years later Ryan was working among Japanese in Shanghai and still publishing *Apostolic Light*. He co-operated with a Japanese church under its pastor, S. Ishakawa. He had a daily Mission School (with two students), a Mission Home in which he lived with two Japanese couples, and daily evening meetings in a Mission Hall.[185]

Robert Atchison of Bethel Gospel Mission in Osaka, a former tramp, arrived as an independent American missionary in 1904 and had regular correspondence with the Pentecostal movement from 1908. He worked separately from the Ryans and mentioned 'four resident native evangelists' working in the area with him. Atchison was another of the shoestring missionaries who had little in financial means, once writing of how he needed money for a coat and waistcoat, which was remarkably supplied by local people, and then of getting a cornet to draw the crowds and save his voice for the preaching. He worked mostly in rural villages but had a building in the city of Osaka where regular services were held.[186] By 1911 Atchison reported that 38 villages were having a weekly service in this area. He returned to the USA in 1912 and continued to write of the ongoing work in Osaka under Japanese leadership. On his return in 1914, he wrote that 150 villages in the Kawachii valley were being reached by his Japan Independent Mission in four stations. He was still there in 1917 when curiously, he writes from Kobe that six missionaries (including his wife and himself) and four foreign businessmen were seeking 'that God will meet with us and baptize every one with the Holy Ghost and fire as on the day of Pentecost'. This is probably the same meeting referred to below, facilitated by other Pentecostals working in Kobe.[187]

There were many other Pentecostal missionaries in Japan, most of whom came from the USA, including Estella Bernauer, who in the wake of M. L. Ryan's departure arrived in Tokyo in 1910 with her daughter to work with English-speaking university students and children. She wrote that 'the power of God has never really fallen in this land' and alluded to the opposition of people and missionaries, especially because of those who had come out as

Apostolic Faith missionaries but had been forced to return through financial hardships. In the same year the first Japanese convert to Pentecostalism, Yoshio Tanimoto, who Bernauer had met as a student in the USA and who had been baptized in the Spirit in Indianapolis, arrived back. By 1913 he reported 25 converts in his work in Hiroshima, which appears to have been the first Japanese-led Pentecostal mission, but we do not hear of him after this. He felt that the need of Japan was not for more foreign missionaries but for 'native workers'.[188] Another Japanese preacher mentioned in the reports was Ichitaro Takigawa, who worked with Bernauer from 1913 and was ordained into the ministry in 1915. Carl and Friderike Juergensen and their three children Marie, Agnes and John arrived in Japan in August 1913 (John came in 1919) to begin a lifetime of service there as Pentecostal missionaries, listed as AG missionaries in Tokyo in 1939. The Barney S. Moores began work in Kobe in 1914 and then moved to Yokohama, where they reported crowded gatherings in their small mission hall and evangelistic meetings in a tent. Their Japanese worker was Hidekichi Soeno.

The PMU supported Mary and William Taylor, a cousin of J. Hudson Taylor and former missionaries in the Japan Evangelistic Band. They were in Nagasaki from 1913 after their return to Japan and sent letters in 1915 reporting individual conversions. The PMU stopped its support in 1916 as no further reports were forthcoming and the Taylors had requested to work independently. They called the mission the Door of Hope Mission, and like their namesake in Shanghai, worked among prostitutes in a special hospital for sexually transmitted diseases. The wife of the naval prison governor in Kobe, Makoto Niki, worked alongside Mary Taylor as a Spirit-baptized Bible woman for several years. In 1917 Mary Taylor was responsible for bringing Leonard Coote, a British businessman in Japan, into Spirit baptism and that year the Taylors were listed as AG missionaries. Coote resigned his job and began a mission in Yokohama in 1919 that helped spearhead the first effective Pentecostal revival movement among the Japanese.[189] Bernauer wrote that this was 'the first real outpouring of the Spirit' that she had known in Japan.[190] Coote and the Grays became Oneness in 1919, which alienated them from the other missionaries, who aligned themselves with the AG. All of these missionaries worked with Japanese workers; they would not have gotten anywhere without them. We do not have the names of all of them in the news reports and letters.[191] In 1923 the Great Earthquake in Tokyo-Yokohama destroyed Pentecostal buildings and killed 100,000 people, including a Japanese Pentecostal pastor Hasegawa and his entire family. The Moores lost everything but their lives and returned penniless to the USA as refugees.

Korea was a country that excited the evangelical imagination, especially after the 'Korean Pentecost' that began in a convention in Pyongyang in 1907 (after an earlier revival in Wonsan in 1903) and continued well into the next decade. Korea had been occupied by Japan after the Russo–Japanese War (1904–5), an oppressive regime that was to last for 40 years, in which all Korean national and cultural aspirations were ruthlessly crushed. This was the context in which welcome relief in the form of Pentecostal revival came. Embracing Christianity was seen as an avenue of resistance to Japanese aggression. The Pentecostal fires ignited by this Great Revival were not mentioned much in

Pentecostal papers at the time, perhaps because this revival was occurring within the Presbyterian and Methodist churches not connected to Pentecostal networks. A brief mention of 60,000 Korean baptisms in 1910 appeared in the Pentecostal press. During the Japanese occupation the numbers of Koreans becoming Christians multiplied, one Pentecostal paper reporting in 1916 that 3,000 conversions to Christianity were taking place every week and later carrying a report on the revival by Jonathan Goforth in 1919.[192]

Although the Taylors and earlier the Turneys from Azusa Street declared their call to Korea, it is a curious fact of history that this country under Japanese occupation and regarded as a land of unprecedented opportunities for Christian mission was not visited by foreign Pentecostal missionaries until much later. It was also a mystery to people like PMU missionary W. J. Taylor in Japan, who wrote of his amazement that 'this land, upon which God laid His Holy Hands and deluged it with His Holy Spirit, adding thousands upon thousands to the Church of Christ, should be without a Pentecostal Missionary'.[193] The AG mouthpiece, *The Weekly Evangel*, reported in 1917 on the remarkable growth and mission zeal of the Korean church amid persecution and oppression, but lamented that 'not one Pentecostal missionary' had gone to this country yet. It continued:

> May the Lord stir up the hearts of His children to arise and take the glad tidings of the Latter Rain outpouring to these humble, earnest Christians in Korea, so that receiving the baptism of the Holy Ghost and fire they may be all the more red-hot with love for Christ and for the souls He died to win.[194]

But these calls went unheeded at least until 1930, when Mary Rumsey, former independent missionary in Japan and Azusa Street convert, moved to Korea. She started a Pentecostal church in Seoul in 1932 with Heong Huh, former Salvation Army worker and later (1957) first Korean superintendent of the Assemblies of God. The rest, they say, is history! The fires of the 'Korean Pentecost' were still burning in the 1920s, especially through the revivalist ministry of Ik Du Kim, whose remarkable healing meetings throughout Korea with crowds of 10,000 in attendance followed the failure of the Korean Independence Movement in 1919. Kim later became moderator of the Presbyterian Church.[195]

Pentecostalism was being planted in other, even more remote parts of the world. Hawaii was one of the first places to which Pentecostal missionaries from the USA west coast went, as it was a refilling post for steamships on the way to East Asia. Henry and Anna Turney from Azusa Street went there for a few months in 1907 to open up a Pentecostal work, and the church thrived among the Filipino and Hispanic population in particular. Juan Lugo, pioneer of Puerto Rican Pentecostalism, became Pentecostal there. Other areas opened up by Pentecostals in the 1910s included Australia and New Zealand, and Suva, Fiji, where Alma Starkenberg and Agnes Johnson went in 1911, followed by Albert and Lou Page in 1913, who worked among Indians there. Eva Caton and Sarah Dowle from Carrie Montgomery's mission joined Starkenberg in 1917, but Caton moved to Honolulu, Hawaii, in 1919 before returning to California. By 1917 Fijians were already going to other Pacific islands as missionaries, one unnamed Fijian Pentecostal having gone to the New Hebrides, and there was also a Pentecostal mission in the Solomon Islands by this time.[196] Pentecostalism only reached Indonesia in 1921, but was to expand there remarkably during the twentieth century.

There can be little doubt that China was the main focus of the earliest Pentecostal missions, perhaps the result of the popular evangelical imagination excited by the stories of the faith missions there. Comparatively little was accomplished elsewhere by Pentecostals in this region. By 1920 there were more foreign Pentecostal missionaries in China than in any other country. The work of the Garrs, the Simpsons, Berntsen, Junk and Moomau was augmented and taken far beyond their sphere of influence by Chinese leaders Mok, Lai, Zhang and ultimately a host of others, who were to make this one of the most thriving Pentecostal missions anywhere.

Notes

1 *LRE* 2:6 (Mar 1910), p.12.

2 *THW*, pp.260–1.

3 *WW* 32: (Jan 1910), p.30.

4 Isaiah 49.12 (AV), translated 'Aswan' in the NIV; Boyd, *Chinese Rainbow*, p.1; *FF* 9 (Jan 1913), p.2.

5 Bays, 'Indigenous Protestant Churches', pp.124–7.

6 Bays, 'Protestant Missionary Establishment', pp.50–1.

7 Chinese people and place names are given in the earlier Wade-Giles transliteration used by the missionaries, except in the case of provinces and well-known cities, where the modern pinyin form is given. Sometimes Wade-Giles and pinyin appear at the same time, for which I apologize, but this is how they appeared in the sources. Law, *Pentecostal Mission Work*, p.2; *Conf* 5:5 (May 1912), p.113; *BM* 129 (15 Mar 1913), p.3; *LRE* 11:8 (May 1919), p.11; 12:12 (Sept 1920), p.20.

8 *AF* 11 (Jan 1908), p.1.

9 *AF* 13 (May 1908), p.3.

10 *BM* 9 (1 Mar 1908), p.4; Sung, 'History of Pentecostal Mission', p. 8.

11 Quoted in Robeck, *Azusa Street*, p.246; Thompson and Gordon, *Alfred Garr*, pp.70, 90–5.

12 Quoted in Bays, 'Protestant Missionary Establishment', p.54.

13 Thompson and Gordon, *Alfred Garr*, p.90; *BM* 12 (15 Apr 1908), p.2; *AF* 13 (May 1908), p.1; *LRE* 6:10 (July 1914), p.19; Sung, 'History of Pentecostal Mission', p.8.

14 *BM* 7 (1 Feb 1908), p.1.

15 McPherson, *This is That*, pp.63–8; *Conf* 2:7 (July 1909), p.147; *BM* 129 (15 Mar 1913), p.3; Thompson and Gordon, *Alfred Garr*, p.106.

16 *UR* 1:7 (Feb 1910), p.54.

17 *WE* 122 (8 Jan 1916), p.12; Thompson and Gordon, *Alfred Garr*, pp.113–72.

18 *BM* 1 (1 Oct 1907), pp.2, 4.

19 *AF* 10 (Sept 1907), p.2.

20 *AF* 12 (Jan 1908), p.1.

21 *AF* 13 (May 1908), p.4; *BM* 9 (1 Mar 1908), p.2; *Conf* 1:5 (Aug 1908), pp.22–3.

22 *TF* 29:1 (Jan 1909), pp.9–10.

23 Quoted in Robeck, *Azusa Street*, p.246; and Thompson and Gordon, *Alfred Garr*, p.97.

24 *BM* 11 (1 Apr 1908), pp.1, 2.

25 *AF* 13 (May 1908), p.3.

26 *BM* 7 (1 Feb 1908), p.4.

27 *Conf* 1:2 (May 1908) Supplement, p.1; *BM* 17 (1 July 1908), p.1.

28 *BM* 38 (15 May 1909), p.2; 50 (15 November 1909), p.3; 54 (15 Jan 1910), p.2.

29 *BM* 78 (15 Jan 1911), p.2; King, *Yet Speaketh*, p.163.

30 *UR* 2:3 (Nov. 1910), p.8; *Conf* 5:6 (June 1912), p.143.

31 *BM* 92 (15 Aug 1911), p.2; *LRE* 4:5 (Feb 1912), p. 15; Law, *Pentecostal Mission Work*, pp.1–2; Woods, 'Failure and Success'.

32 *BM* 4 (15 Dec 1907), p.1; 9 (1 Mar 1908), p.4; 14 (15 May 1908), p.1; 16 (15 June 1908), p.2.

33 *BM* 18 (15 July 1908), p.1; 41 (1 July 1909), p.2.

34 *TF* 29:7 (July 1909), p.158.

35 *TF* 29:5 (May 1909), pp.100–1.

36 *TF* 29:5 (May 1909), p.115.

37 *Trust* 9:3 (May 1910), p.17; Woods, 'Failure and Success'; King, *Yet Speaketh*, pp.167–9; *UR* 2:4 (Jan. 1911), p.7; *BM* 82 (15 Mar 1911), p.1; 104 (15 Feb 1912), p.4; 107 (1 Apr 1912), p.4.

38 *BM* 108 (15 Apr 1912), p.4; 111 (1 June 1912), p.4; *WWit* 9:2 (Feb 1913), p.2; *LRE* 6:1 (Oct 1913), p.15; 7:12 (Sept 1915), p.14; *WE* 117 (27 Nov 1915), p.4; 124 (22 Jan 1916), p.12; 174 (27 Jan 1917), p.12.

39 *BM* 133 (15 May 1913), p.3; *Conf* 7:7 (July 1914), p.137; *CE* 58 (12 Sept 1914), p.4; *TF* 35:4 (Apr 1915), p.88; 37:7 (July 1917), p.161; *WE* 135 (15 Apr 1916), p.12; 146 (1 July 1916), p.12.

40 *LRE* 13:3 (Dec 1920), pp.14–15.

41 *BM* 55 (1 Feb 1910), p.4.

42 *UR* 1:10 (May 1910), p.5; 2:1 (Aug. 1910), p.5; *BM* 84 (15 Apr 1911), p.2; 85 (1 May 1911), p.4; 97 (1 Nov 1911), p.4; *Conf* 5:3 (Mar 1912), p.69; 5:5 (May 1912), p.113.

43 *BM* 97 (1 Nov 1911), p.4; 112 (15 June 1912), p.4; 115 (1 Aug 1912), p.2; 121 (15 Nov 1912), p.4; 123 (15 Dec 1912), p.1; 128 (1 Mar 1913), p.2; 133 (15 May 1913), p.1; *Conf* 5:11 (Nov 1912), p.261; *LRE* 5:3 (Dec 1912), p.12; 5:7 (Apr 1913), p.11; 'Constitution and By-Laws', 1939, p.179; Robeck, *Azusa Street*, p.243.

44 *Trust* 19:3 (May 1920), p.12.

45 *Hongkong Government Gazette*, 22 May 1886, p.449.

46 'Registrar General's Report for the Year 1892', Hong Kong, 1 June 1893, p.257.

47 Letter, S. H. Sung, Superintendent of the Pentecostal Mission, to author, 22 July 2005.

48 *BM* 39 (1 June 1909), p.3; 52 (15 Dec 1909), p.4; *Conf* 2:12 (Dec 1909), pp.282–3; *LRE* 2:3 (Dec 1909), pp.22–3; Law, *Pentecostal Mission Work*, p.2; Bays, 'Protestant Missionary Establishment', p.54.

49 Ho Yan (Connie) Au, PhD candidate, University of Birmingham, 2006, translated Chinese articles in *Pentecostal Truths*.

50 *Pentecostal Truths* 37 (Nov 1914), p.4.

51 *AF* 13 (May 1908), p.1; Woods, 'Failure and Success'.

52 *AF* 13 (May 1908), p.2.

53 *Conf* 2:12 (Dec 1909), p.283.

54 *UR* 1:4 (Sept 1909), p.30.

55 *Pentecostal Truths* 2:4 (Apr 1909), p.1.

56 *Pentecostal Truths* 37 (Nov 1914), p.1.

57 Woods, 'Failure and Success'.

58 *DPCM*, pp.660–1.

59 *Conf* 2:7 (July 1909), p.147; 2:11 (Nov 1909), p.259.

60 Letter of Cora Fritsch to her parents, 23 Jan 1909.

61 Letters of Cora Fritsch to her family, 27 Jan 1909, 5 Feb 1909.

62 *BM* 59 (1 Apr 1910), p.4.

63 *Conf* 2:5 (May 1909), p.115.

64 *Pent* 2:4 (Mar 1910), p.3; *UR* 1:8 (Mar 1910), p.5; 1:10 (May 1910), p.5; *Conf* 3:11 (Nov 1910), p. 251; *WW* 32:12 (Dec 1910), p.379.

65 *BM* 52 (15 Dec 1909), p.2.

66 *BM* 38 (15 May 1909), p.2; *UR* 1:4 (Sept 1909), p.30; *Conf* 2:12 (Dec 1909), pp.283–4; *LRE* 2:3 (Dec 1909), pp.22–3.

67 Letter of Cora Fritsch to her family, 31 Mar 1909.

68 *Pentecostal Truths* 2:4 (Apr 1909), p.4.

69 *BM* 53 (1 Jan 1910), p.2.

70 *UR* 1:7 (Feb 1910), p.54.

71 *UR* 1:8 (Mar 1910), p.5.

72 *UR* 1:9 (Apr. 1910), p.5; 1:11 (June 1910), p.5; *BM* 63 (June 1, 1910), p.1.

73 *UR* 1:12 (July 1910), p.5; *BM* 64 (June 15, 1910), p.1.

74 *BM* 59 (Apr. 1, 1910), p.4.

75 *UR* 1:9 (Apr. 1910), p.5.

76 *Conf* 3:4 (Apr. 1910), p.91.

77 *BM* 69 (Sept. 1, 1910), p.4.

78 *BM* 73 (Nov. 1, 1910), p.4.

79 King, *Yet Speaketh*, p.164.

80 King, *Yet Speaketh*, p.165.

81 *UR* 2:5 (May 1911), p.5.

82 *WW* 33:2 (Feb 1911), p.56; *BM* 79 (1 Feb 1911), p.2.

83 *BM* 124 (1 Jan 1913), p.1; 136 (1 July 1913), p.3; *Advocate* 1:17 (23 Aug 1917), p.7; 4:49 (7 Apr 1921), p.9.

84 *WWit* 9:10 (Oct 1913), p.2; 9:11 (Nov 1913), p.4.

85 *Pentecostal Truths* 37 (Nov 1914), p.1; 38 (Mar 1915), p.1; 39 (Apr 1917), p.1.

86 Law, *Pentecostal Mission Work*, pp.3, 38.

87 *Pentecostal Truths* 39 (Apr 1917), p.4.

88 *Trust* 17:4–5 (June–July 1918), p.12; 17:9 (Nov 1918), p.9.

89 Hongkong Legislative Council report, 18 July 1921, pp.84–5.

90 Letter, S. H. Sung to author, 22 July 2005; Sung, 'History of Pentecostal Mission', pp.8–9.

91 *Trust* 10:4–5 (June and July 1911), p.27.

92 *WWit* 9:11 (Nov 1913), p.4.

93 Bays, 'Indigenous Protestant Churches', p.129.

94 *Conf* 1:7 (Oct 1908), pp.7–8; 2:8 (Aug 1909), pp.174–5; 5:5 (May 1912), p.111.

95 Kay, 'Four-Fold Gospel', pp.64, 66.

96 Letter, T. H. Mundell to A. Kok, 19 June 1914.

97 *Conf* 2:1 (Jan 1909), pp.13–15.

98 *Conf* 2:8 (Aug 1909), p.183; 2:11 (Nov 1909), p.253; 4:3 (Mar 1911), p.67.

99 *Conf* 3:11 (Nov 1910), p.272; 3:12 (Dec. 1910), p.293; 4:1 (Jan 1911), p. 20; 4:3 (Mar 1911), p.69; *BM* 75 (1 Dec 1910), p.4; 108 (15 Apr 1912), p.1; 'Combined Minutes', 1920, p.66.

100 *UR* 2:1 (Aug. 1910), p.6; *Conf* 3:8 (Aug 1910), pp. 199–200; 6:4 (Apr 1913), p.83.

101 Letter, F. Trevitt (Gansu) to T. H. Mundell, 13 Mar 1913; *Conf* 3:11 (Nov 1910), p.270; 4:9 (Sept 1911), p.215; 4:10 (Oct 1911), p.239; *FF* 6 (July 1912), p.5; Taylor, *Pastor Hsi*, p.191.

102 Letter, T. H. Mundell to J. McGillivray, 7 Oct 1925.

103 *FF* 17 (May 1914), p.7.

104 PMU Minutes, 2 Dec 1910, p.88.

105 *Conf* 2:4 (Apr 1909), pp.86–7; *BM* 64 (15 June 1910), p.3; *FF* 38 (May 1916), pp.8–9.

106 Letters from A. Williams to T. H. Mundell, 13 Jan 1911, F. Trevitt to T. H. Mundell, 14 Jan 1911.

107 Letter, A. Kok to T. H. Mundell, 14 Sept 1913; Letter, F. Trevitt to T. H. Mundell, 13 Oct 1913; PMU Minutes, 4 Sept 1913.

108 Letters, H. French Ridley to C. Polhill, 22 Nov 1915; W. Glassby (Bedford) to T. H. Mundell (postcard), n.d.; T. H. Mundell to Maggie Trevitt, 16 May 1916; Maggie Trevitt, Yunnan-fu to T. H. Mundell, 13 July 1916.

109 *FF* 38 (May 1916), pp.8–9.

110 *Conf* 1:2 (May 1908), p.14; 2:4 (Apr 1909) p.91; 2:9 (Sept 1909), p.208; *FF* 5 (Apr 1912), p.4.

111 *FF* 19 (Aug 1914), p.6.

112 Letter, A. Kok to PMU Council, 9 Aug 1912; *Conf* 5:10 (Oct 1912), p.237.

113 *TF* 37:9 (Sept 1917), p.214; 'Constitution and By-Laws', 1939, p.179.

114 Letter, T. H. Mundell to P. Klaver (Yunnan-fu), 14 Nov 1916.

115 Letter, A. Swift to T. H. Mundell, 19 June 1920.

116 PMU Candidates' Schedules: Fanny Elizabeth Jenner, 2 July 1912; Ethel Mercy Cook, 8 Oct 1913.

117 Letters, C. Polhill to A. Kok, 22 Jan 1917; A. Kok to C. Polhill and PMU Council, 19 April 1918.

118 Letters, A. and E. Kok to T. H. Mundell, 17 Aug 1918; A. Kok to T. H. Mundell, 13 May 1919; T. H. Mundell to C. Polman, 11 Aug 1919.

119 Letters, J. H. Andrews to T. H. Mundell, 23 Nov 1921; W. J. Boyd to T. H. Mundell, 12 Apr 1922; P. Klaver to T. H. Mundell, 20 Aug 1923.

120 *UR* 1:8 (Mar 1910), p.5; 1:11 (June 1911), p.8; 2:1 (Aug 1911), p.5; *Conf* 5:7 (July 1912), p.166; *TF* 34:1 (Jan 1914), p.15.

121 Letters, A. Kok to C. Polhill, 13 Aug 1913; E. Cook to T. H. Mundell, 7 Dec 1914 and 6 Sept 1916.

122 *TF* 40:8 (Aug 1920), p.189.

123 Letter, W. J. Boyd to T. H. Mundell, 4 Mar 1920; *TF* 37:4 (Apr 1917), pp.79–82; *LRE* 11:5 (Feb 1919), pp.13–14; *PE* (11 Sept 1926), p.11; Robeck, *Azusa Street*, pp.264–6.

124 PMU Candidates' Schedules, A. A. Swift and C. L. Swift, 22 Dec 1913; Letter, T. H. Mundell to Miss Clack, Springfield, Illinois, 2 Oct 1914; *FF* 20 (Oct 1914), p.4.

125 Letters, A. Swift to T. H. Mundell, 8 Feb 1919; 19 Dec 1919; 20 July 1920.

126 Letters, E. Cook to T. H. Mundell, 19 May 1920; W. J. Boyd to T. H. Mundell, 12 Apr 1922; Boyd, *Chinese Rainbow*, p.iii.

127 Letter, T. H. Mundell to F. Trevitt, 26 Sept 1914.

128 Letter, E. Cook to T. H. Mundell, 6 Mar 1916.

129 Letter, T. H. Mundell to Mr Greenstreet, 26 May 1916.

130 Letters, A. Swift to C. Polhill, 26 Jan 1918; A. Kok to T. H. Mundell, 13 May 1919; P. Klaver to T. H. Mundell, 23 July 1921.

131 Letter, T. H. Mundell to A. Swift, 14 May 1919.

132 *FF* 37 (Apr 1916), p.7; 38 (May 1916), p.5; 40 (July 1916), p.9; 41 (Aug 1916), p.9; 45 (Dec 1916), p.5; *Conf* 9:8 (Aug 1916), pp.138–9.

133 *Conf* 9:10 (Oct 1916), p.171.

134 *FF* (Apr 1917), p.6; (May 1917), p.9.

135 Letter, A. Swift to T. H. Mundell, 30 Jan 1919.

136 Letter, T. H. Mundell to A. Swift, 14 May 1919.

137 Letter, A. Swift to T. H. Mundell, 10 July 1919.

138 Letters, F. Boyd to T. H. Mundell, 16 June 1920; E. Cook to T. H. Mundell, 14 Mar 1921.

139 Letter, D. Leigh to T. H. Mundell, 6 May 1921.

140 Letter, E. Cook to T. H. Mundell, 7 Aug 1915.

141 *Conf* 6:1 (Jan 1913), pp.4–5; *TF* 33:3 (Mar 1913), pp.52–6.

142 *FF* 9 (Jan 1913), p.7.

143 *Conf* 5:7 (July 1912), p.167; *CE* 53 (8 Aug 1914), p.4.

144 PMU Council Minutes, 31 Mar 1914; 3 June 1914.

145 Letter, W. W. Simpson to T. H. Mundell, 5 Feb 1914.

146 Letter, W. W. Simpson to T. H. Mundell, 18 May 1914.

147 *LRE* 8:4 (Jan 1916), p.8.

148 Letter, W. W. Simpson to C. Polhill, 12 Aug 1914.

149 Letter, D. E. Hoste to Cecil Polhill, 4 Jan 1915, enclosing copy of circular letter from Simpson; *CE* 53 (8 Aug 1914), p.4.

150 *FF* 29 (July 1915), p.9.

151 Quoted in Bays, 'Protestant Missionary Establishment', p.60.

152 *TF* 39:6 (June 1919), p.143.

153 *WW* 42:3 (Mar 1920), p.28.

154 *WE* 179 (3 Mar 1917), p.14; *LRE* 12:10 (July 1920), p.15; *WW* 42:4 (Apr 1920), p.29; 42:5 (May 1920), p.30; 'Minutes of the General Council of the Assemblies of God', 4–11 Sept 1918, p.28; *DPCM*, p.1071.

155 *AF* 10 (Sept 1907), p.1; 11 (Oct 1907–Jan. 1908), p.2; 12 (Jan 1908), p.3; *WW* 30:7 (July 1908), pp.218–19; *BM* 26 (15 Nov 1908), p.4; 34 (15 Mar 1909), p.4; 51 (1 Dec 1909), p.3; 64 (15 June 1910), p.4; 67 (1 Aug 1910), p.1; 114 (15 July 1912), p.1; *Pent* 1:5 (Jan 1909), p.2; *UR* 1:3 (Aug 1909), p.5; *WWit* 10:4 (Apr 1914), p.4; 12:5 (May 1915), p.6; *TF* 34:8 (Aug 1914), p.187; Robeck, *Azusa Street*, pp.260–2.

156 Bays, 'Indigenous Protestant Churches', p.130.

157 *Trust* 9:8 (Oct 1910), p.19; *Trust* 10:3 (May 1911), p.19; *BM* 137 (1 Aug 1913), p.3.

158 *BM* 26 (15 Nov 1908), p.4; *UR* 2:4 (Jan 1911), p.7

159 *BM* 32 (15 Feb 1909), p.1; 38 (15 May 1909), p.3; 41 (1 July 1909), p.2; 48 (15 Oct 1909), p.1; 51 (1 Dec 1909), p.1; 53 (1 Jan 1910), p.1; 54 (15 Jan 1910), p.2; 68 (15 Aug 1910), p.1; *LRE* 2:10 (July 1910), p.14; *UR* 2:3 (Nov 1910), p.8.

160 *BM* 57 (1 Mar 1910), p.1.

161 *BM* 59 (1 Apr 1910), p.2; 62 (15 May 1910), p.1; 63 (1 June 1910), p.1; 66 (15 July 1910), p.1; Robeck, *Azusa Street*, pp.258–60.

162 *BM* 75 (1 Dec 1910), p.1; *UR* 2:5 (May 1911), p.5; *Trust* 10:4–5 (June and July 1911), p.26; *LRE* 3:10 (July 1911), p.16.

163 *AF* 11 (Jan 1908), p.3; *Pent* 1:8 (July 1909), p.5; *BM* 44 (15 Aug 1909), 67 (1 Aug 1910), p.1; p.2; 131 (15 Apr 1913), p.4; 135 (15 June 1913), p.3; *WW* 31:12 (Dec 1909),

p.302; *WWit* 9:8 (Aug 1913), p.1; *LRE* 8:10 (July 1916), p.9; *WE* 209 (6 Oct 1917), p.8; Robeck, *Azusa Street*, pp.262–4.

164 *LRE* 12:8 (May 1920), pp.2–6.

165 *Trust* 11:2 (Apr 1912), p.19; *WWit* 8:10 (20 Dec 1912), p.4; Letter, T. H. Mundell to Marcus Wood, Secretary, CIM, 23 Sept 1919.

166 *Pentecostal Truths* 2:4 (Apr 1909), p.4; *BM* 60 (15 Apr 1910), p.4; 87 (1 June 1911), p.3; 109 (1 May 1912), p.2; 140 (15 Sept 1913), p.2; *UR* 1:3 (Aug 1909), p.3; *LRE* 5:10 (July 1913), p.22; 5:12 (Sept 1913), pp.10–11.

167 Deng, 'Indigenous Chinese', pp.452–62; *TF* 37:6 (June 1917), p.127; *LRE* 11:3 (Dec 1917), p.16; 'Constitution and By-Laws', 1931, p.132; Bays, 'Protestant Missionary Establishment', p.58.

168 *WW* 37:3 (Mar 1915), pp.92–3; *WWit* 12:10 (Oct 1915), pp.6–7; *TF* 37:2 (Feb 1917), p.47; *WE* 175 (3 Feb 1917), p.16; 188 (5 May 1917), p.13; 'Combined Minutes', 1920, p.67; 'Constitution and By-Laws', 1939, p.178; Deng, 'Indigenous Chinese', p.442.

169 *LRE* 9:6 (Mar 1917), p.16; 9:8 (May 1917), p.7; 'Combined Minutes', 1920, p.68; 'Constitution and By-Laws', 1939, p.178.

170 Bays, 'Indigenous Protestant Churches', pp.125–6; Bays, 'Growth of Independent Christianity', pp.309–10; Deng, 'Indigenous Chinese', pp.437–66.

171 *TF* 35:2 (Feb 1915), p.47; *WW* 37:3 (Mar 1915), pp.92–3; *CE* 73 (9 Jan 1915), p.4; 77 (13 Feb 1915), p.1; *WE* 202 (11 Aug 1917), p.12; 204 (25 Aug 1917), p.12.

172 Deng, 'Indigenous Chinese', p.442.

173 Deng, 'Indigenous Chinese', pp.441–52;

174 Deng, 'Indigenous Chinese', pp.452–62; *TF* 37:6 (June 1917), p.127; *LRE* 11:3 (Dec 1917), p.16; 'Constitution and By-Laws', 1931, p.132.

175 *Trust* 19:3 (May 1920), p.11; *DPCM*, p.60.

176 *AF* 3 (Nov 1906), p.3; 5 (Jan 1907), p.4; 6 (Feb–Mar 1907), p.2.

177 *Apostolic Light* 183 (29 Aug 1907), pp.1, 3; *AF* 11 (Jan 1908), p.2.

178 *BM* 11 (1 Apr 1908), p.1; 13 (1 May 1908), p.1; *WW* 29:9 (Oct 1907), p.267.

179 *BM* 17 (1 July 1908), p.4.

180 *WW* 30:11 (Nov 1908), p.345.

181 *BM* 22 (15 Sept 1908), p.4; 27 (Dec 1908), p.1; *Pent* 1:4 (Dec 1908), pp.3–5.

182 *BM* 35 (1 Apr 1909), p.4; *Pent* 1:6 (Apr–May 1909), p.5.

183 *BM* 46 (15 Sept 1909), p.3; 72 (15 Oct 1910), p.3.

184 Shew, 'Pentecostals in Japan', p.488–9.

185 *WW* 37:1 (Jan 1915), pp.25, 29.

186 *Pent* 2:11–12 (Nov–Dec 1910), p.4; *WW* 32:11 (Nov 1910), p.342; *BM* 69 (1 Sept 1910), p.2; 75 (1 Dec 1910), p.2; 85 (1 May 1911), p.1; 100 (15 Dec 1911), p.1; 118 (15 Sept 1912), p.2.

187 *LRE* 5:4 (Jan 1913), p.12; 6:11 (Aug 1914), p.17; *WE* 175 (3 Feb 1917), p.15; 188 (5 May 1917), p.12; *WW* 39:16 (May 1917), p.254.

188 *BM* 133 (15 May 1913), p.1; *WWit* 9:9 (Sept 1913), p.4; 9:10 (Oct 1913), p.2; Shew, 'Pentecostals in Japan', p.490.

189 *Trust* 11:7 (Sept 1912), p.19; *BM* 125 (15 Jan 1913), p.4; *WWit* 9:11 (Nov 1913), p.4; *FF* 15 (Dec 1913), p.9; 28 (June 1915), p.13; *LRE* 6:11 (Aug 1914), p.17; 10:3 (Dec 1917), p.8; 11:6 (Mar 1919), p.14; 11:10 (July 1919), pp.22–4; *WW* 36:9 (Sept 1914), p.283; 39:16 (May 1917), p.254; 42:4 (Apr 1920), p.30; *CE* 60 (26 Sept 1914), p.4; *WE* 127 (19 Feb 1916), p.12; 173 (20 Jan 1917), p.12; *TF* 35:4 (Apr 1915), p.88; 37:6 (June 1917), pp.139–40; Letters, T. H. Mundell to W. J. Taylor, Nagasaki, Japan, 27 Nov 1914; T. H. Mundell to W. J. Taylor, Kobe, 26 May 1916; 'Combined Minutes of

the General Council of the Assemblies of God 1914–1917', p.40; 'Constitution and By-Laws', 1939, p.183; Shew, 'Pentecostals in Japan', pp.491–2.

190 *Trust* 18:3 (May 1919), p.20.

191 *WW* 42:10 (Oct 1920), p.10.

192 *LRE* 8:12 (Sept 1916), p.11; 11:6 (Mar 1919), p.14.

193 *FF* 21 (Nov 1914), p.4.

194 *WE* 171 (6 Jan 1917), p.2.

195 *BM* 136 (1 July 1913), p.1; Park, 'Fourfold Gospel', pp.82–4.

196 *WW* 36:7 (July 1914), p.219; *LRE* 9:5 (Feb 1917), pp.13–14; 9:10 (July 1917), p.14; *TF* 37:9 (Sept 1917), p.210; 37:11 (Nov 1917), pp.257–8; 39:10 (Oct 1919), pp.236–7.

6

Stretching Out Hands to God: Africa and the Middle East

'Princes shall come out of Egypt; Ethiopia shall soon stretch her hands unto God.' Here we have Africa in prophecy. Isaiah saw the walls of Israel in ruins; but God saw them complete in His plan of grace and of redemption . . . God sees not the down-trodden heathen, cannibal Africa but He sees her in prophecy. Here we have Ethiopia in the dispensation of God in the Old Testament, not yet, but soon to stretch out her hands.

(Confidence, July 1913)[1]

Pentecostal missionaries went to Africa very early. As in the above quotation written by Swiss Pentecostal missionary in the Congo, Alma Doering, one of the most frequently quoted biblical verses used in connection with Africa in Pentecostal writings was Psalm 68.31: 'Ethiopia shall stretch out her hands unto God.' This text was quoted by missionaries far and wide in this great continent, especially when they found responsive audiences that seemed to confirm this prophecy. Missionary writers like Doering would cite this passage and those in the New Testament referring to Simon of Cyrene carrying Jesus' cross as a symbol of Africa's humiliation and slavery. On the other hand the conversion of the Ethiopian eunuch was a symbol of Africa's exaltation, evidence of God's plan for Africa to 'stretch out her hands to God'. David Livingstone had a few years earlier referred to Africa as the 'open sore of the world', was deeply concerned about the continued slave trade carried out by the Arabs, and believed that British protection and 'civilization' was needed to avert this outrageous practice. Evangelical missions had already been active in Africa for many years before Pentecostals arrived.[2]

Africa was in a period of rapid change in the late nineteenth century. Portuguese traders were followed by ivory poachers and European explorers and missionaries. African societies and states began to adjust to the new situation and rapidly lost their autonomy and territory as a result. Religious ferment was taking place as the tribal religions of time immemorial were brought face to face with a militant Islam on the one hand and a Christianity that followed in the wake of the encroaching colonizers on the other. Africa had neither nation-states nor fixed borders before Europeans began to partition it, and even then, boundaries were usually vague or disputed and often cut across former tribal territories. France and Britain in particular were in constant competition to exert the most influence in the continent and between them they came to control most of it.

The Sultanate of Sokoto was a Fulani Muslim empire that expanded by waging *jihad* (holy war) over much of the present-day interior of Nigeria and

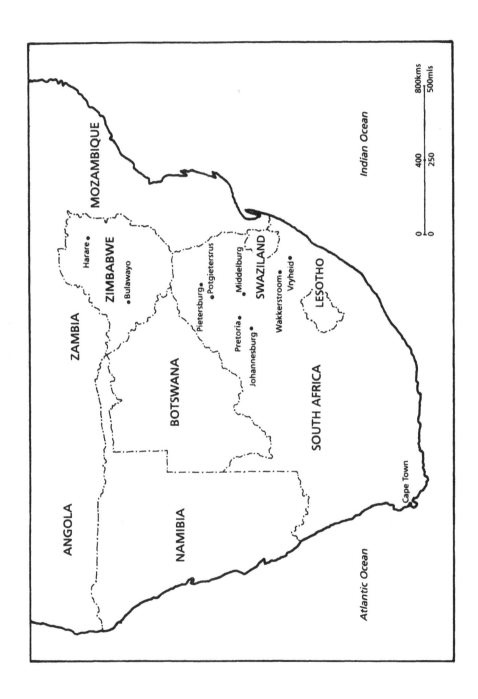

southern Niger until the 1890s. Islam had become a counterforce to European colonial conquest.[3] Africa's need was often highlighted in the Pentecostal periodicals with reference to the advance of Islam and in some cases was touted as the main reason for urgent missionary activity. Cecil Polhill wrote, 'The most urgent missionary world problem is to meet and overcome the Mohammedan advance in Africa.'[4] Elisabeth Sexton stated that 'Moslem propagandists' were taking advantage of the communication improvements made 'by Christian countries' and were advancing through Central Africa with their 'false system of religion'. Many western missionaries were needed in a time when, thanks to colonialism, 'law and order' had taken the place of witchcraft, cannibalism and inter-tribal warfare. The Muslim missionaries on the other hand were 'surging their way through these open avenues with the Koran and the sword; while too many of the Christians in our Christian land are still unarroused [sic] as to the need of earnest missionary activity at this time in Africa'. She asked, 'Shall we claim Africa for Christ? Doors are wide open to us, and God has evidently prepared hearts in Africa who will gladly respond to the full gospel truth.'[5] At least, that was how this editor saw it. Occasional references to this 'encroachment' of Islam in Africa continued to be published in the Pentecostal press. One report stated its alarm that a religion 'so antagonistic to the Cross' had won over powerful African tribes and was raising 'barriers . . . that will make the Christianizing of the natives a thousand-fold more difficult'. It called for 'more strenuous exertions to stem the tide of this false religion that threatens to engulf the heathen'.[6]

The Battle of Isandhlwana in 1879 was the first military engagement of British forces in the Anglo–Zulu War and resulted in the routing of over-confident British forces by a numerically superior but militarily disadvantaged Zulu army. The battle showed that African weaponry and tactical manoeuvres could repel the colonizers, who were not invincible. Similarly, the decisive defeat of Italy by Ethiopia in 1896 at the battle of Adowa had profound significance for western-educated Africans, including church leaders. For them it represented the liberation of African peoples from colonial oppression. The political and religious ferment in Africa in this period created serious tensions and instability across the continent by the beginning of the twentieth century. This was a stimulus for increasing European involvement and the growth of both European Christian missions and independent African churches. European settlers were seeking to appropriate vast areas of African land for themselves, to exploit Africa's rich natural resources for their expanding industries and to control cheap African labour for their own advantage. The 'scramble for Africa' had begun. Africans themselves stood by helplessly or – when they resisted as they sometimes did – they were easily defeated by the superior weaponry, technology and political determination they lacked and by the divide-and-rule strategy of the colonizers.

Of course, although the Europeans won the battles, they could not win the war, and despite harsh repression, African resistance was never entirely subdued. At the Conference of Berlin in 1884–5, most of Africa was carved up between France (who acquired almost a third of the continent) and Britain, with Portugal retaining two large countries in southern Africa, Belgium subsequently taking a large part of Central Africa in the Belgian Congo (1893) and

Germany, Spain and Italy also receiving large parcels of land.[7] Only Abyssinia (Ethiopia) was independent; and Liberia was a quasi-independent state ruled by descendants of former African American slaves. This was the context that greeted Pentecostal missionaries in Africa. Before looking at the situation in the sub-Sahara, the chapter will begin by considering the work of Pentecostals in the Middle East and North Africa.

Pentecostals in the Middle East and Egypt

At the beginning of the twentieth century the Middle East was in a state of political upheaval as the Turkish Ottoman Empire was beginning to fall apart. Egypt was occupied by Britain in 1882; it became a British protectorate in 1914 and was given independence in 1922, but with significant British involvement in her affairs. Britain's control of Egypt led to intervention further up the Nile and the Anglo-Egyptian Sudan was finally created after a long war against the Mahdists in 1898. The Wafd Arab nationalist party in Egypt led a nation-wide revolt against British rule in 1917–19, affecting Pentecostal missionaries there. Palestine (including part of present-day Jordan and Israel), and Lebanon, Syria and Iraq were still under Ottoman rule until the end of the Great War in 1918, when they were mandated to France and Britain as 'protectorates'.[8]

Because of the particular eschatological orientation of Pentecostal missionaries (traced in Chapter 8), Jerusalem, Palestine and Egypt – the so-called 'Bible Lands' – were of particular interest for them and their home churches. The earliest Pentecostal pioneer in this region was the Azusa Street missionary Lucy Leatherman. On arrival in Jerusalem late in 1906 she reported that a 'native minister' from Beirut and a missionary had 'received the baptism' there. Later, when the McIntoshes from Macao joined her, she reported five others receiving Spirit baptism.[9] The work seems to have had a boost, as one report speaks of a convention that Leatherman organized in Ramallah with about three hundred present. Leatherman herself was less optimistic, speaking of 'a few' who had received the Spirit. One was an Egyptian from Asyūt, Ghali Hanna and another a Syrian named Brother Zarub, who was 'turned out' of his denomination when he started preaching about Spirit baptism. Leatherman undertook an arduous and lonely journey, sometimes by mule in mountainous regions through Syria and Galilee, and she held meetings in Beirut. After this, she proceeded to Egypt to see Ghali's work and reported a 'great revival' there and that 'multitudes' had been 'saved, sanctified and baptized with the Holy Ghost and fire'. Later she wrote of a hundred conversions in Asyūt in two weeks. One of those baptized in the Spirit she described as a 'great big lion of a fellow' who was leaving for Khartoum, Sudan to preach the Pentecostal message. Ghali Hanna also wrote of the effects of the visit of Leatherman.[10]

Leatherman left Egypt in February 1909 and moved eastwards through Arabia to India, visiting the missions in the Pune area and meeting up with Carrie and George Montgomery on their round-the-world tour.[11] She moved via Hong Kong and Shanghai (where she visited the missions of Nettie Moomau and the Hansens) to Yokohama, Japan. Her ceaseless activity had taken its toll, for there she was very ill and spent months resting. But from

William Seymour

John Alexander Dowie

A. B. Simpson

William Durham

Charles F. Parham

SOUTH AMERICA

Willis Hoover

Gunnar Vingren

Daniel Berg

The Azusa Street leadership in 1906
(Thomas Junk is second from right, at back)

THE APOSTOLIC FAITH

Pentecost Has Come

Los Angeles Being Visited by a Revival of
Bible Salvation and Pentecost as
Recorded in the Book of Acts

APRIL 1908.   No. 1.

"CONFIDENCE"

A Pentecostal Paper for
Great Britain.

The Latter-Rain Evangel

The days of Heaven on the Earth.

五旬節真理報

PENTECOSTAL TRUTHS.

Volume I, NO.5   HONGKONG, CHINA. MAY, 1908.   Subscription Free.

按期派送不取分文   主降生一千九百零八年五月第五期

The periodicals 1906–08

Ramabai and Manoramabai

Minnie Abrams

Alfred and Lillian Garr

The Hong Kong Pentecostal Mission, *c.* 1910

Mok Lai Chi, *c.* 1918

The Apostolic Faith Mission, Shanghai, 1910

Pentecostal church in Yunnan, *c.* 1915

MISSIONARIES

(back) Amos Williams and Frank Trevitt
(front) Mr and Mrs Sydney Smith and W. W. Simpson

Arie Kok on a mission journey

Clockwise from top left: William Wade Harris;
Shalumbo and Masele; John G. Lake

(L–R at back) James Salter, William Burton, Joseph Blakeney and George Armstrong (seated), 1915

Hettie Burton making a journey

A Congolese preachers' class

Rochester Bible Training School class 1917–18

Japan she went to Manila in the Philippines and was preaching to American military personnel there by the end of 1909. The report in *The Upper Room* in Los Angeles described her as 'this brave woman whom God has made a pioneer in the Gospel'.[12]

Leatherman visited the USA in 1910–11 in poor health, where after her recovery she ministered in conventions before going to Pentecostal centres in Britain on her way back to Palestine. She wrote from Jerusalem in February 1912 where she encouraged the two women missionaries there and was in Beirut that July, from where she intended to relocate permanently in the north of Syria and begin orphanage work. However, in 1913 she was still in Beirut, as her health had again deteriorated. She wrote of the Balkan Wars and her own danger as Christians (especially Armenians) were being killed throughout the Ottoman Empire. She was later that year in Jerusalem planning to return to Egypt, but left for Philadelphia because of the outbreak of war.[13] In 1917 she was travelling through Panama to Valparaiso, Chile and Argentina under the Church of God, until 1921 when she returned to the USA. She was hospitalized with an unspecified serious illness at the end of that year. Although she stated that she intended to return to Jerusalem, she may have died in December 1921 or early 1922.[14]

In February 1911 Elizabeth Brown and Mary Smithson from the Pentecostal Mission in Atlanta, on their way to Jerusalem, visited a Pentecostal church in Beirut. Brown first came to Palestine as a missionary in 1895 but had become Pentecostal in 1908. She worked mainly among Palestinian Arabs. Charles Leonard, formerly of the CMA, was another prominent Pentecostal missionary working in this area and based in Jerusalem at this time together with E. O. Jago (in Hebron, Palestine since 1905) and A. Forder, who had been working among Bedouin Arabs in the area of the Jordan, Sinai and the Dead Sea since 1891. Forder wrote of his deliverance and protection during an Arab rebellion against the Turkish government in Kerak. He travelled by camel in desert areas from place to place seeking out and speaking to nomadic Bedouins about Christ. Leonard moved to Asyūt, Egypt in late 1911 and from there to Cairo in 1912 before returning to America, leaving Brown and Smithson as the only Pentecostal workers in Jerusalem, joined for a short time by Leatherman. Brown and Smithson began learning Arabic with a view to starting a girls' school in Jerusalem. Jago started a mission and a school in Beersheba in 1911. The Leonards rejoined the mission in Cairo in 1913 but moved back to Jerusalem soon afterwards. When the lives of all foreign missionaries in Jerusalem were in danger because of the War (the Ottoman Turks had sided with Germany), the Leonards and other Pentecostal missionaries in Palestine left for the USA in November 1914. But the family contracted smallpox en route and two of their three boys died in England. In early 1915 Forder was imprisoned by the Turks as a prisoner of war in Damascus and was released in 1917 but confined to the city of Damascus with his wife. Three women workers, including Brown and Mrs Forder, were the only Pentecostals left in Jerusalem under conditions that one missionary travelling to Egypt described as 'critical', with starvation and massacre facing them and most Christian work at an end. Brown was forced to go to the USA for furlough in 1917; she returned in 1919 and was an AG missionary in Jerusalem until her death in 1940.[15]

Christian Armenians in the Ottoman Empire were agitating for independence and were decimated through genocide by Turkish Muslim forces over a period of 30 years. An estimated 200,000 Armenians lost their lives in 1895–6 and a further one and a half million were massacred between 1915 and 1922, when a Turkish republic was created and most Armenians fled to safety in the Soviet Union.[16] In Armenian areas of Turkey, a Swiss missionary running a mission home for over 200 Armenian massacre orphans in Cesarea, Maria Gerber, became Pentecostal in 1910. She had heard of people with the experience of Spirit baptism and speaking in tongues that she had herself experienced in 1884. She published books in Turkish on the second coming of Christ and divine healing and did evangelistic work in the surrounding areas. In 1915 Gerber was in the USA raising funds for the orphanage because her European support had been stopped by the war. Her Zion Orphans' Home was requisitioned by the Turkish government as a military hospital in 1917 and the children re-housed, and Gerber died that December, but the buildings were repossessed by the mission in 1919. A Canadian Mennonite missionary, Thomas Ford Barker, in charge of another Armenian orphanage, was mentioned as having become Pentecostal in 1913. These institutions were greatly affected by the Armenian massacres in 1915.[17]

Two Persian (Assyrian) missionaries from Chicago, Bob Lazarus and Saul Baddell, wrote of severe persecution (including whippings) and hunger they endured in the city of Urumia in 1911. After 18 months of this hardship Baddell returned to Chicago in 1913 to work in Andrew Urshan's 'Persian' church, while Lazarus remained.[18] Urshan himself, son of an Assyrian Presbyterian minister, left for Urumia in November 1913, leaving the Chicago church in the hands of Baddell. By June 1914 Urshan was reporting 'latter rain' with 50 conversions during two weeks of street preaching and 30 receiving Spirit baptism. Severe opposition from the Russian Orthodox Church brought a halt to the Pentecostals' street preaching. A group of young women who had become Pentecostals were shot at while on their way to an evening meeting. A 15-year-old girl Sophia died as a result and two were seriously injured. Urshan said that their workers' lives were in danger and requested prayer. A little later that year he reported four assemblies having opened. But as the war raged on in 1915, thousands of Armenian and Assyrian Christians were slaughtered and their homes destroyed – including three Persian Pentecostals: Andrew the leader in Sophia's congregation, Urshan's main assistant Jeremiah Eshoo (both killed by Kurdish insurgents) and Elisha. Urshan's mother died of typhoid, he lost all the contents of his home and on one occasion was horsewhipped. During this conflict, at least half a million Christians lost their lives in Turkish territories, mostly Armenians, in a horrendous wave of what today would be termed 'ethnic cleansing'. In late 1915 Urshan left the country with his family and other Pentecostal workers via Russia to return to the USA. The work in Urumia continued under Urshan's remaining team of Bob Lazarus, Timothy Urshan (Andrew's brother), Joseph Yohanan, Yohanan Baboo and unnamed women workers. Urshan made an appeal for better financial support for them in 1917.[19]

Egypt was an Islamic country that especially attracted Pentecostal missionaries, again motivated by biblical prophecies about the eschatological blessings upon Egypt in the last days.[20] Asyūt on the upper Nile was the centre for Pentecostalism in Egypt to which a number of western missionaries went, first invited by Ghali Hanna.[21] Egyptian Christians had also heard of the Pentecostal movement through Alexander Paul, an Egyptian who had been Spirit baptized in 1907 in the USA. The first Pentecostal missionaries in Egypt after Leatherman's visit were George and Lydia Brelsford from Colorado Springs, invited by Ghali Hanna and other Pentecostal believers there. After several delays, they arrived in Asyūt in March 1909, reporting that the Egyptian Christians had already rented a building for the mission and that between 30 and 40 people were 'tarrying for Pentecost'. The Brelsfords were joined by several others by the end of the year making a total of ten, including Frank Moll (who would later leave for Kenya) and Sarah Smith from Indianapolis – a 'frail little woman, gray-haired' in her late sixties. The following year they were joined by the experienced Pentecostal minister A. H. Post, originally from Azusa Street. Reports were written of miracles of healing resulting in conversions – they estimated praying for 'two thousand sick people' in two months – itinerating in surrounding villages and publishing a quarterly paper in Arabic from Cairo called *The Message of God and the Good Report*, edited by H. E. Randall. A second mission home was opened in Nikhela, south of Asyūt. Alexander Paul and his American wife Carrie came as missionaries in Cairo and were joined by Sarah Smith in 1912, who first worked among Coptic women. They held services nightly and Paul acted as interpreter for missionaries and translator and editor for the Arabic paper. During 1911 the Brelsfords visited the USA and returned to Asyūt that October. The following September George Brelsford died from cancer and his wife and two daughters returned to the USA.

Lillian Trasher (1887–1961) and her sister arrived in Egypt in 1910 to begin her life-long ministry in Asyūt, announcing the opening of her famous orphanage a block away from the Pentecostal mission and reporting the kindness of the Egyptians in making them feel at home. She struggled with nervous exhaustion during her first year, but missionaries continued to come to work in Asyūt, including Trasher's mother and a newly converted former alcoholic from New York, Albert Juillerat. By 1913 there were at least 18 foreign Pentecostal missionaries in Egypt in seven different stations. There were also seven full-time Egyptian preachers. After a needed rest, Trasher resumed work in her orphanage in 1913 and had 50 children there by 1916, and was assisted by an Egyptian teacher, Shaker Gadallah and two Egyptian women.[22] In 1913 Leatherman again visited Egypt and named two Egyptian workers who had become Pentecostals six years earlier during her ministry there. One she calls Ayub and the other Nashed Boulos, in charge of the mission at Beni Suief. Another Egyptian leader was Ayad Abdel Malik in Minya, who wrote letters to American periodicals. The role of Ghali Hanna by this time is unclear, but he identified himself with the Pentecostal mission in Asyūt. After the departure of the foreign missionaries during the War he corresponded with the Pentecostal papers in 1916 and gave news of the work of eight Egyptian workers in nine stations. Habid Yousif was another Egyptian pastor who corresponded with the foreign press and reported on the progress of the work in Cairo and Alexandria during the absence of the expatriates.[23] Two Egyptian workers Matta Bohnam and Fahmy Nan were at Beni Suief, and Botros Labib wrote to Pentecostal papers in 1919. One missionary described the seven Egyptian workers as those 'God has chosen and qualified, and they have forsaken all to follow Jesus'. He continued, 'Some have stepped out under great persecutions, having had their lives threatened, locked up and beaten with rods, but they have been faithful to the One who called them. Praise His name! In Egypt it is a disgrace to the family for one to go out in the work of the Lord without a salary', but these workers had made this sacrifice.[24]

Ansel H. Post (c. 1850–1931), who had been a Baptist minister for over 30 years, received Spirit baptism in June 1906 at Azusa Street. He was numbered with the 'Spirit-filled workers' from Azusa Street in Santa Barbara, and was in charge of work in Pasadena.[25] In August 1907, leaving his family behind, he travelled via Cape Town to Sri Lanka, where he spent three months in Kandy and went on to India for several months, where he ministered (among other places) in Coonoor, travelling mainly to CMA missions. He reported that 'a very blessed Pentecostal work has been going on in many of the Alliance stations'. While there he met up with Daniel Awrey on his first round-the-world tour. Post also reported 'fully a thousand or more' Indian Christians who had 'received the baptism'. Awrey and Post travelled from there to Egypt together, and Post remained in Asyūt, probably in response to the Egyptian call for Pentecostal missionaries. He was in Sunderland, England for the International Pentecostal Congress in May 1909 on his way back to Los Angeles, but returned to Asyūt in 1910 at the age of 60 with his wife Henrietta, intending to remain there. He helped establish new Pentecostal missions, going to Cairo with a party of eight new missionaries in 1912 and the following year took charge of the mission in Alexandria, where Nicola Rafael was the permanent Egyptian worker. Post looked after the Asyūt mission after the death of Brelsford in 1912 and by 1913 reported eight stations in the Pentecostal mission in Egypt, two of which were under the leadership of 'native brethren'. The number of expatriate Pentecostal missionaries in Egypt was decimated after the outbreak of war in 1914 and by early 1917 all except Lillian Trasher had returned home.[26] Post left for the USA in 1915, affiliated with the AG and went back to Egypt in 1917, writing of how much the Egyptian pastors and Christians had welcomed him. The pastors had 'held on amidst some real privations and severe trials' and in some places 'the flock' had scattered, but he was happy to report that 'no Mission has closed on this account' and that revival was needed to bring many people together again. He remained in Egypt until his death in 1931 at the age of 81.[27]

Lillian Trasher hardly ever visited the USA, so consumed was she with her life's mission to Egyptian homeless children. When pressed in 1917 for a report on her work, which she was so reluctant to provide, she wrote the following characteristic reply:

I'm interested in every little thing. It is my very *life*. My work is my reward. I don't want any other. The love of my children has replaced the love of my relatives. The Orphanage is my home and if I am away from it for a few days I count the hours until I am back again. I am loved by all the people and I love them. I would never be happy to live in America again; my life would be too empty. Truly I never thought I could be so happy on this earth. I was as happy when I received my baptism but that was the joy of a blessing received; this is the joy of a blessing given which you must know is even better.[28]

By that time she had finished paying for her building and a large annex and had 62 children housed. Sarah Smith joined her in 1917 but died of pneumonia after only a few months, and Trasher was the only expatriate there again. Later that year she had a forced furlough in the USA after a harrowing experience when Asyūt was looted by Arab raiders and nationalist rioters and all foreigners were ordered to leave. She left the orphanage children under the care of her Egyptian matron Zackiah until her return in February 1920. She was to remain working with her beloved Egyptian orphans until her death in 1961 at the age of 74 after 50 years in Egypt. Although affiliated originally to the CG in Cleveland, Tennessee, she joined the AG in 1919. One of the remarkable things about her work from the beginning was the recognition, esteem and support she received from the Egyptian government and the financial support she received from Egyptian people, Muslims and Christians alike. They saw this work as theirs and readily helped Trasher put up buildings when needed. Her orphanage today houses 650, is known as the Lillian Trasher Memorial Orphanage, and she is buried there.[29]

There were other areas in North Africa where early Pentecostals were found. Ellen and James Hebden, founders of the first Pentecostal congregation in Canada (Toronto), went to Algiers, Algeria as missionaries in 1910, where James died some nine years later. We do not know anything about their work. Josephine Planter was a Pentecostal missionary in Tunis from 1912. After two years learning French and Arabic, she reported three Muslims and two French women converted. One young Muslim man went to Cairo to the Pentecostal mission and received Spirit baptism. Pentecostalism in the Muslim world did not exactly make a big impact, but these pioneers were tenacious in extremely difficult circumstances.

Apostolic Faith Missionaries in the Sub-Sahara

Samuel and Ardelle Mead had been Bishop Taylor's Methodist missionaries in Angola for 21 years when they came to Azusa Street to be baptized in the Spirit.[30] Ardelle Mead believed that she had been given 'an African dialect', but Samuel Mead was more hesitant about whether the tongues they had received would be used in 'a foreign field'. The veteran missionary said simply, 'As for myself I cannot say. My God is able, this I know.'[31] The African American preacher who had locked her church door against William Seymour, Julia Hutchins, left for Liberia in September 1906 with her husband Willis and niece Leila McKinney. She seemed to have motivated others to follow, including Lucy Farrow, another African American leader at Azusa Street and Parham's former governess who had introduced Seymour to Parham's message of Spirit baptism. By the following month there were 8 missionaries from Azusa Street going to 'the foreign field' beginning to gather in New York, and 30 'workers' going to various parts of the USA. By the time they sailed in December 1906 there were 16 missionaries in all leaving New York for Liverpool. George and Daisy Batman and their three children, the Hutchins and McKinney, the F. M. Cooks, Mrs Lee and Farrow sailed from Liverpool to Monrovia, Liberia, while the Meads and Robert and Myrtle Shideler left on another ship bound for Benguela, Angola. The Meads were to return permanently to the USA within a year (after spending some time in Sunderland, England), and the Shidelers' fate is unknown. In 1912 Alexander Boddy visited the Meads in California (apparently then in retirement) and preached at the Azusa Street Mission.[32]

The S. S. Slingerlands, who received Spirit baptism in Salem, Oregon in December 1906, arrived in Berbera, British Somaliland (Somalia) as early as December 1907, but found this a very hard place to work and were not heard of again.[33] Clyde and Lila Miller were the first and among the most isolated Pentecostal missionaries in Africa. They arrived in British East Africa (Kenya) in late 1908, to Ogoda Mission Station near Kisumu by the eastern shore of Lake Victoria. Conditions were difficult, they built a grass house to live in and progressed well with language learning. In 1911 the mission moved to Nyangori and the following year Frank Moll arrived from Egypt. The mission opened a children's school and sought to break down the fear of white people caused by brutal colonial oppression. By 1913 there were seven American Pentecostal workers there and a Norwegian Pentecostal mission with another seven workers was only 18 miles away. The Millers and their team worked with very little financial support, finally building a more permanent dwelling with an iron roof in 1913. Miller reported that 250 were attending Sunday services held in a pole and mud, thatched church building completed that year.[34] By this time the J. R. Buckleys had been with the mission some 18 months and wanted to start a new mission among the Nandi people to the east, stressing the importance of getting a former CMS property there soon before another mission got it. Buckley wrote that there were already too many workers at Nyangori.[35] Miller lost his wife and in 1919 his only remaining co-worker Frank Moll in Nyangori. He left at the end of that year for furlough in the USA and did not return. In German East Africa (Tanzania), the Mount Horeb Pentecostal Mission at Itigi was established in 1913 by Karl and Marian Wittich – Karl died three months after arriving there. Marian Wittich returned in 1920 to marry Otto Keller, a Canadian Pentecostal missionary and former co-worker, and they worked in Miller's former station at Nyangori. The Kellers were to work in Kenya for many years, affiliating in 1924 with the newly formed Pentecostal Assemblies of Canada. From their mission Zakayo Kivuli began the independent African Israel Church Nineveh. Otto Keller died in 1942 and Marian retired four years later.[36]

Liberia was a favourite place for African American missionaries, who perhaps were encouraged by the contemporary movement advocating emigration to Africa. But missionaries did not find Liberia an easy place to live in and soon returned to the USA. First, there was considerable unrest among the native Liberians, especially in the Cape Palmas area where the Kru (including Grebo) people lived. An insurrection against the Liberian government took place in 1909 escalating to the full-scale Grebo War in 1910.[37] There was extensive exploitation of indigenous Liberians by the Americo-Liberian minority that lasted for much of the twentieth century. Slavery was only out-lawed there in 1936 and aboriginal people were denied voting rights. Pentecostal missionaries started arriving there in 1907. *The Apostolic Faith* reported that African American evangelist Lucy Farrow, who had first accom-panied Seymour to Los Angeles from Houston, would be in the first party of Azusa Street missionaries who left for Africa. In Liberia, Mrs Cook, Mrs Lee and the whole Batman family died of tropical fever within a few weeks. *The Apostolic Faith* did not announce their tragic deaths, which soon became a source of great embarrassment and criticism for the new Apostolic Faith movement. Some Holiness periodicals used the deaths as proof of the 'delu-sion' taught at Azusa Street and charged Julia Hutchins with 'kidnapping' a young Kru girl from Monrovia because she had returned with an African child.[38] Farrow returned after seven months in Johnsonville, Liberia, where she worked among the aboriginal population, reporting that 20 had 'received their Pentecost' and that she had been able to speak and preach two sermons in the Kru language. The paper concluded the report on Farrow by saying that some of 'the heathen' had spoken 'in English and some in other tongues'. The Lord had shown Farrow when she was to go, the time she was to return, and pro-vided the fare in time, the paper said. Farrow was now home safely, and being used in Virginia and in the southern states.[39] She continued to minister at Azusa Street for a few months after her return before returning to Houston.

Other early African American missionaries to Liberia were the Frank Cummings, Church of God in Christ missionaries who left in 1907, and Edward and Mollie McCauley, leaders of the mixed Apostolic Faith congrega-tion in Long Beach, California. With an associate Rosa Harmon, the McCauleys arrived in Monrovia in November 1907 and established a thriving work there among Kru people. Canadian John Reid visited Monrovia briefly on his way to Cape Palmas in December 1908 and reported how he stumbled upon the Apostolic Faith Mission hall, met with McCauley and learned that he had 145 members. Harmon reported 154 Kru members the following year. On an overnight stop in Monrovia, Daniel Awrey, a global travelling American preacher reported a thriving, 'large congregation in the Apostolic Faith Church' there in October 1913, less than two months before his own death from malaria at the Pentecostal mission near Cape Palmas.[40]

The foundation of a large AG mission in Liberia goes back to when John Reid from Winnipeg, Canada and trained at Lupton's college in Alliance, Ohio arrived in Cape Palmas in December 1908, after spending some time with Boddy in Sunderland before sailing from Liverpool. He built a 'native house' 70 miles inland (three days by wagon) for the missionary party of eight work-ing among the Barobo people consisting of new graduates of Lupton's college and experienced missionaries. But Reid spent the first two months recovering from tropical fever and died after only six months there,[41] the first of many Pentecostal missionaries buried in Liberia. John Harrow, a Canadian mission-ary from Toronto was probably the leader of this party. He wrote in 1910 from Cape Palmas of two schools with 90 students and three new stations being opened, while John and Jessie Perkins were working in the Borobo 'Bush Country' in that area, running two boys' homes – they arrived in 1909. Both Harrow and Perkins were formerly Methodist Episcopal missionaries, Harrow having first gone to Liberia in 1894 under William Taylor. Perkins reported having 66 in the mission and of teams of preachers fanning out into the surrounding villages preaching against 'ju-jus' (fetishes).[42] They also operated a successful fruit and vegetable farm for the support of the homes and their workers. Martha Hisey and Rhodema Mendenhall (who married Harry Bowley in 1917 shortly before she died), both from Lupton's school and probably also in the original party, were in a station further inland where they ran a school for 50 children. Harrow stated that they had six white and three African workers and took 'purely native heathen' into their home where they provided food, clothing and education 'so that they can read the Bible for themselves' (presumably, English Bibles). He made appeals for more workers, saying that he was exhausted and that the native workers were discouraged.

By 1911 a team of ten Pentecostal missionaries was working in this mission in four stations, including a new station operated by William and Jennie Johnson, who had already been in Africa 15 years. This mission concentrated on bringing converted individuals (especially young men) out of their towns and villages into the mission compound, teaching them to read and write and then sending them back as preachers to their own people. Harrow mentions three 'native workers' by name in 1912: Jasper Toe, who assisted Perkins and in 1914 took charge of a station, Friday Sebo and John Aner, who went to their own people to start Pentecostal work. It seems that these were former associates of Harrow, for he later said that those who were converted when he was in the Methodist mission 'came into Pentecost'.[43] Harrow said that his main work was ministering to these and other workers. In 1918 Jasper Toe went as a missionary to the Gold Coast (Ghana), the first African leader to do so from this mission.[44]

Liberia was to be the burial ground for many Pentecostal missionaries. In 1912, the mission lost three women: Mrs Harrow and two new workers, Mary Staub and a young woman from Kilsyth in Scotland, Maria Tee, who died after only two weeks in Liberia. The next year claimed more missionary lives. Altogether, ten missionaries in this mission died of tropical diseases in the first eight years of the mission, and some returned home.[45] Conditions for these workers were far from easy. Johnson wrote of travelling 'through forest and jungle, fording rivers and wading swamps until almost exhausted' in order to reach remote villages with the gospel, but he also asked for prayer for his wife's nervousness of the 'many snakes and rats, and insects of every kind' that she had to endure. An African American couple who had been active workers in Chicago's Stone Church for five years, Isaac and Mattie Neeley, joined the mission at the end of 1913 and were soon reporting revival taking place in the interior, with a chief and 45 others getting baptized. By 1915 they had started a new station among Dorobo people and were soon afterwards ministering 'revival' in Methodist missions along the coast and engaging in itinerant revival work. This was bringing these missions into the Pentecostal 'baptism', and they were invited to speak at the Methodist conference in Cape Palmas in 1916.[46]

New missionaries arrived in 1916–17 including two more Canadians and a party with Harrow after his furlough, but at that time civil war had broken out again between tribal Liberians and the Americo-Liberian government. A young Canadian woman died of malaria two weeks after arriving at her station. There were now a total of 18 missionaries in this field led by Harrow, with seven Liberian preachers helping them. A division between the missionaries occurred in 1917 when Perkins and Johnson asked Harrow to step down as superintendent and he left the mission. All except four of the 18 missionaries plus two new ones were now affiliated with the AG, where John and Jessie Perkins remained in charge at least until 1939. John Harrow died in Liberia in 1920.[47]

Sierra Leone was the only other country in West Africa that received Pentecostal missionaries this early. The James Hares went from Chicago to Freetown in December 1910 as Pentecostal missionaries. They may have been African Americans. Mrs Hare had been in Sierra Leone for some time before she was married and was now returning with her new husband. On their arrival they started work among the Creoles (descendants of the freed slaves and the first settlers in the country), and they engaged in evangelistic work in the local military barracks among the various tribes from the interior who had moved to Freetown. They reported various healings taking place and expected a couple from Canada to join them in late 1911. Little more is known about their work, except that they were still there four years later. In 1914 the Wesley Longstreths arrived in Freetown and eventually began an Apostolic Faith Mission 165 miles into the interior, living in a mud house at Mayattah, near Kunso. They were there for at least six years. In 1917 a bush fire destroyed all the buildings on the mission, but they began building a new mission in 1920. In 1917 Ira and Ita Shakley were also working in Freetown, where they remained as AG missionaries at least until 1939. The Wilbur Taylors and Harry White were the first to travel from Sierra Leone to the interior of the French Sudan (present-day Burkina Faso) to begin Pentecostal work among the Mossi people under the AG in 1919.[48]

Pentecostalism and West African Independency

The pressures of religious change occurring in colonial Africa at the end of the nineteenth century resulted in many movements of resistance. The 'Ethiopian' independent churches in Southern Africa and the 'African' churches in West Africa were not as much movements of religious reform and innovation as were the later 'prophet-healing' churches, but were primarily movements of political protest, expressions of resistance against European hegemony in the church. Although they rejected the political dominance of white-led churches, they framed their protest in familiar Protestant categories and therefore did not seriously contest its social, religious and cultural components.[49] Their more lasting significance lay in the fact that they were the first to overtly challenge social structures of inequality and oppression in the church and to give a religious ideology for the dignity and self-reliance of the black person, thus foreshadowing the African nationalist movements and forming a religious justification for them. These secessions were often the result of tension between an increasingly self-aware African Christian community and a multiplying number of zealous European missionaries with colonial expansionist sympathies. The secessions that began in South Africa and Nigeria were to set a pattern for the next century. Secession was not a peculiarly African phenomenon, as we have seen. Africans were simply continuing what had become commonplace in European Protestantism. By the end of the nineteenth century there were already hundreds of new denominations, 'faith missions' and other mission societies springing up in the West, from where missionaries were sent to Africa. These multiplied denominations and societies were reproduced there, and it is hardly surprising that it was considered quite a natural thing for secessions to occur – urged on by the mission policies and colonial politics of the time that were highly prejudicial to Africans.[50] Nevertheless, the African and Ethiopian churches were part of the struggle against colonialism and were ecclesiastical forerunners of the African nationalist movements. The Freedom Charter that marked the creation of the African National Congress in South Africa in 1912 had several prominent Ethiopian church leaders as signatories. These churches were also seeking to make Christianity more African and therefore more appealing and relevant for ordinary people.

In West Africa, there was also the particularly aggravating dimension of the perceived failure of Samuel Ajayi Crowther's Niger Mission. The result was that new, young white missionaries were virtually unanimous in their view that Africans were unfit for church leadership – a view that was to persist for half a century. In 1890, a 'purge' involving unsubstantiated charges of immorality against almost all the African clergy and other workers in the Niger Mission took place. The actions of young English missionaries forced Bishop Crowther to resign from the committee of which he was Chair. The elderly Crowther was humiliated by white missionaries in their twenties, and died a year later to be replaced by an English bishop.[51] At the same time and rubbing salt in the wound, the numbers of young European missionaries to Nigeria increased significantly after 1890.[52] But there were deeper religious and socio-cultural issues at stake. The entrance of Pentecostalism into the African melting pot had the effect of stimulating new and more radically transforming forms of independent churches. The 'African' and 'Ethiopian' churches were overshadowed in the early twentieth century by new, rapidly growing 'prophet-healing' or 'spiritual' churches – so named because of their emphasis on the power of the Spirit in healing, prophecy and speaking in tongues.

Along the West African coast, churches associated with the Liberian prophet William Wade Harris and the Nigerian Garrick Sokari Braide emerged. They were later followed by churches known by the Yoruba term 'Aladura' ('owners of prayer') from the 1920s onwards in south-western Nigeria. In 1913, one of the most remarkable preachers in the history of Christianity began preaching in the Ivory Coast and from there to the Gold Coast (Ghana). William Wade Harris (1865–1929) was a Grebo of the indigenous Kru peoples of Liberia from the Cape Palmas area, the people most involved in the insurrections against the Americo-Liberian government. Raised and educated in a Grebo Methodist minister's house, Harris became a Methodist lay preacher who could speak English well, and he worked respectively as a seaman, a bricklayer, an Episcopalian school teacher and finally a government interpreter. He lost his job when he became involved in political activities and was imprisoned on a charge of treason. He had suggested (following his mentor Edward Blyden, a former Liberian Vice-President) that Liberia should become a British colony rather than be ruled oppressively by Americo-Liberian settlers. He was arrested in 1909 for allegedly pulling down the Liberian flag and planting the British flag in its place, and for leading a Grebo uprising.

After he had received the first of many visions in prison, he believed that his God-given mission was to be a prophet to take God's word to those who had never heard it. In order to accomplish this (as he later told a French Protestant missionary), the Spirit came on him as on the Day of Pentecost and he spoke in tongues.[53] There is the distinct possibility that he came in contact with and knew the Pentecostal missionaries working with Kru people in the Cape Palmas area, Harris's home, especially as many of them were former Methodists. One of them, William Johnson from Levi Lupton's school, spoke of working with Kru people from a Methodist school, and John Perkins was also working in this area.[54] It is also likely that Harris had heard of African American preachers of the Apostolic Faith Mission like Edward McCauley, who had a thriving Kru Pentecostal congregation in Monrovia from 1908 at least until 1913.

We may never know the extent of Harris's contact with Pentecostalism, but his personal experience of Pentecost was to signify a dramatic change in the direction of his life. The date of his release from prison is unknown, but could have been as late as 1912. When he emerged, it was with a calling to be a prophet to preach repentance and faith in Jesus Christ. He began walking eastwards to the French colony of Côte d'Ivoire and as far as the western Gold Coast (Ghana), a British colony at the time. He was one of the first African Christian prophets and certainly one of the most influential, his preaching resulting in the beginning of an unprecedented movement of mass conversions to Christianity. He preached from the Bible about one true God, healing from disease, and the rejection of fetishes and practices associated with traditional religions. His practices have precedent in the activities of the Pentecostal preachers in Liberia, where William Johnson described one of their African preachers in the Cape Palmas area in 1911 whose main work seems to have been exhorting people to 'destroy their jujus or idols'.[55] Going a step further by rejecting western clothing and walking barefoot, the white-bearded Harris wore a long white calico robe, a round white turban, and black bands crossed around his chest. He carried a Bible, a gourd rattle, a bowl, and a staff in the shape of a cross, striking an imposing figure not unlike a biblical prophet.[56] Harris was accompanied initially by two women assistants who were also dressed in white. At this time, a few hundred Catholics were probably the only Christians throughout the entire Ivory Coast. The effect of Harris's ministry was electrifying, as 'the whole population of the regions through which he passed accepted him as the authentic voice of God', and that Harris was God's messenger 'to revitalize their religion and society . . . in a time of crisis'.[57]

Harris and his companions would approach a village singing songs accompanied by calabash rattles. Local people would gather and Harris would preach fervently, inviting them to renounce traditional religious practices and believe in God. The thousands that did so were immediately baptized from the water in Harris's gourd dish in the name of Father, Son and Holy Spirit, and the Bible was placed on their heads. The fact that they were given no instructions before baptism worried the Catholic missionaries, but their baptism signified that they were purified of their sins and protected from evil during their transition from the old to the new, as they received Christian teaching. Sometimes people possessed by evil spirits and traditional deities were invited to touch the prophet's staff and were sprinkled with holy water, and many ecstatic manifestations were reported during this revival. It is said that several miracles were associated with Harris's ministry, most of which served to demonstrate the superiority of the power of God over traditional deities and healers. Harris sometimes carried a large brass tray to which people brought their fetishes, whereupon he burned them. This too was common Pentecostal practice.

At first, French colonial authorities considered him a 'harmless maniac', but they became increasingly concerned. They imprisoned him on at least one occasion and kept him under constant surveillance.[58] He is believed to have baptized some 120,000 adult Ivorian converts in one year (over 300 a day), often baptizing whole villages and thereby causing a minimum of disruption to customary structures. Unlike the European missionaries, Harris tolerated polygamy and some think he practised it. People travelled from distant places to hear him and be baptized. As a result, his message penetrated deep into the Ivorian and Ghanaian interiors where he had not been himself. He also sent out disciples to carry his message and methods far and wide. On the Ghanaian coast, Harris confronted and confounded traditional priests, many of whom were converted as a result. It was estimated that 1,000 new people came to hear him each day, until opposition from the Catholic missionaries caused him to return to Côte d'Ivoire.[59] The French administration and the Catholic missionaries then accused him of intimidation and fraud. Harris and three women assistants were arrested, and he was beaten and deported from Côte d'Ivoire towards the end of 1914. Over the next ten years, Harrist believers were systematically suppressed and village prayer houses destroyed. Harris returned to Liberia to relative obscurity until his death in 1929.

Harris never intended to form a separate church and he seemed to have favoured European missionaries. He directed people to existing churches, but also encouraged converts to build their own prayer houses where there were no churches, led by a minister and twelve 'apostles' chosen by the village community. Thousands of his followers formed these village churches in the Ivory Coast and the Gold Coast. This was noted by a Methodist missionary some seven years later, who said that these Harrist Christians had mostly abandoned traditional beliefs and practices. Harris told his followers to wait for teachers with Bibles who would instruct them in their new faith. Many of his converts joined the Catholic Church and later even more joined the Methodist Church after missionaries arrived in Côte d'Ivoire in 1924. Ivorian Methodists identify their beginnings with Harris's mission there in 1914.[60] He is regarded as the father of Christianity in the Ivory Coast. His unparalleled success seems to lie in his complete identification with ordinary people, his simple lifestyle and forceful personality, and his ability to make converts without unduly creating social tensions.

But he was far more than that. He both claimed and demonstrated that God had chosen an African person to be a prophet, with all the power that accompanied that calling. His outward accoutrements were not specifically African (although quite similar to Hausa garments), and the message he proclaimed was in radical discontinuity with much of African pre-Christian religion. He saw himself as a specifically Christian prophet, but found some Old Testament symbols appropriate for the people to whom he ministered. Yet Harris personified all there was about African religion that was good and reassuring for people plagued by evil forces and disease. In the eyes of his followers, he demonstrated that the God of the Bible was more powerful than the ancient divinities, ancestors and nature spirits had been, relevant to the needs of Africans under the yoke of colonial oppression. He accepted the African spirit world as reality, but regarded the spirits as the work of Satan to be cast out. It was this message that made him so popular on the West African coast, transcended the efforts of white missionaries and made him a pattern for many African prophets to follow.[61]

Thousands of Harris's followers soon found themselves at odds with Methodist policies, their prohibition of polygamy and the foreign liturgy so different from the African style of hymn-singing and dancing practised by Harris. They formed the Harrist Church, apparently after receiving the prophet's approval to do so. Just before Harris died in 1929, he is believed to have sent back an Ivorian delegation of three men with permission to organize a new church under one of them, John Ahui.[62] Like other African independent churches elsewhere at this time, this Harrist movement was severely persecuted by the colonial administration and its adherents had to meet secretly. Although it continued to have a strong emphasis on divine healing and the ministry of prophets, the Harrist movement that emerged in the 1930s was very different from western Pentecostalism and may no longer be considered a 'Pentecostal' movement without considerable qualification. The same is true of other churches that emerged out of Harris's ministry, like the Twelve Apostles Church in Ghana and its secessions. Many African independent churches developed in ways that have departed from their more 'Pentecostal' beginnings, but these beginnings still have to be recognized.

The popular Anglican revivalist in the Niger Delta, Garrick Sokari Braide (c. 1882–1918), was formerly a Kalabari (Ijo) fisherman and trader with little formal education. He was the first of many Nigerians to be recognized as a Christian prophet and prayer-healing evangelist. His reputation as a prophet and healer grew and he emerged from about 1912 until 1916 as a fiery preacher urging the destruction of fetishes and shrines, the rejection of alcohol and healing through prayer. Like Wade Harris, his message was simple: renounce traditional practices and believe in God. He named his hometown Bakana-Israel, and multitudes flocked there and spread his message all over the Niger Delta. The chief beneficiaries of this mass conversion movement were Anglicans, but Braide's increasing popularity and exploits were regarded as a threat to both the colonial authority and the Anglican missionaries. There is evidence that the area's alcohol trade decreased drastically as a result of Braide's preaching and consequently the colonial excise revenue fell. Braide, like Harris, advocated the use of African music in Christian worship with clapping and ecstatic dancing and encouraged the development of African leadership. On one occasion he was reported to have said publicly that the time had come for Africans to assume responsibility for themselves, which was interpreted as anti-colonial incitement. In 1916, Anglican auxiliary bishop James Johnson (an African), who had confirmed Braide four years earlier, was asked by Braide's supporters to recognize his ministry. Instead, the bishop declared him a 'devil-inspired' heretic and suspended any clergy supporting him. A month later the colonial authorities had Johnson's written encouragement to arrest Braide for seditious behaviour, incitement to commit violence, and wilful damage to property, in this case traditional shrines. He spent most of the next two years in prison and died after his release in 1918, perhaps as a result of the influenza epidemic. Although Braide remained a faithful Anglican until his death, while he was in prison in 1916 some 43,000 of his followers formed the Christ Army Church, the first 'spiritual church' in Nigeria, but it was soon racked by internal dissension.[63] Braide died in the year that the Aladura movement began to emerge further west.

The Aladura movement had its roots in the Anglican (CMS) Church in Nigeria. There were no foreign Pentecostal missionaries in Nigeria until much later, and this was an African reaction to European-dominated Christianity. A lay leader at Ijebu-Ode in the Yoruba country in south-western Nigeria, Joseph Shadare (d. 1962), formed a prayer group in 1918 together with a woman schoolteacher, Sophia Odunlami, who had a vision in which she was commanded to preach healing and reject medicines. This group was known as the Precious Stone (Diamond) Society, created to provide spiritual support and healing for victims of the influenza epidemic. In 1922 the society left the Anglican Church, rejecting both infant baptism and the use of medicines. It began a branch in Lagos and affiliated with a church in Philadelphia called Faith Tabernacle, whose literature had reached Nigeria and who emphasized divine healing and adult baptism by immersion. Contact with the church in the USA was severed in 1925 after doctrinal differences over the Pentecostal gifts of the Spirit (particularly speaking in tongues) favoured by the Africans, the apparent failure of the Americans to support the church in Nigeria, and the American leader's alleged immorality.[64] After a remarkable revival in 1930 under Joseph Babalola, the group forged links with the British Apostolic Church and later developed into the independent Christ Apostolic Church, one of the largest Pentecostal churches in Nigeria.

Another Anglican member, Moses Orimolade Tunolashe began preaching in about 1915 after partially recovering from a long illness. Crowds came to him for prayer for healing during the influenza epidemic of 1918. His emphases caused him to be known as Baba Aladura ('praying father') – a title used by subsequent leaders of the church that he founded. He was called upon to pray for a 15-year-old girl, Abiodun Akinsowon, to awake from a trance. She afterwards related her visions of heaven, out-of-body experiences and instructions to use special prayers and holy water for healing. Like the earlier movement, this began as a prayer group within the Anglican Church but withdrew from it because of heavy criticism. The members of this movement claimed a special relationship with angels, whom they represented on earth. Abiodun and Orimolade took the revival to other parts of Yorubaland on extended missionary journeys, and they challenged witchcraft openly. This brought them into considerable conflict with both traditional and colonial authorities. In 1925, they founded the first Aladura church, and gave it the name the Eternal Sacred Order of Cherubim and Seraphim Society. There were to be several schisms in the Cherubim and Seraphim movement.

The Aladura movement was a Pentecostal revival movement of massive proportions, later influenced by western Pentecostalism but usually only on the invitation of African church leaders. This movement fundamentally changed the face of West African Christianity. As they did to the African churches before them, so the Aladura churches themselves were overtaken and impacted by a new wave of Pentecostalism that swept over Africa in general and West Africa in particular in the second half of the twentieth century – but that is another era and another story.[65] Like the Zionists and Apostolics in southern Africa (who had more Pentecostal influence), these churches presented a more penetrating challenge to older European churches than the earlier independent churches had done. Their growth posed fundamental questions about the essence of Christianity in Africa and its leadership. In southern Africa, they were sometimes aided and abetted by foreign Pentecostal missionaries, who worked with them for a while but whose ideas African leaders borrowed from freely yet selectively. This was a specifically *African* Christian response, despite the outward trappings of rituals and customs that were innovations rather than continuations of African symbols. In this regard, these new African churches represented a radical reformation of African Christianity.[66]

Pentecostal Missionaries in Southern Africa

At the other end of the continent and with a milder climate due to its high altitude in the interior and distance from the tropics, South Africa was one of the earliest and most-favoured places for Pentecostal missionaries. Among the first Pentecostal missionaries to South Africa were Henry (1850–1920) and Anna Turney. Turney was an evangelist in Alaska when he heard about Azusa Street. He went there in 1906 for his personal Pentecost, then travelled on to San Jose, California, where he opened up Pentecostal work. He wrote, 'I am soon expecting to start around the world preaching full salvation as I go, trusting my heavenly Father to supply all my needs.'[67] In early 1907, Turney was in Honolulu, Hawaii, opening up a Pentecostal centre. He wrote that he and his wife had both spoken in Korean, and that therefore Korea would be their 'next field of labor'.[68] But by January 1908 the Turneys were on their way to Africa via England, where they stayed over a year. They were with Cecil Polhill in Bedford and ministered in several places, including Birmingham and various places in Kent, and they held the first Pentecostal meetings in Paris – where the first two to receive Spirit baptism in France were the basis for a Pentecostal Mission under Michel Mast. The Turneys started work with Hannah James (from the Railway Mission in Bedford and one of the Turneys' converts) in the Transvaal in South Africa in early 1909, at first working with the Apostolic Faith Mission (AFM) in Pretoria and from 1911 with the Pentecostal Mission at

Doornkop near Middelburg. By 1916 their work had affiliated with the American AG, the first AG work in South Africa. Turney reported on his work to several Pentecostal papers, including itinerating by donkey cart in the Pietersburg district where African evangelists had started Pentecostal churches. In 1911 opposition to the work caused Turney to make an urgent appeal for funds to secure a new mission site in Doornkop, where he remained until his death in 1920.[69] Anna Turney and Hannah James were listed as American AG missionaries in 1931, still stationed in Middelburg.[70]

Thomas Hezmalhalch (1847–1934), who with John G. Lake (1870–1935), Jacob Lehman and others began the Apostolic Faith Mission in South Africa in 1908, was an itinerant preacher of British stock in his sixties in Glendale, California. He had been a Holiness pastor who had received Spirit baptism at Azusa Street. At various stages he was found preaching in different parts of Colorado, to the Mojave Amerindians in California, and leading a church in Indianapolis and a new Pentecostal outreach in Zion City, Illinois, where he became acquainted with Lake. Lake was a former elder there who had received Spirit baptism through the ministry of Parham in Zion City in 1906 and was involved in Glen Cook's meetings in Indianapolis in early 1907. The team was identified with the Pentecostal work in Indianapolis and sent from there to South Africa. Because of his seniority, Hezmalhalch was regarded as leader of this group and became the first president of the Apostolic Faith Mission, although Lake was the more charismatic.[71] Lily and Jacob Lehman were returning missionaries who had been six years in South Africa (Lehman had gone to Bulawayo, Southern Rhodesia in 1901), they were able to speak Zulu and had received Spirit baptism at Cook's meetings in Indianapolis.

With hardly enough funds for the voyage, the Pentecostal missionary party of seven adults and seven Lake children sailed third-class for South Africa via Liverpool in April 1908, after being 'called' during a missionary convention in Indianapolis that February.[72] The Zionist connections of the American missionaries proved extremely fruitful. Pieter L. le Roux, a former Dutch Reformed missionary working in Wakkerstroom near the Natal border, had joined Dowie's Zionist movement in 1902 or 1903 and become an elder, together with some 400 African fellow-workers and converts, a group that had reached 5,000 by 1905. They were baptized in 1904 by Daniel Bryant, Dowie's appointed Overseer for South Africa.[73] Le Roux, an Afrikaner, was to become the first South African president of the Apostolic Faith Mission of South Africa (AFM), a position he held for more than 30 years. There were other fortuitous circumstances for the Pentecostals. Bryant, on his return to the USA in 1906, had become disaffected with Dowie's successor Wilbur Voliva and had left the movement. He had also encouraged his followers to seek a deeper baptism in the Spirit. It seems that his disaffection had spread to his South African followers, who welcomed the Zionists-turned-Pentecostals with open arms. Carrie Montgomery also records that Bryant led a large faction in Zion City and that the Pentecostal faction united with Bryant's church for services in which she preached. A letter of Lake to Bryant referring to some of his former converts in Johannesburg appeared in Pentecostal publications and Bryant was actually a featured preacher in a Pentecostal convention in Indianapolis in 1910.[74] The Zion converts of le Roux in the Wakkerstroom area became the source out of which eventually a whole series of African Zionist denominations emerged throughout southern Africa. Two of the Zulu leaders associated with le Roux were Daniel Nkonyane and Fred Lutuli, both of whom already had hundreds of followers of their own by 1905 and were to found significant African independent Zionist churches after breaking with the AFM from 1910 onwards.[75]

The American missionaries were soon writing back to their supporters of the amazing things that had happened since their arrival. They had been offered a house free of charge by an American woman they met by divine appointment at the Johannesburg station. Lake wrote of how God had 'wonderfully blessed their work in Johannesburg and Pretoria so that 'manifestations of the Spirit have been intense in their power and depth of character beyond anything I have known'. Daily meetings with packed audiences with 'instant' healings, people falling to the ground 'under the power' and other manifestations of the Spirit were reported. Back in the USA, these events were regarded as the most remarkable of the reports from Pentecostal missionaries anywhere in the world. 'In fact', exuded Lake, 'it is the most wonderful Apostolic Faith work I have yet seen'. He said that 'Johannesburg was never so religiously stirred before', and that he was receiving so many enquirers that he had 'hardly been able to eat, let alone sleep'.[76] The services began in an American Congregational 'native' church in Doornfontein, an area inhabited mainly by 'Coloured' (Afrikaans-speaking mixed race) and African people. This soon became too small, and the Pentecostal team were given the unrestricted use of the 500-seater Zion Tabernacle in Bree Street, Johannesburg. Lehman observed 'the prejudice that exists with the white people against the natives' and that because of the whites coming to the meetings, 'the natives became timid and were crowded out'. The Zion Tabernacle's larger capacity had seemingly solved the problem temporarily, soon becoming the Central Tabernacle of the Apostolic Faith Mission, and the 'Doornfontein Tabernacle' continued as a venue for 'Coloured' services.[77]

Their activities included healing services, meetings in various homes throughout the city, and meetings in mine compounds among labourers from many parts of southern Africa.[78] By August 1908 Hezmalhalch had travelled to Wakkerstroom – it seems, at le Roux's invitation – and from there he went on to Vryheid in Natal, working among the hundreds of Zionist Africans in that area and reporting many healings. One report put the number of healings at 'at least 2000' during a six-week trip. Louie Schneiderman and Jacob Lehman soon joined him there and reports continued of another 500 'instantly healed'.[79] The reports refer to 'native evangelists' but, as usual, do not mention names. We do know that one of those working in this region with le Roux was Daniel Nkonyane, who later led one of the first African secessions from the AFM. It appears that the growth of South African Pentecostalism among the African population was initially as a result of Zionist leaders joining the movement and reports of healings, and that American missionaries used these Zionist contacts to promote their work. Lehman reported exuberantly that 'God has already raised up more than a score of workers consisting of English, Dutch [Afrikaner] and natives of various tribes who are baptised with the Holy Ghost, and the signs follow them as well as they do us. Hallelujah!'[80] Lake lost his wife Jenny to rheumatic fever in December 1908, leaving him with seven children to care for alone.

A long letter to Levi Lupton published in May 1909 was written just before Lake's departure to Volksrust for a conference with the 'native preachers under our baptized brother, Elder le Roux'. Le Roux had joined the movement with 'thirty-five native preachers ministering to five thousand people'. Lake pleaded for 'divine order and system' in Pentecostal activities. He wrote that there were now 'at least fifty thousand' people for whom the AFM was responsible, and he mentions other South African missionaries with whom he was working, Edgar Mahon and Jack Armstrong. Mahon was also a former Zionist leader and earlier a Salvation Army captain who had a large following in the Orange Free State. Lake gives his opinion that because these white South African missionaries already spoke 'Dutch' and 'native languages' and did not 'live in the luxurious way that the Americans have been accustomed to', they were 'a better class of missionary than the average foreign missionary'. He asked for support for these workers. The majority of whites joining the Apostolic Faith Mission were Afrikaners, and Lake was soon to plead for support for Afrikaner workers who were 'far superior to any that can come from America' because they had 'always lived among the natives' – although he stated that the Afrikaner was like the American Southerner with 'strong prejudice on his part against the blacks' that only the Holy Spirit could remove. The American missionaries appealed for funds for two overseers in particular, one of whom was undoubtedly le Roux, 'a strong, clear-headed Africander [sic] who understands the natives and their customs' and had a 'native work touching 35,000 people'. Support for such a person would be 'worth as much in the extension of the Kingdom of God as twenty American missionaries would be'.[81] While these statements might not have endeared Lake to his American readers and fellow-missionaries, he seemed to have won the hearts of many Afrikaners with his anti-British views (perhaps gleaned from Dowie in Zion City) and his sympathy with the Afrikaners' plight since the recent Anglo–Boer War.

A number of other Pentecostal missionaries arrived in 1908 and 1909, apparently independently of each other, including Charles and Emma Chawner from Toronto, who took over Hezmalhalch's work in Vryheid, Natal among the Zulu. Archibald Cooper, a former British soldier during the Anglo–Boer War who had remained in South Africa as a British shipping agent and joined the new Pentecostal movement, was prominent in the formation of the Pentecostal Mission, later the Full Gospel Church, after the rupture with Lake (see below). Cooper, running the Pentecostal Mission mainly among the Afrikaner farmers in Middelburg, worked with William Elliott from Ohio, in charge of the 'PMU' (Lupton) work among Africans. Elliott had been influenced through *The Apostolic Faith* newspaper and became a Pentecostal in May 1907. He gave up his business and went to Levi Lupton's school for 15 months before leaving with his wife and four children for Cape Town in November 1909. From there they went to Johannesburg and concentrated on work in the mine compounds and 'native meetings' in their house, before starting the Doornkop mission in 1910, a year before the Turneys went there. The work at Doornkop was reported on regularly in the periodicals by Elliott,

Turney, Edgar Slaybaugh and other workers, and there was a growing network of 'native preachers' representing this mission who took the Pentecostal message abroad.[82]

The first executive council of the AFM was appointed in 1909, made up of five Americans: Elliott, Lehman, Turney, Lake and Hezmalhalch; and two Afrikaners: R. H. van der Waal (usually spelled van de Wall) and Schuman (Schoeman). By 1910 the executive consisted of only two Americans: Lake and Hezmalhalch (the latter was dismissed as President that year); and five Afrikaners, including van der Waal, a former Dutch Reformed minister and le Roux.[83] A meeting between white representatives of the Zion church and the AFM executive in 1909 agreed that le Roux would be in charge of the Zion mission work (African churches) in the Transvaal, and that these two organizations would 'mutually acknowledge each other's [preaching] certificates'. Pentecostalism did not take the place of Dowie's Zionism in South Africa, but the new message of the power of the Spirit was simply added to it. The executive council resolved in 1910 that 'whereas the natives deem the name of Zion so essential that this portion of our Mission be known henceforth as the Zion Branch of the Apostolic Faith Mission'.[84] Van der Waal gave a comprehensive account of the various places where white AFM workers were holding services at the end of 1909, most of the names being those of Afrikaners. Besides four different venues in Johannesburg, the work had spread to 17 other towns and districts throughout the Transvaal, Natal, the Orange River Colony (Free State) and Basutoland (Lesotho). Letters appearing in the Pentecostal periodicals reported on extensive work being carried on in the Free State and Lesotho (largely through the efforts of Edward Lion and Edgar Mahon), and large 'native conferences' were held every year by Lake and his team in Bloemfontein. The seeds of division had already formed. Africans leaders with their proven talents were simply left out of all administrative authority. Lehman was forced to have the Africans worship in the same building in Commissioner Street, Johannesburg (at different times to the whites), but this was clearly a temporary measure until he could procure a separate building for them.[85]

South African Pentecostalism was very quickly segregated. Although the very first meetings in the Zion church in Johannesburg were integrated, within a few months segregation was practised. This led to a whole series of secessions from 1910 onwards, when Daniel Nkonyane started the first 'Zulu Zion' church.[86] In a letter to his American supporters, Lehman commented on the 'very unsatisfactory' arrangements in the Zion tabernacle and the 'terrible barrier of race distinction' that 'could be our greatest difficulty'. This had caused the 'native work' in Johannesburg to be independent of the 'white work' from March 1909. Lehman thought that 'no one else had the burden of the natives of Johannesburg on their hearts', and he secured a separate hall rented by the Africans themselves. He worked for a time with Edgar Slaybaugh in the mine compounds, hospitals and prisons, and by this method the Pentecostal message spread as far as Nyasaland (Malawi) and Portuguese East Africa (Mozambique), Slaybaugh writing of preaching to 'the Blantyre [Malawi] tribe of Central Africa' in 1910. Lehman continued his work in the mine compounds and hospitals around Johannesburg for eleven years, but made occasional trips further away, one being to the Soutpansberg district in the Limpopo province with James Brooke of the Apostolic Faith Church from Britain in 1912. Slaybaugh had become a Pentecostal at Lupton's school in 1907 and had arrived in South Africa at the end of 1908.

Lake and Hezmalhalch returned to the USA and visited (among other places) Durham's mission in Chicago in September 1909 and the Upper Room in Los Angeles. During their absence, van der Waal was left in charge of the Central Tabernacle in Johannesburg, assisted temporarily by le Roux.[87] During 1910 the two missionaries fell out, with Hezmalhalch being influenced by other missionaries (initiated by E. M. Scurrah and including Archibald Cooper and George Bowie, another American missionary), who had charged Lake with financial irregularities, being 'a second Dowie', and failing to forward funds sent for African workers. Lake, however, continued to get the support of all the Afrikaner and African AFM workers. There were also rumours of exaggerated reports made by the missionaries, George Berg in India lamenting those who had been 'misled by big reports from South Africa' resulting in 'thousands of dollars' being sent there letting 'God's work suffer elsewhere'.[88] This complaint came from someone who would soon suffer similar accusations and go home in disgrace. The Upper Room in Los Angeles (Lake's largest financial supporter) published a full vindication of Lake in November 1910, stating that they were fully satisfied with Lake's integrity with regard to the charges against him. The AFM executive minus Hezmalhalch wrote a letter of support for Lake through its secretary van der Waal, stating that the accusations were 'petty jealousies' which South Africans were not taking notice of, as they were 'chiefly for the eyes of the saints in America'; and the African leader Elias Letwaba wrote a letter of support for Lake, stating that the accusations were 'all lies'. Hezmalhalch was dismissed from the presidency and returned to California, leaving Lake in charge of the AFM.[89]

This event seemed to mark the first denominational schism in South African Pentecostalism, with Lake, le Roux, Letwaba, Frank Dugmore (another American missionary) and most Afrikaner Pentecostals in the AFM; and Bowie, Cooper, Lehman, Turney and their converts associated with the Pentecostal Mission – although Lehman had by then joined the PHC – an affiliation he maintained until his return to the USA in 1920, because of his wife's ill health. He ministered in Long Beach, California and joined the AG in 1926. Lake returned to the USA in 1913, when le Roux took over as president of the AFM, but remained in contact. His son Wilford was a visiting evangelist in the AFM Central Tabernacle in 1917.[90] The Pentecostal Mission under George Bowie and Cooper in Middelburg included Turney's mission at Doornkop and Lehman's work in Johannesburg. This group was to split again into the Full Gospel Church and the Assemblies of God, and eventually into further factions. They held their first convention in Middelburg over Christmas and New Year 1910–11.[91]

Expatriate Pentecostal missionaries continued to come to southern Africa. Frances Taylor, a Miss Harris (who was killed in a riding accident) and Maggie Gourlay, English missionaries in contact with Alexander Boddy, were working in Mbabane, Swaziland, in 1910. Kenneth Spooner, an African American, arrived in 1915 and worked with Lehman in the PHC, looking after several congregations in the Rustenburg area west of Johannesburg for several years.[92] William Wallis left from the Stone Church in Chicago in 1910 and stayed with the Armstrongs in Pretoria, working in that area with interpreters into Dutch while waiting for direction to go north to the Zambezi and the Congo. By 1914 he was in Bulawayo in Southern Rhodesia (Zimbabwe) at the mission of George and Johanna Hitchcock, the first permanent Pentecostal missionaries in Zimbabwe and former Salvation Army officers who spent the rest of their lives in Bulawayo working under James Brooke in the Apostolic Faith Church and after a schism in the 1920s, the United Apostolic Faith Church.[93] The AFM's Frank Dugmore was arranging for a permanent mission station with a white worker in Gwanda, Zimbabwe in 1917 where Elias Kgobe was working and 400 had been baptized. The Luttigs went to Gatooma (Kadoma) in the centre of the country in 1918 and other white South African AFM missionaries followed.[94] There were also Pentecostal missionaries from the Rochester Bible Training School in New York (Elim Tabernacle), Roy and Blanche Vernon, who went to Kasempa, Northern Rhodesia (Zambia) in 1914 (Mrs Vernon died of a fever in 1915), and Ernest Hooper of the Pentecostal Mission was opening churches in rural parts of Mozambique by 1919, but living in South Africa.[95]

In June 1910 a party of three young American missionaries – the newly-wed David and Marie Gillies and Edgar Slaybaugh – left Middelburg on a four-day, third-class train journey to Salisbury, Rhodesia (now, Harare, Zimbabwe). They found living in the town too expensive and so procured a tent in which to live a mile outside the town.[96] It appears that they had intended to proceed across the Zambezi towards the Congo by ox-wagon, but Slaybaugh turned back after reaching the Zambezi valley. The reason Slaybaugh gave for the change in plans was that he had found 'the natives very few in number compared to the thickly settled multitudes in the Northern Transvaal' (not an accurate assessment); and so he returned to Doornkop to help in the establishment of a 'Bible school' for training in evangelistic work. He makes an interesting observation on the difference between the 'native work' and the 'white work' that there was 'a readiness for the reception of the truth, a depth of spirituality, sacredness of worship, and a spiritual sweetness of the presence and approval of God upon the native meetings that cannot be found in the white work'.[97] The Gillies continued on their journey and proceeded to Elisabethville (Lubumbashi) in Katanga, Congo, where Marie Gillies died and her husband probably returned to South Africa as he is not mentioned again. John and Thomas Armstrong went to Rhodesia late in 1910 with their families as missionaries where John died of a fever, to be followed by their father in the Congo five years later.[98]

African Leaders in South Africa

There is much less information on the many early African Pentecostal leaders in South Africa than there is on Lake and his expatriate missionaries. These African leaders made this movement vigorous and dynamic, missionaries and pioneers in their own right with influence far beyond their own churches' spheres. They played a remarkable role in the future history and development of Christianity in South Africa. Clearly, the work of Lehman and others in the gold mines employing contract workers from several southern African countries was an important means of spreading Pentecostal ideas in ways that the western missionaries could not have imagined, and certainly played a significant role in the increasing pentecostalization of newly emerging independent churches. In 1910 Lake reported that there were 250 'native preachers' and 100 white preachers in the AFM. Lehman referred to several African workers by their first names only, including Timothy, Johannes, Ingraham and Soloman, all of whom had returned to their homes (mostly in Zululand) as Pentecostal preachers, with success mingled with persecution. Lehman wrote that he had several 'native helpers' who were in 'secular work', but he needed full-time African workers like Lohabalala who were 'able evangelists whom God is using in our midst'. Lehman was one of the few who attempted to give credit to African workers.[99] Elliott made mention of the African preachers working with him in itinerant preaching from Doornkop: David Mokwena (later in the AFM), Josiah Mokabane, Daniel Mogoane and Asaph Tlaka. Slaybaugh mentioned an African preacher at the Premier Mine called Nehemiah, and Turney mentions David Mokwena and Elias Kgobe as prominent African evangelists in their work.[100] Kgobe, a relative of Elias Letwaba, became a Pentecostal in about 1911 and worked with the AFM after the split with the Pentecostal Mission took place, and was responsible for church planting in areas as far away as Zimbabwe and the Transkei. In 1920 he was based in Springs. Mokwena was first mentioned by name as one of the evangelists going from Doornkop to the Cullinan Mine in 1910 and to the Pietersburg district in 1911, where he is called 'our native minister'. Turney made appeals for funds to support the opening of new mission stations in the Northern Transvaal. In charge at the mission school at Chief Manamela's village was Evangelist Joseph Sono, while Evangelist Josiah Mokabane was in charge at the Premier Mine.[101]

Elias Letwaba (c. 1870–1959) was one of the first African preachers to become Pentecostal and certainly one of the best known. William Burton was to publish his biography in 1934 in which P. L. le Roux wrote in a brief foreword that 'the name of Letwaba is known as no other of our native preachers and workers'.[102] Letwaba was born in Potgietersrust (now Limpopo province) in about 1870. His mother received a remarkable revelation about his future. His father, an Ndebele Christian who spoke Dutch at home, did not allow his son to attend the customary initiation school, and Letwaba was raised in a Christian environment. At the age of 14 he rescued a white man from drowning in a river and felt called by God 'to rescue men and women out of the black river of sin and death'.[103] At this time he received a Bible from his farmer employer, and in 1887 he joined the Berlin Lutheran Mission and went into training as a preacher. Besides being fluent in several African languages, Letwaba learned German, could speak English and Dutch/Afrikaans, and he read many books. During his lifetime, like many other Africans, he became fluent in several languages and was for the most part self-educated. In 1890 he joined the newly formed Bapedi Lutheran Church (an independent 'Ethiopian' church founded by a disaffected Berlin missionary) where he worked for 19 years. Letwaba travelled through hundreds of villages preaching and made 'thousands of converts' during this period.[104]

Not much else is known about his early ministry, but it seems that when he met Lake at the beginning of 1909 he had joined the Zionists and was a respected minister in the Zion Apostolic Church. Burton recorded an incident when Letwaba first attended one of Lake's meetings: 'Lake put his arm about the black man's neck and kissed him, calling him "My brother", while many of the unconverted white men in the hall booed and hissed at him.'[105] Letwaba was so impressed by the miracles of God's power that he decided to stay with Lake in his home to learn from him – further evidence of Lake's ambivalent position with regard to the race issue. He accompanied Lake on his journey to Bloemfontein and received the Pentecostal 'baptism' there in February 1909. Lake, who was usually patronizing and racist in his comments about 'native workers' who could not function (he thought) without white supervision, made an exception of Letwaba who he conceded was 'equal to many white workers'.[106] Hezmalhalch also reported remarkable miracles and healings in Letwaba's ministry, including four people reported to be raised from the dead.[107] Letwaba is mentioned in the executive council minutes of the AFM in February 1909 and in missionary letters. He was married to Jessie, also a very capable Pentecostal worker. One of the American missionaries called Letwaba 'our best native Basuto missionary' – he was not 'Basuto', but spoke 'Sesuto'. Theo Schwede, a young American who worked closely with Letwaba in the Waterberg district, wrote that Letwaba was 'the most godly man I ever saw' – high praise indeed.[108] Van der Waal listed him and J. M. Morivane, 'a qualified native minister', as 'presiding elders' in the AFM in 1909, with widespread responsibilities to supervise 'native work' throughout the country. Other native workers mentioned by name then are J. Mokwena and Jesayo Mphaphane. Van der Waal describes Letwaba as 'the native minister' in the Waterberg district and 'of princely blood . . . strong in his humility and trust in God'. His ministry had been 'especially blessed in the prayer of faith for the sick and suffering'.[109] A mission house was opened in Potgietersrus in 1910, from where Letwaba's brother Wilfred worked as pastor and a small school was run by a teacher, E. M. Makgatha, whom Schwede described as a 'Holy Ghost man and a good missionary'.[110]

Occasional reports of Letwaba filtered through to the overseas Pentecostal press, who reported that he was 'such a godly and blessed fellow laborer in preaching the gospel to the natives in South Africa'.[111] In April 1910 Letwaba, based at Potgietersrus, was working with Schwede in the Waterberg district of what is now the Limpopo Province, and they reported 329 baptisms, with six places of worship in the district and 12 local preachers. Schwede left to return to the USA in June that year suffering from physical exhaustion, but Letwaba commended him warmly: 'He is the man who did sleep with the natives in their huts; he ate their food, which I myself, as a native, sometimes could not eat; God put us together and made us one.'[112] This was a remarkable testimony in 1910 South Africa, the year that the former Boer republics and British colonies united as the Union of South Africa. The first prime minister was an Afrikaner and former Boer general. Africans were never given voting rights and the die had been cast for the National Party government in 1948 and apartheid ideology.[113] Clearly, African Pentecostal preachers and some missionaries did not accept social customs that forced segregation.

But Letwaba was a victim of his time and his experience of integration short-lived. By 1913, he was holding his own conferences for his followers and had a considerable following. He preached a gospel of salvation, healing and Spirit baptism and lived on a salary of five pounds a month. His first convert to Pentecostalism was his father, who also received Spirit baptism. Letwaba asked Lake's team to join him on an evangelistic tour of Limpopo province, but they were not able to complete this journey because the missionaries found the conditions physically too strenuous. Letwaba continued on his own in what was his home country, walking 'many hundreds of miles, along dusty roads, and twisting paths, and through tangled thorn-tree scrub'.[114] He encountered considerable persecution.[115] Letwaba's ministry was characterized by reported healings and miracles.[116] Lake himself wrote about Letwaba in 1912 in one of the early editions of the AFM's periodical *The Comforter*, in which he spoke of a 'great drought' in that part of the country. Letwaba was preaching to a large crowd when 'the Lord caused him to prophesy that before the next morning there should be abundance of rain'. Lake went on, 'He continued in prayer all night, apparently submerged in the Spirit, and was only aroused by the rain falling upon him . . . the Chiefs called a thanksgiving meeting. The Holy Ghost fell mightily upon the people, with pungent [sic] conviction for sin.' Letwaba had reported that 'hundreds were saved'.[117] On another occasion, which Lake afterwards related to Seymour in Los Angeles, Letwaba prayed for a boy who had fallen and broken his neck. Lake left the room because he 'did not have faith for a broken neck' and did not want to 'interfere' with Letwaba's faith. Letwaba carried on praying, and the boy was reported healed.[118]

In 1921 Elias Letwaba and David Mokwena were appointed as the first African marriage officers in the AFM, which meant they were the only ones given full ministerial responsibilities in this denomination.[119] Perhaps this was a gesture on the part of the white leaders in order to arrest the secessions that were beginning to proliferate. Letwaba felt that he should develop his ministry of healing and for two years he travelled far and wide (even going to Zimbabwe), reporting over 10,000 healings and 100,000 conversions by the late 1920s.[120] Although it goes beyond the timeframe of this study, one of the highlights of Letwaba's achievements was the establishment in 1930 of the Patmos Bible School, the first theological training facility for Blacks in the AFM, started on Letwaba's own initiative and without financial help from the white AFM. He ran a three-year course there and did much of the teaching himself, being a gifted Bible expositor. It took another two decades before an 'official' AFM Bible school was created, but in one report 'many thousands of graduates' from this school were 'teaching and preaching the Gospel throughout Africa'.[121] Elias Letwaba died in 1959, and he was buried in the Waterberg district in the Limpopo province where he had spent most of his life and ministry. Significantly, influential American Pentecostal leader Gordon Lindsay considered that it was Letwaba more than any other person who has 'carried on the great work started by John G. Lake in Africa. It is still going on today.'[122]

In 1916 this remarkably significant letter by the then Secretary of the AFM, Frank Dugmore was published, of which I reproduce a large portion:

Our policy is, and has been from the beginning, one of trusting the native. It would seem that right here has been the failure in all the Mission work that has been done in South Africa. The natives have been trusted, and have failed; the trust has been withdrawn, and color has been blamed, and confidence has been destroyed.

God has put in no color bar in His Word, and the example of our Lord was to choose ignorant fisher men to be His representatives, and to endue with His heavenly power.

The natives are able preachers, and, though they sometimes err in doctrine, they are mighty in faith. The native peoples of South Africa are awakening from their dark past. Self-consciousness and national conscious-ness is dawning among them. This is naturally evident among their leading thinkers, who are usually religious men also.

Before the event of the Apostolic Faith Mission in South Africa, Ethiopian-ism (a word used to describe a spirit of Independence and refusal to recog-nize European control among the natives of South Africa) was a strong force. Within the AFM they have found that they are trusted, and given scope to work for the Lord, so that today Ethiopianism is nothing like the same force that it was, and this forward movement among the natives which is out of touch with the Government, has the touch and sympathy of the Europeans of the Apostolic Faith Mission.

We have big responsibilities resting upon us, and a situation that always needs the most delicate handling. Could we take hold of this movement among the natives for God, in the manner and measure that I think God would have us do, it could sweep right through South Africa, and not only South Africa, but Central Africa, and the Soudan.[123]

Amazing as this letter appeared, Dugmore was still an American whose enlightened views were certainly not shared by all white South African Pentecostals at the time. Clearly, Letwaba was one of these trusted 'natives' referred to in his letter. Just as clearly, the AFM saw itself as a catalyst for the channelling of African preachers into their work rather than into independ-ency. As the following years were to show and despite Dugmore's admirable intentions, they did not handle this very well (to put it mildly) and Africans began to resist the domination of white overseers over what was largely their work. Some missionaries felt that Dugmore's policy was a step too far. Burton wrote that Lake had been caught out into adopting Ethiopian churches that were often 'turned into breeding grounds for anti-European political propa-ganda' and 'start to teach freedom from the European rule'.[124] God forbid that *that* should ever happen! And of course, many early African leaders did not maintain the same harmonious relationship with the white AFM leaders that Letwaba enjoyed. The trust broke down and in the majority of cases the Africans began to work independently of the whites. In what follows we will focus on two of the most prominent examples.

The first is Edward Lion, also known as Edward of Basutoland (Lesotho) or Edward Motaung (Sotho for 'lion person'), who chose the name 'Lion' for him-self after a disagreement with other members of his father's family, Motaung. We do not know much about him or how he came to be Pentecostal, but he seems to have been one of Edgar Mahon's first converts and according to one observer, 'the most spectacular of the Sotho Zionists of an earlier generation'.[125] The reports about him have become legendary and at least as long as he was in the good books of the white missionaries, several brief hagiographical accounts of his ministry are extant. On one occasion he baptized 130 converts in the Caledon River – 'the first mass baptism in that Sotho Jordan'. Lake also wrote about the healing ministry of Lion, who was from a poor background and 'until a few years ago, didn't even wear clothes'. Lake gushed over with superlatives. When 'a multitude of sick folk' were brought to Lion, 'the power of God came upon him and he went upon the mountainside, stretched out his hands over the sick below, and poured out his heart to God. In a minute, hundreds were healed! Healing power fell upon them.'[126]

Lake also told of an occasion in Lesotho on Christmas Eve 1912, where 75 healed lepers were given Communion by 'a black fellow whose sole raiment when we first knew him was a goatskin apron' – Lake was probably referring to Lion.[127] But Edward Lion was no ignoramus. Frank Dugmore attended an AFM convention in Basutoland led by Lion in 1914 and not only did he report that 'rich blessing' followed his itinerant ministry, but he commented on how impressed he was by his preaching skills. Dugmore heard him 'present the contrast between the old and new covenants in a way that delighted my soul'.[128] Gordon Lindsay (following Burton) wrote that Edward 'Lyons' was a great preacher after his Pentecostal experience, and crowds of five to six thousand would gather to hear him preach, sometimes for the whole day. He had a remarkable healing ministry, and 'thousands' were reported healed as a result of his prayers. He is reputed to have spent whole nights praying for the sick until his strength was gone, after which he would ask his assistants to direct the long line of sick people to the stone on which he had sat, that they might also sit there and be healed.[129]

Lion was given oversight of the AFM work in Basutoland – it was largely his work, after all. He may have met the AFM (and possibly Lake) in Johannesburg in 1910 and joined in 1912. In any case, he was working with Vera Barnard, another American missionary in 1913. She wrote of 'healings and blessings' accompanying the team of 'natives, Edward Lion and party'.[130] In 1916 a British Pentecostal missionary, David Fisher, moved to Mafeteng in Basutoland to help Lion, who he wrote was 'being used by the Lord to the healing and salvation of very many', his converts were coming to 'repentance and true conversion', and were baptized and 'led to expect the baptism in the Holy Spirit'. Fisher also was in contact with another significant African founder of an independent church in Lesotho, Walter Matita, who at that stage was still 'connected with the Paris Society', but 'also has received the full baptism'.[131] Archibald Cooper also visited Lion's work in Lesotho, and was equally impressed that 'the works of an apostle have been done there'. He continued:

> God has given Brother Edward Lion and others (all natives) mighty ministries in the power of the Holy Ghost, and has especially used Brother Edward among the sick. He claims positively that the dead have been raised, that at least three deaf and dumb persons were wholly delivered; that many

blind ones have received their sight, and cripples healed through the laying on of hands, as well as other awful diseases. Many lepers also have been healed. This fact is indisputable. One of them I came in contact with and she gave me her own testimony. This woman had lost parts of four fingers and two thumbs before the Lord healed her of this terrible disease. It is truly the simplicity of the natives' faith that enables God to work so wonderfully among them.[132]

Just why Lion left the AFM is not clear, but among all the reasons it was probably as much connected to his being denied real leadership in the church on which he had had such an impact. In the minutes of the AFM executive council in 1921, Lion was still considered leader of the AFM in Lesotho. His apparent lack of submission to the white leaders 'as other native leaders do' made these leaders think it necessary to send a white man to 'take control' of his work – probably without much success. Unknown to the white leaders, however, Lion had already seceded to form the Zion Apostolic Faith Mission in 1920. Lindsay says that as the result of a lack of 'spiritually mature teachers' Lion 'got into error and gave fanciful and absurd prophecies which soon resulted in his being discredited'.[133] Nevertheless, this was a Pentecostal leader who was greatly influential in his time and one of the first early African Pentecostals intent on founding a 'city of Zion' after the pattern of Dowie – a very significant development, as future events were to prove.

The second example of an African leader who resisted white ecclesiastical domination was the founder of the Zion Christian Church, the largest denomination in South Africa. Engenas Lekganyane (c. 1880–1948), a preacher associated with the AFM, was so impressed by Lion that he joined him in about 1920 (possibly when he seceded), eventually leaving Lion's church to form the Zion Christian Church in 1925. The influence of Lion on Lekganyane was considerable, and Lekganyane even named his son Edward after him. Lekganyane was born in Thabakgone in the Mamabolo area of Limpopo province somewhere between 1880 and 1885. He was an evangelist in the Free Church of Scotland when he met le Roux and the AFM in Johannesburg soon after it started in 1908.[134] It appears that he was working in the area at the time and had suffered from an eye disease for many years. He had a vision in which a voice told him that if he went to Johannesburg he should join the church that baptized by triune immersion and thus find healing for his eyes. So, he joined the AFM, was baptized in the Spirit and at first was a member of a congregation near his home, at the time called the Zion Apostolic Church. This may have been one of Letwaba's congregations. He met the Mahlangu brothers, Elias and Joseph (or Johannes) on his arrival in Johannesburg in 1912, probably the same 'Elias' that Elliott reported on at the Premier Mine in 1910, who had received the Spirit in a remarkable way and had spoken in several languages. (Elias's Ndebele name Mahlangu supports this possibility, as the mine is in an Ndebele area.) Elliot remarked that this wonderful event took place 'without any white missionary being there'. Elias and Johannes Mahlangu are also mentioned as being part of a team of AFM African preachers and missionaries at a conference in Basutoland in 1914. Another Zulu independent church leader, Ezra Mbonambi, is also mentioned in this report as being in the AFM party.[135]

It is difficult to reconstruct the sequence of events in Lekganyane's early ministry. One report has it that Mahlangu baptized Lekganyane and he was healed of his eye sickness. Another account suggests that Lekganyane may have been baptized by Mahlangu and could have visited Johannesburg on an earlier occasion, when he met le Roux. A Zionist historian Lukhaimane admits that Lekganyane and le Roux 'knew each other closely' and that Lekganyane got his preaching credentials from le Roux.[136] In 1916 the strains of the relationship were beginning to tell. Lekganyane was ordained and there was a split in the local congregation over the name of the church – Lekganyane favoured the name 'Zion Apostolic Church' rather than Apostolic Faith Mission. He started his own congregation in his home village Thabakgone, but soon rejoined an AFM congregation under the leadership of Timothy Mamabolo.[137] These events probably coincided with Mahlangu leaving the AFM in 1917 and forming the Zion Apostolic Church of South Africa. Lekanyane seems to have been part of this secession. Mamabolo died in 1918 and Lekanyane became the leader of Mahlangu's Zion Apostolic Church in the Limpopo province. He was a powerful preacher and won many converts. In 1917 Lekganyane prophesied the defeat of Germany by Britain and when this happened a year later his prestige as a prophet and 'man of God' grew. It seems that he continued with Mahlangu for about three years after his break with the AFM but that differences soon developed between them. Customs that were promoted by Mahlangu and which Lekganyane found objectionable were the wearing of white robes, the compulsory growing of beards by (adult male) members, and taking off shoes before services. These practices are found in many Zionist and Apostolic churches, but have not been observed by the Zion Christian Church. His final break with Mahlangu came in 1920, when he went to Lesotho and joined up with Lion's Zion Apostolic Faith Mission. There he was ordained as bishop for this church in the northern provinces.

At about this time, while praying on a mountain near his home, Lekganyane had a revelation through a whirlwind that a multitude of people would follow him. He was encouraged by this encounter to have faith, because God would give him strength to found a large church. Lekganyane's marriage to a second wife precipitated the break with Lion, who opposed polygamy. But the main reason for Lekganyane's break with Mahlangu and later with Lion was probably a leadership power struggle. Once again, differences emerged, mainly on administrative matters, and at the end of 1924 or the beginning of 1925 he returned to Thabakgone to found his own church, the Zion Christian Church. In 1925, when he first applied for government recognition (refused), he claimed 926 adherents in 15 congregations in the Limpopo and Mpumalanga provinces and in the urban townships of Gauteng (around Johannesburg).[138] The church was to grow rapidly in the twentieth century to have government statistical membership of five million by 2001, twenty times the size of the AFM, the country's largest classical Pentecostal denomination. There are eight million more people who joined the thousands of Zionist and Apostolic churches that now exist in South Africa.[139]

The existence of these strong independent churches today has much to do with early Pentecostal missions. There are indications that Pentecostal missionaries tapped into a new phenomenon that was particularly strong in South

Africa. Lehman wrote of a whole tribal community in the north-west of the country that had with their chief seceded from 'a certain missionary society' because of the highhandedness of and exploitation by the missionaries. The reference is obscure, but he may have meant the event in 1885, when Tswana chief Kgantlapane helped found a church seceding from the London Missionary Society in Taun, Botswana, called the Native Independent Congregational Church. Near Middelburg, Lehman, Cooper and Elliott held services to welcome a group of secessionists into the Pentecostal fold and Lake visited an 'Ethiopian' church conference that was seeking affiliation with the AFM. Lake wrote of a 'native missionary', Paul Mabiletsa, who told Lake about a paralysed woman healed through prayer in the Germiston district. Mabiletsa founded the Apostolic Church in Zion in 1920, to become one of the larger Zionist churches whose leadership remained in the Mabiletsa family. Lake himself reported that 24 'native Catholic churches' and 'five large Ethiopian churches' had decided to affiliate with the AFM in 1910, and that the 'African Catholic Church' with 78 preachers joined in January 1911. Again in 1911 the 'Ethiopian Church' affiliated with Pastor Modred Powell to become the Apostolic Faith Church of South Africa. Clearly, many of the early Pentecostal 'converts' in South Africa were already members of Christian churches, especially African independent ones.[140] But the flow went both ways – by 1915 there were several secessions from the Pentecostals, especially from the AFM. Turney also complained of African women who had 'risen up refusing to acknowledge any authority in the church' and who were now 'trying to establish a church of their own, with a native as leader'.[141]

For the purposes of this study it is important to note the role of Pentecostalism and expatriate Pentecostal missionaries in the early years of African, Indian and Chinese independency and the links with some of its most significant leaders. The independent 'Zionist' and 'Apostolic' churches in South Africa together form the largest grouping of Christians in the country today. Although the independent churches may no longer be described as 'Pentecostal' without further qualification, the most characteristic features of their theology and praxis is overwhelmingly Pentecostal and, in the case of South Africa, also influenced by the Zionist movement of John Alexander Dowie. Healing, prophecy, speaking in tongues, and baptism by immersion (usually threefold), and even the rejection of medicine and the eating of pork, are some of these features that remain among these African churches. Whatever their motivation might have been, Pentecostal missions in South Africa were unwittingly catalysts for a much larger movement of the Spirit that was to dominate South African Christianity for the remainder of the twentieth century. Although these Zionist and Apostolic churches have gradually increased the distance between themselves and 'classical' Pentecostalism in liturgy and practice, their growth and proliferation are further evidence of the rapidly 'spreading fires' of the Spirit in Africa and deserve to be accounted for in any historical research on Pentecostalism.

The Congo Evangelistic Mission

Central Africa, and in particular the vast unexplored region of the Congo, held a particular fascination for the more intrepid missionaries. Although there were attempts to penetrate this vast region as early as 1910, Pentecostals were not really involved there until 1914, when British missionary Fred Johnstone was sent by the PMU to work with the Congo Inland Mission at Djoko Punda in Kasai among the Baluba.[142] Meanwhile, in the same year George Bowie and three other Americans from the Pentecostal Mission proceeded from British East Africa through present-day Kenya, Uganda and Rwanda to establish a mission in the Congo. One turned back, two contracted malaria, and one, Richardson, died in Rwanda. But Bowie and Ulyate walked 1,000 miles to the Congo river, went south by riverboat and secured a site for a station from the local chief before they returned to South Africa, where Ulyate soon died.[143]

William F. P. Burton (1886–1971) felt a special calling when he was six years old and an African American former slave turned evangelist, T. L. Johnson, visited his home in Surrey, England and prayed for him to be sent to Africa.[144] He became a Pentecostal in 1910 and trained under Thomas Myerscough in Preston and at the PMU training school in London. Controversy followed his unorthodox and independent ways, and brought him into conflict with the PMU Council,[145] but his mentor and supporter was Myerscough until his death in 1932. After pastoring churches while waiting for doors to open, Burton finally sailed for Africa in 1914, spending a year in South Africa and Lesotho before being joined by his friend James Salter. They headed north to the Belgian Congo (now the Democratic Republic of the Congo) in 1915 together with two Pentecostal Mission workers, George Armstrong and Joseph Blakeney. Arriving in Elizabethville (now Lubumbashi) they were treated favourably by the colonial authorities and among other things were given a licence 'to shoot all animals excepting elephants'. They proceeded to their first mission station at Mwanza Kasingu among the Luba people, but the older man Armstrong died of malaria before their arrival and Blakeney left to return to South Africa a month afterwards, leaving Burton and Salter alone. They began the urgent task of language acquisition and after a month were trying to preach in Kiluba, but recognized their great limitations in human communication. By the end of 1915 they were joined by two American women sent from Johannesburg by Bowie, Julia Richardson (an experienced missionary in Africa and the widow of the man who died in the Congo a year earlier) and Anna Hodges. They established a new station south of Mwanza but left the mission in 1917 through ill health.[146]

Burton, by profession an engineer, was an extremely talented person, being (among other skills) an adept linguist, author of many books, and a skilled builder, artist, poet, photographer, surveyor and cartographer. He benefited from a middle-class and public school background in England. After a few months at Mwanza, Burton and Salter were joined by a group of 14 emancipated Bekalebwe slaves from Angola led by a former slave raider, Shalumbo Kisoka. These had become evangelical Christians in Angola and were now returning to their homeland to preach the gospel. They immediately joined up with the new mission, which represented a quantum leap for the new mission

– so impressed was Burton by Shalumbo that he wrote one of his first books about him. Shalumbo became the first African evangelist in Burton's mission, working there for the next 20 years preaching and healing, resulting in much of its early success. In 1917 Burton wrote of 'two beloved and faithful black brothers, Shakayobo and Shalumbo', who with their wives and a younger man Shakitu 'never weary in the work of God, going out continually'.[147] The same year Shalumbo went with Salter on an extended preaching trip during which Salter contracted blackwater fever, and Burton wrote that Salter was 'raised up by the faithful prayers of our beloved black friend Shalumbo'.[148] He went on to describe the work of these African evangelists, who were 'never weary in the work of God, going out continually when we are needed nearer home, telling with eager earnestness of "this *Great Salvation*," and never so happy as when they come marching home with a handkerchief full of charms to burn'. He wanted them to rest, but they replied, 'Now we realize that war and famine are sounding out Jesus' coming, and we want everyone to know.' He went on, 'Their lives, their love, their prayers and their faithfulness are exemplary. We praise God indeed for these black co-workers, and trust that they may soon meet their fullest desire, in being filled with the Holy Spirit.' A year later Burton recorded that each of six 'native evangelists' held two to six meetings a day in six to eight villages a week, with an average weekly attendance of 6,300 people.[149] It seems that Shalumbo and the other evangelists from Angola only received Spirit baptism after the 'Luban Pentecost' at Mwanza in 1920 and had been resistant to this teaching at first.[150]

In 1917 Burton constructed a chapel and school building at Mwanza, partly in reaction to Catholic opposition. Because Catholics were teaching young people and sending them out as catechists, there was a possibility that villages won for Pentecostalism would be taken away from them – so it was necessary to teach the Christians in these villages 'to read, put Testaments in their hands, and send them out'. This underlined the urgent need for the mission to train 'native evangelists', he wrote.[151] The stage was set for the multiplication of mission stations after the model of the older missions. In 1918 Burton married a South African, Helen (Hetty) Trollip, and returned with her to Mwanza. By this time there were three new missionary 'recruits' from South Africa (two women and one man), and one American woman and a Brother Gatzke, who had arrived a year earlier (but was soon to leave), making a total of six. The new missionaries were immediately put to language learning.[152] Burton himself by 1920 had written down a Kiluba vocabulary of 15,000 words. By 1928 he was to institute a strict regime by which any missionary who could not preach in the local language after six months in the field would be sent home. In 1919 Shalumbo and the Burtons visited Shalumbo's birthplace 200 miles north of the mission in the Bekalebwe villages. He introduced the missionaries there, resulting in the Johnstones (the former PMU missionaries) establishing a station there in 1921. By 1922 there were 15 white missionaries and between 30 and 40 'native evangelists' in the mission.[153] The church formed by their converts was eventually called the Pentecostal Community of the Congo.

Shalumbo and his wife Masele eventually moved even further north to establish work in another unreached area at Mukombo Katanga. Eventually in their old age, they settled in Kipushya where they pastored a church at least until the 1930s, when Masele died. By 1937 Shalumbo was remarried and living and working in a neighbouring village and the record ends there.[154] Burton remarked that this man was responsible for 'revival after revival' and 'the opening up of great new areas of Central Africa for the Gospel of the Lord Jesus'.[155] Burton often referred incidentally (and sometimes anonymously) to such workers as Shalumbo, who were instrumental in spreading the Pentecostal gospel among their own people in the early stages, such as when Burton reported in February 1917 about 'one of our native christians' who had had just returned from a trip reporting 'splendid meetings', where 'ten adults, as well as children and young people, yielded to the Lord Jesus, bringing their charms and fetishes to burn'.[156]

Another of the CEM workers whom Burton chose to describe in his writings was Kangoi – like Shalumbo, one of the group of former slaves freed in Angola. Kangoi left Mwanza with his wife and children in about 1916 to travel east for some days to evangelize the village Bunda, a chief's village, and set up classes so that people could read the Bible. Among his first converts was the chief's brother Nongo, who persuaded the chief to allow the stranger to remain and continue his work in their village, although the chief himself opposed the work vehemently and eventually became a Catholic. On hearing of the plans of Catholics to set up a school in 'their' village to force them out, Burton immediately set out for Bunda, rounding up people on the way to help him carry building materials there, and he set up a chapel a day before the Catholic priest arrived. The scramble for Africa had reached the Catholics and the Pentecostals. When tin mining commenced in the district, Kangoi visited the compounds to evangelize the workers, but unfortunately, he left the mission and the district in order to seek a more affluent lifestyle. Behind his 'fall' was discontent with the 'wage' of 30 francs he was receiving from Mwanza. The work at Bunda received a serious setback, young Christians left to work in the mines, but it was continued by Nongo and another worker Fataki, until a trained evangelist, David Katontoka and his wife Yunishi, were sent to the village. The mission began to make steady progress again, including receiving the favour of the chief Penge and the chief's eventual and dramatic conversion.[157]

Burton's work had only just begun. A Bible school for the training of workers was started at Mwanza and the 'most promising' of the young evangelists who had already proved themselves in the different stations (as Burton put it) were trained there for two years.[158] Many of the African evangelists in the CEM were severely persecuted for their faith, being opposed by chiefs and witchdoctors, and they were lashed and beaten, imprisoned and poisoned. But the work of the CEM continued to grow in the region. Burton was to remain at Mwanza for 45 years in all, directing his mission until 1960, when the civil war in the Congo on the gaining of independence forced him out, now 74 years old. He wrote books about the mission, about the south-eastern Congo and its inhabitants, and about the things he had learnt there. From 1919 onwards Burton's mission was an independent one called the Congo Evangelistic Mission, although only officially organized as such in 1922, when Salter became Home Director in England.[159]

The earliest Pentecostal missions in Egypt, Liberia and South Africa, followed by missions in Kenya and the Congo and isolated missionaries elsewhere, were fraught with the real dangers of war, tropical disease and physical hardships for missionaries unprepared for the rigours of the African bush. Pentecostalism did not really thrive in Africa until later, but its pioneers had sown the seed for the explosive growth of Charismatic forms of Christianity that were to fundamentally alter the identity of African Christianity in the twentieth century.

Notes

1 *Conf* 6:7 (July 1913), pp.147–8.

2 *UR* 1:3 (Aug 1909), p.6; *LRE* 2:11 (Aug 1910), p.22; 2:12 (Sept 1910), p.20; 5:7 (Apr 1913), p.15; 6:2 (Nov 1913), p.19; *BM* 69 (1 Sept 1910), p.2; 129 (15 Mar 1913), p.1.

3 *THW*, p.238.

4 *FF* 9 (Jan 1913), p.2.

5 *BM* 68 (15 Aug 1910), p.1.

6 *LRE* 5:12 (Sept 1913), p.4.

7 *THW*, pp.240–1.

8 *THW*, pp.244–7, 258–9.

9 *AF* 1 (Sept 1906), p.4; 13 (May 1908), p.1.

10 *Conf* 2:1 (Jan 1909), p.22; *Pent* 1:5 (Jan–Feb 1909), p.5; *BM* 29 (1 Jan 1909), p.1; 32 (15 Feb 1909), p.1; 33 (1 Mar 1909), p.2.

11 *WW* 31:8 (Aug 1909), p.168; *TF* 29:6 (June 1909), p.125.

12 *UR* 1:6 (Jan 1910), p.6; 1:7 (Feb 1910), p.6.

13 *Pent* 1:8 (July 1909), p.6; 1:10 (Sept 1909), p.4; *BM* 44 (15 Aug 1909), p.2; 48 (15 Oct 1909), p.2; 50 (15 Nov 1909), p.1; 52 (15 Dec 1909), p.3; 56 (15 Feb 1910), p.1; 76 (15 Dec 1910), p.4; 97 (1 Nov 1911), p.4; 102 (15 Jan 1912), p.2; 107 (1 Apr 1912), p.2; 111 (1 June 1912), p.3; 127 (15 Feb 1913), pp.2, 3; 137 (1 Aug 1913), p.2; *Conf* 3:2 (Feb 1910), p.39; 5:3 (Mar 1912), p.59; 5:8 (Aug 1912), p.185; *UR* 2:2 (Sept–Oct 1910), p.4; *WW* 36:11 (Nov 1914), p.342.

14 *WW* 39:16 (May 1917), p.254; 43:12 (Dec 1921), p.7; Robeck, *Azusa Street*, p.242; *DPCM*, p.23.

15 *WE* 121 (1 Jan 1916), p.13; 209 (6 Oct 1917), p.5; 'Constitution and By-Laws', 1939, p.186.

16 *THW*, p.228.

17 *Conf* 1:7 (Oct 1908), pp.20–1; 3:7 (July 1910), p.172; 4:1 (Jan 1911), p.11; 5:1 (Jan 1912), p.18; *WW* 32:8 (Aug 1910), p.251; 33:1 (Jan 1911), p.23; 36:11 (Nov 1914), p.323; 37:4 (Apr 1915), p.118; *LRE* 3:1 (Oct 1910), p.11; 4:8 (May 1912), p.11; 5:4 (Jan 1913), p.13; 5:5 (Feb 1913), pp.13–14; 5:10 (July 1913), p.21; *BM* 82 (15 Mar 1911), p.2; 84 (15 Apr 1911), p.4; 104 (15 Feb 1912), p.4; *Trust* 10:1 (Jan 1911), p.30; 33:3 (Mar 1911), p.90; 17:1 (Mar 1918), p.15; 18:8 (Oct 1919), p.16; *UR* 2:5 (May 1911), p.5; *WE* 166 (25 Nov 1916), p.12.

18 *Conf* 4:12 (Dec 1911), p.285; *WW* 34:2 (Feb 1912), p.56; *LRE* 3:11 (Aug 1911), p.17; 3:12 (Sept 1911), p.13–14; 5:11 (Aug 1913), pp.2, 4.

19 *WW* 35:12 (Dec 1913), p.380; 36:11 (Dec 1914), pp.323, 341; 37:11 (Nov 1915), pp.302–3; *FF* 19 (Aug 1914), p.7; 21 (Nov 1914), p.7; 30 (Aug 1915), pp.8–9; *TF* 35:4 (Apr 1915), pp.82–5; 35:10 (Oct 1915), p.238; *Conf* 8:5 (May 1915), pp.91–2; *LRE* 8:1

(Oct 1915), p.17; 8:2 (Nov 1915), p.13–14; 8:11 (Aug 1916), pp.2–6; 9:3 (Dec 1916), p.13; *WE* 209 (6 Oct 1917), p.9.

20 Isaiah 19.24–5. *BM* 110 (15 May 1912), p.4.

21 *Conf* 1:1 (Apr 1908), pp.15–16; *BM* 23 (1 Oct 1908), p.1; *WW* 30:10 (Oct 1908), p.311; 30:11 (Nov 1908), pp.346–7; Frodsham, *With Signs Following*, p.235.

22 *WE* 135 (15 Apr 1916), p.13; *DPCM*, p.712.

23 *BM* 22 (15 Sept 1908), p.1; 41 (1 July 1909), p.1; 47 (1 Oct 1909), p.2; 60 (15 Apr 1910), p.4; 61 (1 May 1910), p.2; 68 (15 Aug 1910), p.1; 76 (15 Dec 1910), p.1; 86 (15 May 1911), p.1; 97 (1 Nov 1911), p.4; 99 (1 Dec 1911), p.1; 108 (15 Apr 1912), p.2; 110 (15 May 1912), p.1; 111 (1 June 1912), p.1; 125 (15 Jan 1913), p.2; 133 (15 May 1913), p.1; 134 (1 June 1913), p.3; 146 (15 Dec 1913), p.2; *WW* 31:7 (July 1909), p.141; 35:5 (May 1913), p.157; *Pent* 1:8 (July 1909), p.8; 1:12 (Nov 1909), p.4; 2:9–10 (Sept–Oct 1910), p.4; 2:11–12 (Nov–Dec 1910), p.5; *Conf* 3:7 (July 1910), pp.165–6; 3:8 (Aug 1910), p. 189–90; 5:12 (Dec 1912), p.285; 6:7 (July 1913), p.146; *LRE* 3:2 (Nov 1910), p.11; 5:2 (Nov 1912), p.11; 6:12 (Sept 1914), p.11; 9:1 (Oct 1916), pp.14–15; *WWit* 8:6 (Aug 1912), p.3; 8:8 (Oct 1912), pp.3–4; 9:1 (Jan 1913), p.2; 9:6 (June 1913), p.1; 9:10 (Oct 1913), p.2; 10:8 (Aug 1914), p.4; *Trust* 12:3 (May 1913), p.19; *WE* 179 (3 Mar 1917), p.12; 190 (19 May 1917), p.13.

24 *BM* 136 (1 July 1913), p.2; 139 (1 Sept 1913), p.3.

25 Robeck, *Azusa Street*, pp.204–8, 243.

26 *AF* 3 (Nov 1906), p.1; 4 (Dec 1906), p.4; 5 (Jan 1907), p.4; 11 (Jan 1908), p.2; 13 (May 1908), p.4; *BM* 13 (1 May 1908), p.4; 25 (1 Nov 1908), p.1; 38 (15 May 1909), p.4; *Conf* 2:6 (June 1909), p.137; 3:7 (July 1910), p. 165; *WW* 30:10 (Oct 1908), p.312; 30:11 (Nov 1908), p.346; 32:10 (Oct 1910), p.315; 39:16 (May 1917), p.254; *UR* 1:10 (May 1910), p.7; 1:11 (June 1910), p.8; 2:2 (Sept–Oct 1910), p.7; *LRE* 5:2 (Nov 1912), p.11; 5:5 (Feb 1913), p.11; 5:7 (Apr 1913), p 15; 5:12 (Sept 1913), p.16; *WWit* 8:8 (Oct 1912), p.4; 9:2 (Feb 1913), p.2; *CE* 72 (26 Dec 1914), p.4; Bartleman, *Azusa Street*, p.61.

27 *TF* 37:11 (Nov 1917), p.259; Robeck, *Azusa Street*, p.208.

28 *LRE* 9:6 (Mar 1917), p.13.

29 *WE* 191 (26 May 1917), p.12; *TF* 38:4 (Apr 1918), p.90; *LRE* 11:9 (June 1919), p.11; 11:12 (Sept 1919), pp.14–19; 12:1 (Oct 1919), pp.7–8; *DPCM*, p.1153.

30 *AF* 1 (Sept 1906), p.2.

31 *AF* 3 (Nov 1906), p.3.

32 *AF* 2 (Oct 1906), p.1; Robeck, *Azusa Street*, p.274; *BM* 118 (15 Sept 1912), p.3; *Conf* 5:11 (Nov 1912), p.247.

33 *Conf* 1:3 (June 1908), p.23.

34 *Pent* 1:9 (Aug 1909), p.4; *WW* 32:3 (Mar 1910), p.89; *BM* 65 (1 July 1910), p.2; 104 (15 Feb 1912), p.2; 120 (1 Nov 1912), p.2; 129 (15 Mar 1913), p.2; 131 (15 Apr 1913), p.2; 132 (1 May 1913), p.4; *Conf* 4:6 (June 1911), p.141; 6:7 (July 1913), p.146; *LRE* 5:9 (June 1913), p.12; 5:10 (July 1913), p.22.

35 *BM* 136 (1 July 1913), p.4.

36 *WE* 176 (10 Feb 1917), p.12; *Conf* 13:1 (Jan–Mar 1920), p.13; 13:2 (Apr–June 1913), p.29; *LRE* 11:9 (June 1919), p.6; *WW* 42:2 (Feb 1920), p.20; *Trust* 19:7 (Sept 1920), p.15; *DPCM*, p.818; Anderson, *African Reformation*, pp.156–7.

37 Haliburton, *Prophet Harris*, pp.28–35.

38 Robeck, *Azusa Street*, pp.269–70.

39 *AF* 11 (Jan 1908), p.2.

40 *AF* 13 (May 1908), p.1; *Conf* 2:4 (Apr 1909), p.92; 7:2 (Feb 1914), p.36; *UR* 1:3 (Aug 1909), p.7; Robeck, *Azusa Street*, pp.271–2.

41 *Conf* 1:9 (Dec 1908), p.8; 2:4 (Apr 1909), p.92; 2:8 (Aug 1909), p.184; 2:9 (Sept 1909), p.209.

42 The word 'fetish' is used here as West African Christians use it, to denote 'jujus': traditional charms, images, 'medicines' and amulets, etc. used to ward off evil or to do someone else harm.

43 *LRE* 8:11 (Aug 1916), p.20.

44 *LRE* 11:7 (Apr 1919), p.13.

45 *UR* (Aug 1910), p.6; *LRE* 2:11 (Aug 1910), p.21; 3:10 (July 1911), p.17; 3:11 (Aug 1911), p.17; 5:3 (Dec 1912), p.12; 6:2 (Nov 1913), p.2; 8:11 (Aug 1916), pp.18–21; *BM* 67 (1 Aug 1910), p.4; 69 (1 Sept 1910), p.2; 75 (1 Dec 1910), pp.3, 4; 79 (1 Feb 1911), p.4; 81 (1 Mar 1911), p.4; 104 (15 Feb 1912), p.2; 106 (15 Mar 1912), pp.1, 3; 130 (1 Apr 1913), p.4; *Trust* 10:1 (Mar 1911), p.19; 10:2 (Apr 1911), pp.15–16; 11:8 (Oct 1912), p.19; *Conf* 6:2 (Feb 1913), p.39; 6:9 (Sept 1913), p.184; *CE* 55 (22 Aug 1914), p.4.

46 *LRE* 5:6 (Mar 1913), p.17; 6:2 (Nov 1913), pp.2–3; 6:10 (July 1914), pp.22–4; 8:1 (Oct 1915), p.15; 9:6 (Mar 1917), pp.21–2; *Trust* 15:9 (Nov 1916), p.24.

47 *WE* 172 (13 Jan 1917), p.12; 178 (24 Feb 1917), p.12; 179 (3 Mar 1917), p.12; 213 (3 Nov 1917), p.13; *LRE* 11:7 (Apr 1919), p.13; 'Constitution and By-Laws', 1939, p.177.

48 *LRE* 3:10 (July 1911), p.17; 4:2 (Dec 1911), pp.18–19; 6:2 (Nov 1913), p.2; 9:6 (Mar 1917), p.14; 9:10 (July 1917), p.15; 13:1 (Oct 1920), pp.6–7; *Conf* 7:9 (Sept 1914), p.176; 8:5 (May 1915), p.95; 8:12 (Dec 1915), p.236; 9:10 (Oct 1916), p.170; *Trust* 16:9 (Nov 1917), p.2; 19:8 (Oct 1919), p.16; 'Constitution and By-Laws', 1939, p.177.

49 Comaroff, *Body of Power*, p.176.

50 Hastings, *Church in Africa*, p.499.

51 Sanneh, *West African Christianity*, p.169.

52 Sanneh, *West African Christianity*, p.172; Webster, *African Churches*, pp.17–21, 32–3, 40–1.

53 Haliburton, *Prophet Harris*, pp.30–2, 35.

54 *LRE* 2:12 (Sept 1910), p.16; *BM* 99 (1 Dec 1911), p.1.

55 *LRE* 3:12 (Sept 1911), p.13.

56 Haliburton, *Prophet Harris*, p.1.

57 Haliburton, *Prophet Harris*, p.38.

58 Haliburton, *Prophet Harris*, pp.49, 51, 57; Walker, 'Message as the Medium', pp.11–14.

59 Haliburton, *Prophet Harris*, pp.79, 88–9.

60 Walker, *Religious Revolution*, p.63.

61 Haliburton, *Prophet Harris*, pp.2–3, 47.

62 Walker, 'Message as the Medium', pp.19–20.

63 Turner, *History*, pp.122, 138–44; Sanneh, *West African Christianity*, pp.180–4; Tasie, 'Christian Awakening', pp.299–306; Tasie, 'Prophetic Calling', pp.99–115.

64 Turner, *History*, pp.11–12.

65 Anderson, *African Reformation*, pp.172–6.

66 Anderson, *African Reformation*, pp.51–64.

67 *AF* 4 (Dec 1906), p.3.

68 *AF* 6 (Feb–Mar 1907), p.1; 9 (June–Sept 1907), p.1.

69 *AF* 11 (Jan 1908), p.1; *BM* 22 (15 Sept 1908), p.2; 32 (15 Feb 1909), p.4; 85 (1 May 1911), p.2; 93 (1 Sept 1911), p.4; *Conf* 2:11 (Nov 1909), p.263; *LRE* 3:3 (Dec 1910), p.8; *Trust* 10:10 (Nov 1911), p.17; 19:8 (Oct 1920), p.16; *WE* 144 (17 June 1916), p.4.

70 'Constitution and By-Laws', 1931, pp.131–2.

71 *AF* 5 (Jan 1907), pp.3, 4; Robeck, *Azusa Street*, pp.274–80; Burpeau, *God's Showman*, pp.44–5.

72 *AF* 6 (Feb–Mar 1907), p.3; *Pent* 1:1 (Aug 1908), p.2; *LRE* 13:2 (Nov 1920), pp.20–3; Burpeau, *God's Showman*, pp.44–5; Burton, *When God Makes*, pp.30–1.

73 *Leaves of Healing* 15:25 (8 Oct 1904), pp.853–4; 18:11 (30 Dec 1905), pp.314–20.

74 *BM* 29 (1 Jan 1909), p.4; *WW* 32:7 (July 1910), p.213; *TF* 30:9 (Sept 1910), p.195; Oosthuizen, *Birth of Christian Zionism*, p.30; Burton, *When God Makes*, p.31.

75 Sundkler, *Zulu Zion*, p.51; *Leaves of Healing* 18:11 (30 Dec 1905), p.317.

76 *Pent* 1:2 (Sept 1908), p.2; *WW* 30:11 (Nov 1908), pp.344–5; *Conf* 2:2 (Feb 1909), p.28.

77 *Pent* 1:1 (Aug 1908), p.7; *UR* 1:7 (Feb 1910), p.7.

78 *TF* 29:2 (Feb 1909), p.38–9; *Pent* 1:4 (Dec 1908), p.7.

79 *Pent* 1:5 (Jan–Feb 1909), p.6.

80 *Pent* 1:4 (Dec 1908), p.2.

81 *Pent* 1:7 (June 1909), p.2; *BM* 115 (1 Aug 1912), p.1.

82 *UR* 1:3 (Aug 1909), p.6; *BM* 51 (1 Dec 1909), p.4; 56 (15 Feb 1910), p.1; 58 (15 Mar 1910), p.1; 61 (1 May 1910), p.2; 64 (15 June 1910), p.1; 66 (5 July 1910), p.4; 73 (1 Nov 1910), p.4; 78 (15 Jan 1911), p.4; 85 (1 May 1911), p.2; 101 (1 Jan 1912), p.2; *LRE* 2:11 (Aug 1910), p.15; *Conf* 3:8 (Aug 1910), p.188; Watt, 'Assemblies of God', p.8; Sundkler, *Zulu Zion*, p.53.

83 *BM* 45 (1 Sept 1909), p.2; *UR* 2:3 (Nov 1910), p.6.

84 Quoted in de Wet, 'Apostolic Faith Mission', pp.34, 64.

85 *WE* 214 (10 Nov 1917), p.13.

86 Sundkler, *Zulu Zion*, pp.55–6, n54.

87 *Pent* 1:5 (Jan–Feb 1909), p.4; 1:10 (Sept 1909), p.4; *Conf* 2:3 (Mar 1909), p.74; *BM* 38 (15 May 1909), p.4; 39 (1 June 1909), p.4; 47 (1 Oct 1909), p.2; *UR* 1:1 (June 1909), p.3; 1:5 (Oct–Nov 1909), p.1; 1:7 (Feb 1910), p.7; 2:4 (Jan 1911), p.6.

88 *WW* 32:4 (Apr 1910), p.121.

89 *UR* 2:3 (Nov 1910), pp.1–2, 6–8; Burpeau, *God's Showman*, pp.120–5.

90 *Advocate* 1:8 (21 June 1917), p.10; 4:49 (7 Apr 1921), p.10; *PE* 656 (17 July 1926), p.3.

91 *UR* 1:7 (Feb 1910), p.7; 2:5 (May 1911), p.6; *BM* 62 (15 May 1910), p.4; 82 (15 Mar 1911), p.1.

92 *WW* 42:7 (July 1920), p.13.

93 *LRE* 2:12 (Sept 1910), p.20; 5:1 (Oct 1912), pp.19–20; *BM* 70 (15 Sept 1910), p.4; 108 (15 Apr 1912), p.1; *Conf* 4:1 (Jan 1911), p.16; *WE* 109 (25 Sept 1915), p.4; 157 (16 Sept 1916), p.11; *WWit* 12:10 (Oct 1915), p.6; personal correspondence with E. T. Hitchcock, Aug 2006.

94 *WE* 188 (5 May 1917), p.12; 192 (2 June 1917), p.13; *WW* 40:29 (21 Sept 1918), p.15.

95 *Trust* 14:11 (Jan 1916), p.2; 15:3–4 (May–June 1916), p.26; 15:8 (Oct 1916), p.2; *WW* 42:3 (Mar 1920), p.27.

96 *BM* 68 (15 Aug 1910), p.4.

97 *BM* 72 (15 Oct 1910), p.3.

98 *Conf* 4:4 (Apr 1911), p.89; 4:6 (June 1911), p.141.

99 *BM* 56 (15 Feb 1910), p.1; 58 (15 Mar 1910), p.3; 74 (15 Nov 1910), p.2; *Pent* 1:7 (June 1909), p.1–2; 1:10 (Sept 1909), p.3.

100 *UR* 1:10 (May 1910), p.5; *BM* 86 (15 May 1911), p.4.

101 *BM* 80 (15 Feb 1911), p.1; 81 (1 Mar 1911), p.4; 85 (1 May 1911), p.2; 86 (15 May 1911), p.4; 112 (15 June 1912), p.2; *WW* 42:12 (Dec 1920), p.14.

102 Burton, *When God Makes*, p.ix.

103 de Wet, 'Apostolic Faith Mission', p.66; Burton, *When God Makes*, pp.11, 14–16.

104 Burton, *When God Makes*, pp.21–2; Lindsay, *John G. Lake*, p.42.

105 Burton, *When God Makes*, p.51.

106 *UR* 2:2 (Sept–Oct 1910), p.5; Burton, *When God Makes*, p.55; Lindsay, *John G. Lake*, pp.43, 45.

107 *BM* 45 (1 Sept 1909), p.2; *UR* 1:3 (Aug 1909), p.6.

108 *BM* 43 (1 Aug 1909), p.4; *UR* 1:3 (Aug 1909), p.6; 2:4 (Jan 1911), p.8.

109 *UR* 1:7 (Feb 1910), pp.7–8.

110 *UR* 1:11 (June 1910), p.5.

111 *UR* 1:10 (May 1910), p.6.

112 *UR* 1:11 (June 1910), p.5; 1:12 (July 1910), p.5.

113 *UR* 2:1 (Aug 1910), p.8.

114 Lindsay, *John G. Lake*, pp.47–8.

115 de Wet, 'Apostolic Faith Mission', p.68.

116 Lindsay, *John G. Lake*, p.48.

117 de Wet, 'Apostolic Faith Mission', pp.73–4.

118 Lake, *Adventures in God*, pp.32–3; Burton, *When God Makes*, pp.81–2.

119 de Wet, 'Apostolic Faith Mission', p.68.

120 Lindsay, *John G. Lake*, p.51.

121 Lindsay, *John G. Lake*, pp.51–2; de Wet, 'Apostolic Faith Mission', pp.68, 130–1; Burton, *When God Makes*, pp.90–7.

122 Lindsay, *John G. Lake*, pp.51–2.

123 *WE* 126 (12 Feb 1916), p.16.

124 Burton, *When God Makes*, p.84.

125 Sundkler, *Zulu Zion*, p.65.

126 Lake, *Adventures in God*, p.38.

127 Lake, *Adventures in God*, p.87.

128 *CE* 66 (7 Nov 1914), p.4.

129 Lindsay, *John G. Lake*, p.49; Burton, *When God Makes*, pp.85–7.

130 *WW* 35:12 (Dec 1913), p.379; Sundkler, *Zulu Zion*, p.65.

131 *Conf* 9:6 (June 1916), p.106.

132 *LRE* 8:6 (Mar 1916), p.16.

133 Sundkler, *Zulu Zion*, p.65; de Wet, 'Apostolic Faith Mission', p.126; Lindsay, *John G. Lake*, p.50; Burton, *When God Makes*, p.87.

134 Lukhaimane, 'Zion Christian Church', p.9; Hanekom, *Krisis en Kultus*, p.39.

135 *BM* 73 (1 Nov 1910), p.4; *CE* 66 (7 Nov 1914), p.4.

136 Lukhaimane, 'Zion Christian Church', pp.14–17.

137 Hanekom, *Krisis en Kultus*, p.40.

138 Lukhaimane, 'Zion Christian Church', pp.18, 20.

139 'South African Population Census 2001, by gender, religion recode (derived), population'; Anderson, 'Lekganyanes and Prophecy', pp.285–312.

140 *BM* 52 (15 Dec 1909), p.4; *UR* 1:10 (May 1910), p.6; 2:2 (Sept–Oct 1910), p.3; 2:4 (Jan 1911), pp.6, 8; 2:5 (May 1911), p.6; *Conf* 4:12 (Dec 1911), p.284; Anderson, *African Reformation*, p.97.

141 *WE* 124 (22 Jan 1916), p.13.

142 *FF* 91 (Nov 1914), p.6.

143 Burton, *God Working*, p.4.

144 Moorhead, *Missionary Pioneering*, p.2.

145 Letter, Alma Doering (St Croix, Switzerland) to T. H. Mundell, 11 Feb 1914.

146 *WE* 140 (20 May 1916), p.11; 199 (21 July 1917), p.12; Burton, *God Working*, pp.18–19; Moorhead, *Missionary Pioneering*, pp.20, 24, 45–6; Womersley and Garrard, *Into Africa*, pp.29, 51, 56.

147 Moorhead, *Missionary Pioneering*, p.74.

148 *WE* 212 (27 Oct 1917), p.4.

149 Moorhead, *Missionary Pioneering*, pp.103–4.

150 Moorhead, *Missionary Pioneering*, pp.198–207.

151 Moorhead, *Missionary Pioneering*, p.72.

152 Moorhead, *Missionary Pioneering*, pp.108–9, 114, 163.

153 Moorhead, *Missionary Pioneering*, pp.215–16; Womersley and Garrard, *Into Africa*, pp.66–7.

154 Burton, *When God Changes a Man*, pp. 45–9, 76, 107–13, 121–2, 128–30; Moorhead, *Missionary Pioneering*, pp.160–96.

155 Burton, *When God Changes a Man*, p.131.

156 Moorhead, *Missionary Pioneering*, p.64.

157 Burton, *When God Changes a Village*, pp. 28–42, 59–74, 80–102, 135–44.

158 Burton, *God Working*, p. 108.

159 Womersley and Garrard, *Into Africa*, pp.110, 115–16.

7

The Neglected Continent: Latin America and the Caribbean

Why . . . were one-twentieth of the world's inhabitants not represented? It is only another reason for calling South America 'The Neglected Continent'. It is preeminently the neglected continent, and now neglected by the combined missionary force of the world. Is it not a mission field?

(*The Bridegroom's Messenger*, 1912)[1]

Latin American independence between 1806 and 1825 had greatly reduced the empires of Portugal and especially of Spain, who fiercely attempted unsuccessfully to retain her considerable colonies. For the next hundred years the newly emerging states were trying to find themselves, with a series of dictatorships and coups-d'état until the situation was relatively calm in the early twentieth century. A number of relatively liberal Latin American rulers considered Protestantism to be a better option for progress in their countries compared to what they considered the backward-looking Catholicism of their former colonial oppressors, and they allowed Protestant immigration to encourage trade with the USA and Western Europe. Religious tolerance and anti-clericalism led to secularization in education and an easier environment for Protestant missionaries to work in at the beginning of the twentieth century.

The author of the quotation above drew attention to a Christian missionary exhibition in Boston that had encouraged interest in world missions but had completely ignored Latin America. Similarly, the Edinburgh missionary conference of 1910 had left Latin America out of the programme altogether, regarding it (like all Europe), as already Christianized and therefore not needing missionaries. To Pentecostals in the North, like their evangelical cousins in the early twentieth century, South America was the 'neglected continent' because in the opinion of established mission organizations it was already Christian.[2] But in contrast, Pentecostal missions, like evangelicals at that time, were stridently anti-Catholic. They saw Latin America as a 'Romanist' stronghold and their letters and reports abounded with allusions to the 'darkness' and 'delusion' of popular Catholicism in this region. Evangelical and Pentecostal missionaries were at pains to point out that Catholicism was 'Christopaganism' or 'baptized paganism' and that such things as the burning of (Protestant) Bibles, the veneration of Mary and images, 'pagan' religious festivals and rampant immorality were evidence that South America was anything but a 'Christian' continent. Furthermore, they pointed out, there were millions of indigenous Amerindians who were totally without any

Barquisimeto• •Caracas
VENEZUELA
GUYANA
SURINAME
FRENCH GUIANA
COLOMBIA
•Quito
ECUADOR
Belém
Amazon River
Recife•
PERU
BRAZIL
BOLIVIA
Lake Titicaca
•La Paz
•Cochabamba
PARAGUAY
Embarcación•
São Paulo•
•Rio de Janeiro
•Jujuy
(prov.)
Pacific Ocean
Porto Alegre•
Sante Fé •
Valparaiso•
CHILE •Santiago
•Gualeguaychu
Buenos Aires•
Vienticinco de Mayo•
URUGUAY
Rosario de Santa•
ARGENTINA
Atlantic Ocean
Isla de Chiloè•
Falkland Islands
Tierra del Fuego•

0   800kms
0   500mls

knowledge of Christianity at all. As the indomitable Lucy Leatherman, pioneer Pentecostal missionary in three continents, put it near the end of her life:

> In South America it is said there is only one ordained missionary for 200,000 people. There is said to be fifteen million Indians, some tribes as yet untouched by white man's civilization. The Lord has given a burden to me, that many more missionaries be sent forth. Will the saints pray our Lord to send forth laborers into this 'Neglected Continent'? Pray He may send out fifty missionaries at once. All things are possible with God ... O! God hasten missionaries to South America for your glory.[3]

Evangelical Christians thought that South America was the 'most neglected field in the whole world', having so few qualified workers but being wide open to American missionaries in particular. One paper thought that South Americans would 'be looking to the United States as they never have in the past'. It was necessary therefore for the opportunity to be grasped so that God could 'find faithful workers whom He can thrust forth into this most neglected field of the whole world, for truly the fields are white already unto harvest', this Pentecostal paper declared.[4] Calls for increased missionary awareness of and activity in the 'neglected continent' went largely unheeded in mainline Protestant denominations – but as the rest of the century was to prove, Latin America soon became the stronghold of Pentecostalism.

Some Pentecostal denominations were established in Latin America several years before the major ones in the USA were founded from which they are sometimes erroneously presumed to have emerged. The origins of much of Latin American Pentecostalism took place at a time when North American Pentecostal denominations were still forming. The movement in the South therefore is quite different from that of the North, and we should not regard it wholly as a North American creation or importation, especially not in the case of the two largest Pentecostal countries at that time, Chile and Brazil. In the case of all these Latin American countries except Chile, where Pentecostalism began with a large number of established Methodist believers and an experienced minister, the movement had a very slow start and it took decades before it became significant in numbers. Nevertheless, by the end of 1910, Pentecostal missionaries were already operating in several Latin American countries, including Guatemala, Nicaragua, El Salvador, Puerto Rico, Cuba, Bolivia, Venezuela, Brazil, Chile and Argentina. The next decade would see them reaching into Mexico, Panama, Colombia, Ecuador and Peru. This is their story.

Mexican, Central American and Latin Caribbean Missions

Missionaries from Azusa Street first went to Central America and Mexico. The Pentecostal papers carried reports from different Latin American places where Pentecostal missionaries were active. Amos and Effie Bradley were American missionaries in San Jeronimo, Guatemala who received Spirit baptism there in 1908 and corresponded regularly with *The Bridegroom's Messenger* in Atlanta and other periodicals. In Guatemala, the R. S. Andersons were writing to

Pentecostal papers in the USA by 1911 and their work in Coban consisted of a printing press and a day school. They were assisted by Eula Fay Watson (who arrived in 1910) and a 'native teacher'. Conway G. Anderson was writing regularly the following year from Zacapa, and James Taylor was also active in Guatemala in itinerant preaching. By 1913 a Brother Butler was at Coban, and (Miss) Willie Barnett was assisting Watson, with plans for a boarding school and orphanage. There was a Scandinavian Pentecostal, H. A. Johnson, relating to Barratt's church in Oslo and evangelizing in Mexico in 1911 or 1912, but nothing else is known about him.[5]

Romanita Carbajal de Valenzuela, an elderly Mexican woman, converted to Pentecostalism in Los Angeles by 1912, possibly at Azusa Street. She moved back to Villa Aldama, Cumpas, in the northern Mexican province of Chihuahua in 1913 with her husband Genaro and nephew Miguel Garcia. There they commenced services in a Protestant church until meeting stiff opposition from its pastor. In 1914 the Valenzuelas founded what was probably the earliest Pentecostal denomination in Mexico, Iglesia Apostólica de la Fe en Cristo Jesús (Apostolic Church of the Faith in Christ Jesus), soon to take a non-Trinitarian (Oneness) position and baptize in Jesus' name. Their first ordained minister was the former Methodist pastor Rúben Ortega. Romanita, who is regarded as the mother of Oneness Pentecostalism in Mexico, returned to the USA in 1918 where she died. Other Mexican Oneness churches resulted from her original work after schisms in the movement from the 1920s onwards, including two large ones, Luz del Mundo (Light of the World, 1926) and El Buen Pastor (The Good Shepherd, 1942), which have been actively spreading over the Spanish-speaking world. Carrie Judd Montgomery visited San Jose, Mexico where the Valenzuelas were holding evangelistic meetings in October 1913 and Chonita Morgan and her husband were also working in that area as Pentecostal missionaries. There were other Mexican evangelists in northern Mexico, including a Mr Guzman who itinerated with a donkey in mountain villages and a Yaqui Amerindian named Sijuri. The Mexican Oneness Pentecostals had early contact and co-operated with the Pentecostal Assemblies of the World, whose missionary Manuel Walker worked in this region. Axel and Esther Andersson came to Mexico from Lewi Pethrus' Filadelfia Church in Sweden to begin a work there in 1919 that would last beyond Axel's death there in 1981 at the age of 90. The Anderssons' 60 years' work resulted in the creation of several significant Trinitarian independent Mexican Pentecostal churches, including the Iglesia Christiana Independiente Pentecostés (Christian Independent Church Pentecost) and the Unión de Iglesias Evangelicas Independientes (Union of Evangelical Independent Churches). Scandinavian Pentecostal ecclesiology favouring local autonomy has clearly encouraged the creation of independent Mexican churches, as it has in other parts of the world.[6]

In the USA itself, the Assemblies of God had established its Mexican work as an independent district of the denomination by 1929, mainly through the earlier efforts of missionaries Henry and Sunshine Ball and Alice Luce (1873–1955), who operated at the Texas border among Mexican refugees and into Mexico itself. Luce was English and a former CMS missionary in India who had received Spirit baptism through the ministry of Shorat Chuckerbutty in Allahabad. Ball was a Methodist missionary to Mexicans in 1914 when he received Spirit baptism and joined the AG, and Luce joined this work in 1916. The following year the first AG Mexican missionaries, Loreto and Paulita Garza were sent over the border from the USA to Bargos. Luce began a night school to train Mexican preachers and spent two years working in Monterrey, Mexico (1917–19) with a team of women including Sunshine Marshall (later Mrs Ball). This work was interrupted by the civil war and Luce relocated to Los Angeles and later to San Diego, where she founded the Berean Bible Institute in 1926 for Hispanic pastors. She worked there almost three decades until her death at the age of 82. Also working along the western Mexican border among the Mexicans in these years were the George Thomases (who moved to Mexico at Nacozari in 1920) and Mrs C. Nuzum, a popular author of Christian devotional articles.

Francisco Olazábal (1886–1937), a Mexican-born Methodist minister, friend of Carrie Judd Montgomery and AG missionary from 1917, began a Pentecostal work in El Paso, Texas in 1919, hiring a hall in the city centre and paying the rent from the Mexican members. As late as September 1920, during a missionary convention of the AG in Springfield, Missouri, a report mentions by name several prominent white Americans in Mexican work along the borders and then refers simply to a 'native Mexican evangelist' who spoke at this conference and was now working in El Paso, Texas. The name of this graduate of Moody Bible Institute is not even mentioned, but he was of course Olazábal, by then leading one of the biggest Hispanic Pentecostal works in the USA.[7] It is little wonder that there were several schisms of Hispanics from the AG, mainly over the question of autonomy. A significant schism took place in 1922 when Olazábal and a group of churches for whom the AG had refused further autonomy, withdrew and founded the Concilio Latino-Americano de Iglesias Cristianas (Latin American Council of Christian Churches). Olazábal was one of the most effective Pentecostal preachers and organizers of the time, establishing Hispanic churches all over the USA, Puerto Rico and Mexico.[8]

The date of Pentecostalism's introduction to El Salvador is disputed, one account placing it in 1904 with the Canadian missionary Frederick Mebius, who was influenced by Charles Parham. Amos Bradley, however, wrote from Guatemala that Mebius had come from Mexico, had been a CMA missionary in South America, and had received his Pentecostal baptism in 1909. In any event, Mebius established a church among coffee workers in a remote area of El Salvador, by 1927 growing to several hundred members in 24 congregations, each with an 'apostle' and a 'prophet'. From these rural beginnings began the two largest Salvadoran Pentecostal denominations, the Assemblies of God and the Church of God as well as several independent churches in El Salvador, Guatemala, Nicaragua and Honduras. We know that Mebius was working among Mexicans in El Paso, Texas in 1914 and may have been an itinerant preacher. The Bradleys moved to Sonsonate, El Salvador in early 1911 and reported regular meetings with 25 Amerindian Christians. They lived in difficult circumstances in a two-roomed house with a kitchen having nothing but a mud-and-brick stove covered with roof sheet-iron. By 1913 the Bradleys were in Ahuachapan in El Salvador, now working with the PHC. They wrote of their congregation of 21 members and the physical opposition they were experiencing from local thugs. By 1917 they were in Guatemala City, but they returned to the USA in 1918.[9]

The first Pentecostal missionary in Nicaragua (and perhaps in the whole of Latin America) appears to have been Edward Barnes, who arrived there in 1907 and remained at least until 1917, when he was in Leon and affiliated to the AG.[10] We have no information about when and how he became a Pentecostal. In 1912 B. Austin and Marie Schoeneich went with their family and Marie's mother Mrs Yaegge to Matagalpa, Nicaragua, where they encountered stiff opposition from the Catholic priest, threatening excommunication for any who associated with the Pentecostals. They itinerated in a remote mountain area using mules and donkeys to reach isolated villages. They opened a Mission Home for orienting new Pentecostal missionaries to Latin America, a church called the Apostolic Evangelical Mission and a school for children. It was slow work: after five years they had only ten Spirit-baptized people, but others had been immersed in water baptism. There were six foreign Pentecostal missionaries in Nicaragua by 1916, and two more women arrived the following year to help at Matagalpa in the school. Mrs Yaegge died there in 1918. The Schoeneichs were in Leon, Nicaragua in 1931 as AG missionaries, and by 1937 their pioneering work in Matagalpa was built on by Lois and Melvin Hodges, one of the most influential AG missionaries and mission strategists.

J. Wilson Bell was a Pentecostal worker in the Canal Zone of Panama, but was reported insane and institutionalized in 1915. In 1917 he briefly re-appeared as a CG evangelist to Jamaica, where he again fell foul of the law. Pentecostals were also active in the Latin Caribbean islands. By 1913 the first Pentecostals in Cuba were the J. M. Shirlens, who were working from Madruga and Aguacate. In 1920 May Kelty helped establish the AG in Cuba and returned to work there permanently in 1931 together with a Puerto Rican couple, Esther and Francisco Rodríguez.[11]

Juan (John) Leon Lugo (1890–1984), a Puerto Rican, was one of the most significant pioneers of Latin American Pentecostalism. Lugo was converted in Hawaii in 1907 by missionaries from Azusa Street and was part of a Hispanic Pentecostal congregation there, later moving to California in 1914. He left a Pentecostal church in San Jose, California for Ponce, Puerto Rico in 1916 after 16 months in the USA as an AG missionary to Hispanics. He was later that year joined by his friend Salomón Feliciano Quiñones (also a Puerto Rican who had become Pentecostal in Hawaii in 1913), and his wife Dianicia. They worked with Lugo for a year before going to the Dominican Republic to begin a church there. On arrival in Ponce, Lugo was invited to preach in the Methodist Episcopal Church but soon the Protestant churches joined together in oppos-ing the new Pentecostal movement. The Pentecostals in turn had little regard for Protestant comity arrangements and evangelized all over the island, mainly in street preaching and meetings in homes. According to Lugo, the Protestant churches there were 'as dry as a piece of wood'.[12] These mission-aries began with street preaching in Ponce and were invited to a home for the first meeting indoors, where this family became their first converts and an assembly was founded. Although it was difficult at first to get a permit to preach and Lugo was told by Protestant pastors that he lacked the training, by the end of 1916 there were 87 converts amid great opposition and persecution from civil authorities and other churches. Lugo reported people crowding their 100-seat hall every night with some falling under the power, receiving Spirit baptism and remarkable healings, but the Pentecostals were given a court order to close services at 10.30 p.m. People who were baptized in the Spirit at these meetings were put out of their churches, but the number of Pentecostals grew steadily.

Another Puerto Rican, Frank (Francisco) Ortiz, Jr, also known as 'Panchito', his wife Santitos and his father Francisco Ortiz, Sr (who had been Lugo and Feliciano's pastor in both Hawaii and California) arrived from San Jose, California in 1917. The younger Ortiz began a congregation in Arecibo (the fourth on the island) and his father established a periodical before his sudden death in 1922. A Methodist minister who became Pentecostal and a future missionary to Cuba, Francisco Rodríguez, was in charge of a congregation in Don Alonso, and there was another congregation in San Antone. In Lares another Methodist preacher, Thomas Alvares joined the Pentecostals. In 1921 Lugo founded what is now the largest non-Catholic denomination in Puerto Rico, the Iglesia Pentecostal de Dios (Pentecostal Church of God). In 1929 Lugo went to New York to pastor the first Puerto Rican Pentecostal church there, which now flourishes in the north-east USA as the Latin American Council of the Pentecostal Church of God of New York. The Pentecostal Church of God has sent missionaries all over Latin America and to the USA, Spain and Portugal. It was affiliated with the AG until 1956, when it became an independent denomination.[13] Feliciano was the first Pentecostal missionary to the Dominican Republic, first going there in 1917, but in 1920 he and Lugo were still listed as AG missionaries in Ponce. Feliciano's work and that of several other Puerto Rican missionaries in the Dominican Republic was eventually taken over by the American AG in 1941.

Missions in the British West Indies

Pentecostalism in the British West Indies began in the Bahamas. Rebecca and Edmond Barr, probably the first African Caribbean Pentecostals, received Spirit baptism in Florida in early 1909 and returned to their home church in Nassau, the birthplace of Pentecostalism in the Caribbean. There the Barrs engaged in itinerant ministry throughout the islands and reported great success among both the black and white population. Later that year the first missionaries sent out by the CG in Cleveland, R. M. and Ida Evans, went to these islands. They joined up with the Barrs, whom they referred to as 'our colored co-laborers . . . faithful and abundant in labours, but the field before them is appalling, except to faith in an omnipotent God'.[14] The Pentecostal missionaries found two particular things 'appalling' about the British-ruled Caribbean: the cohabitation of most couples with children outside formal marriage bonds, and the mixture of African spiritism with western Christianity that prevailed in these islands. The Pentecostals saw these two practices as the first to be confronted by their preachers. The Barrs and Evanses were joined in 1910 by Flora Boever, also from Cleveland, but her stay seems to have been short-lived. So was that of the W. C. Hocketts from California, who went independently in 1911 and preached to Pentecostal groups in Nassau and Curent Island. One of the more flamboyant of the early American Pentecostal leaders, A. J. Tomlinson, overseer of the CG, was in the Bahamas on a two-month evangelistic tour in 1911 with W. C. Hockett. He toured several outlying islands with a 12-person brass band and a big tent, but the trip was cut short because of the critical illness of Tomlinson's wife in Cleveland, and he returned home. An African American worker from Miami, Anna Marshall, established a Pentecostal congregation at Rock Sound on Eleuthera island in early 1912 but the Evanses complained that the three 'native helpers' (African Caribbeans) had had to seek work in Florida through financial hardships. It seems that the Barrs returned to Florida that year, when Tomlinson ordained Edmond Barr as overseer of the 'colored' work in Florida.[15] The Evanses, the only American Pentecostals on the island, returned to Florida in 1912 because of a shortage of funds and ill health. Leadership passed to William Franks, appointed overseer in 1918 and having a ministry in the Bahamas of some 60 years. Most of the Bahamian churches joined Tomlinson in his new church in 1923 and eventually became the Church of God of Prophecy.

In Antigua and Barbuda, Canadians Robert and Elizabeth Jamieson were working as independent Pentecostal missionaries in 1911 after spending six years in the Caribbean with another society. In 1914 they arrived in Jamaica but soon moved on to Montserrat where there was an established Pentecostal work under a local leader. Their practice was to raise up local leaders and then move on to another island. In Montserrat they worked with five different centres and held regular conventions, one in October 1914 reporting 'revival' with 44 baptisms. In 1915 they went to work in Newfoundland because of the war, but were in Bridgetown, Barbados in 1919 reporting eight Pentecostal stations under local leaders the J. T. Hurleys. The Jamiesons moved to Trinidad in 1920 and took Pentecostalism from there to Grenada and continued the work in Montserrat. They reported that three 'missions' in Trinidad had joined their work with the AG. They affiliated with the Pentecostal Assemblies of Canada in 1926 and their work in these various islands became known as the Pentecostal Assemblies of the West Indies. This church sent Trinidadian missionaries to Montserrat, Barbados and Martinique.

The largest and most populous of the British-ruled Caribbean islands was Jamaica. Apart from a brief visit by the Jamiesons in 1914 and early activity that year by the African American led Pentecostal Assemblies of the World, J. Wilson Bell was the first American Pentecostal to stay there. Bell affiliated with the CG in about 1918 but was arrested after a few months and imprisoned for refusing medical intervention for his daughter who subsequently died. The work passed to a Jamaican farmer, Rudolph Smith, who together with his two converts Henry Hudson and Percival Graham were responsible for spreading the Pentecostal message through the island. From these three and from Tomlinson's schismatic withdrawal from the CG in 1923 came the two largest Pentecostal churches in Jamaica, the New Testament Church of God with Hudson as overseer and the Church of God of Prophecy under Smith. But Pentecostalism arrived in Jamaica relatively late. The CG missionary leader James Ingram had his first assignment in Bermuda, arriving there in 1921.

Ingram was an influential figure in the subsequent development of this church in the Caribbean and Central American regions, so that the CG is now the largest Pentecostal work in the British Caribbean.[16] A feature of British Caribbean Pentecostalism is the fact that the work was established by local residents rather than by expatriate missionaries. As in other regions, Pentecostalism has become one of the most significant expressions of Christianity in the Caribbean islands and wherever their inhabitants have spread.

Missions in South America

In continental South America, there were four main regions of activity for early Pentecostal missionaries. The most northerly of these was in Venezuela and the beginning of Pentecostalism there is linked to CMA missionaries. Gerard Bailly, who had been a missionary in Caracas with the CMA since 1896, returned there in 1908 after receiving Spirit baptism in Los Angeles – the link appears to have been with Elmer Fisher's Upper Room Mission. He established a training school for 'native workers' in 1909 near Los Teques and a church in Caracas by 1910. These CMA Pentecostals received considerable opposition from local Catholic priests. New, larger premises were obtained in 1912 for the school and half of the eight men being trained for ministry there were from Puerto Rico. Several of these Puerto Ricans went to other parts of Latin America as missionaries, including Castulo Rivera, who went to Colon in Panama to work among the Amerindians in 1917. The Baillys' main associates, Frank (or Fred) Bullen and Toma Salazar, a Venezuelan, both died in 1914, and apart from a brief association with Frederick Bender, the Baillys continued at their mission alone. Increasing opposition within the CMA leadership to tongues as evidence of Spirit baptism led to the Baillys leaving the CMA that year. They founded an independent Pentecostal church that eventually became known as the Iglesia Apostólica Venezolana y Misionera (Venezuelan and Missionary Apostolic Church). In 1918 Bailly started working with the newly wed Frederick and Christina Bender, German Americans and products of the CMA who had just arrived. After involvement with Bailly's work they fell out with him and began leading an independent Pentecostal denomination from Barquisimeto, Venezuela, which joined the AG on the retirement of the Benders to the USA in 1947.[17]

The second region of Pentecostal activity was in the Andean states. In 1909, Earl W. Clark, a CMA missionary who had turned Pentecostal arrived in Bolivia with a team to open a mission station with an industrial school for Amerindian boys, a flour mill and shops. He opened the school three nights a week in Brother Baker's mission in La Paz early in 1912 and by 1913, on furlough in Chicago, was planning a 'Pentecostal colony' for a hundred American families to settle in Bolivia and evangelize the Amerindians. However, he got diverted in the USA when he worked as an assistant preacher for Maria Woodworth Etter in her campaigns and married her granddaughter. He began his own itinerant preaching in the USA, established a ministry in Washington DC and nothing was heard of his Bolivian project again.[18] The first permanent missionaries in the region were Howard and Catherine Cragin, who arrived in Quito, Ecuador as Pentecostal missionaries in 1911 after a short and unsuccessful stay in Callao, Peru. They were joined two years later by the L. B. Slys, who called it a 'hard field' but were still there in 1917. The Cragins went from Ecuador to Bolivia in 1913 together with their son Paul, daughter Helen and son-in law Vern Vandermain. They located at Lake Titicaca and then near Cochabamba working among Aymara and Quechua peoples, but the Cragins afterwards returned to Peru where they worked for many years. In 1914 Frederick and Lizzie Stevens were working in northern Peru. Other American missionaries began arriving there in the 1920s mainly to work with the AG, the largest Pentecostal denomination in Peru.[19]

The third region of Pentecostal missionary activity in South America was in the southern cone of Argentina and Chile. Pentecostalism arrived in Argentina early in 1909, when Italian Pentecostals from Chicago, Luigi Francescon, Giácomo Lombardi and Lucía Menna founded the Iglesia Asamblea Cristiana (Christian Assembly Church) among Italian immigrants in Buenos Aires. May Kelty and her mother Harriet from the USA and Alice Wood from Canada arrived in early 1910 in Gualeguaychu, Entre Rios province, 100 miles north of Buenos Aires, working from a former CMA station handed over to the Pentecostals in Gualeguaychu. This station was followed by a second CMA one given to them at Gualeguay, 50 miles west, to which the Keltys moved to take charge. May Kelty soon reported that all the CMA missionaries in a station near Buenos Aires had 'been baptized into the Holy Spirit' and that another band of CMA missionaries nearby were 'tarrying also'. But their work did not yield much in the way of local converts and they worked with women and children in the area amid stiff opposition.

Alice Wood, who had already been a CMA missionary in Venezuela for 12 years, reported that the revival had 'really come' to Argentina in August 1910 and that 'God is pouring out of His Spirit' upon the missionaries in two CMA stations. Berger Johnson, a Norwegian missionary, joined this mission in 1911 and engaged in itinerant work among Protestant missions, also doing the work of a Bible colporteur. Alice Wood suffered a breakdown that year and the Keltys moved back to Gualeguaychu to assist her. At first they confessed that there was little happening among the Argentines and that their ministry had concentrated on sharing their Pentecostal experience with other missionaries. In 1912 the Keltys moved to Rosaria de Santa Fe, where they planned to work with German missionaries among Amerindians. Two years later they moved with the R. S. McBrides 1,000 miles north to work among the Chiriguano people in the Jujuy province near the Bolivian and Chilean borders. There they opened a school for children and an industrial school for men and women. Alice Wood was joined by a Danish Pentecostal worker, Annina Bejlstrup, in 1913 in Gualeguaychu, but she continued to describe the difficult conditions with little results. She joined the AG in 1914. Wood's work received a boost when a Spanish evangelist, Juan Barrio, joined her in 1915. In 1917 Wood, Barrio and Anita Kildegaard relocated to Veinticinco de Mayo, 100 miles south-west of Buenos Aires in the Pampas, from where they soon reported 30 attending services and the opening of a mission hall. The congregation was led by Barrio, who married Elisa Seppe later that year. Clearly, the move to Veinticinco de Mayo was advantageous for the missionaries, who found the area more receptive to their message than their earlier mission had been. Wood was still at this station in 1939 listed as an AG missionary and she remained there until just before her death in 1951.[20]

Johnson bought land in the far north-west at Embarcación among the Amerindians, and another Danish missionary, Nils Sorensen, arrived in 1913 to marry Bejlstrup and move from Gualeguaychu to the north near Johnson. But in 1916 they returned to Gualeguaychu because of ill health and from there a year later to Bolivar in the south-west. Johnson apparently disagreed with having women in the ministry and he split with Alice Wood and the Pentecostals further south. He sought affiliation with Willis Hoover in Chile.[21] The world-travelling senior missionary Lucy Leatherman was in Argentina in 1918 holding services in two suburban villages near Buenos Aires – she spent four years in South America affiliated with the CG before returning to the USA. In 1920 she complained that in the largest city in the southern hemisphere there was but one Pentecostal mission (Iglesia Asamblea Cristiana) which was only for Italians, led by Brother 'Narruci' from Chicago – this was Narcisco Natucci, who was sent by Francesconi in 1916 with Fransico Anfuzzo to revitalize this Buenos Aires congregation. This church was 'in a flourishing condition', wrote Leatherman. She pleaded for more workers to come to this the 'Neglected Continent', and her plea is quoted at the beginning of this chapter.[22] There was slow progress in the Pentecostal work in Argentina (compared to Chile and Brazil) during the first 30 years – Pentecostalism was only really to take off in this country after the healing evangelism campaign of American evangelist Tommy Hicks in 1954.[23]

The Chilean Revival

Many of the first Pentecostals in Latin America were Chileans and in the early years this was the most successful of the different Pentecostal missions in the continent. This is all the more surprising when so little coverage of the dramatic events in Chile and Brazil appeared in the English-language Pentecostal periodicals and these two areas of greatest expansion received almost no support from North American churches. One of the reasons for this in the case of Chile was that this was a national movement with very little influence from the North. Chile presents a different scenario from that of the rest of Latin American Pentecostalism in several respects. Although its leader was an American, his ejection from an American Methodist mission meant that he relied on Chilean people for his support, his infrastructures and his workers. As a result, the Methodist Pentecostal Church was almost immediately a self-governing, self-supporting and self-propagating church – probably the first in Latin America. The origins of Pentecostalism in Chile are associated with Willis C. Hoover (1858–1936), an American revivalist minister in Valparaiso, a former physician who had been in Chile since 1889, pastor of the largest Methodist Episcopal congregation in Chile (700 strong) and a district superintendent. Like fellow Pentecostal leaders T. B. Barratt in Norway, Minnie Abrams and Albert Norton in India, and J. M. L. Harrow and John Perkins in Liberia, he too was a product of Bishop William Taylor's missionary zeal.

Thanks to Hoover's own accounts we have much more information about the Pentecostal revival in the Methodist Church in Valparaiso, Chile, where Hoover was the pastor. There is some evidence that the Hoovers received Pentecostal papers from the USA, but that these were only circulating after the revival began in April 1909. Willis Hoover himself wrote that it was his wife May Louise receiving in the mail in 1907 a copy of Minnie Abrams' 1906 booklet *The Baptism of the Holy Ghost and Fire*, thus learning of the outpouring of the Spirit in Mukti, India, and May Louise Hoover's subsequent correspondence with Abrams, her former fellow student in the Chicago Training School (for women missionaries), that stimulated the Chilean Pentecostal revival. The Hoovers also made contact with a Swedish pastor in Chicago, Alexander and Mary Boddy in Sunderland and their paper *Confidence*, and others like fellow Methodist Barratt, thus learning of the Pentecostal revival movement taking place in various parts of the world.[24] The Methodist Episcopal Church in Valparaiso was stirred to pray for and expect such a 'Holy Ghost revival' and daily prayer meetings 'for the outpouring of the Holy Spirit upon our church' began in January 1909. These 'seeking' meetings happened to coincide with the opening of their new church building, the largest Protestant edifice in Chile.

By July 1909, after six months of prayer, the expected revival arrived in Valparaiso during one of these prayer meetings and many unusual and ecstatic manifestations occurred. These included weeping, uncontrollable laughter, groaning, prostration, rolling on the floor, revelatory visions, and singing and speaking in tongues, with people repenting and confessing sins, so that there were more than 200 conversions in a year.[25] Those baptized in the Spirit felt compelled to rush out onto the streets to tell of their experiences. This, together with the noise generated by the revival meetings, caused a hostile reaction from the civic authorities, the local press and eventually from the Methodist Church hierarchy. In Santiago, some of the revivalists were arrested, including a young English-born woman from Valparaiso, Nellie (Elena) Laidlaw, a former prostitute who Hoover described as having 'remarkable manifestations and gifts'. She had been refused permission to prophesy in two Santiago Methodist churches and a majority of the members thereupon resigned from those churches and began holding meetings in homes. Hoover's support for Laidlaw was his undoing as far as the Methodist Church was concerned and he became the subject of a flurry of scurrilous reports.

There were other positive and independent reports of this revival. Earl Clark wrote from Bolivia that the 'Pentecostal fire' had broken out in Chile and that throughout the country 'great blessing is following in its wake' with 'hundreds' being 'saved'. He wrote that these fires were 'breaking out in missions where I spent two years in the work'.[26] A. B. Simpson visited Chile early in 1910 and preached to almost a thousand people in Hoover's church in Valparaiso, which visit was reported in several Pentecostal papers. He wrote that Hoover was 'the most successful missionary in Chile' and that the revival there was 'accompanied by many of the remarkable manifestations which have come to our [CMA] work in India, South China and many parts of America', including simultaneous prayer, speaking in tongues and divine healing. Hoover was, Simpson wrote, 'overflowing with the love of God and unction of the Spirit, and yet sane and Scriptural in his views and methods'. Simpson prophetically warned that sending Hoover back to the USA 'would break up the largest Protestant church in Chile and probably lead to the forming of an independent mission' and that 'the gravest issues are hanging in the balance', especially if the Methodist Church were to 'dismiss him or try to coerce his people'.[27]

The warning went unheeded. In 1910, the Methodist Conference met in Hoover's own Valparaiso church building and in the presence of his members, Hoover was charged with conduct that was 'scandalous' and 'imprudent' and with propagating teachings that were 'false and anti-Methodist . . . contrary to the Scriptures and irrational'. Reminiscent of Charles Parham's similar denunciation of the Azusa Street revival just over three years earlier, the Conference in its official statement derided the manifestations of the revival as being 'offensive to decency and morals' and involving 'hypnotism'.[28] Pressure was put upon Hoover to leave Chile and return to the USA, and he almost agreed to this plan. The presiding bishop Bristol removed Hoover as district superintendent and told him that either he had to leave Chile or leave the Methodist Church. Meanwhile the Santiago revivalists had decided to form a new church they called the Iglesia Metodista Nacional (Methodist National Church) and the Valparaiso congregation officials and the majority of its members joined them. Although 'in a moment of weakness' Hoover agreed to leave Chile as the bishop had instructed him, he changed his mind, took the bishop's second option and resigned from the Methodist Episcopal Church and its missionary society in May 1910. He stated that he was not separating himself either from Wesley or from Methodism. The Methodist leaders tried to have him arrested and deported but the Chilean authorities released him. To this day the MPC has maintained its Methodist doctrines and practices, including infant baptism and other Methodist and episcopal structures. In the Valparaiso congregation, 450 of Hoover's 700 members and all the members of the two congregations in Santiago had already resigned. Hoover was invited to become superintendent of the new church, whose name he suggested be changed to Iglesia Metodista Pentecostal (Methodist Pentecostal Church, MPC), to make it clear that the division did not come out of nationalism and that they were still essentially Methodist. Hoover was supported entirely by a Chilean church, probably the first self-supporting church in Latin America, referred to by at least one Pentecostal paper as 'an independent Methodist mission'. Hoover himself referred to his church as an 'independent, self-supporting body'. Within the first year, not only had Hoover's Valparaiso congregation grown by 150 new members, but five years later there were congregations of the new denomination in twelve different cities, some 1,200 members, and 'several other considerable groups affiliated' with the MPC, all wholly self-supporting.[29] Chilean missionaries also planted MPC congregations in Argentina and Peru in the 1920s.

The closeness to Methodism differentiates Chilean Pentecostalism from North American classical Pentecostalism. Significantly, this Chilean movement with origins in the Mukti revival in India was not connected to American Pentecostal churches and Hoover was founder of an autochthonous Chilean church. Chilean Pentecostalism, like the movement at Mukti, did not follow white American classical Pentecostalism's doctrine of 'initial evidence'. Since Hoover's time it has seen speaking in tongues as one of many of the manifestations of Spirit baptism. As has been the case all over the world, many secessions have taken place in the MPC, the first when Carlos del Campo left to start the Iglesia del Señor (Church of the Lord) in 1913; and later the Iglesia Evangélica de los Hermanos Pentecostales (Evangelical Church of the Pentecostal Brethren). In time, Hoover would clash with the majority of the Chilean pastors in the MPC over (among other things) the use of popular music and instruments in the church. Hoover himself led a secession in 1932 and founded the Iglesia Evangélica Pentecostal (Evangelical Pentecostal Church), which he led until his death in Santiago four years later. The MPC was led by Manuel Umaña Salinas, who became its bishop. The vast majority of Chilean Pentecostals belong to churches whose origins are in the MPC.

At this early stage, only one other Pentecostal work in Chile is known. Norwegian Pentecostal missionaries were working at Ancud on the island of Chiloe in the south of Chile from 1912 onwards, N. O. and Marie Gunstad, Martha Olsen and Kirsti Melbostad, who were later joined by a Brother Jakobsen. They worked in the islands there, including Sebastiana, where a congregation was established with a local leader.[30]

The Brazilian Phenomenon

The fourth, the largest and ultimately the most prolific region of Pentecostal activity in South America was in the enormous Portuguese-speaking country of Brazil. The two earliest forms of Pentecostalism there (at different ends of the country) have common connections to the Chicago ministry of William Durham. He had prophesied that his associate since 1907, Luigi Francesconi (1866–1964), a former Waldensian and leader of the first Italian Pentecostal church, would preach the Pentecostal message to Italian people. Francesconi established Italian congregations throughout the USA and in Argentina in 1909. In 1910, he went to São Paulo, Brazil with a small team to begin working among the large Italian community there, at that time over a million strong. He preached on the baptism in the Spirit to Italian Presbyterians and was expelled from their church. The result was the formation of a Pentecostal denomination, Congregacioni Christiani (Christian Congregation), the first Pentecostal church in Brazil. In about 1935 it began to adopt Portuguese in its services and to attract native Brazilians, and is now known by its Portuguese name as Congregação Cristã, one of the largest Pentecostal denominations in Brazil.[31]

Two Swedish Baptist men, Gunnar Vingren and Daniel Berg, loosely associated with William Durham, were responsible for the beginning of Pentecostalism in north-east Brazil. Vingren, graduate of the University of Chicago's Divinity School and pastor of a Swedish Baptist church in South Bend, Indiana and Berg, a layman in Chicago, received separate prophecies that they should go to 'Pará'. When Vingren discovered in the public library where that place was, they travelled to Belém in the northern Brazilian state of Pará in 1910, the same year that Francesconi went to São Paulo in the south. Unable to speak Portuguese, they began prayer meetings in the cellar of a Baptist church pastored by a Swedish missionary and waited for revival. Some received Spirit baptism and began evangelism in their neighbourhood. A group of 18, a majority of the members, was expelled from the church in June 1911 and Vingren became their pastor. Berg and Vingren could speak Portuguese in six months and in three years they had over 100 converts in Pará. In five years there were 400 Pentecostals in northern Brazil and ten churches. The first named Brazilian preacher associated with Vingren and Berg was Adriano Nobre. Berg assisted Vingren as a freelance evengelist, supporting the mission as a shipping agent and colporteur distributing Bibles along the rail and river-boat routes, making converts as he went. In 1917 he reported 126 baptisms and 11 missions established along the Amazon River and its tributaries; two years later there were 26 assemblies and 500 people in the movement. As in other parts of Latin America, violent mobs were organized against the Pentecostals and some followers were thrown in prison. The Pentecostal missionaries believed that these mobs had been instigated by local Catholic priests.[32] Like the Hoovers in Chile, Vingren and Berg adopted Brazil as their own country and the church grew as a Brazilian church from the beginning. Vingren made it clear that the work spread through Brazilians who 'caught the fire' and spread it in other parts of the country – first to the Amazon interior, then further south, along the railroad and along the coast. As he put it: 'There was not a missionary there when the Lord poured out His Spirit and started a big church.'[33]

The resulting church was first called the Apostolic Faith Mission but regis-tered in 1918 as the Assembléia de Deus (Assembly of God), but not affiliated to the North American version. The denomination grew rapidly, particularly through its practice of prayer for healing. Tragically, Vingren left Brazil in 1932 with stomach cancer, but the work quickly became completely autochthonous. Brazilian Pentecostal missionaries were sent out very early in their history. Not only did Pentecostals from Belém begin evangelizing the Amazonas region and spread to the big cities of Recife, Rio de Janeiro, São Paulo and Pôrto Alegre, but in 1913 José Plácido da Costa left Belém for Porto, Portugal, the first Pentecostal there to be followed by another Belém Pentecostal in 1921, José de Mattos. Brazilian Pentecostals emphasized healing and establishing churches in cities, where there was remarkable expansion.[34] The denomination spread to every state in Brazil, an autochthonous movement without financial support or personnel from elsewhere (apart from Vingren's early support from Sweden and the USA). Lewi Pethrus in Stockholm, a fellow Baptist until 1913, was one of these supporters. Members were recruited initially from the lower strata of Brazilian society, and Pentecostalism appealed to Amerindian, black and mixed-race (mulatto) Brazilians, the majority in this church.[35]

There was also an early Pentecostal mission in Rio de Janeiro, where the Welshman James Roberts and his wife, who were baptized in the Spirit in England, operated an orphanage and held regular healing services. They reported in 1915 over 150 baptisms and many 'wonderful cases of healing' bringing about conversions. He was working with 'Plymouth brethren so-called' churches in the city.[36]

Pentecostalism in Latin America would develop into one of the most impressive success stories in the history of missions, certainly during the twentieth century. From its rather chaotic, persecuted and fragile beginnings this movement has grown to be by far the largest 'evangelical' or 'Protestant' movement in the southern hemisphere. Most of this growth, however, took place in the second half of the twentieth century. By 2000 it constituted possibly as many as half of all the 'classical' Pentecostals in the world. Brazil alone had one of the largest populations of Pentecostals globally with growth rates that cannot fail to impress all observers, whether sympathetic with its methods of expansion or not. It is hoped that some of the causes of this phenomenal change in the religious landscape of Latin America will at least be better understood or placed into a more comprehensive historical and religious context by the story of its beginnings.

Notes

1 *BM* 104 (15 Feb 1912), p.4.

2 *BM* 59 (1 Apr 1910), p.4.

3 *WW* 42:1 (Jan 1920), p.14.

4 *WE* 144 (17 June 1916), p.8.

5 *BM* 31 (1 Feb 1909), p.1; 36 (15 Apr 1909), p.4; 51 (1 Dec 1909), p.1; 58 (15 Mar 1910), p.2; 62 (15 May 1910), p.3; 82 (15 Mar 1911), p.4; 93 (1 Sept 1911), p.1; 104 (15 Feb 1912), p.3; 106 (15 Mar 1912), p.3; 120 (1 Nov 1912), p.3; 127 (15 Feb 1913), p.2; 133 (15 May 1913), p.3; *WW* 32:10 (Oct 1910), p.314; *UR* 2:4 (Jan 1911), p.7; *DPCM*, pp.176–7.

6 *BM* 133 (15 May 1913), p.3; *TF* 33:12 (Dec 1913), pp.270–1; 37:3 (Mar 1917), p.66; 37:7 (July 1917), pp.156–8; *DPCM*, pp.175–8, 1169; Espinosa, 'Ordinary Prophet', pp. 38, 53.

7 *LRE* 13:3 (Dec 1920), p.12.

8 *WE* 91 (22 May 1915), p.4; 198 (14 July 1917), p.13; *TF* 37:3 (Mar 1917), pp.53–4; 37:7 (July 1917), p.158; 182 (31 Mar 1917), pp.12–13; 39:3 (Mar 1919), pp.71–2; *DPCM*, pp.175–8, 323–4, 936.

9 *Advocate* 1:1 (3 May 1917), p.13; 4:49 (7 Apr 1921), p.10; *WE* 210 (13 Oct 1917), p.10.

10 *WE* 212 (27 Oct 1917), p.12.

11 *BM* 68 (15 Aug 1910), p.4; 127 (15 Feb 1913), p.2; 128 (1 Mar 1913), p.2; 129 (15 Mar 1913), p.3; 133 (15 May 1913), p.3; 135 (15 June 1913), p.2; 137 (1 Aug 1913), p.3; 145 (1 Dec 1913), p.2; *LRE* 4:12 (Sept 1912), p.14; 5:5 (Feb 1913), p.8; 8:6 (Mar 1916), p.15; 8:10 (July 1916), p.24; *TF* 34:6 (June 1914), p.136; 37:3 (Mar 1917), p.65; 37:10 (Oct 1917), p.235; *WWit* 10:3 (Mar 1914), p.4; 12:7 (July 1915), p.5; *WE* 174 (27 Jan 1917), p.12; *WW* 42:1 (Jan 1920), p.13; *DPCM*, pp.161–4, 175–8, 323–4, 724.

12 *WE* 160 (7 and 14 Oct 1916), p.12; 171 (6 Jan 1917), p.12.

13 *WE* 154 (26 Aug 1916), p.14; 155 (2 Sept 1916), p.13; 164 (11 Nov 1916), p.13; 166 (25 Nov 1916), p.13; 172 (13 Jan 1917), p.12; 178 (24 Feb 1917), p.12; 182 (31 Mar 1917), p.12; 197 (7 July 1917), p.12; 200 (28 July 1917), p.13; 212 (27 Oct 1917), p.13; *DPCM*, pp.77–9, 81–3, 209–10, 845, 949–50; 'Combined Minutes', 1920, p.67.

14 *BM* 58 (15 Mar 1910), p.2; 64 (15 June 1910), p.4; 66 (15 July 1910), p.3; 68 (15 Aug 1910), p.1.

15 Hunter, 'Journey Toward Racial Reconciliation', p.285; Tomlinson, *Diary*, pp.182–91; *DPCM*, p.30.

16 *BM* 70 (15 Sept 1910), p.3; 85 (1 May 1911), p.2; 101 (1 Jan 1912), p.2; 107 (1 Apr 1912), p.1; 122 (1 Dec 1912), p.2; *WW* 33:12 (Dec 1911), p.362; 36:6 (June 1914), p.186; 36:7 (July 1914), p.216; 36:9 (Sept 1914), p.282; 36:11 (Nov 1914), p.348; 37:1 (Jan 1915), p.28; 42:1 (Jan 1920), p.13; 42:3 (Mar 1920), p.31; 42:6 (June 1920), p.13; 42:7 (July 1920), p.13; *LRE* 12:7 (Apr 1920), p.14; *DPCM*, pp.51–3, 143.

17 *Pent* 1:6 (Apr–May 1909), p.3; 2:4 (March 1910), p.1; 2:9–10 (Sept–Oct 1910), p.4; 2:11–12 (Nov–Dec 1910), pp.4, 5; *LRE* 3:4 (Jan 1911), p.3; 5:4 (Jan 1913), pp.19–22; *BM* 90 (15 July 1911), p.2; 102 (15 Jan 1912), p.2; 105 (1 Mar 1912), p.1; 123 (15 Dec 1912), p.4; *FF* 14 (Oct 1913), p.4; 21 (Nov 1914), p.7; *CE* 60 (26 Sept 1914), p.1; *TF* 35:2 (Feb 1915), pp.46–7; 36:11 (Nov 1916), p.257; *WWit* 12:5 (May 1915), p.6; *WE* 181 (17 Mar 1917), p.11; 219 (22 Dec 1917), p.10; *DPCM*, pp.279–81.

18 *Pent* 1:6 (Apr–May 1909), p.3; 2:4 (Mar 1910), p.1; 2:9–10 (Sept–Oct 1910), p.4; 2:11–12 (Nov–Dec 1910), pp.4, 5; *LRE* 3:4 (Jan 1911), p.3; *BM* 90 (15 July 1911), p.2; 102 (15 Jan 1912), p.2; 105 (1 Mar 1912), p.1; 123 (15 Dec 1912), p.4; 132 (1 May 1913), p.2; *WW* 6:6 (June 1914), p.186; 36:7 (July 1914), p.219.

19 *BM* 146 (15 Dec 1913), p.4; *WW* 36:9 (Sept 1914), p.284; 36:10 (Oct 1914), p.315; *WWit* 10:4 (Apr 1914), p.4; 12:5 (May 1915), p.6; *Trust* 14:7 (Sept 1915), p.19; *WE* 187 (28 Apr 1917), p.11; *DPCM*, p.199.

20 'Constitution and By-Laws', 1939, p.184; *DPCM*, p.23.

21 *BM* 62 (15 May 1910), p.3; 71 (1 Oct 1910), p.2; 72 (15 Oct 1910), p.1; 73 (1 Nov 1910), p.4; 82 (15 Mar 1911), p.1; 87 (1 June 1911), p.1; 100 (15 Dec 1911), p.1; 110 (15 May 1912), p.1; 118 (15 Sept 1912), p.4; 136 (1 July 1913), p.2; 137 (1 Aug 1913), p.1; *WW* 32:12 (Dec 1910), p.381; 33:5 (May 1911), p.158; 33:7 (July 1911), p.222; 37:2 (Feb 1915), p.58; 39:12 (Apr 1917), p.191; *LRE* 4:10 (July 1912), p.9; *WWit* 10:7 (July 1914), p.4; 12:5 (May 1915), p.5; 12:8 (Aug 1915), p.3; *WE* 103 (14 Aug 1915), p.4; 121 (1 Jan 1916), p.12; 162 (28 Oct 1916), p.13; 179 (3 Mar 1917), p.12; 181 (17 Mar 1917), p.13; 192 (2 June 1917), p.12; 214 (10 Nov 1917), p.13; *DPCM*, p.23.

22 *WW* 40:30 (Sept 1918), p.15; 42:1 (Jan 1920), p.14; 42:7 (July 1920), p.14; *TF* 40:5 (May 1920), pp.104–5; Saracco, 'Argentine Pentecostalism', p.48.

23 Saracco, 'Argentine Pentecostalism', pp.66, 210–16.

24 Supplement to *Conf* 2:6 (June 1909), p.12; *LRE* 3:7 (Apr 1911), p.19.

25 Hoover and Hoover, *History*, pp.9, 18–20, 29–32, 36, 68–73; *UR* 1:6 (Jan 1910), p.5; *WW* 32:3 (Mar 1910), p.94; *Trust* 9:8 (Oct 1910), p.18.

26 *Pent* 2:4 (Mar 1910), p.1.

27 *WW* 32:5 (May 1910), pp.156–7; *UR* 1:10 (May 1910), p.5; *TF* 30:6 (June 1910), pp.26–7.

28 *LRE* 3:7 (Apr 1911), p.20; *DPCM*, pp.770–1.

29 Hoover and Hoover, *History*, pp.74–100, 240–7; *Trust* 9:8 (Oct 1910), p.19; *UR* 2:5 (May 1911), p.5; *LRE* 3:10 (July 1911), pp.21–4; 6:9 (June 1914), p.19; 13:4 (Jan 1921), pp.2–5; *BM* 97 (1 Nov 1911), p.4; *TF* 32:2 (Feb 1912), p.48.

30 *WWit* 9:11 (Nov 1913), p.4; 10:4 (Apr 1914), p.4; *WE* 168 (9 Dec 1916), p.12; 198 (14 July 1917), p.13.

31 Hollenweger, *The Pentecostals*, pp.85–92.

32 *WWit* 9:10 (Oct 1913), p.2; 10:3 (Mar 1914), p.4; *LRE* 8:4 (Jan 1916), pp.14–16; 12:3 (Dec 1919), p.11; *WE* 213 (3 Nov 1917), p.13.

33 *LRE* 8:4 (Jan 1916), p.14.

34 Hollenweger, *The Pentecostals*, pp.75, 78; Chesnut, *Born Again*, pp.26–7; *DPCM*, p.208.

35 Chesnut, *Born Again*, p.30.

36 *FF* 34 (Jan 1916), p.9.

Part Three

Theology and Praxis

8

With Signs Following: Evangelism, Healing and Eschatology

The great and last call of God has been given to the church in the Pentecostal move-ment. It is a call to push the missionary work; and this means that every nation must be visited with the living, saving Gospel of our Lord Jesus; and that those who are sent must measure up to Bible standard, equipped as the disciples were after Pentecost, full of burning messages of love and life and accompanied with signs following. Nothing short of this kind of missionary effort will prepare the people for translation or for that great and terrible day of the Lord, the tribulation, which not all Christians shall escape.

(*The Bridegroom's Messenger*, 1910)[1]

The mission emphasis of early Pentecostalism almost always saw mission as first and foremost a worldwide and intense evangelism. As a consequence of this, there was also an almost uniformly negative approach to other faiths, which attitude the next chapter will examine. Evangelism in Pentecostal practice, however, differed significantly from that of the older evangelical and 'faith' missions. The Pentecostal task was to preach a 'full' or 'fourfold'/'fivefold' gospel (depending which kind of Pentecostal you were). This 'full' gospel included a message of salvation, healing (sanctification), baptism in the Spirit, and the return of Christ. This gospel was intrinsically part of their proclamation and could not be separated from it. As we will see in this chapter, these emphases were not without their challenges.

The great Edinburgh Missionary Conference of 1910 was an important mile-stone in Protestant missions and gave birth to the ecumenical movement of the twentieth century. This was also a conference that put great stress on evangelism, and the motto of its organizer John Mott was 'the evangelization of the world in this generation'. But there is little evidence that it had any influence on Pentecostal missions. After all, Pentecostals were not invited to this event, quite understandable at a time when they were not yet organized into structures. Furthermore, Edinburgh 1910 did not foresee the massive transformation in the nature of the Church that was to take place during the twentieth century, in which Pentecostalism played a major role. There were very few references to Edinburgh in the Pentecostal literature of the time. One of these was by Elisabeth Sexton in *The Bridegroom's Messenger* and was decidedly negative. Although this was 'undoubtedly the greatest missionary gathering the Christian world has ever known', she doubted whether the applauded unity was really that of the Spirit uniting them in Christ or was rather out of respect for the occasion. She decried Catholic par-ticipation and concessions to 'heathen religions', holding out 'little hope for great results for our God' as an outcome of the conference. She saw the conference as a lost opportunity, especially as it had in her view missed the urgent eschatological dimension of missions and the power of the Spirit that were thrusting out Pentecostal missionaries all over the world in the shortest possible time.[2]

Cecil Polhill, leader of the PMU had a broader experience with his Anglican background and CIM involvement. His assessment of Edinburgh was more positive. The conference was 'evidently ordered in the Plan of God', he wrote, and its reports brought the Church 'face to face with the world's needs in detail' while they concentrated on the 'unparalleled opportunity' and the 'Church's responsibility'. He drew special attention to the 'Report of the Commission for Carrying the Gospel to All the Non-Christian World' and highlighted its emphasis on the unprecedented opportunities for evangelization. But he said that the Church had not responded to these calls and that the Pentecostal movement had arisen to rectify this grave omission.[3] Two PMU missionaries, Percy Bristow and John Beruldsen, were official delegates to a continuation conference of Edinburgh 1910 conducted by John Mott in Beijing in 1913.[4] So Pentecostals were not entirely absent.

The Priority of Evangelism

As a result of the various revival emphases, the power of the Spirit in Pentecostal thinking is always linked to the command to preach the gospel to all nations. Pentecostal preachers had to proclaim this gospel everywhere with attendant signs that demonstrated the Lord's presence. This task was also given urgency in view of the impending return of Christ. *The Bridegroom's Messenger* described graphically what motivated early Pentecostals in their feverish mission activities: the world was about to end and Christ had sent the new Pentecost to prepare for his coming. The nations of the world had to be evangelized through the power of the Spirit and with 'signs following' before this cataclysmic event occurred. Sexton later elaborated on this theme, writing in 1912 that any church 'alive to the interests of the kingdom of God' and with 'a real spirit of revival' would always show this by an 'intense interest in the return of their Lord and by active missionary enterprise'. Their hope would be of 'speedily propagating the word of truth in all nations before He comes'.[5] The letters from Pentecostal missionaries were filled with one overriding concern: to evangelize the nations of the world as quickly as possible before the return of Christ. In order to accomplish this supreme task the power of the Spirit was needed. Minnie Abrams thought that 'only a small portion of the Christian church' had as yet 'awakened to her responsibility of evangelizing the masses of the heathen world'. But she urged that there be no shirking this work 'given to us by our Lord', so that Christians could 'stand before Him uncondemned'. 'As yet', she continued,

we have reached only a few, while hundreds of millions still lie in darkness. Jesus said, 'This gospel of the kingdom shall be preached in the whole world for a testimony unto all the nations,' Matt. 24:14. How are we to do it? The church has sufficient machinery to accomplish this work and sufficient workers, but the workers lack power.[6]

Not only were those from the English-speaking world motivated by 'Great Commission' texts like Matthew 28.19 ('Go ye therefore, and teach all nations') and Mark 16.15 ('Go ye into all the world and preach the gospel to every creature'), but were even more often fired by the eschatological text of Matthew 24.14 referred to by Abrams above and by Old Testament prophecies like 'Ask of me and I shall give thee the heathen for thine inheritance' (Psalm 2.8), and 'Ethiopia shall soon stretch out her hands unto God' (Psalm 68.31). These texts were both the motivation and the justification for their evangelistic activities.[7] The power to preach the gospel and evangelize all nations permeated the activities of the missionaries and their converts, but not to the exclusion of all other activities. Frequently missionaries quoted the words of Christ that the 'fields are white unto harvest, but the labourers are few', and wrote of the great need of the multitudes of 'heathen' in the nations for more evangelizing missionaries. The outpouring of the Spirit had made this known to the Church and so it was its urgent task to get on with the job of preaching the 'full gospel' to the 'heathen'. Many prophecies had been spoken in unknown tongues and many visions about the 'soon coming' of Christ, *The Apostolic Faith* declared. 'The heathen must first receive the gospel. One prophecy given in an unknown tongue was interpreted, "The time is short, and I am going to send out a large number in the Spirit of God to preach the full gospel in the power of the Spirit".'[8]

This itinerating evangelism in the Spirit's power was the main activity required, at least as far as some were concerned, and this was to govern the mission policies of the few Pentecostal mission societies and later denominational missions departments. The British PMU Secretary Mundell expressed this priority in a letter to one of the PMU missionaries in 1914 that the 'first and great need of course, of China and Tibet' was 'the Evangelization of the Masses so that the Gospel is preached as our Lord desired "to all nations"'. He wrote that the Council did 'not feel justified in carrying out a policy of establishing large missions in any part of a locality beyond what is necessary for itinerating thoroughly the district in which our missionaries are to be placed'.[9] Pentecostals saw their task made both easier and more effective because of the power of the Spirit. This view sometimes brought them into sharp tension with older and more experienced evangelical missionaries who had laboured for many years at individualistic evangelism with only limited results. The conflict became even sharper when newly Spirit-baptized missionaries declared that their previous efforts had been virtually futile, and that they had found that the freedom of the Spirit gave them faster and more efficient methods than the bureaucratic machinery of established mission societies. The veteran missionary in China who became Pentecostal in 1912, W. W. Simpson, described his evangelistic job as follows:

I know by practical experience and actual work that the evangelization of the Heathen can be carried on now exactly as in the days of Peter, Paul and Phillip. This knowledge had revolutionized my whole work and methods, I now see the complete evangelization of China in the course of two or three years as a practical possibility within our grasp. Not by opening large mission stations and establishing extensive plants and institutions and cumbering the work with elaborately organized machinery, not by boards and committees and high sounding phraseology, not by suasive words of wisdom and discussions and councils, but by the foolishness of preaching in the demonstration of the Spirit and the power is the work to be done.[10]

No wonder the established missions were threatened by this sort of 'propaganda'. Jacob Lehman wrote from Johannesburg that 'In His name demons are cast out, the vilest sinners saved, and the most stubborn diseases are healed'. He added that 'through these manifestations of His presence people are drawn to Christ and reconciled to God'.[11] The evangelistic methods used by foreign missionaries were (at least by today's standards) quaint and anachronistic. Pentecostals would visit busy places like markets and main streets and set up preaching points in the open air. There they would use a portable organ, concertina or other musical instrument to gather a crowd and would then begin a service with testimonies and preaching. Crowds began to gather, probably as much from amusement as curiosity. Sometimes, as when there were great Hindu festivals in India, they would divide their workers into two groups of men and women, because the pilgrims were divided according to gender. Then they would distribute and sell tracts and gospel portions there, and preach in the open air. They used similar techniques of evangelism in Buddhist festivals in Sri Lanka and China.[12] Ethel Cook has given a description of these methods, writing a personal letter from Yunnan, China in 1914 after she had been on an itinerating preaching tour on horseback with her senior missionary, Sigrid McLean:

We live native fashion here – only two meals a day . . . mostly of rice & vegetables, in bowls, eaten with chopsticks . . . Last Friday we started after morning meal for a Village two miles away; arrived at a nice open space, we borrowed some straw seats (like thick hassocks) to sit on, & our singing, with Mrs McLean's Autoharp, soon collected a big crowd. As far as we can tell they had not heard the Gospel before, & how they listened! We kept on singing & preaching & talking for 1½ to 2 hours & we believe the Lord worked in many hearts. Two young men asked our Mr Chiü all kinds of intelligent questions . . . We gave away some tracts, taught a tiny prayer, then closed in prayer & left them.[13]

A year later Cook used a similar technique as she travelled from village to village with a Chinese evangelist and sometimes a 'woman helper', but instead of the autoharp they sang hymns in Chinese while she played a violin – 'which never failed to draw a group of listeners'. Once a large enough group had gathered they took it in turns to preach to them, an activity that took 'some time'. For reaching the women, Cook would walk up and down the open-air market selling gospels and speaking to small groups. She rued the fact that there were no results to report on from all these daily activities.[14]

There were other emphases linked to the Pentecostal priority of evangelism, not least of which was the importance of sustained prayer. Writing about the Lake-Hezmalhalch team in Johannesburg in 1908, W. J. Kerr expressed the importance of prayer in the missionaries' strategy of evangelism. They had emphasized 'the necessity of much prayer, and most of the meetings are largely prayer meetings, either before or after the usual gospel service'. It was customary for the workers to be in a back room of their meeting place 'for one or two hours either praying with people, or waiting on God for His blessing', he said.[15]

It would be a mistake, however, to conclude that this 'spiritual' kind of evangelism was the only activity with which early Pentecostal missionaries were engaged. Nothing could be further from the truth. What is most remarkable about these missionaries was their preoccupation with rescue missions, famine relief, feeding the poor, and especially the creation of orphanages and schools to care for the many destitute children they came across. It was not just a case of preaching the full gospel and leaving their converts to take care of themselves. Looking after the physical needs of their converts and of needy children was an integral part of the gospel they proclaimed.

The Practice of Healing

Pentecostal missionaries regarded 'signs and wonders' to be such an indispensable part of their evangelism, without which their preaching was powerless. They considered this evidence that the 'apostolic' power was as available as it had been in the time of the New Testament. At the beginning of the twentieth century, there was a general expectation in radical evangelical and revivalist ideas that 'signs and wonders' would accompany an outpouring of the Spirit.[16] Elisabeth Sexton wrote that unbelievers would be convinced by 'the supernatural manifestation of His power in His saints' and that the world had the right to expect signs to follow their ministry. She believed that this power in Jesus' name was being realized in Pentecostal people.[17] William Burton wrote much about this. Christ's command to heal the sick had never been withdrawn. His apostles continued his healing and miracle ministry to the end of their lives. The present days were 'apostolic days' and God was still sending apostles to the nations of earth. Jesus had given the example of a method of evangelism and he expected it to proceed in like manner, with 'signs following', just as had happened from the beginning of his mission in the Congo.[18]

Pentecostals see healing as good news for the poor and afflicted. Early twentieth-century Pentecostal newsletters and periodicals abounded with 'thousands of testimonies to physical healings, exorcisms and deliverances'.[19] Divine healing was an evangelistic door-opener for Pentecostals by which the full gospel is demonstrated in a physical and personal deliverance.[20] Early Pentecostal missionaries such as Lake in South Africa, Burton in the Congo, Berg and Cook in India, and especially the later healing evangelists expected miracles to accompany their evangelism, and as McGee points out, they 'prioritized seeking for spectacular displays of celestial power – signs and wonders, healing, and deliverance from sinful habits and satanic bondage'.[21] The 'signs and wonders' promoted by independent evangelists have led to the rapid growth of Pentecostal churches in many parts of the world, although they have seldom been without controversy.[22]

In many cultures of the world, healing has been a major attraction for Pentecostalism. In most ancient cultures of Africa and Asia, the religious specialist has extraordinary power to heal the sick and protect from evil spirits and sorcery. Because of the possibility and proclamation of healing and miracles in Pentecostalism, people could relate to it in their own context and saw it as a 'powerful' religion to meet human needs. G. S. Brelsford expressed the convictions of many of these early Pentecostal missionaries, writing from Egypt in 1910 that if only the missionaries could 'get into God's way of doing things, He can work'. God had worked 'some precious miracles' in Egypt that had given 'an entrance to the Gospel in that land'. People had come from distant places bringing the sick for prayer, and had begged the missionaries to come to their towns and villages. He went on, 'This Gospel in its primitive power will open the doors. If God had had a better way to reach the heathen nations He would have given it. If we will take His way the doors will open.'[23] For some Pentecostals, faith in God's power to heal directly through prayer resulted in their rejecting other methods of healing. Even some of the more moderate PMU missionaries had these convictions. J. H. Boyce wrote from India that he had noticed that 'those who refused medicine and trusted the Lord were healed, and recovered sooner than those who took medicine, and in addition received blessing in their souls' and in some cases, 'instantaneous deliverance from fever was given as they cried for the administration of the remedy prescribed in James v. 14'.[24]

Healing permeated the writings and activities of many early Pentecostal missionaries. The numerous healings reported by them confirmed that God's Word was true, his power was evidently on their missionary efforts and the result was that many were persuaded to become Christians. As Burton put it, healing was one of the missionaries' 'credentials' that they carried with them. Above all of the 'signs' promised in Mark 16, he declared, was that 'again and again, we lay hands on the sick in the Name of Jesus and they recover, whereas the witch doctors' fetishes could not, in some cases, heal them'. Furthermore, in contrast to the traditional healers who charged for their services, Pentecostals offered their healing power free. Burton wrote that healing was 'the very foundation of pioneering missionary work'.[25] It was, in effect, this power confrontation with traditional healers that won converts for the Pentecostals. This healing activity was played out in many different contexts and occasions, often spreading much quicker through 'native' agency. A Pentecostal missionary in South Africa wrote in 1909 that God was 'doing marvelous things amongst the native people'. When Africans got 'saved' and 'healed', they also had 'faith in God for the salvation and the healing of others'. He continued, 'It goes like wildfire from one to another. It is the ministry of healing that carries the Gospel. Missionaries without faith for healing do not amount to much here. There are plenty of them here now who cannot touch the people.'[26] Tom Hezmalhalch wrote in similar vein about healing being an indispensable part of the gospel and the most effective means of evangelism. He said that healing was 'one of the greatest essentials of the Gospel'. He thought that 'to see a lame man get up and walk by the power of Jesus, and the blind receive their sight, and the dead raised to life again, does more to get the truth of God home to the hearts of the nations, and will do more good than all the preaching and ecclesiastical machinery has ever done or can do'.[27] W. J. Kerr described the important role of divine healing to his readers, 'one of the greatest powers we have', he wrote, and the means by which people were 'brought to Jesus'. He declared that he 'could fill a fair sized newspaper with detailed accounts' of people 'completely healed in answer to prayer'.[28]

But it was not always power and glory for the early Pentecostal missionaries. Some doubted the authenticity of all the many reports of healing, especially issuing from South Africa and India, and some were later proved to be exaggerated. There was a certain dilemma for many Pentecostal missionaries on the subject of healing. Occasionally, missionaries reported cases of failed healings and of course, many of these early missionaries succumbed themselves to sickness and even to diseases that resulted in death. There is little evidence that they were any different from those missionaries who were not Pentecostal. Tragically, many of these itinerant western missionaries died in their adopted countries after only a short time. Among them was Aimee Semple MacPherson's first husband, Robert Semple, who died in Hong Kong in 1910 after only ten weeks there, leaving his wife with their baby girl, Roberta, to return to America. Several missionaries died of smallpox, among them the entire Batman family in Liberia in 1907, Antoinette Moomau's assistant in Shanghai, Leola Phillips in 1910 and Amos Williams in 1915.[29] Cora Fritsch Faulkner wrote home to Seattle in 1909 that because she could not get a reduction in the fare to return to the USA, 'perhaps the Lord would have me stay a few years longer and learn the language'. Six years later she too died.[30] There were many others.

Some early Pentecostals' views on healing were strikingly reminiscent of the present-day 'Word of Faith' teaching that believes that all sickness is from 'the devil' and does not belong to a Christian believer, so that when we 'feel' sick we have the symptoms, but not the sickness itself. This came from a missionary suffering from dysentery in India:

In Him we are perfectly safe, and though Satan has the power and is permitted to put upon us feelings of sickness (only the appearance, I don't believe the reality), they cannot harm or touch us unless we give way to them, and so open the door to the enemy. We are branches in the vine and His perfect life flows through each one of us. The branch cannot be diseased within unless the tree itself is affected, for the same sap flows through each. The branch may be attacked from without by the enemy, and then (praise Him) it is the work of the husbandman to purge it and deal with the enemy.[31]

Some were more realistic in their approach to their own physical weaknesses. Minnie Abrams, struggling against ill health during her furlough to the USA in 1909–10, spoke of her views on the subject in a convention address in Rochester, New York. She said that during the outpouring of the Spirit in Mukti they were praying for sick people and although 'the Lord wrought many wonderful things', 'not one' of them was 'a perfect work'. They came to the conclusion that unbelief among their workers stopped the healing power of God.[32] Abrams also believed that Christians would be able to survive death until the coming of the Lord. On her last recorded public speaking engagement in the All India Pentecostal Convention in Faizabad, she preached that because the last enemy to be destroyed would be death, so Pentecostal believers would be able to conquer death as they had conquered sickness and pain, and be alive at the coming of Christ. She died less than a year later of a longstanding affliction.[33] Lillian Garr, who herself died soon after her return to the USA and lost both her daughter and her nanny to smallpox soon after their arrival in Hong Kong, wrote of the loss of the two children of other missionaries there. These children they had to 'give up', she said, because God was preparing them for 'higher ministry'. As a result of their 'double sorrow' they would 'come forth as gold'.[34] As she nursed her terminally-ill husband in China, Maggie Trevitt struggled with the conflict between her faith in divine healing and the reality of her husband's tuberculosis. They did 'not understand why deliverance does not come', she wrote. They had both searched their hearts and had 'asked the Holy Spirit to search us and anything that was revealed we confessed it and asked for cleansing and forgiveness, but still deliverance is withheld and the Lord must have a purpose in it'.[35] Her husband died a short time after this letter was written.

Allan Swift stressed the need for careful medical screening of PMU missionary candidates because 'when one after another goes to the Doctor, our testimony for healing has no value in this city'. He felt that there was a weakness in those missionaries who had 'a painful lack of being able to trust the Lord in times of sickness'.[36] These words were written before the Swifts lost their only son to smallpox. Many missionaries lost children to disease, often using their belief in the near coming of Christ as a comfort in their grief. A heartfelt letter from George Hansen in Shanghai in 1910 is not an isolated example, written after his son had died of smallpox.

> It pleased our heavenly Father to call home to Himself our dear little son, George, seven years and four months old, the ninth of August. He rejoiced to go home to the heavenly land. We asked him if he wanted to go to Jesus, he answered, 'Yes, it is much better, it is so warm here in China. I do not want to stay here.' He smiled, looked up, lifted up his little hands, as though he wanted to receive something . . . Only a little while and we will meet with the dear one gone before us.[37]

Sometimes, letters appeared in the Pentecostal press from people who had had contact with Pentecostal workers, had had prayer for their severe illnesses and had not been healed. Such letters were rarely published, but on one occasion an Indian writer was asking for prayer 'for the recovery of my disease'.[38]

The central role given to healing is probably no longer as prominent a feature of western Pentecostalism as it once was, but in the Majority World the problems of disease and evil still affect the whole community and are not relegated to a private domain for individual pastoral care and prayer. These communities were, to a large extent, health-orientated communities and in their pre-Christian religions, rituals for healing and protection were prominent. Pentecostals responded to what they experienced as a void left by rationalistic western forms of Christianity that had unwittingly initiated what was in effect the destruction of familiar spiritual values. Pentecostals declared a message that reclaimed the biblical traditions of healing and protection from evil, they demonstrated the practical effects of these traditions and by so doing became heralds of a Christianity that was really meaningful. Thus, Pentecostal missionaries went a long way towards meeting physical, emotional and spiritual needs of people in the Majority World, offering solutions to life's problems and ways to cope in what was often a threatening and hostile world.[39] But sadly, this message of power has become in some instances an occasion for the exploitation of those who are at their weakest.

Early Pentecostal missionaries seldom confessed to failure in the realm of healing, but occasionally we get glimpses that it did not always happen. Berntsen in China wrote in 1909, 'We have results in praying for the sick, but we like to see more', and went on to list all the things God had 'promised to confirm His word with signs and wonders'.[40] Burton struggled with the issue of taking quinine as protection against malaria after he discovered how many missionaries had died of malaria in southern Africa, as 'The Apostolic Faith and Pentecostal Mission have 33 graves of splendid men and women who refused quinine and died'. He asked the rhetorical question, 'But now these malaria victims are dying, and of course some of the Spirit filled missionaries are taking quinine, and they don't die, and they ask me which gives God most glory? To take this stuff and live, or refuse it and die?'[41] These were some of the dilemmas and heartaches faced by Pentecostal missionaries in the practice of healing.

Eschatological Mission

A particular kind of eschatological expectation was also a dominant theme in Pentecostalism, further adding to the urgency of mission service. There was a shift from the optimism of the postmillennialism that prevailed in early nineteenth-century Protestantism to a pessimistic, premillennialist 'secret rapture' dispensationalism that swept through evangelical circles later that century. This shift occurred gradually in the Holiness movement as a result of several factors, but was precipitated by the teaching of John Nelson Darby of the Plymouth Brethren in Britain. A monthly periodical *The Prophetic Times* commenced in 1863 and prophetic conferences like D. L. Moody's annual Prophecy Conference in Massachusetts from 1880 prominently advocated Darby's eschatological views. Popular preachers A. T. Pierson, A. B. Simpson and A. J. Gordon all expounded premillennialism; eventually it was accepted by a majority of American evangelicals, and it became a prominent theme of the Keswick conventions in England. With a few exceptions, most of the Holiness movement, many evangelicals and subsequently most early Pentecostals accepted premillennial eschatology, although several prominent Methodist and Holiness leaders of the Wesleyan persuasion were actively opposed to it. The reasons for its widespread acceptance are complicated, and include a pessimistic reaction to theological liberalism and the 'social gospel' that increasingly came to identify the main Protestant denominations. But more significantly, premillennialism was based on the same modernistic assumptions as those of the emerging 'liberalism' that these evangelicals were trying to counteract. Their complex and intricately woven eschatological system was a product of a highly rationalistic approach to biblical apocalypticism. Because the Keswick movement was at first an expression of Reformed evangelicalism, it accepted premillennialism at an early stage. Faupel has shown that as most other Holiness groups gradually accepted the pneumatological centre of the Keswick position through exposure to their teachers, they also accepted its eschatology with its stress on the coming of a new Pentecost to usher in the soon return of Christ.[42]

The demise of postmillennialism in nineteenth-century evangelicalism with its optimistic view of a coming 'golden age' of material wealth and progress was replaced by an increasingly pessimistic premillennialism that believed that the world would get progressively worse until the return of Christ. So, the missionary task was to rescue individuals from imminent peril rather than seek to transform society. One missionary, writing from China, expressed this well, as she said at the beginning of a new year that their hearts were 'thrilling with the thought "He is coming soon". Oh! may we win many souls for the Master . . . How evident it is that we are in the last days; the general indifference, coldness, deadness, & iniquity waxing worse & worse. Yet, praise God, here & there – a gleam of light.'[43] But this premillennialism was not entirely pessimistic, for there was a certain tension between the negative view of the world and the very positive view of their place in it. The outpouring of the Spirit in the last days made mission and evangelizing the nations possible. The eschatological link between revival and missions was expressed by the founder of the CIM, James Hudson Taylor, who had apparently declared ten years before his death that 'the next great series of events on the world's stage of action would be a great war between Russia and Japan in which Russia would be defeated. Then would follow the greatest spiritual revival the world has ever known, and soon after would follow the coming of Jesus.'[44] This was a remarkable prophecy, but the last part had not been fulfilled, at least not as soon as Taylor had thought. Pentecostals believed that they were in that revival and that their mission work was a direct consequence of it.

The differences between these various interpretations of biblical apocalyptic literature were vast. Postmillennialists held that Christ would return after a thousand-year period and therefore they laid greater stress on social activism in order to make the world a better place to live in. Their mission work included educational, philanthropic and medical activities as well as evangelism and church planting, but the latter was given less attention. In contrast, premillennialists believed that Christ's return could be imminent and before the thousand-year period, so their view of the world was decidedly negative, where its activities were to be rejected and it was seen as a temporary place in which Christians were merely brief visitors. Pentecostal periodicals were full of exhortations about the imminent return of Christ. It has been a feature of Pentecostalism throughout its history that current events are taken as signs of the times, proof that the Lord was coming back soon. Their mission work consisted particularly (but not entirely) of feverish evangelism and church planting, and together with most of the newly established 'faith missions', they began to propagate this eschatology. Maria Woodworth-Etter, a prominent healing evangelist, helped popularize these ideas in radical evangelical circles in the USA at the end of the nineteenth century. That the 'last times' had come was evident and the coming of the Lord was 'very near' because the power of the Spirit was causing God's people to dream dreams and see visions in fulfilment of Joel's prophecy.[45]

But we must also remember that most early Pentecostal missions had philanthropic and educational activities, especially in the creation of orphanages, schools and rescue centres – Albert Norton's work in India, Mok Lai Chi's in Hong Kong and Lillian Trasher's in Egypt being prime examples. Norton wrote disapprovingly of those missionaries who fraternized with European colonialists in their sports and amusements 'to ignore and deny the existence of the sufferings of the poor'.[46] The evangelism of the Pentecostals did not therefore obliterate all other concerns, although it must be said that all other activities were usually seen as subservient to the primary task of getting individuals 'saved' and filled with the Spirit. The first Pentecostals saw the soon coming of Christ as the prime motivation for the urgent task of preparing the world for this cataclysmic event. Prophecies, tongues and interpretations and visions affirmed this expectation almost on every occasion. Declared *The Apostolic Faith* in 1908:

'Jesus is coming soon,' is the message that the Holy Ghost is speaking today through nearly everyone that receives the baptism with the Holy Ghost. Many times they get the interpretation of the message spoken in an unknown language and many times others have understood the language spoken. Many receive visions of Jesus and He says, 'I am coming soon.' Two saints recently in Minneapolis fell under the power were caught up to Heaven and saw the New Jerusalem, the table spread, and many of the saints there, both seeing the same visions at the same time. They said Jesus was coming very soon and for us to work as we had little time.[47]

The second coming of Christ would occur when the gospel had been proclaimed to every nation, they declared, and so it was necessary to engage in the most rapid evangelization possible. Despite their optimism about their role in this end-time mission, their view of the world around them, especially the religious world, was decidedly negative. They saw the increase of 'false prophets', the expansion of Islam, theological liberalism (especially 'Higher Criticism', anathema to these premillennialists) and the spread of heterodox Christian groups like Mormons and Jehovah's Witnesses (then called 'Millennial Dawn') – all signs of the impending doom.[48] Pentecostal missionary H. M. Turney, from Azusa Street and itinerant evangelist before settling in South Africa, wrote that he expected to leave on a round-the-world trip 'sounding the golden trumpet, heralding the year of jubilee'. He continued, 'For the coming of the Lord is near, even at the door. And he wants the heathen nations to hear the glad tidings and be ready for His coming.'[49] The Scripture most often linked to this eschatological motivation for mission was Matthew 24.14: 'And this gospel of the kingdom shall be preached in all the world for a witness unto all nations; and then shall the end come.'[50] An American woman,

Mary Courtney (later married to Will Norton), used this verse to plead for prayers that doors would open for her to enter Tibet or Nepal, 'perhaps through His own healing power' – although they might need to live in tents and 'eat native food', yet 'the gospel must be preached, and if some fall, others will be raised up to take our places', she wrote.[51] In fact, for so many of these Pentecostal missionaries and their children, the 'soon coming of the Lord' was realized in their premature death through diseases – especially smallpox, malaria and, from 1918, the influenza epidemic.

One of the clearest expositions of this link between mission and premillennial eschatology was made by Elisabeth Sexton in an editorial discussing (rather negatively) the great Edinburgh missionary conference of 1910. It was not the frantic and increased activity in itself that would achieve God's purposes, she wrote, but the haste that was needed in these last days was in 'preparation for that blessed day, and the making ready of the Bride of Christ'. Any missionary activity that did not have this end in view would 'miss the highest privilege of this age'.[52] On the other hand, two years later Cecil Polhill was more positive in drawing attention to the calls of the conference for making the most of the unprecedented opportunities to engage in world evangelization. There had never been a decade like the second decade of the twentieth century where doors all over the world were opened.[53] Sadly, the Great War was to put pay to these opportunities and leave the world reeling from its devastation. Missionaries made premillennial eschatology part of their preaching wherever they went and the seeming delay in Christ's coming did not deter them. A missionary in North India preached in a village about the soon coming of Jesus, and when challenged because a long time had already elapsed, replied that 'the signs of the times show that He will soon come'.[54]

There was also an implied link between this eschatology and the expectations regarding the 'holy land', Palestine, until 1918 occupied by the Ottoman Turks. One of the ideals of this Christian eschatology was that the Jews would return to their own land, and that political events 'from a human standpoint' showed that 'everything promises to be working towards the occupancy of the land at no distant future by the only people who have a God-given right to it'.[55] This belief in an exclusive, 'God-given right' belonging to the Jews concerning Palestine persists in Pentecostal circles to this day. During the Great War the conviction among premillennialists grew that Turkey would be defeated and Palestine pass into the control of the Allies, thus paving the way for the return of the Jews to their 'holy land' and the setting up of the nation of Israel. When British troops marched into Jerusalem in 1918 the prophecies seemed to have been fulfilled. Linked to these events would be the final battle of Armageddon, when Palestine would be invaded by Russia in the north, it was believed.[56] Most premillennialists held that before this final battle, the 'saints' would be 'raptured' (snatched away) from the world in the time of the 'Great Tribulation' and the world would be left to its own fate of bloodshed, unimaginable horror and eventual destruction. After this period Christ would return and set up a thousand-year reign on earth when Satan and his demons would be confined to a tortuous prison (Hades). At the end of this Millennium, Satan would be released for a short period until his final destruction in the 'lake of fire' (Hell). So when Pentecostals preached about the imminent return of Christ, many of them had this whole complicated panorama in mind. It was not a simple case of Jesus coming back soon.

Minnie Abrams also linked the power of the Spirit with the evangelization of the nations in the last days and penned the following in her booklet *The Baptism of the Holy Ghost and Fire*. She wrote that there was only a short time left 'to gather out from these thousand millions of unevangelized people the Lord's portion'. She went on:

> If we do not do this work, their blood will be required of us. No Christian is exempt from this responsibility. It is time that we seek the fulness of the Holy Ghost, the fire that empowers us to preach the word in the fulness of love and with signs following. It is our unbelief that is keeping us from receiving this power to evangelize the nations.

She concluded with a bold call for missionaries who would go out in the power of the Spirit. When 'those anointed to preach the gospel' would be 'bold enough to accept and exercise the gifts of the Spirit, and to do the signs and miracles authorized in the word of God, in three years time the gospel will spread more rapidly and bring more under its power, than it has in the past 300 years'. She ended this exhortation, 'Awake, O Zion, put on thy strength, and thus prepare a great host to meet the coming King!'[57]

Some were not as sure about the overemphasis on hastening the coming of the Lord and that the coming of Christ was conditional upon their faithfulness in mission. This was particularly the case in Europe, expressed by the principal of the PMU Men's College, H. E. Wallis, and published in *Confidence* in 1913. He wrote that it was 'a sad truth that with some of the Lord's dear saints the fact of His near return for His own is having the very opposite effect that it should have upon their missionary zeal'. These Christians, he thought, were 'so engrossed with the horizon of the glorious hope of His coming that they fail to see the intervening landscape of daily obedience to the Lord's last command to send the Gospel message to earth's farthest bounds'. He considered that these Christians argued 'that the Lord's return warrants an undue haste or a superficial carrying out of His commands'. This was unacceptable to a person so engrossed in the proper preparation of Pentecostal missionaries.[58] He went on to say that the power of the Spirit had been given to Pentecostal people for the express purpose of witnessing to the nations of the earth, and that the Lord would not come back until this command had been obeyed.

War and the Coming of Christ

Eschatology was the primary reason for the opposition of early Pentecostals to war. For most of them, the outbreak of the Great War in August 1914 was further evidence that the end had come and that the world, of which they were certainly no part, was involved in a bloody conflagration that would lead to the final battle of Armageddon preceding the return of Christ. As believers they would be snatched away from the world's conflicts, and therefore they should have no part in this war. Pentecostals believed that the Great War or the First World War as it is now called, was predicted in the Bible. Some quite remarkable prophecies were printed in Pentecostal periodicals before the event, such as one in early 1912 that declared:

> We are on the eve of one of the greatest upheavals in Europe that the world has ever seen; the bloodiest battles, with the most terrific carnage both on land and sea, will take place very shortly, engaging almost all the great powers of this continent, when prophecy will be fulfilled to the very letter ... Europe at the present moment may be likened to a vast armed camp, with fourteen million soldiers enrolled and ready for a terrible butchery of each other. Every deadly instrument which modern science and human ingenuity can devise has been adopted for this hellish purpose of the destruction of human life. On every sea, also, are crowded those ugly, infernal engines of death called Dreadnoughts, ready to vomit forth death and destruction upon each other, and to send hundreds of souls to eternity in a few moments.[59]

How true these words were to prove.

Pentecostal periodicals in the USA almost unanimously saw the outbreak of war as pointing to the end times, although they were hesitant to say it was Armageddon. After a summary of recent events leading to the declarations of war, *The Latter Rain Evangel* asked: 'Is this the final conflict? Are we at Armageddon?' Even more significantly, the paper looked at the potentially devastating effects of the war on missions, lamenting:

> How shall we answer to the heathen to whom we carry the Gospel, for the cruel, murderous warfare among the so-called Christian nations? The press has very aptly cartooned the heathen chiefs looking on in derision. The present conditions cannot help but cripple missionary effort in foreign lands, and there is little doubt that we are in the tribulation days.[60]

Christianity as a whole had lost credibility through the determination of so-called 'Christian nations' to exterminate each other.

Some American periodicals were even more definite in linking the outbreak of war with Armageddon, while the British periodical *Confidence* was just as adamant that this was not the final war before the coming of Christ. The official periodical of the AG, *The Christian Evangel*, headlined that the war was preliminary to the dawning of the Great Tribulation prophesied in the Book of Revelation, although hastened to add that this was not Armageddon but 'the beginning of the great wars which will wind up in the battle of Armageddon'.[61] As the USA got drawn into the war, American Pentecostals were divided on the meaning of this and whether they should support the president's decision. In early 1917 W. W. Simpson published a vision he had seen in 1912 and declared that after the war in which Germany would be defeated, a League of Nations would be set up and at its head was the Man of Sin, the Antichrist of 2 Thessalonians 2.[62] In April 1917 the official mouthpiece of the AG *The Weekly Evangel* published an article by Booth-Clibborn against participating in war as

Christians, and a testimony by an English Pentecostal conscientious objector.[63] Because of their conviction that war was sinful and part of the evil world system, many Pentecostals were pacifists during the First World War and some remain so until the present day. Some Pentecostals were imprisoned for their stand. Secretary of the PMU, T. H. Mundell, wrote against involvement in the war to his missionaries and William Burton praised the anti-war stand taken by Pentecostals in Britain.[64]

Among the more vocal advocates of pacifism was the former Quaker turned Salvationist and then Pentecostal, Arthur Booth-Clibborn, Irish husband of Catherine, daughter of General William Booth. Booth-Clibborn's anti-war book *Blood against Blood* was mentioned but clearly not endorsed by Alexander Boddy – the book was banned in Britain after conscription was introduced in 1916. Across the Atlantic, however, the AG enthusiastically endorsed the book as a 'most striking, realistic and forceful book' that presented 'war from a Christian standpoint'. Their Gospel Publishing House was the USA distributor for it, offering the book at a special price. It was widely publicized in other American Pentecostal periodicals.[65] The Assemblies of God press recommended that its readers 'purchase it and become imbued with the spirit of its contents, in a complete opposition and protest against war and the shedding of blood'.[66] On his return from Europe in 1915, Frank Bartleman prolifically expressed his opinion in articles concerning the futility of war, the exploitation of British colonialism and warned of the dangers of the war to the USA. These articles were given a high profile in leading Pentecostal papers.[67] Bartleman's censure of Britain would probably find more sympathetic (and certainly interested) ears in a later generation as he wrote, 'A nation trained to sporting, running down poor little foxes with a regiment of men, women, horses, and dogs must make professional killers.' And then he delivered his coup de grace: 'Great meat eating nations make brutal people.'[68] One article even suggested that the recruiting of men into the war that was taking place in some churches in Canada amounted to the Antichrist 'getting possession of the House of God'.[69]

The periodical of the AG made an official statement titled 'Pentecostal Saints Opposed to War' and said the following:

> The Pentecostal people, as a whole, are uncompromisingly opposed to war, having much the same spirit as the early Quakers, who would rather be shot themselves than that they should shed the blood of their fellow-men. Because we have given this bit of war news is no reason that we are in favor of war, but rather that our readers may have some knowledge of how the war is actually affecting our own people, who, through force of circumstances are compelled to be in the midst of the terrible conflict.[70]

The AG General Council adopted a resolution in 1917 'toward any Military Service which Involves the Actual Participation in the Destruction of Human Life', declaring itself in favour of conscientious objection. It stated that while the AG affirmed its 'unswerving loyalty to Government of the United States', it was 'constrained to define our position with reference to taking of human life'. Quoting various Scriptures against killing and in favour of peace, the resolution went on to declare that 'these and other Scriptures have always been accepted and interpreted by our churches as prohibiting Christians from shedding blood or taking human life' and stated:

> Therefore, we, as a body of Christians, while purposing to fulfill all the obligations of loyal citizenship, are nevertheless constrained to declare we cannot conscientiously participate in war and armed resistance which involves the actual destruction of human life, since this is contrary to our view of the clear teachings of the inspired Word of God, which is the sole basis of our faith.

It followed this with a resolution declaring its 'unswerving loyalty to our Government and to its Executive, President Wilson', and 'our fixed purpose to assist in every way morally possible, consistent with our faith, in bringing the present "World War" to a successful conclusion' (the last phrase was omitted after the end of the war). This article remained in the By-Laws of the AG at least until 1939.[71]

South African Pentecostals similarly declared themselves 'clear cut on the issue of taking up arms against our fellows, and refuse to do it'.[72] Not all American Pentecostals were pacifists, however. The official organ of the Pentecostal Holiness Church, *The Apostolic Evangel*, published an article in 1917, 'Can a Christian go to War and keep his Christian Experience?' which it answered in the affirmative. Alexander Boddy quickly retorted that 'conscientious objectors should obtain this copy'.[73] Aimee McPherson preferred to take a softer line as America became involved in the war in 1917, but made the eschatological link to the Great War as a sign of the end times.[74] By 1917 Pentecostals were softening their beliefs that the war was the final battle before the coming of Christ, and the AG's *Weekly Evangel* published an article by Charles Leonard, missionary in Palestine, who said that he did not believe that the war in Palestine was 'the last great struggle before He comes, but rather that there will be a short time to preach the Gospel of the kingdom before the coming of the King'.[75]

The First World War had more of an effect on western countries than it had on the continents of the South and East. Even so, missionary giving to the PMU in Britain and to various independent missions in the USA showed signs of slowing down. Postal services became less reliable and took longer; in some countries it was difficult to transfer funds from overseas, travelling on the sea became much more difficult, some missionaries found their supplies and transportation cut off, the cost of living escalated, unemployment increased, and missionaries like Berg with German support found their income drying up. American papers assured their readers of the safety of their missionaries and the protection of the American consulates for those in most danger, but they made urgent appeals for more sacrificial giving to missionaries for what was undoubtedly a financial crisis.[76] In some of the most dangerous areas such as the Middle East and continental Europe missionaries began to leave for home. However, for the most part Pentecostal missionaries were remarkably unfazed by these tumultuous events and their attitudes to these world conflicts, including their pacifism, was seen as further evidence of their convictions that this was the end of the world. On hearing news in China of the outbreak of war, the PMU missionaries in Yunnan instituted special Bible studies on the 'Second Coming', believing that 'our Lord is coming now very very soon', as Ethel Cook wrote.[77]

PMU Secretary Thomas Mundell wrote letters to the missionaries stating his views against war, typical of most Pentecostals who took a pacifist stance. He believed that war was 'not a thing for Christians to take part in as the Word of God is very distinctly against it'.[78] But his opposition to war was also clearly linked to his eschatology. He wrote that is was 'very difficult to keep one's soul clear of the war spirit but the children of God have to do with another Kingdom than that of this world and many enlightened Christians in England are seeing that they cannot take a vindictive part against even the Germans and that they cannot on any account go to fight against them'.[79] He was one of these 'enlightened' ones, although his age may have precluded him from the labour camps that younger Pentecostal men with the same views had to endure. As far as he was concerned, Christians could 'have only one attitude towards this war which is clearly set out in our Lord's teaching'. He said that the war was 'essentially of the world and I hold that no Christian ought on any account take part in actually destroying and killing his fellow men'. Further, the present war was 'undoubtedly one of God's Judgments upon the nations, England included, and I feel that we are on the very verge of the Coming of the Lord and that prophecy is being rapidly fulfilled'. He went on to link this to biblical prophecy: 'Many believe that evolving out of this terrible conflict will be the setting up, of Anti-Christ when Daniel 7 and Rev. 13 will have quick fulfilment.'[80] Towards the end of the war, Mundell wrote, 'The outlook for the coming of the Lord is a very bright one. I expect you will have seen the declaration on behalf of our government that the Jew is to have Palestine at the end of the War.'[81]

For their pacifist stand, many Pentecostal men were imprisoned in Britain and sent to forced labour camps. In Germany, some Pentecostals were executed for refusing to bear arms. When the PMU Men's Training Home in London had to be closed, former students were sent to work camps and prison. Such information could not be published in the periodicals because of censorship, but PMU Secretary Mundell reported that only one had enlisted, while 'the other dear men are in various parts and positions in England, some of them suffering for Christ's sake very acutely'.[82] One American woman missionary in the Congo suggested on the eve of the USA's entering the war that instead of laying down their lives in the 'fearful carnage' as British young men had done, they should come to Africa as missionaries.[83]

The American AG reiterated its opposition to bearing arms and killing in a statement released in its *Weekly Evangel* in August 1917, just as the USA was being drawn into the war. This article, 'The Pentecostal Movement and the Conscription Law' is remarkable, stating clearly what the AG considered to be the position of Pentecostals everywhere:

From the very beginning, the movement has been characterized by Quaker principles. The laws of the Kingdom, laid down by our elder brother, Jesus Christ, in His Sermon on the Mount have been unqualifiedly adopted, con-

sequently the movement has found itself opposed to the spilling of the blood
of any man, or of offering resistance to any aggression. Every branch of the
Movement, whether in the United States, Canada, Great Britain or Germany,
has held to this principle. When the war first broke out in August of 1914,
our Pentecostal brethren in Germany found themselves in a peculiar position. Some of those who were called to the colors responded, but many were
court marshalled and shot because they heartily subscribed to the principles
of non-resistance. Great Britain has been more humane. Some of our British
brethren have been given non-combatant service, and none have been shot
down because of their faith.[84]

The AG sought exemption for its members from military enlistment on the
basis of these principles. But not all Pentecostals were pacifists. Some, like
Anglicans Boddy and Polhill, took a stand in favour of a 'just war' against
the oppressing German regime, Boddy serving in France to help tend the
wounded troops.[85] At the beginning of the war, which had been declared soon
after one of the most successful Sunderland conferences with the full participation of a German contingent, Boddy bemoaned the 'almost unthinkable' fact
that 'our beloved German brethren . . . should be separated from us by this cruel
state of things'. He asked for the Lord to end it quickly, adding 'may be by His
coming in the air for His own'. But *Confidence* soon became a strong defender of
the 'just war' doctrine and published news on the progress of the Allied troops
and patriotic literature, including a statement by the Bishop of Durham holding
that this was a 'Holy War' against the 'unprecedented peril' of 'tyrannous
domination of a single great State'.[86] Polhill similarly thought that war was the
means of bringing about 'manliness, patriotism, then righteousness, holiness
and godliness'. Nevertheless, by 1918 the PMU Council had made the 'unanimous decision' that if any missionaries volunteered for war service, they would
have 'entirely severed their connection with the PMU'.[87] By the close of the
war, even the pacifist Mundell began to see that Germany's defeat was a spiritual victory as the result of two days of national prayer in Britain.[88]
   It seems that the PMU officially favoured non-combatant service. One
missionary candidate after the war, James Andrews, who was imprisoned for
refusing to take this up, confessed to the PMU Council, 'You was [sic] right and
I was wrong in this so please forgive me my foolishness and lack of discrition
[sic] in this matter.'[89] Among other reasons, the fundamental difference
between the pacifist and non-pacifist views within British Pentecostalism was
ultimately to lead to the separation of Boddy and Polhill from the movement
in the 1920s and the setting up of the Assemblies of God. Not until the 1960s
would British Anglicans again be involved in Charismatic activities. Early
British Pentecostal denominations were essentially pacifist organizations and
this issue effectively ended their relationship with the patriotic Anglicans.
Boddy regularly publishing patriotic statements, news and letters from British
soldiers in *Confidence* must have alienated many British Pentecostals who
believed strongly that they should abstain from any involvement in this
end-times conflagration. In any event, the Great War effectively ended the
leadership of Boddy and Polhill over the British Pentecostal movement and its
missionaries.

Evangelism, healing and the coming of Christ were essential parts of the Pentecostal missionary mandate, but not exclusively so. Their premillennialism gave them a negative view of the world and its events, and led most Pentecostals to reject involvement in war, at great personal cost. The central theme of their mission remained pneumatological, as the Spirit had baptized them in the last days to preach the gospel of individual salvation and to heal the sick, doing 'signs and wonders' to authenticate their gospel and to demonstrate that King Jesus was coming soon. Indeed, there was no time for anything else.

Notes

1 *BM* 69 (1 Sept 1910), p.1.
2 *BM* 69 (1 Sept 1910), p.1.
3 *FF* 9 (Jan 1913), p.3.
4 *Conf* 6:4 (Apr 1913), p.83.
5 *BM* 110 (15 May 1912), p.1.
6 *WW* 35:4 (Apr 1913), p.117.
7 *BM* 58 (15 Mar 1910), p.3; 59 (1 Apr 1910), p.1.
8 *AF* 3 (Nov 1906), p.2.
9 Letter, T. H. Mundell to A. Kok, 14 June 1914.
10 Circular letter, W. W. Simpson to missionaries in China, undated, likely 1914.
11 *BM* 64 (15 June 1910), p.4.
12 *BM* 95 (1 Oct 1911), pp.3–4.
13 Letter, E. Cook to T. H. Mundell, 7 Dec 1914.
14 Letter, E. Cook to T. H. Mundell, 8 Dec 1915.
15 *Conf* 2:2 (Feb 1909), p.28.
16 McGee, '"Power from on High"', pp.317,324.
17 *BM* 91 (1 Aug 1911), p.1.
18 Moorhead, *Missionary Pioneering*, pp.76–9.
19 McGee, 'Pentecostals and their Various Strategies', p.206.
20 McClung, 'Spontaneous Strategy', p.74.
21 McGee, 'Power from on High', p.329.
22 McGee, 'Pentecostals and their Various Strategies', p.215.
23 *LRE* 3:2 (Nov 1910), p.10.
24 *Conf* 9:10 (Oct 1916), p.171.
25 Moorhead, *Missionary Pioneering*, pp.39–40.
26 *Pentecost* 1:7 (June 1909), p.2.
27 *BM* 47 (1 Oct 1909), p.2.
28 *Conf* 2:2 (Feb 1909), p.29.
29 *UR* 2:4 (Jan. 1911), p.7.
30 Letter, Cora Fritsch to her mother, 31 Mar 1909.
31 *FF* 3 (Jan 1912), p.5.
32 *Trust* 9:8 (Oct 1910), p.13.
33 *BM* 99 (1 Dec 1911), p.1.
34 *BM* 84 (15 Apr 1911), p.2.
35 Letter, Maggie Trevitt to T. H. Mundell, 9 Oct 1915.
36 Letters, A. Swift to T. H. Mundell, 26 Jan 1918; 20 April 1918.

37 *BM* 73 (1 Nov 1910), p.3.

38 *BM* 97 (1 Nov 1911), p.2.

39 Anderson, *Zion and Pentecost*, pp.120–6.

40 *BM* 52 (15 Dec 1909), p.1.

41 Moorhead, *Missionary Pioneering*, pp.12, 15.

42 Faupel, *Everlasting Gospel*, pp.99, 104–5, 110–12.

43 Letter, Jenny Boyd to T. H. Mundell, Kaihua, 8 Jan 1919.

44 *WW* 30:5 (May 1908), p.142

45 Joel 2.28–9; *TF* 10:1 (Jan 1890), p.22.

46 *BM* 97 (1 Nov 1911), p.1.

47 *AF* 11 (Jan. 1908), 3.

48 *BM* 94 (15 Sept 1911), p.1; Stanley, *Bible and Flag*, p.76.

49 *AF* 5 (Jan. 1907), 1.

50 Matthew 24.14, AV.

51 *BM* 46 (15 Sept 1909), p.2.

52 *BM* 69 (1 Sept 1910), p.1.

53 *FF* 9 (Jan 1913), p.7.

54 *BM* 129 (15 Mar 1913), p.1.

55 *WW* 31:11 (Nov. 1908), p.347.

56 *WE* 102 (7 Aug 1915), p.3.

57 *WW* 35:4 (Apr 1913), p.119.

58 *Conf* 6:10 (Oct 1913), pp.201–2.

59 *LRE* 4:7 (Apr 1912), p.15.

60 *LRE* 6:12 (Sept 1914), p.13.

61 *WW* 36:9 (Sept 1914), p.262; *Conf* 7:9 (Sept 1914), p.163; 7:11 (Nov 1914), pp.203–8.

62 *WE* 179 (3 Mar 1917), p.2.

63 *WE* 187 (28 Apr 1917), pp.5, 7.

64 Moorhead, *Missionary Pioneering*, p.91.

65 Booth-Clibborn, *Blood Against Blood*; *Conf* 8:1 (Jan 1915), p.6; *WWit* 12:7 (July 1915), p.8; *LRE* 8:8 (May 1916), p.24.

66 *WE* 95 (19 June 1915), p.1.

67 *WWit* 12:6 (June 1915), p.5; *WW* 37:11 (Nov 1915), pp.300–1; 37:12 (Dec 1915), pp.332–3; 38:15 (Aug 1916), pp.296–7; *WE* 93 (5 June 1915), p.3; 98 (10 July 1915), p.3; 102 (7 Aug 1915), p.1; Bartleman, *Azusa Street*, p.159.

68 *WW* 38:15 (Aug 1916), pp.296

69 *WE* 140 (20 May 1916), p.13.

70 *WE* 95 (19 June 1915), p.1.

71 *WE* 190 (19 May 1917), p.8; 'Combined Minutes of the General Council of the Assemblies of God', 1920, p.31; 1921, pp.35–6; 1923, pp.43–4; 'Constitution and By-Laws of the General Council of the Assemblies of God', 1939, p.42.

72 *WE* 113 (30 Oct 1915), p.4.

73 *Apostolic Evangel* (Apr 1917), p.16; *Conf* 10:3 (May–June 1917), p.39.

74 *WW* 39:38 (Nov 1917), pp.633–4.

75 *WE* 175 (3 Feb 1917), p.9.

76 *CE* 58 (12 Sept 1914), p.1.

77 Letter, E. Cook to T. H. Mundell, 8 Aug 1914.

78 Letter, T. H. Mundell to Jenner, de Vries, Cook and Millie, 23 April 1915.

79 Letter, T. H. Mundell to A. Kok, 8 Nov 1914.

80 Letter, T. H. Mundell to F. E. Jenner, 8 Jan 1915.

81 Letter, T. H. Mundell to A. Kok, 14 Nov 1917.
82 Letter, T. H. Mundell to W. J. Boyd, 21 Oct 1916
83 *WE* 199 (21 July 1917), p.12.
84 *WE* 200 (4 Aug 1917), p.6.
85 Letter, T. H. Mundell to the Swifts, 17 July 1915.
86 *Conf* 7:9 (Sept 1914), p.163; 7:11 (Nov 1914), pp.203–8; 8:1 (Jan 1915), p.5.
87 Letter, T. H. Mundell to A. Swift, 28 May 1918.
88 Letter, T. H. Mundell to A. Swift, 30 Nov 1918.
89 Letter, J. H. Andrews to PMU Council, 28 Jan 1919.

9

The Powers of Evil:
Religions, Culture and Politics

The powers of evil are no myth in this land. Do you know that in some places where we go to carry the gospel we feel the unseen forces wrap like a cloak around us? The experience is too awful to describe. We only know the reality of it, and the conflict baffles description.

(Pentecostal missionary in India, 1910)[1]

The missionary who penned these words felt 'unseen forces' or 'powers of evil' that were 'too awful to describe'. These powers restricted her freedom and feeling of well-being that she was accustomed to in her home country. They affected everything she did, said or felt in the dark, foreign land she was now living in. They pervaded every part of her being, and she did not know how to handle it or describe it. As we will see in this chapter, this fundamental sense of alienation affected expatriate missionaries in their attitudes to other religions, cultures, politics and societies. In these spheres, Pentecostalism had emerged in a particular context of marginalization that has not been given sufficient recognition in popular histories. Its background in radical evangelicalism and revivalism, and its missionaries' own socio-political context in the western world had certain consequences. Among those consequences examined in this chapter are the ways that expatriate Pentecostals approached other cultures and religions, political issues, and how they were influenced by racial and cultural stereotypes. The result was not always a pretty picture.

Religions and Contextualization

The awareness of the supernatural pervaded the religions of the peoples to whom Pentecostal missionaries went and formed a fertile seed-bed for a message of spiritual power. The head of the CMA, A. B. Simpson, described his impressions following a world tour in 1896 that included India, China and Japan, in what he called the 'shadows of heathenism'. In it he portrayed 'some pictures that may deepen upon your hearts the conviction which I am sure has been settling down upon us all, these days, the need of the evangelization of the world'. His language was stark – he saw nothing whatsoever that attracted him to 'the foreign heathen races', only destitution, misery, shame and degradation of 'idolatrous races', and religions he described as 'the heathendom of the East, the religions of the Orient, that have been painted in such false colors', which were 'but a covering of an awful skeleton'.[2]

These dichotomies were created to give greater effect to the emphasis on recruiting more missionaries. But as a result of colonialism a culture of difference had also been formed during the nineteenth century that would be very difficult to erase. The urge for world evangelization was made all the more acute through stark assumptions made about the religious and cultural conditions of the people to whom foreign missionaries went. By the beginning of the twentieth century, a prevalent missionary assumption was that 'the baneful influence of idolatry extended to all aspects of a people's culture and society'.[3] The evangelical missionary movement of the nineteenth century almost unanimously saw all other religions except Protestant, conservative evangelical Christianity as 'idolatry' and 'heathenism', sometimes with the exception of Islam, whose strictly conservative morality they admired.[4] This was the inheritance of the Pentecostal missionaries who went from western countries to Africa, Asia and the Pacific. The other religions they encountered were invariably condemned in the most negative terms. Western missionaries saw the societies and cultures around them as degraded and benighted of all hope by these 'idolatrous' religions, for which only western 'civilization' could provide the antidote. Two evangelical missionaries writing from Pune in 1901, for example, typified this attitude: 'There is nothing connected with Hinduism but darkness and blackness and hellish cruelty.' This attitude reflected the views of evangelical leaders.

Western Pentecostals went out to 'foreign fields', as many other Christian missionaries had done before them, with a fundamental conviction that the North Atlantic was a 'Christian' realm, that they were sent as 'light' to 'darkness' and that the ancient cultures and religions of the nations were 'heathen', 'pagan' and 'demonic', to be 'conquered' for Christ.[5] Western culture was 'Christian' culture and all other cultures were dark and foreboding problems to be solved by the light of the gospel, replacing the old 'paganism' with the new 'Christianity'. Over a decade later, Aimee Semple McPherson reflected on her three-month experience of Hong Kong in 1910, where her first husband died, saying that she felt there 'as never before the need of the Holy Spirit as a Comforter, and found it much more difficult to pray through'. It seemed to her 'as though the air were filled with demons and the hosts of hell, in this wicked, benighted country, where for many centuries devil worship has been an open custom'. She said that in China, 'ancestral worship is observed by almost all'.[6] These authoritative pronouncements were made after only three months, in which most of the time she was heavily pregnant, giving birth to a daughter and tending to a dying husband in hospital.

Missionaries went out from places like the PMU Missionary Training Homes with the conviction that their 'future labours' would be among 'the poor heathen in darkness'.[7] Pentecostal periodicals regularly gave reports about the negative qualities and failings of the ancient religions of Asia. Even when other missionaries were more appreciative of Asian religions, religious intolerance and bigoted ignorance were common features of some of the Pentecostal missionary reports, illustrated by a lament from a British PMU missionary in India in 1914, who exclaimed, 'Oh, what a dark, sad land this seems to be, and the longer one lives in it, the more one feels the darkness all around.' She referred to a discussion she overheard among other missionaries where the subject was the contribution of Hinduism to Christianity, and she felt it 'a pity to see young missionaries occupying their time and thoughts with such things, instead of studying and pondering over the Word of God . . . Why, the best thing any Hindu can do is to die to all his Hinduism and all its distinct lines of thought, and to be baptised into Jesus Christ.'[8] Almost four years later, the same missionary was writing about Hindu temples as 'the works of the devil', and that 'Ram' was 'a favourite god of the Hindus . . . supposed to be an incarnation of the second person of the Hindu Trinity'.[9]

With such an approach it was not surprising that these missionaries found it difficult to get a hearing, although they did not always understand why people were not queuing up to hear them. One Pentecostal missionary was totally surprised by the seeming indifference of Hindu people to her message, and such a 'strange thing' it was that 'among all the hundreds to whom we must have preached, we have never met anyone who has been a seeker after the true God and who, after hearing the truth from us, has admitted that he was dissatisfied with his heathen religion, and was really longing for the light. No, not even one have we met', she despaired.[10] Another missionary discussed Hinduism, quoting the apostle Paul ('they sacrifice to devils, and not to God', 1 Corinthians 10.20) and said that 'The Devil' was 'at the bottom of all their worship'.[11] At a missionary convention in London in 1924, Walter Clifford, on furlough from Ceylon, described Hinduism as 'a religion of fear, not a religion of love' and that many of the Indian holy men were 'demon possessed', because 'you can see the devil shining out of their eyes. They have given themselves over to him.'[12] In present-day Pakistan, A. L. Slocum complained about the opposition of Muslims, using pejorative terms: 'Satan seems so entrenched in these Mussulmans that my efforts seem only a drop in the bucket.'[13] PMU worker Frank Trevitt (who died in China in 1916) sent back a report from 'dark China', where he had observed 'heathendom truly, without light or love, not even as much as a dumb beast would have'. They had 'seen much of this spirit, which truly is the "Dragon's" spirit, which is as you know, China's ensign'. He exclaimed, 'Oh, how one's heart longs and sighs for the coming of Christ's glorious Ensign, to be placed where the Dragon holds such sway.'[14] Trevitt's obviously identifying a treasured Chinese national symbol with the devil was bound to cause offence. Later he referred to Tibetan Lama priests as Satan's 'wicked messengers', and that 'Satan through them hates Christ in us'.[15]

Another PMU missionary John Beruldsen reported on a visit to a Mongolian 'Lama Temple' in Beijing and described a priest worshipping 'a large idol from 90 to 100 English feet high'. He commented that 'One could almost smell and feel the atmosphere of hell in these places. Poor benighted people! The power of God could save them from it all, if only they knew it.'[16] Apparently they did not. A Canadian Pentecostal missionary to Mongolia, Thomas Hindle, remarked that 'all heathen religions are more or less demon worship'. The theological basis of all these statements lay in Paul's admonition to the Corinthians that 'what the heathen sacrifice to idols they sacrifice to demons'.[17] Satan was the cause of it all. This all-embracing influence of 'the devil' in other religions included ancestor veneration in China. One missionary, observing religious rituals in Yunnan, wrote, 'the heathen spent one whole day in worshipping the graves of relatives – burning incense and weeping and wailing. Oh the mockery of it all. How Satan blinds their minds!'[18] Another reported from Yunnan on a visit to a Tibetan Buddhist lamasery and remarked that 'the seat of Satan might be a good name for such a place' because 'the demonic power was keenly felt, and the wicked faces of these lamas haunted us for many days after'.[19] Another was even able to make parallels between Buddhism and the much-feared Roman Catholicism, telling of the 'tortures of the Buddhist Purgatory' and even more amazingly, how she was 'anew impressed with the strong resemblance between Roman Catholicism and Buddhism'.[20] Sometimes these Pentecostals conflated their views of the 'demonic' nature of the 'heathen' religions with the culture and identity of the nation itself, one writing that 'China is almost the very seat of the devil'.[21]

In Africa, the situation was just as bad. Africa's religions were, it seemed to these missionaries, totally in the grip of demonic power. One Pentecostal in the Belgian Congo (who had not been there long) was able to make authoritative generalizations about all Africans, what was called Africa's 'Satanic power'. 'The whole of Africa', this missionary declared, 'is a superstitious people, and they know not God; but they have an idea that there is a God who wants to rob and eat them, and they believe all sickness is due to demon possession.' He went on, 'They will bleed and cut one, and through suction try to spit out the demon, but, oh, the saddest thing I have seen, is this fearful fear of God and of demons, that when anyone is ill and the witch doctor cannot help them the people are carried out into the jungle, there to await death.'[22]

Missionary reports were intended to be entertaining, and in the days before audio-visual media nothing was more entertaining than a report about exotic and fearful, 'demonic' religious practices confronted by the valiant foreign missionary. Such reports would guarantee a readership and reinforce stereotypes about the 'savages' who needed the Christian gospel and western 'civilization'. A British Pentecostal missionary gave graphic illustrations of his confrontations with 'the powers of darkness'. He wrote of his encounter with 'three of Swaziland's greatest witch doctors, dressed in the most fearsome costume (?) of their devilish trade'. He described them 'chanting a weird lewd song' and that 'a word from Heaven's Court assailed and broke down the arrayed power and splendour (?) of Satan's assembly' so that they 'had to disband'.[23] Later he described a 'large heathen Kraal' with a family gathering for a traditional ritual killing, where 'all are called by the father to lay their hands on the sacrifice, while he calls upon Satan and his demons to behold their devotion, begging that sickness be kept from the Kraal'.[24] In yet another report, he described 'all their demon and ancestral worship paraphernalia', which include a big drum, a 'demon designed and a demon-looking headgear', spears and axes, 'several bundles of "muti" (charm medicines), dishes on which food was wont to be offered to demons and to Satan himself', baskets and clothes that were used 'at no other time and for no other purpose than in such devil worship, and by no other than a fully initiated medium'.[25] The African ritual in question was not 'devil worship', it would certainly not have addressed 'Satan' or the 'demons' at all, for no reference would be made to biblical concepts, and the offerings he described would be to appease the ancestors. The fact that so many inaccurate, confrontational and tendentious comments were published in leading British Pentecostal periodicals not only displays the ignorance and prejudices of these missionaries, but also is in itself a reflection of the prevailing cultural and religious ethos of early Pentecostals. This is a far cry from the strategy of Paul, who used existing religious concepts to proclaim his message and was even commended for not blaspheming the goddess Artemis.[26]

Islam was not usually seen as 'idolatrous', but was nevertheless regarded as an enemy, an 'Anti-Christ' religion to be overcome by proclaiming the Christian message. An address by G. S. Brelsford in Egypt during his furlough in the USA typifies this approach. He said that 'very little is really known about Jesus' in Egypt; it was 'almost exclusively Mohammedan', which meant to Brelsford that it was 'anti-Christ, completely against Christ as the Son of God', who was 'recognized in the Koran, and mentioned as a prophet; they are willing to acknowledge Him as a prophet, as a man, but not as the Son of the living God'. He continued, 'That makes a great difference, takes away the divinity of Christ and of the atonement through that precious blood. So it becomes necessary to preach Jesus in that land as the Son of God.'[27] What missionaries sometimes saw as Egypt's mixture of Islam and ancient Coptic Christianity came in for particular criticism. C. W. Doner had only been there two months when he wrote of his labours among 'the downtrodden in darkest Egypt' where 'superstition and heathen darkness reigns'. There, he asserted, the Muslim 'worships their false prophet' and the Copt 'falls down to a fallen Priestcraft, and neither worship God nor serve Jesus Christ'. Their job as missionaries was simply to 'wage persistent warfare by prayer and the sword of the Spirit, the Word of God' and to proclaim 'liberty and deliverance from all the power of the devil'.[28] For most of these missionaries, it was a simple truth–error dichotomy between their kind of Christianity and their superficial observations of the other religion.

Sometimes missionaries applied their negative evaluations of world religions to their home countries, especially when it came to theological liberalism. Albert Norton, veteran missionary to India, commented on what he saw as the apostasy of the West in an article published in 1910. Because the Bible had lost its authority in England and America and was now rejected by their leaders, this turning away 'from the God of Revelation, the God and Father of the Lord Jesus', meant they had 'discarded Christianity for Pantheism, the degrading religion of the Hindoos'.[29] Western Pentecostal missionaries inherited from their evangelical cousins an attitude that can mostly be described as condemnatory and exclusivist. Often these denunciations made use of broad generalizations. Elizabeth Sexton expressed this in an editorial when she wrote, 'All religions of the heathen world are dead formalities, ceremonies, and idol worship. Their gods have no life-giving power. They cannot save from sin or transform a sinful life.'[30] Stanley writes of the 'extreme negativism which characterised the missionary approach to other religions for most of the nineteenth century', and the evangelical missionary enterprise was seen as a 'crusade against idolatry'. Throughout Asia missionaries denounced the religions around them; in Africa they described the religious practices in exclusively negative terms. In Latin America they mostly denounced Catholicism and its 'idolatrous images' of the crucifix and the Virgin Mary, even calling it 'baptized paganism'.[31] Albert Norton described India as 'this dark land of heathenism', and such depictions of India and Hinduism pervaded missionary literature. One Pentecostal missionary described Indian holy men, their clothing and their practices in derogatory terms and contrasted them with Christian preachers.[32]

China fared little better. American evangelical missionaries writing from Macao in 1905 exclaimed: 'Oh, you cannot realize how dense is the darkness in a heathen heart. No conception of God or heaven or purity or right.'[33] The same attitude was shown by Ethel Cook describing the funeral of the mother of a Christian-educated Chinese governor in Yunnan, who invited the missionaries to 'feasts'. 'But of course' she said, they did not go, but she witnessed 'a grand procession with all the usual heathen paraphernalia on an extensive scale' where 'the very skies seemed to shew their displeasure, for rain fell heavily nearly all day'. Her conclusion was that Christian education had no effect 'if the Holy Spirit is not working in [the Governor's] heart'.[34] One wonders how much more would have been accomplished for the missionaries' cause if they had accepted the Governor's invitation and shown solidarity with him and his community in their grief. On another occasion, the Christians held a prayer meeting for rain after 'the heathen had an idolatrous fast for a few days'. The letter did not say (but of course it assumed) which prayer effort, Christian or 'heathen', resulted in the 'abundance of rain' that fell thereafter, but this time the rain signified God's bounty and not God's displeasure.[35] Cook continued in her tirades against Buddhism in particular, writing of 'the utter depravity and filthiness of the heathen mind'.[36]

Pentecostal missionaries, in common with their evangelical counterparts, expected their converts to make a radical break with the past 'idolatrous' religion. This was often expressed by a ceremony in which the convert brought 'idols', charms, incense urns, potions and other religious accoutrements to be publicly burned. In China, paper writings to the ancestors and 'heaven and earth tablets' in Christian homes were to be removed, burned, and replaced with Scripture texts. The same happened in Africa, where one of the first signs of conversion was that the professed Christians should publicly burn their charms and 'fetishes'. But as British Pentecostal missionary leader William Burton pointed out in the Congo, he did not want people to think 'that baptism or fetish-burning or any such thing [other than faith in Christ] is salvation'.[37] In his books Burton often wrote remarkable and insightful ethnographic descriptions about the religions and customs of the people among whom he was working in his mission. But even though he was positively enthusiastic about the cultural achievements of African people and their skilful crafts, he was diametrically opposed to their religions. He was convinced that the religious practices of the people in Lubaland (what he called 'African idolatry and superstition') – particularly those practices associated with witchcraft and sorcery that were so prevalent – were evil practices that needed to be eliminated through Christian evangelism and instruction. He wrote that despotic local government, bribery and trial by ordeal had to be replaced by western systems of governance and justice.[38] Alma Doering, Swiss Pentecostal missionary working with the Congo Inland Mission, believed that the peoples of Central Africa had 'no religion whatever' and that things like 'worship, praise and prayer' were absent.[39] Such obvious ignorance of African religion was prevalent in missionary writings.

This is only one side of the story, however. By and large, the worldview of the Pentecostal missionaries, unlike that of their Protestant cousins, was one of spirits and evil forces that were prevalent everywhere, that could be overcome and exorcized by the superior power of the Christian God through the Holy Spirit. In many aspects this worldview was identical to that of the peoples outside the European and North American rationalistic Enlightenment sphere of influence. In actuality, despite the seeming confrontation and intolerance, there was general acceptance by Pentecostal missionaries of the genuineness of the spiritual experiences of the people in Africa and Asia. And even more significantly, Pentecostal converts and local preachers began to relate their message of the transforming power of the gospel to their own religious worlds, creating continuity between certain aspects of the old religions and this new form of Christianity. Birgit Meyer has called this 'translating the devil', when the Christian idea of a personal devil (Satan) was applied to African deities and spiritual phenomena with little, if any change.[40] We saw the missionary in Swaziland do that in the earlier example.

The crusading mentality of these missionaries was especially directed at other religions, including Islam, but always excluding Judaism. Pentecostal periodicals in the West, like evangelical ones, continued to foment ignorance and prejudice against Islam. 'Mohommedanism [sic]', they declared, was the 'curse of Eastern life' that had spread and left 'bondage and superstition and sin in its wake'.[41] But not every Pentecostal shared these negative views about Islam. Some like Andrew Urshan, an Assyrian Pentecostal, spoke appreciatively of the positive aspects of Muslim devotion. His 'countrymen' were 'not heathen as many people think'. He thought that Muslims were 'the most religious people you ever saw'. He went on:

> If we were as faithful in prayer as they are in their forms of prayer we might have converted them ere now. They have set times of prayer and will pray even on the streets no matter how many people are passing. They are a temperate people and the liquor traffic is under a curse in their religion. Some of them know the Bible better than some of us do. In order for us to make those Mohammedans believe that Jesus is the Son of God we will have to show them the power of the glorious Gospel; preaching doctrines will not do it.[42]

Although the explosive growth of Pentecostalism in the twentieth century is often implicitly assumed to be largely the work of 'white' missions, the truth is a little more sobering. There can be little doubt that many of the secessions that took place early on in western Pentecostal mission efforts in Africa, India and China (and elsewhere) were at least partly the result of cultural and social blunders on the part of foreign missionaries. Perhaps Pentecostal missionaries cannot be blamed with the same enslavement to rationalistic theological correctness and cerebral Christianity that plagued many of their contemporary Protestant missionaries. In the first place, they were not as educated in western theology as their counterparts were. Missionary training schools did not demand much formal education from their candidates. Nevertheless, sometimes there were hints of a more informed attitude to other nations. *The*

Bridegroom's Messenger carried a brief paragraph criticizing 'the haughty Anglo-Saxon who regards all other races as his inferiors', by pointing to the outstanding achievements of a hundred Filipino boys educated in the USA 'in competition with American boys'.[43]

But many of the letters and missionary addresses published in the periodicals showed blatant ignorance of other religions. This was even the case of missionaries who had been a long time in their adopted countries, like Minnie Abrams, who considered Parsees (Zoroastrians) in Bombay as 'fire worshippers' who were also 'worshipping the sun'.[44] Sometimes their evangelistic efforts were directed at 'heathen' priests. Ethel Cook wrote of a young imprisoned Taoist priest who became a Christian in jail where he was serving a life sentence. The sign of his becoming a Christian was that his long hair was cut off and burned together with his priestly clothes, after which he was 'most diligent in studying the New Testament'.[45] Cook also wrote of how difficult it was to persuade Buddhist women to give up their vegetarianism – apparently the missionaries expected this from them on conversion to Christianity – giving the reason that 'according to Buddhist doctrines they "accumulate merit" by not eating meat'. She added that she had 'found them self-righteous indeed'. Of the village tribal folk in Yunnan, she wrote, 'their minds are saturated with the superstition of centuries & darkened by demon powers'. She asked for prayer that the power of God in the Pentecostals would help them convert to Christianity.[46]

However, Pentecostal missionaries from the western world who went into Africa, Asia and Latin America did not have to face the secular and rationalized cultures they knew at home. There, the very existence of God was doubted or at best, God was thought of as a remote supreme being not involved in everyday human life. There was a fundamental difference between the religious approach of Pentecostal missionaries and that of most of their Protestant counterparts. For the latter, local cultures and religions, including beliefs in witchcraft, ancestors and shamanism, were ignorant superstitions to be overcome by education, and disease was a problem to be solved by medical science. To be sure, Pentecostal missionaries usually adopted a confrontational approach to other religions and cultures (and often with insensitivity), but did so with a conviction that the evil they thought they were confronting was real – that an active God was able to break through into this world of ancestors, spirits and sorcery and give protection and power to cope with stresses in daily life.

William Burton expressed this positive connection between the Pentecostal message and African religious beliefs at the beginning of his ministry in the Congo in 1915. He wrote that being filled with the Spirit would not be hard for Africans to understand, because 'every day they can see their own witch-doctors under the possession of demons'. They naturally expected 'to see supernatural manifestations accompany the Gospel, and this is where we have the key to the whole situation'.[47] Even though he sometimes used language that would be considered today as racist, Burton was one of those rare examples of a foreign missionary who considered Africans just as 'civilized' as Europeans were. He pointed to their skilled labourers, including blacksmiths, salt, cloth and basket makers, potters, boat makers, tailors, and those who transmitted messages hundreds of miles by drums: 'civilized, but with a civilization of their own'.[48]

From the perspective of some of the hearers of the new Pentecostal message, these missionaries offered a real alternative that resonated with their belief in the involvement of the divine in the mundane affairs of life. In particular, the independent churches influenced by Pentecostalism provided many examples of innovative approaches whereby popular culture and religious practices were adapted and transformed with Christian meanings. Pentecostal missionaries proclaimed a pragmatic gospel that sought to address practical issues like sickness, poverty, unemployment, loneliness, evil spirits, witchcraft and sorcery – issues that were fundamental to the pre-Christian religions of the local people. In varying degrees and in their many different forms, and precisely because of their inherent flexibility that belied their outward coating of biblical literalism, Pentecostals were able to offer answers to some of the basic questions asked in local contexts. A more sympathetic approach to their converts' cultures and the retention of certain cultural practices in their free liturgies were undoubtedly major reasons for their attraction. At the same time, both local and foreign Pentecostal missionaries confronted existing beliefs about sorcery with a declaration of a more powerful protection against sorcery and a more effective healing from sickness than either the existing missions or popular rituals had offered. Healing, guidance, protection from evil and success were some of the practical benefits offered to faithful members of their churches. The cultures and religions of the people to which the Pentecostal missionaries went were a fertile soil for their message of salvation and deliverance.

So, the new Pentecostal expression of Christianity was rather less encumbered by western cultural forms. As it encountered other living religions, however, transformation took place in two directions. First, the Pentecostal message challenged, confronted and changed whatever seemed incompatible with it or inadequate in the other religions and cultures. But second, the other religions and cultures transformed and enriched the Christian message as proclaimed by the Pentecostal missionaries, so that it was understandable and relevant within the worldview in which it was submerged. In this way Christianity (as understood by the Pentecostals) became more relevant and comprehensible to both those to whom it was shared and to those missionaries who shared it. It was not a case of a western Christianity replacing or superseding a 'pagan' religion or culture. There was an appropriation and transformation taking place within a particular context which involved all the participants. The Pentecostals' message of the power of the Spirit found familiar ground in countries where spiritual power was absolutely basic to the popular understanding of the universe. This is perhaps one of the main reasons for the proliferation of Pentecostal and independent churches throughout the Majority World during the twentieth century. Popular beliefs were transformed in these churches so that Christianity was presented as an attractive and viable local alternative. Pentecostal missionaries encountered and confronted popular religions and provided answers to a host of perplexing questions that seemed inherent there.

Although this analysis is not exhaustive, at least from a Pentecostal perspective it appears that the popular or 'folk' religions their missionaries encountered were inadequate on several fronts. The local divinities often seemed distant and unfathomable, the human ancestors on whom people relied appeared sometimes fickle and unpredictable, and the diviners, local healers and shamans seemed limited by the omnipresent fear of evil powers that might be greater than their own. The solutions offered in these religions and cultures, at least from this Pentecostal perspective, seemed to be seldom completely satisfying and left people uncertain, threatened and fearful. Problems caused by a loss of power and life through the malicious workings of sorcery, magic and witchcraft, and through those capricious spirits who often demanded more than humans could provide, demanded a Christian, power-filled response. What was attractive about Pentecostals to many local people was that they *did* offer answers to these problems. But in their encounter with the 'strange' religions and cultures they were themselves challenged and enriched concerning the content of their message, which would have been impoverished and foreign without this encounter. Their message of the power of the Spirit challenged evil powers and what were roundly declared to be the work of Satan. The ancestors were confronted as impersonating demons from which people needed deliverance, and evil spirits were exorcized in the name of Christ. Sorcerers, witches, and even shamans and healers were boldly (sometimes insensitively) declared to be agents of the devil. Pentecostal missionaries acknowledged all these various forces as real problems to be overcome, and not as ignorant superstitions from which people simply needed enlightenment. They offered realistic solutions by accepting these problems as genuine, conscientiously attempting to provide authentic explanations, and expecting to resolve the problems through faith in the Christian God. Believers did not need to fear these things because they had received the power of the Spirit enabling them to overcome any onslaughts against them. The Pente-costal response involved prayer to an all-powerful God for deliverance from the evil, protection from its possible future occurrences, and the restoration of that well-being found in Christ. In the eyes of these Pentecostals the out-come was that God was glorified as demonstrably more powerful than other divinities and powers.

Missionaries and Culture

The early Pentecostal missionaries were ill prepared for the rigours of inter-cultural and interreligious communication. Everything had happened at great speed, for the early missionaries believed that these were the last days before the imminent return of Christ, and there was no time for proper preparation through such things as language learning and cultural and religious studies. Pentecostal workers from the white Anglo-Saxon Protestant world usually saw their mission in terms of from a civilized, Christian 'home' to a Satanic and pagan 'foreign land', where sometimes their own personal difficulties, preju-dices (and possible failures) in adapting to a radically different culture, living conditions and religion were projected in their newsletters home. Western culture was 'Christian' culture and all other cultures were foreboding problems to be solved by the light of the gospel, replacing the old paganism with the new Christianity. Missionaries went out with the conviction that their future labours would be among 'the poor heathen in darkness'.[49] These were the fundamental presuppositions that coloured the work, the attitudes and the letters of early Pentecostal missionaries, and we cannot fail to notice this here. From the perspective of those who received them, these missionaries were rather a curious sight, with strange customs of their own, and some may be forgiven for wondering how it was that these strange tongue-speaking Christians not only could not communicate with them in their own language, but usually depended totally on educated local people who could already speak the missionaries' language and two or three other languages also!

It must be said that some Pentecostal expatriate missionaries had a moderate understanding and appreciation of the cultures among which they worked. One such was a German associate of George Berg in India, J. L. Bahr, who wrote of the 'real privilege' of eating by invitation with Indian people and of living on 'native food' for a month.[50] Arie Kok of the PMU made his way into the hearts of the Hsi-fan people (in Chinese, 'western barbarians') and identified with them by saying that he was also from the West from a people who were regarded by the Chinese as barbarians. He related the story of the Flood to the Na-hsi villagers, referred to in their own religious literature.[51] William Burton was one of the most appreciative of African culture among the Pentecostal missionaries. He wrote that the Luba people of the Congo were 'intelligent people, expert in fishing, trapping, basket-making and agriculture . . . exceedingly rich in the oral literature and folk-lore, using hundreds of proverbs in everyday conversation, displaying a profound philososphy'.[52] He pointed out that 'the black man is not such a silly, primitive being as some people have painted him' but is 'far-sighted, astute . . . as intelligent as the average white man . . . artistic'. An agricultural specialist after ten years in Africa had decided that 'there was little which he could teach the black men, but a great deal which he could learn from them'. Nevertheless, Burton's positive assessment was drastically tempered by his view of the religious substrata to African society: their 'whole social machinery and outlook lies under the hideous curse of a dark, menacing cloud . . . the supposed influence of the dead upon the living', which 'paralyses effort, cramps initiative, and causes its victims to live in a constant state of apprehension and fear'.[53] Burton favoured the practice of other missions in advising their male converts in polygamous marriages to put away all but one of their wives (considering this to be 'Christ's teaching'), resulting in much hardship and suffering for women and children thus abandoned. Yet some years later Burton wrote on the subject of polygamists who became Christians, stating that 'polygamy is not immorality' and that 'many a polygamous husband is the soul of virtue' and that there were great dangers in asking converted polygamous men to divorce their wives. He wrote that the Bible was silent on the subject and therefore 'there can be no universal law laid down' and that 'no two cases are alike'.[54]

But early Pentecostal missionaries frequently referred in their newsletters to their 'objects' of mission as 'the heathen' and were slow to recognize local leadership.[55] Missionary paternalism was widely practised, even if it was 'benevolent' paternalism. Often the letters written by missionaries and published in periodicals would depict the places in which they were working as areas of intense darkness and indescribable evil.[56] In country after country, white Pentecostal missionaries followed the example of other expatriate missionaries and kept control of the churches and their indigenous founders, and especially of the finances they raised in Western Europe and North America. Most wrote home as if they were mainly (if not solely) responsible for the progress of the Pentecostal work there. The truth was often that the churches grew in spite of (and not because of) these missionaries. As Gary McGee has remarked, 'most Pentecostal missionaries paternally guided their converts and mission churches until after World War II (for some to the present)', and that 'in their zeal to encourage converts to seek spiritual gifts ... they actually denied them the gifts of administration and leadership'.[57] This is an issue with which expatriate Pentecostal missionaries are still struggling.

There are allusions in the missionary newsletters to the cultural and racial tensions that existed. The Garrs, who first went to India and Hong Kong with an African American nanny, Maria Gardner, who died in Hong Kong, seemed to have been fairly well off, making several trips between their homeland, India and China and eventually purchasing a large house as a 'missionary home' in Hong Kong in 1909. They did not learn Chinese. There was no segregation intended, but in a letter published in the USA, Mok Lai Chi, the senior Chinese pastor in this mission wrote that although he had been offered place in the home, he had declined the offer because it was 'too small, and my family of nine persons cannot be squeezed in two rooms of 12 feet by 18 feet each'.[58] Missionaries often curried the favours of the colonial administrations. Lillian Garr, during their final visit to India in 1910, recounts an incident during a major Hindu festival when they were afforded protection from both the crowds and the sun by English police officers, who were not averse to controlling the crowds with bamboo canes.[59]

Expatriate missionaries made cultural blunders frequently and here are just a few examples. American missionary E. T. Slaybaugh wrote of a double missionary wedding at a mission station in South Africa where a 'large company of natives' were excluded from the supper even though they were present singing 'on the veranda' and had brought gifts for the wedding couples.[60] This, of course, ran contrary to African custom where weddings are community affairs to which everyone is invited. Henry Turney, after all a product of Azusa Street with its African American leadership and one of the first Pentecostal missionaries in South Africa, wrote presumptuously and paternalistically about Africans. He said that his readers should never forget 'that the natives are only, after all, "grown-up children" and require much training and instruction, even after they become Christians'. Because most of the adults could not read, the teaching had to be verbal, and had to be 'repeated many times before these poor darkened minds can thoroughly grasp and understand it'.[61]

Missionaries found it difficult to make cultural adjustments, especially when it came to 'native food'. John G. Lake wrote about his missionaries' inability to live like the people did in South Africa. They were unable to live on African food, he said, for if they did they 'would all die'. So they were 'compelled to live as we did in America'. He thought that American missionaries could not 'change their manner of life suddenly in this respect', and that their party of missionaries had 'very little attention given them by the Pentecostal people in the home land'. It seems that they had not been well supported by the American churches, and so they were struggling to maintain their American lifestyle. He went on wryly, 'It is beautiful to talk and say nice things concerning missions and missionaries, but when you are on the field under a boiling sun with an empty stomach, it is then that you will find out the kind of goods that the Lord has put in your soul. It is so much different from shouting in meetings after coming from a good supper.'[62]

Foreign missionaries were less than complementary of local workers in their letters. Allan Swift wrote to the PMU Council that although the Chinese workers were 'indispensable', they lacked initiative and the Chinese background of Confucianism 'tended to make not leaders but followers'. He wrote that foreign missionary supervision was absolutely essential. His letter also made plain the basic problem of missionary organizations like the PMU where foreign workers were settled with other, more 'experienced' foreign workers, getting their cues from them and not from the local people.[63] Another PMU missionary wrote of Chinese workers who did 'not spend sufficient time in prayer & Bible reading', and a worker who had 'no fire, no zeal for souls, no joy, and very little light on Divine things'.[64] Yet another, newly arrived missionary who had not yet been indoctrinated by other expatriates was far more positive. She thought it 'a treat to hear' the Chinese preachers on that particular Sunday morning, 'Mr Suen the Evangelist and Mr Wang the converted Buddhist'. She said that 'both appeared so mellow in Spirit as they clearly expounded to the others what fighting the good fight of faith meant'. She thought, rather condescendingly, that 'for a Chinaman to grasp this great truth is indeed a great thing'.[65]

The PMU missionaries in China generally had better relationships with the people and were not as disparaging in their comments as those in other fields. Whether this was because of the influence and experience of Cecil Polhill or due to the fact that China (unlike India and Africa) was never colonized, is an interesting speculation. Nevertheless, by 1916 the PMU missionaries were leaving the organizing of a Christmas conference in Lijiang entirely to the Chinese, with whom they shared meetings, meals and accommodation; and the missionaries declared that they were 'indeed a happy family'. However, these reports continued to carry innuendos, as a few sentences further the same report quipped, 'The Chinese are not renowned for their truthfulness!'[66] But there were exceptions. A particularly interesting account of missionary identification was provided for his home church in 1923 by Alfred Lewer, who donned Lisu garb and ate as a Lisu in the presence of the Chinese official at New Year festivities. Lewer had obviously made cultural decisions, forbidding the wearing of pigtails for Christians, and wrote, 'We have taught our Christians that they must not bow down to anyone' – a contravention of Chinese custom, especially for the Lisu, a subjugated people. His comments mixed insight with innuendo, as was almost always the case, even with the most liberal of missionaries on cultural ethics. 'From a Chinese point of view', he observed, 'it was awful for me, a foreigner, to eat with slaves, but through the grace of God we are all of one family, Hallelujah!' He went on, 'One has to think Yellow out here, and I assure you it is a queer way of thinking at times.' This incident was 'one of the greatest victories we could have had' and Lewer was quick to point out that this did not constitute 'any sacrifice to me, it was all enjoyment'. His motivation for this action, he said, was love: 'Yet I do think love changes things, for a lover will do anything for the one he loves, and I believe we need a real love for our work at home and abroad.'[67]

In some ways the Dutch PMU missionaries were more culturally sensitive than some of the British ones were. The Klavers objected to the appointment of Andrews as their replacement partly because he was not 'entirely *one* with the natives', and therefore did not have 'the respect of the natives here, even though we have pointed it out to him again & again he will not listen, & observe Chinese custom, which is a great necessity to successful work in the interior'.[68] Foreign missionaries, like other contemporary expatriates, were used to having house servants and their letters sometimes complained about their ineptitude. Sometimes their sheer possessions separated them from the local people. One missionary superintendent complained about a newly arrived missionary who came to China with too many things: 'the large amount he expended on his outfit', including a stove, collapsible bath, and six pairs of rubber soles and heels.[69]

Pentecostal missions were used to thinking in expansionist terms. Sometimes the expansionist mentality brought Pentecostal missionaries in conflict with other missions, partly because the Pentecostals had no comity agreements (nor wished to have them) and partly because the other missions saw the Pentecostals as encroaching on their territory and so opposed them vigorously. There was also the fact that Pentecostals sought to 'convert' other Protestant missionaries, which added considerably to the tensions. In particular, Pentecostals saw Catholics as their enemies and refused to co-operate with their missionaries, sometimes resulting (in Catholic-dominated areas like Latin America) in conflict with the governing powers. In undeveloped areas of African countries like the Congo, colonial administrations operated a policy that the first mission to build a church or a school in an area would have exclusive rights to operate there. Burton complained that Catholic priests went out of their way to frustrate the CEM's evangelistic strategy to go to areas where no Christian missionaries had ever been. Often the Pentecostal missionaries were given favour by local chiefs simply because they were more acceptable than the Catholics, who were seen as agents of the hated colonial regime.[70]

Some of the foreign Pentecostal missionaries were observed by neutral observers favourably. Boddy reproduced a long report written by D. W. Kerr in the South African missionary periodical *Africa's Golden Harvest*. He had approached the American Pentecostal missionaries 'very cautiously', especially as they had arrived in the country 'without any reputation'. He decided 'to investigate before deciding anything', and he observed that they had come to South Africa 'in simple trust in God, determined, as they said, to follow His leading, whatever that was; prepared to go wherever He directed, no matter how vile the surroundings were'. This had impressed Kerr favourably, 'considering that they settled without a murmur in a district, and at once began work, amid the vilest surroundings of perhaps any place in Africa; it all seemed to indicate the genuine spirit of Christ', he concluded.[71]

Roland Allen's books on indigenous churches and the earlier writings of Methodist missionary bishop William Taylor were beginning to circulate in Pentecostal circles as early as 1921.[72] Alice Luce, an early Assemblies of God missionary, wrote a series of three remarkable articles entitled 'Paul's Missionary Methods'. Although she acknowledged the important contribution to her thinking of Allen's book *Missionary Methods* (which she read as a CMS missionary in India), she could not remember the name of its author. Luce wrote that her initial Pentecostal experience received in India had taught her that 'there is such a thing as doing an apostolic work along apostolic lines'. She was surprised at how very quickly the 'heathen' were able to recognize 'the difference between those who went to them with a hidden sense of their own superiority and those who really had the spirit of a servant'. She said how important it was to declare the equality of all nations before God and to train 'native workers', the 'only ones' who would ever accomplish the evangelization of their own nations and who had 'many advantages over the foreigner'. Paul's aim was to found everywhere a 'self-supporting, self-governing and self-propagating church', with trained leaders who were independent of the foreign missionary and missionaries in their own right. She wrote that although it might be necessary for new churches to have 'foreign supervision' for a long time, this was only because of maturity and experience and had nothing to do with nationality or race. Once there were 'spiritually qualified leaders' in the native church, the foreign missionary must 'be subject to them, and to let them take the lead as the Spirit Himself shall guide them'.[73] William Burton discussed the principle of indigenization in a 1933 publication, stating that the idea first found prominence among Pentecostal missionaries 'at about the time of the Great War'. He wrote that 'white missionaries' were 'a mere passing phase in the introduction of Christianity to a heathen people' and that native Christians are given 'from the very commencement, the responsibility for the support and propagation of the young church' (significantly, Burton also mentions self-government, thus supporting the 'three-self' principle).[74]

But sadly, despite these early exhortations that so greatly influenced the policies of Pentecostal missions, there are still many areas of the world Pentecostal movement dominated physically, financially and ideologically by foreign missionaries. It appears from the records that the ideal of a 'three-self' independent church was slow in being realized in most of the expatriate mission efforts outlined in this book. Only occasionally were there exceptions. George Kelley wrote from Sai Nam in South China in 1920 about one of their missions which had 'assumed the support of all the workers and the work as a whole, with the exception of the preacher'. Elders and deacons had been ordained and the work had 'a desire to be wholly self-supporting next year'.[75]

The cultural and religious contexts of Pentecostal missionaries must be given serious consideration. Although they were not as closely associated with colonial governments as their more 'respectable' and generally better-educated Protestant counterparts were, and their attitudes and activities were probably not as greatly influenced by imperialism and colonialism, the Pentecostal missionaries who hailed from the same background did not escape these dangers. Their Christocentric message was very similar to that of their evangelical contemporaries, but like them too, these missionaries living and working in the zenith of European colonial expansion and imperialism were beset by a host of problems, presuppositions and prejudices on the mission field.

Missionaries and Politics

How did the early western missionaries respond to the strange context in which they found themselves? Their reaction to culture has just been noted and their response to religious ideas and practices was examined. Political events were sometimes commented on by Pentecostal missionaries and reveal some ambiguity. May Law was willing to go to print against Japanese imperial policies in China. She clearly respected the Chinese nation and its customs, seeing it as a 'great nation'; and was opposed to the Japanese attempt to make Buddhism the state religion, to enforce military rule and 'twenty other unjust demands'. 'God pity China', she declared.[76] Other Pentecostal missionaries wrote with an implicit disapproval of the Japanese-supported Manchu government in China, and the violent unrest in South China that ensued. Others had tropical diseases to contend with, including a plague in India, typhoons in China and the influenza epidemic of 1918.[77]

There is little doubt that the Pentecostal expatriates, in common with other contemporary missionaries, saw the colonizing process as part of God's provision to facilitate the spread of the gospel. Their patriotism usually blinded them to the harsh realities of oppressive colonialism as experienced by the colonized peoples. Lillian Denney wrote of the British encroachments on the independent kingdom of Nepal, in which the 'King Emperor' George V reciprocated the Nepalese monarch's lavish gifts to him 'representing the arts and treasures of the country' with photographs of himself and Queen Mary! Denney saw the new 'friendship' between the two rulers as evidence of God breaking down 'prejudice, fear and suspicion' against the English and thus enabling their work to be favoured.[78] But expatriate Pentecostals in India were under no illusions about the nationalistic tendencies of the people they were among. Will Norton wrote in 1913 about India's 'critical stage', where Muslims were 'turning against' Britain because of 'her attitude regarding the Turkish war' and Hindus 'are, of course, all the time more or less against England', with 'plotting going on all the time'.[79]

American Pentecostal missionaries, like their government, favoured the republican revolution led by Sun Yat Sen against the Manchu dynasty in China – naturally, it had to be 'a republican form like that of the United States'. The result would be, it was assured, a greater 'opening up of China for the Gospel'. Of course, Pentecostals were enamoured by the news that Sun Yat Sen's mother-in-law attended a Pentecostal church in Shanghai, and when the new president of China publicly declared his Christian faith in 1913 and Christian churches were asked to set aside a day of prayer for the new republican government, this was confirmation that God was using the politics of the day to bring about a greater response of the Chinese to Christianity.[80] Similarly, Cecil Polhill expressed his approval of the impending Chinese annexation of Tibet, because he believed that this would result in the opening up of this hitherto closed country for Christian missionaries. This British patriot, unlike the Americans, believed that a constitutional monarchy was the best solution for China's woes, supporting the Manchu Prince Regent Yuan in his efforts to win back the Republicans. Arie Kok, Dutch PMU missionary wrote that because Tibet was 'closed to the Gospel', many Christians trusted that the Chinese Revolution would bring about 'a breakdown of the Lama-power, and a splendid opening for the Gospel of Christ'.[81]

On the other hand, another Pentecostal missionary felt that Tibet's desire for British protection from China would make this country amenable to British missionaries and Russia's securing trade rights in Afghanistan meant 'the beginning of European influence in Cabul [Kabul], and the beginning of the downfall of the intolerance and isolation of that country' (little did he know what the next century would bring). These political events, he felt, were the answer to the prayers 'to break open those doors hitherto fast locked against His messengers'. But he was by no means exonerating the colonial powers, adding that the 'doors and barriers' had been 'erected and butressed [sic] by the political ambitions and greed of the empires surrounding these benighted lands – by China, Russia and Great Britain'.[82] During 1915 there was a rebellion in Yunnan province staged by the military, ostensibly against President Yuan Shih-kai's rumoured intentions to reinstate the monarchy. The missionaries were clearly against the rebellion, as they felt that Yuan was the only person capable of holding the Chinese nation together in peace.[83] Another missionary in China saw the increasing 'socialistic' and 'suffragette' views of the Chinese as evidence that the biblically prophesied lawlessness was increasing in the last days, but at the same time brought with them an unprecedented openness to the Christian message.[84]

Amos Bradley in El Salvador was concerned about the American policy of charging all other nations for using the Panama Canal while American vessels went through free and for refusing to allow Japan to build another canal through Nicaragua. This, he said, was adding to what was 'already a repulsive feeling against North Americans' and if the USA persisted, it was 'likely to stir up war with all Central America and probably with other nations'. He obviously disapproved of the American policy.[85] Another American, May Kelty wrote with disapproval of the plight of Amerindians in Argentina. Although she thought the 'Indians' were 'generally savages', she decried their being 'kept down with cruel, unjust treatment, being driven from pillar to post'.[86] The Pentecostals also saw their revival movements as the solution to all political and social ills. This is illustrated by the words of a group of young women from India and Ceylon and published by Carrie Montgomery, who spoke of the wonderful 'heart-hunger for deliverance which is growing so apparent among the people'. This heart-hunger took many forms in people's minds; some thought it was 'the "tyranny" of the government, some of caste, some of poverty, and others of other oppressions'. But actually the task of the missionary was 'to show that the bonds are the bonds of Satan and sin – that nothing but the Blood of Jesus can set free – that His is freedom indeed'.[87]

Pentecostal missionaries and workers, like the Holiness movements from which they emerged, were expected to refrain from 'worldliness' in their daily conduct with each other and outsiders. Their ascetic requirements for 'separation from the world' were sometimes severe, certainly by today's standards.

One PMU superintendent complained that three of the young women that had been sent to his station seemed 'not to have got quite weaned away from the worldliness which manifests itself in MUCH Novel reading, and too much love of Social life'.[88] In today's world we would say that these missionaries were not much fun and were not allowed to have any.

At the beginning of this chapter we noticed the unholy relationship that existed between missionaries and the colonizing powers, and how the missionaries depended on imperial protection and patronage. But occasionally these powers were condemned for their atrocities. Most of the western Christian world recoiled at the atrocities committed in King Leopold's private fiefdom, the Belgian Congo. *Word and Work* reprinted an article from the *Church Herald* on 'The Congo Outrages':

> The atrocious crimes of King Leopold, Belgium's king, against the natives of the Congo Free State, which are more murderous than Nero and more merciless than a Borgia, are now attracting the attention of civilized nations ... this infamous king, the most murderous and merciless of modern times, has violated all his pledges and is killing the natives by the most unspeakable tortures, cutting off their heads, feet, etc. He is practicing cannibalism on a large scale ... And yet with these unspeakable crimes and wickedness continually on the increase throughout the world, they tell us it is getting better.[89]

This was not the last time the atrocities of the Belgian colonial government were denounced in the Pentecostal press. One author wrote that while the whole world stood aghast at the suffering of Belgium during the Great War, most were unaware of the 'awful atrocities which were perpetrated in the Belgian Congo under the sanction of this same government'. Belgium was now under the judgement of God, for it had 'sowed the wind and reaped the whirlwind'.[90] Whether the Belgian policies in the Congo changed so much in a few years to become as Burton alleged, 'no more humane set of laws in Africa' is unlikely, but his statement does illustrate how often Pentecostal missionaries were either deceived by or ignorant of the perniciousness of colonialism.[91] Subjugated people were certainly not subjects of humane laws, but missionaries of that era would not have thought otherwise. It is true that Pentecostals generally tried to stay out of political affairs, but this approach lay them open to the charge that they were 'pie-in-the-sky' preachers who were not really concerned about the oppression under which the people they professed to love were suffering.

Racism and Social Segregation

There were darker and more sinister issues at stake relating to race and society that affected missionaries and stemmed from their background in a culture dominated by Enlightenment thinking, colonialism and social Darwinism. Early Pentecostal missionaries were mostly paternalistic, often creating dependency, and sometimes were overtly racist.[92] The attitudes of some of them left much to be desired (to put it mildly), and with the benefit of hindsight, their actions, words and attitudes would now be crude and insulting. In one shocking report, Fred Johnstone, a missionary writing to *Confidence* from the Congo in 1915, speaks of the 'practically nude natives' who were 'very raw and superstitious'. The missionaries had carriers, who not only bore their heavy luggage for many days on end, but also piggybacked the missionaries across streams and swamps. Some of the carriers became drunk and violent – and the missionaries' solution was to give them 'a thrashing with a stick', after which there was 'perfect peace'. Arriving at their destination, Johnstone reported, 'The natives came to meet their new "mukelenge" (or white chief) for fully a mile from the mission station.'[93]

Two months later, *Confidence* published another report from Johnstone from 'the wilds of darkest Africa', where he describes the Lulua as a 'very raw, superstitious, and indolent race' who were 'gradually becoming a little more accustomed to the white man and his ways and, praise God, His message of love'.[94] His routine on preaching trips was to have carriers who hauled him through the forests and long grass, and over streams and rivers in a hammock. He had a young man (probably his own age) he called 'my boy' to cook his meals.[95] He thought that Africans had tougher bones than other people had, for when a woman was wounded on the head by a large hailstone, he commented, 'It generally needs a hard knock to hurt a native on his hard skull.'[96] But fortunately, this missionary was still on a learning curve. A year later, as he left his mission for furlough in England he wrote: 'It was very hard to say good-bye to the dear natives whom I had learned to love so much, especially the young teachers in training . . .'[97]

Early Pentecostals were subject to making the same racial stereotypes as their contemporaries. Sometimes these stereotypes were reinforced in the missionary meetings during conventions in the 'homelands'. One at the Stone Church in Chicago in 1914 changed the words of the chorus 'Bringing in the Sheaves' to 'Bringing in Chinese' and one missionary from Africa followed this with 'Bringing in Black Boys'. The correspondent commented: 'We saw by faith many going forth sowing the seed and bringing in the sheaves from every kindred, tribe and nation, and laying them at the Master's feet.'[98]

Even the most saintly were no exception. Alexander Boddy addressed the subject of race in one of his tours of the USA in 1912, referring to the first 'Coloured' (African American) church service he attended, an Episcopal church where during the singing of a solo, he observed, 'If I had closed my eyes I would not have known that he was a negro', as if African Americans would inherently sing differently from Anglos. He also commented on an encounter with a young black Christian waiter, whose 'dark, ugly countenance' lit up so much, wrote Boddy, that he 'hardly looked the same'. Another African American Christian he met he described: 'His black face in the darkness seemed almost that of a demon.' He observed that the two races never mixed, even among church ministers, and this did not seem to bother him much. He had seldom heard white people 'speak kindly of the black ones' and he remarked on how remarkable this made the Pentecostal revival in Los Angeles.[99] On another trip to North America in 1914, Boddy was reluctant to declare himself 'White' on a southern train, but did not disapprove of the segregation either.[100]

Racial slurs and innuendos were not uncommon among early twentieth-century Europeans. *Confidence*, the premier Pentecostal publication in Europe until the First World War, published photographs of missionaries sitting in the centre of groups of 'natives' on their front pages. One such photo published in 1913 showed a group of 'Pentecostal Zulus' in which Canadian missionary Chawner is surrounded by a group of 11 Africans who are named only by their 'Christian' names: Lisa, Salome, Solomon, etc.[101] A well-known Swiss Pentecostal missionary from the Congo, Alma Doering, considered the African 'native' to be 'naturally indolent'.[102] The conference address published in *Confidence* in 1915 by Doering, 'Leopard's Spots or God's masterpiece, which?' referred to African people as follows:

The savage is God's opportunity, the masterpiece of our common creator, who delights in tackling impossibilities . . . unless the superior races are ready to humble themselves, we may yet witness such an awakening of the despised races as will put to shame the pride of their superiors.[103]

The so-called 'superior races' of Europe were at that very moment engaged in such a horrible and dehumanizing war that the rest of the world could be forgiven for wondering who were actually the 'savages'. The term 'native' was in constant use in missionary correspondence, and distinguished the local people from expatriate missionaries. The term 'native preacher' was used often to refer to the local people who assisted the expatriates and often did most of the work of ministry. Some considered 'native' a neutral term, but at least one missionary, Albert Norton's son Will, who was born in India, pointed out that it was in fact a term of reproach, 'a word of contempt', he put it, when referring to himself as a 'native of India and take my stand with those people over there as my brethren'.[104]

Early missionaries were sometimes patronizing, impolite and racist. Racial stereotyping by missionaries expressed itself most often in the denying of real leadership to local people and undoubtedly caused the withdrawal of these potential leaders into independent churches. Typical of this more subtle form of racism was that of a PMU missionary, whose opinion was that 'a native, under the supervision of a foreigner, can be mightily used of God'. He added, 'they can go where we are forbidden and open the way for us and the precious Gospel'.[105] Perhaps this was not intended, but the obvious implication of these words is that without the 'foreigner' there was no 'precious Gospel' and without foreign supervision, no effective 'native' ministry. Of course, the opposite was often and probably usually the case: the less supervision by foreigners, the more effective the 'native' minister was!

This attitude played its way out in different ways. Early in the formation of the Apostolic Faith Mission in South Africa, African pastors were given only nominal and local leadership opportunities, the races were almost immediately separated in baptisms and church gatherings, and apartheid had become the accepted practice of the church. The same pattern pertained in all white-led Pentecostal denominations until the 1990s. In 1920, J. O. Lehman's appointed assistant in the PHC made remarks which were not atypical of attitudes of white missionaries at the time. He thought that 'the native' was 'indeed a very peculiar creature to deal with'. They had 'strange ideas about the white man toward them', which of course comes as no surprise in South Africa where Africans were completely disenfranchised. He went on as if he had to convince his American readers:

> You would have been convinced of the truth of my statement if you had heard for yourself what I heard only a couple of days back from a native's mouth. Only the Lord's Spirit can let them see how dreadful and unthankful much of it is. But I believe the Lord God will in some way meet the need as we pray, and let Him use us.[106]

This tension between Pentecostal spirituality and racism and the ambiguous relationship white Pentecostals had with their African fellow-believers was to manifest itself many times in twentieth-century South Africa. Although African pastors and evangelists were largely responsible for the growth of the movement in South Africa, they were written out of history (with the possible exception of Nicholas Bhengu) and such racist views have abounded. It cannot be wondered that the schisms that occurred within the AFM from 1910 onwards resulted in hundreds of other denominations and the creation of the largest church in South Africa today, the Zion Christian Church. These African Pentecostal churches, although perhaps not 'classical Pentecostals' in the usual sense of the word, now represent almost half of the African population, compared to about 10 per cent who belong to 'classical' Pentecostal and Charismatic churches of white origin.[107]

John G. Lake made a less-than-flattering description of South African 'natives' when writing about their 'tremendous native work' and asking for 'REAL MISSIONARIES' (capitalization in the original). But Lake was quick to point out that he did not want any person to come to Africa 'with the thought of a lot of "brand new American ideas" to teach to the natives', and said that 'one of the curses of American missionaries is that when they come here they forthwith are teaching social equality between the white people and the natives'. Lake would have nothing of that in his mission, because he thought that 'the African native is a very different man from the American negro'. The African, he declared, was 'a heathen' and the proof of this was because 'he does not wear anything but a blanket, until he is taught and Christianized'. So he warned that missionaries coming to South Africa should come 'prepared to come and learn, and in these days when God is calling men out into the mission field, they want to come in wisdom and strength, and knowledge, too'.[108] This attitude caught on very quickly, as another American Pentecostal missionary, Theo Schwede, who had only just arrived in South Africa, in his first letter home wrote that 'some American missionaries' had made 'a great mistake in trying to put the natives on an equality with the white man'. The result of this would be disastrous, he thought, for there was 'danger of the unchristianized natives being stirred up by some wicked leader', with the result that 'they could in a short time extinguish the whites altogether'. Schwede was, however, to change his mind as he got to admire Elias Letwaba, one of the most effective and godly of the early South African Pentecostals.[109]

Lake, although praising the faith of his 'native workers', was still putting out letters that betrayed his inner prejudice. African men, he thought, were 'crude and many things in their lives do not appeal to us as the right thing at all times'. He said that that he had to frequently 'deal with them strongly and clearly and exercise a good deal of discipline to keep them out of sin'. The reason for this necessary discipline was that 'the native is still a child-man though he is saved, and like a child, it is easy for him to fall back into sin'. But all was not hopeless for Lake, because 'nevertheless you see, brother, that God honors them', and even though he thought that the African was 'just an animal yet, and the animal in him predominates', yet 'the submergence of the animal comes gradually as the Spirit of God in him is permitted to develop and obtain power over him'. Later, Lake wrote that the idea that Africans could 'christianize' themselves was a false one, for 'all undeveloped natives retrograde fast when left alone'. Only 'the better energy of the white man' could 'stir them to activity', he declared, but 'of course, Letwaba is an exception . . . equal to many white workers'.[110]

There are many examples of what would today be very offensive language in Pentecostal missionary writings. Frances Taylor, a missionary writing from Mbabane, Swaziland in 1910, spoke of the work among 'the native boys', quickly explaining that 'all [African males] are called "boys" – from infancy to grey hairs'. Another Pentecostal missionary in Johannesburg writes of the 'Holy Spirit coming down on these black boys [mine workers] in such power', and William Burton often refers to African men and evangelists as 'boys', and African children as 'pickaninnies'.[111] The use of 'boys' to refer to grown African men was a common practice among Pentecostal missionaries, as it was among the colonizers. Burton's mission made it a policy that each missionary should have a full-time housekeeper ('house boy') and gardener ('garden boy'), paid at sixpence a day, compared to a British labourer being paid forty times that amount at that time.[112]

Many of these and similar struggles were evidence of cultural misunder-standings and insensitivity that could have been avoided. Sometimes Pentecostal missionaries found conditions in the 'field' quite intolerable. S. S. Slingerland writing from Berbera, British Somaliland in 1908, probably expressed the pent-up feelings of many when he wrote that the great majority of people there were Muslims, and were 'very ignorant and superstitious, and poverty reigns supreme among thousands of them'. He thought that 'lying, stealing, and begging are the principal occupations of the poor class, and they do not think it any disgrace to have it known'. But this missionary did believe in a solution: 'Nothing but the mighty power of God manifested in a miracu-lous way will ever waken them to a sense of their great spiritual need.'[113] It seems that this particular missionary did not send any further letters after this picture of hopelessness, and disappears from the records.

It was not only in Africa that this language was used; it was also frequently in the writings of missionaries in India. One constantly referred to the young Indian men who were preaching in Nepal as 'our boys'.[114] Two British missionary women in India wrote home in 1912 to complain about the fact that because no Europeans lived in that district 'there is no house where we could live, there are only the Indian native houses'.[115] A PMU missionary from Tibet likewise described Tibetan food and said, 'only those who know anything about Tibetan life will fully understand how unpleasant it really is.'[116] In fact, there was an underlying belief among expatriate missionaries that one could not live healthily on 'native food' alone and that a missionary needed the sustenance that western food brought. Some attributed disease and even death to living for too long on 'native food', and one missionary suggested that the cause of her husband's 'seriously impaired' stomach was his 'living a long time on Chinese food'.[117] Even as late as September 1920, during a missionary convention of the AG in Springfield, Missouri, a report mentions by name several prominent white Americans in Mexican work along the borders, and then refers simply to a 'native Mexican evangelist' who spoke at this conference and was now working in El Paso, Texas. The name of this graduate of Moody Bible Institute is not even mentioned, but he was none other than Francisco Olazábal, leading one of the biggest Hispanic Pentecostal works in the USA.[118]

Social segregation was invariably practised between European or American missionaries and 'native workers'. Even in a case where two American women were accompanying Indian workers on a mission trip to outlying villages with an Indian woman leader, the two American workers travelled by cart while the eight Indian workers walked, and they used a separate tent to that of the five Indian women (the men slept in the cart).[119] The AG missionary conference held in St Louis, Missouri in 1917 resolved that it disapproved of any intermarriage between 'missionaries and natives' and that it should be prevented, and that missionaries should avoid 'too great familiarity' by living 'in the same quarters as a family' with the 'native workers'. New missionaries should seek the advice of 'senior missionaries . . . especially with regard to their relationship to the native people'.[120]

As we will see later, almost from its inception in South Africa, the Pentecostal movement favoured segregation – a practice that was to endure throughout the twentieth century. This was particularly true in the case of the AFM, which provides an illuminating example of the general trend. Only four months after the founding of the AFM, the Executive Council minuted in September 1908 that Lake had spoken of 'the necessity of getting adequate accommodation for the holding of services in Doornfontein especially for the coloured people'. Less than two months later, after complaints by white followers, the Executive decided that 'the baptism of Natives shall in future take place after the baptism of the white people'. At the Executive meeting in February 1909 it was decided that the superintendent over the 'Native work' had to be a white man.[121] The minutes of July 1909 read: 'In future, the baptism of Whites, Coloured and Natives shall be separate.'[122] By 1910 separate annual national conferences were being held for white and African members. A 'Native Council' was formed in that year consisting of three white and three African members. All decisions of this council could be revised by the all-white Executive Council.[123] By 1915 the racist attitude had become even more pronounced, when the AFM Executive Council declared that no ordination or leadership appointment could be made by an African church official except with the consent of the white superintendent.[124] One wonders to what extent this apparent lack of trust of African leadership in the AFM contributed to the schisms that took place from this time onwards. In 1917 an ambiguous resolution was adopted by the Executive Council, illustrating clearly the prevailing racial prejudice:

> We do not teach or encourage social equality between Whites and Natives. We recognise that God is no respecter of persons, but that in every nation he that feareth Him and worketh righteousness is acceptable to Him. We therefore preach the Gospel equally to all peoples, making no distinctions. We wish it to be generally known that our White, Coloured and Native peoples have their separate places of worship, where the Sacraments are administered to them.[125]

In 1925 the Executive Council decided that all African districts should be under the control of a white overseer, failing which under the chairman of the white district. On several occasions during this period decisions were made by the whites for the African AFM members, who had simply to obey or leave the church.[126]

There were exceptions to this general malaise among early Pentecostal missionaries. There was the selfless dedication of Thomas Junk, one of the earliest of all Pentecostal missionaries, who identified with the people he was working with in North China to the extent that he saw himself as poor with them, writing in May 1911 about his work living together in a compound with a 'family' of over 50 people rescued from depredation and abandoned children, where God had 'enabled me to become a Chinaman'.[127] Anna Deane recognized the religious propensities of the Chinese. She wrote that they were 'hungry for God' and that even the 'heathen' were 'a worshipful people' with a 'profound respect for a temple or church'. She observed that 'when they are really converted they would put any American congregation to shame'.[128]

William Burton – whose wife was South African – published his opinion on the 'race problem' in South Africa in 1934. In one respect, he was reluctant to come out strongly against white South African policies, but in another, his views were pragmatic. He saw 'the spirit of resentment and mutual distrust' being periodically stirred up by extremists on either side. Although he believed in the inevitability of 'the black man' ousting 'the white man' (and that thinking blacks were justified in their resentment against the wrongs their people suffered), he thought that segregation was 'for the present . . . the most humane suggestion offered' – there it is again: Burton used 'humane' to cover a multitude of sins. Although he was convinced of the equality of people in the eyes of God, he was much less convinced about the advisability of integrated worship or mixed marriages in the church. Burton did not attempt to suggest solutions to the problem, but merely to state the 'difficult conditions' that had made South Africa 'one of the least missionary countries of the world'.[129]

Pentecostals followed the practice of other missions in considering the original names of their converts to be 'heathen' names, that needed to be replaced with 'Christian' ones. Mary Courtney, writing from Uttar Pradesh in India, described a river baptism conducted by Albert Norton and said that some of the girls being baptized 'gave up their heathen names and took Christian names, such as Rebekah, Leah, and Rachael'.[130] These Hebrew-derived English names from the Old Testament were considered 'Christian', while the Indian names were 'heathen'.

This neo-imperialism has caused tension between US Pentecostal mission-aries and national leaders, and certainly the perceived hegemony bolstered by US economic and military muscle emerging after the First World War has not helped the negative image. Nevertheless, Pentecostalism in many parts of the world has always been influenced by the USA in particular and the worldwide dominance of US forms of Pentecostalism continues into the twenty-first century. The seeds of this global dominance were sown early in the twentieth century. But this domination is mitigated by the fact that the centres of Pentecostalism are no longer mainly based in the USA. Pentecostalism has rapidly become a poly-nucleated phenomenon where US forms, while still hegemonic and representing the US-invented tradition that is to be emulated, are in an intense relationship of competition and assimilation with varieties of Pentecostalism from the South and East. The resultant Pentecostalisms in different regions and nations are no longer influenced only by US American forms but are emerging with their own character and centres of influence, and these in turn sometimes relate to centres of Pentecostalisms in other parts of the world. Although Pentecostalism with its offer of empowerment for all without preconditions was possibly more effective in raising up local leader-ship than other missions were, Pentecostal missionaries were also impas-sioned with ideas of global spiritual conquest, an expansionist conviction influenced by their premillennial eschatological expectations that the nations of the world had to be conquered for Christ before his imminent coming to rule the earth. This expansionist tradition had been around for some time, rooted in the nineteenth-century Evangelical Awakenings, but also present in older European missions, including among the Catholics.[131] There was also an imperialism that accompanied that tradition, as both Catholic and Protestant missions were linked to particular countries. Undoubtedly, for American missionaries the belief in the 'manifest destiny' of the USA further influenced missions used to thinking in expansionist terms.

Notes

1　*TF* 30:11 (Nov 1910), p.261.
2　*TF* 16:1 (Jan 1896), p.1.
3　Stanley, *Bible and Flag*, pp.64–5.
4　Stanley, *Bible and Flag*, pp.64–5.
5　*FF* 35, Feb 1916, p.4.
6　McPherson, *This is That*, p.64.
7　*FF* 49 (May 1917), p.40.
8　*Conf* 7:12 (Dec 1914), p.238.
9　*Conf* 11:3 (July–Sept 1918), p.57.
10　*FF* 23 (Jan 1915), p.8.
11　*Conf* 10:1 (Jan–Feb 1917), p.11.
12　*Redemption Tidings* 1:2 (Oct 1924), p.17.
13　*The Pentecostal Witness* 1 (July 1924), p.4.
14　*Conf* 4:8 (Aug 1911), p.191.
15　*Conf* 5:9 (May 1912), p.215; 5:12 (Dec 1912), p.286.

16 *Conf* 6:4 (Apr 1913), p.84.

17 *LRE* 9:8 (May 1917), p.7.

18 *Conf* 8:6 (June 1915), p.118.

19 *FF* 48 (Apr 1917), p.29.

20 *Conf* 8: 6 (June 1915), p.119.

21 *LRE* 10:11 (Aug 1917), p.7.

22 *Conf* 6:7 (July 1913), p.148.

23 *Things New and Old* 1:4 (Oct 1921), p.32 (question marks in original).

24 *Things New and Old* 2:3 (Aug 1922), p.11.

25 *Things New and Old* 2:5 (Dec 1922), p.7.

26 Acts 19.37.

27 *LRE* 3:2 (Nov 1910), p.7.

28 *LRE* 6:6 (Mar 1914), p.14.

29 *WW* 32:12 (Dec 1910), p.362.

30 *BM* 97 (1 Nov 1911), p.1

31 *LRE* 4:10 (July 1912), p.8.

32 *UR* 2:3 (Nov 1910), p.5; *BM* 89 (1 July 1911), p.1.

33 *WW* 27:8 (Aug 1905), p.210.

34 Letter, E. Cook to T. H. Mundell, 7 Aug 1915.

35 Letter, E. Cook to T. H. Mundell, 1 Apr 1915.

36 Letter. E. Cook to T. H. Mundell, 14 Mar 1921.

37 Moorhead, *Missionary Pioneering*, pp.63, 64; Letter, E. Cook to T. H. Mundell, 5 June 1916.

38 Burton, *When God Changes a Village*, pp. 17–25.

39 *LRE* 4:9 (June 1912), p.18.

40 Meyer, *Translating the Devil*.

41 *Pent* 2:11–12 (Nov–Dec 1910), p.5.

42 *LRE* 5:11 (Aug 1913), p.3.

43 *BM* 1:2 (1 Nov 1907), p.2.

44 *LRE* 2:11 (Aug 1910), p.7.

45 Letter, E. Cook to T. H. Mundell, 1 Apr 1915.

46 Letter, E. Cook to T. H. Mundell, 8 Dec 1915.

47 Moorhead, *Missionary Pioneering*, pp.38–9.

48 Moorhead, *Missionary Pioneering*, pp.83–6.

49 *FF* 35 (Feb 1916), p.4; 49 (May 1917), p.40.

50 *BM* 112 (15 June 1912), p.2.

51 *Conf* 7:1 (Jan 1914), p.16.

52 Moorhead, *Missionary Pioneering*, p.34.

53 Burton, *God Working*, pp.29–31.

54 Moorhead, *Missionary Pioneering*, p.128; Burton, *When God Changes a Village*, pp. 153–60; Burton, *God Working*, p.33.

55 *Conf* 1:2 (May 1908), p.19; 2:5 (May 1909), p.110.

56 *TF* 30:11 (Nov 1910), p.261.

57 McGee, 'Pentecostal Missiology', p.279.

58 *BM* 54 (15 Jan 1909), p.1.

59 *BM* 63 (1 June 1910), p.3.

60 *BM* 66 (15 July 1910), p.4.

61 *BM* 115 (1 Aug 1912), p.1.

62 *Pent* 1:7 (June 1909), p.3.

63 Letter, A. Swift to T. H. Mundell, 4 Aug 1920.

64 Letter, E. Cook to T. H. Mundell, 14 Mar 1921.

65 Letter, Gladys Eaton (Kuang Hsi Cheo, Yunnan) to T. H. Mundell, 23 Apr 1923.

66 *Conf* 10:2, Mar–Apr 1917, pp.15–17.

67 *Things New and Old* 3:2 (June 1923), p.9; *Redemption Tidings* 1:3 (Dec 1924), p.14.

68 Letter, P. Klaver to T. H. Mundell, 20 Aug 1923.

69 Letter, W. J. Boyd to T. H. Mundell, 8 Mar 1921.

70 Moorhead, *Missionary Pioneering*, pp.71–2; Burton, *When God Changes a Village*, pp.38–40.

71 *Conf* 2:2 (Feb 1909), p.27.

72 Allen, *Missionary Methods*; McGee, 'Pentecostals and their Various Strategies', p.212.

73 *PE* 374–5 (8 Jan 1921), pp.6–7; 376–7 (22 Jan 1921), pp.6, 11; 378–9 (5 Feb 1921), pp.6–7.

74 Burton, *When God Changes a Village*, pp.127–8.

75 *LRE* 12:6 (Mar 1920), p.15.

76 Law, *Pentecostal Mission*, p.36.

77 *BM* 87 (1 June 1911), p.1.

78 *BM* 108 (15 Apr 1912), p.2.

79 *Trust* 12:3 (May 1913), p.2.

80 *LRE* 4:3 (Dec 1911), p.13; *FF* 15 (Dec 1913), p.6.

81 *FF* 1 (Oct 1911), pp.4–5; 2 (Nov 1911), p.5; *Conf* 5:5 (May 1912), p.111.

82 *BM* 146 (15 Dec 1913), p.3.

83 *FF* 35 (Feb 1916), pp.7–8.

84 *BM* 116 (15 Aug 1912), p.4.

85 *BM* 145 (1 Dec 1913), p.2.

86 *BM* 102 (15 Jan 1912), p.2.

87 *TF* 30:11 (Nov 1910), p.247.

88 Letter, A. Swift to T. H. Mundell, 20 Apr 1918.

89 *WW* 29:1 (Jan 1907), p.19.

90 *LRE* 9:6 (Mar 1916), p.16.

91 Burton, *God Working*, p.25.

92 McGee, 'Pentecostals and their Various Strategies', p.211.

93 *Conf* 8:5 (May 1915), pp.98–9.

94 *Conf* 8:7 (July 1915), p.139.

95 *FF* 40 (July 1916), p.11.

96 *Conf* 9:12 (Dec 1916), p.200.

97 *FF* 53 (Sept 1917), p.72.

98 *LRE* 6:9 (June 1914), p.8.

99 *Conf* 5:9 (Sept 1912), pp. 203, 208–9.

100 *Conf* 7:8 (Aug 1914), p.147.

101 *Conf* 6:8 (Aug 1913), p.149.

102 *LRE* 5:6 (Mar 1913), p.18.

103 *Conf* 8:8 (Aug 1915), p.154.

104 *LRE* 9:7 (Apr 1917), p.15.

105 *Conf* 9:10 (Oct 1916), p.171.

106 *WW* 42:6 (June 1920), p.14.

107 Anderson, *Zion and Pentecost*, pp.46–9.

108 *UR* 1:1 (June 1909), pp.2–3; *Pent* 1:7 (June 1909), p.3.

109 *UR* 1:1 (June 1909), p.7; 1:3 (Aug 1909), p.6.

110 *UR* 2:2 (Sept–Oct 1910), p.5.

111 *Conf* 4:1 (Jan 1911), pp.16, 18; *Pent* 1:8 (July 1909), p.8; Moorhead, *Missionary Pioneering*, pp.11, 35, 38, 44, 87, 160.

112 Moorhead, *Missionary Pioneering*, p.117.

113 *Conf* 1:2 (June 1908), p.23.

114 *BM* 94 (15 Sept 1911), p.2.

115 *Conf* 5:2 (Feb 1912), p.47.

116 *Conf* 5:5 (May 1912), p.167.

117 *LRE* 11:5 (Feb 1919), p.13.

118 *LRE* 13:3 (Dec 1920), p.12.

119 *BM* 129 (15 Mar 1913), p.2.

120 *WE* 209 (6 Oct 1917), p.10.

121 De Wet, 'Apostolic Faith', pp.160–1.

122 Sundkler, *Zulu Zion*, p.54.

123 De Wet, 'Apostolic Faith', pp.93, 95–6.

124 De Wet, 'Apostolic Faith', p.100.

125 Quoted in De Wet, 'Apostolic Faith', p.165.

126 De Wet, 'Apostolic Faith', pp.135, 163.

127 *UR* 2:5 (May 1911), p.5.

128 *BM* 59 (1 Apr 1910), p.4.

129 Burton, *When God Makes*, pp.2–7.

130 *BM* 62 (15 May 1910), p.2.

131 Stanley, *Bible and Flag*, p.62.

10

Persons of Average Ability: Pentecostal Ministry

Believing that in foreign lands, as in our own, there are masses who can be influenced by persons of average ability – baptized with the Holy Ghost and with fire – the design of this school is to take any who give evidence of being called of God, and give them such an education as should be specially adapted to lead them to become soul-winners in foreign lands. This will include such teaching and practice as will tend to physical, mental and spiritual development.

(*Triumphs of Faith*, 1885)[1]

Generally, early Pentecostals did not place great store on theological training and most of their early missionaries had little of it or none at all. Many of the early Pentecostal missionaries and pastors in many parts of the world have been those with little or no formal theological education. The emphasis in Pentecostal leadership usually has been on the spirituality of the leader rather than on intellectual abilities or even ministerial skills. This was the legacy of the evangelical 'Bible schools' and 'missionary training schools' instituted in the late nineteenth century for the training of missionary candidates and pastors, often no more than rudimentary short courses in Bible study. For example, a 'Bible School for Christian Workers' was opened in Springfield, Massachusetts in 1899 by the Christian Workers' Union led by S. G. Otis, later a Pentecostal. This organization had set up 'an unsectarian band of Spirit-filled Christian workers for humble, practical missionary work at home and abroad'. The Bible school was to give its students 'a practical training for aggressive missionary work'. The curriculum was set up with the purpose being 'for the study of the Word of God, development in holy living and preparation for Christly service in the home land or the foreign fields'. The courses of study that were offered included 'Lessons in the Life of Christ', 'The Beginning of things' and 'The Word of God applied to our daily living'. Significantly, two of the three resident teachers were women. Because this was 'a Faith work', entrance to the school was free, but 'every one is expected to make "Freewill" offerings each week as God prospers them and as the needs require'. The advertisement for the school stated that they were 'depending upon the Holy Ghost to send whoever He wants identified with the School and to keep or send away all that He does not want'. It added, 'No shirkers or jerkers need apply'.[2]

Towards the end of the nineteenth century, evangelical groups hastily created institutions for the training of an increasing number of missionary candidates. The quotation heading this chapter was the stated purpose of the Mission Training School set up in Niagara Falls in 1885 for the training of women missionaries and would be reproduced in Pentecostal circles. Carrie

Judd Montgomery set up a 'Missionary Training School' in 1894, where the stated aims were 'to provide for the special training in the most direct and speedy manner, of such as should be led to dedicate themselves to the Foreign Missionary Service'. This was 'not a Theological School or course, as such, but a careful study of the Word itself along the fundamental lines of human ruin, and the Divine plan of redemption'. The purpose of this training course would be to 'equip the student for direct soul-winning and evangelistic work in heathen lands' and 'to teach the student how to tell the message of salvation fully, and in the simplest possible way'.[3] This school, later called the Shalom Training School, decided three years later that the urgency of the times was so great that the training period had to be reduced. Because it was the time of the 'last call' and for 'eleventh hour laborers', there was 'every evidence that the work of training must be done in the shortest possible time, and that it must consist in essential work'. All that was needed was for the missionary to possess 'the essence of Christianity in the life and power of the Holy Ghost'. So the course was reduced to 'six weeks for Home Workers, and, at most, four months for the Foreign Field'.[4]

The focus on training national leadership to emerge in Pentecostal churches was not exclusively Pentecostal for it came out of this background of evangelical missions. By the end of the nineteenth century there were fund-raising appeals for 'native workers' who were called 'substitutes' for foreign missionaries. H. B. Gibbud in Massachusetts, for example, ran a 'Self Denial Substitute Band' whose aim was 'supporting native preachers and Bible women in the foreign field'.[5] The American Baptists declared that 'the great need of Christian missions' was 'the raising up of native evangelists endued with mighty power', and affirmed that there was 'no lack in the missionary work which may not be overcome by this means'. It continued: 'The great successes of Christian missions in the past have nearly all been due to native evangelists filled with the Holy Ghost and power, preaching the gospel to their own people in their own tongues.' The pressing need in all Christian missions was 'the development of high spiritual leadership in some of the converts', giving the example of the Congo as a 'most encouraging element of missions', where there were 'frequent reports of evangelistic journeys undertaken by the native Christians, self prompted and self sustaining, often even without the knowledge of the missionary'. If this was one of the 'conspicuous features' of a mission that 'may be small at present', this was 'far more promising than one which can number many thousands of converts who are supinely relying upon American or European missionaries, not only for support, but for leadership and that initial energy and enthusiasm which is the essential of all successful evangelistic work'. The report ended with a prayer that 'the Lord will pour out his Holy Spirit upon the native converts and raise up among them everywhere men of power and leadership'.[6]

Early Pentecostals believed, following Paul, that God had called the weak and foolish things of this world to confound the wise, or as the passage above puts it, 'persons of average ability' who had been baptized in the Holy Spirit and were specially called by God to 'become soul-winners in foreign lands'. Even though there was spontaneity and a rather chaotic flurry of mission activity in early Pentecostalism, these missionaries did not just happen. They went through a process of calling from many different walks of life, preparation, (in some cases) training, sending and learning, before they actually began the work that they believed they were to do. This chapter discusses this process, including the different kinds of preparation and training, the use of and training of local workers and ministers, the use of women in ministry, the hardships they met on the field and the beginnings of organization, division and ultimately, schism.

Preparing Pentecostal Missionaries

The first training schools among Pentecostals were generally of about eight months' duration after which trainees were sent out into the 'field', either 'home missions' or 'foreign' missions. Some of the first missionaries that went out only five months after the Azusa Street revival had begun were untrained, self-supporting and without financial backing from any organization. Most of them went without any theological or practical missionary training and although they usually received funds for their outward journey, they certainly did not expect to return 'until Jesus comes'. They sometimes went in teams of a dozen or more at a time. Although a number of these early Pentecostals were short-term itinerant missionaries, many saw their work as a lifetime commitment to be continued until they died on the field (which many did) or until Jesus returned – whichever came first. Not many had training for their task, but that was soon to change.

Early Pentecostal conventions in North America and Europe made among their chief activities to motivate and promote the recruitment of new missionaries to join those already in the field. Earnest appeals were made for young people to offer themselves for missionary service, citing great needs in these exotic foreign places and often stating how much the people there were looking forward to the arrival of western missionaries. In its report on a convention in Pennsylvania in 1910, *The Latter Rain Evangel* wrote of 'the great needs of the heathen world' that 'were laid heavily on many hearts'. The convention had listened to missionaries 'who had been in the thick of the battle' and new recruits had offered themselves 'eager to be thrust forth into the field'. The result of the appeals from the missionaries on furlough had 'filled many a heart with a burning zeal they had not had before as they told of the crying need and the hungry hearts that were awaiting the coming of the Gospel'.[7] This passionate appeal was typical of the enthusiasm that accompanied appeals for missions in Pentecostal circles. The motivation for these hundreds of mostly young people who offered themselves for 'foreign service' in Pentecostal churches across the western world was much the same for all, with the spiritual needs of the 'heathen' world being paramount. For example, William Boyd, from the Full Gospel Assembly in Belfast, Ireland was fairly typical, writing in his pro forma application to the PMU in 1912 that 'the reason why I offer for the Foreign Field is that the kingdom of our Lord and Saviour might be extended and that our Heavenly Father might be glorified in very many precious souls being brought into His kingdom and delivered from the power of darkness'.[8]

Pentecostal missionaries cannot be accused of the same enslavement to rationalistic theological correctness and cerebral Christianity that often plagued many of their contemporary Protestant missionaries and often made them less adaptable to the local cultures. In the first place, Pentecostals were seldom educated in western theology like their other Protestant counterparts were. This is not to say that they had no theological training at all, but that it was presented in a very different way. Levi Lupton was a Quaker minister and prominent Pentecostal missionary leader until his fall from grace through marital infidelity in 1910. His Missionary Training Home was to be 'from one to three years careful, practical training, and real study of the Word of God', as Lupton himself explained.[9] His biographer stated that in 1911 75 Pentecostal missionaries had 'gone to foreign lands from the Missionary Home training school or from one of its auxiliaries'. The list given here, however, seemed to name everyone (often misspelt) who had ever visited the Home at any time (no matter how fleetingly) or had been 'supported through the efforts of Mr Lupton'. It included many of the best-known Pentecostal missionary names, such as Minnie Abrams, Albert Norton, J. O. Lehman, Lillian Trasher, H. M. Turney, George Berg and M. L. Ryan. Most of these, directly or indirectly, were products of Azusa Street or of the Mukti Mission in India.[10] Nevertheless, Lupton's Home was probably the first significant American Pentecostal centre for the training and sending out of Pentecostal missionaries.

Although there were evangelical and 'undenominational' schools like Gordon Bible and Missionary Training School that used the best available scholarship,[11] there is evidence that whatever few training schools were put in place by Pentecostals they followed similar aims and patterns to those of the more radical and rudimentary schools. There the emphasis was on thrusting out workers into the 'harvest fields' as soon as possible, for the Lord's coming was near. The early Pentecostals generally put priority on the calling and empowerment of the candidate rather than on age or education. As *The Latter Rain Evangel* put it in 1911, many of those Pentecostals who had gone into the mission field 'would never be accepted by boards, but God called them and they have obeyed Him'. The recruits 'going forth to the foreign field' included one woman who was 'about sixty-five years of age', whereas the missionary society boards would not accept anyone over 35. It stated: 'God is not limited to age, and wherever He can get a willing vessel to carry His message He will use it.'[12] But not all Pentecostals agreed with this open-ended invitation for mission service and societies like the PMU, itself modelled on the CIM, generally did not accept anyone over 35. It was to take 50 years before Pentecostals began to have higher education centres. Although Pentecostals were not as thoroughly immersed in western theology and ideology as their counterparts, they soon realized that if the Spirit had not given them the languages of the nations in which to preach their gospel they had better learn them themselves. Great effort was put into language learning. The PMU, for example, made it a compulsory condition for further service in the field, and would even consider recalling its missionaries if they did not make satisfactory progress.

The first Pentecostal mission society, the PMU, constituted in Sunderland, England in January 1909, provided rudimentary training for missionary candidates but stated initially that their qualifications had simply to be 'a fair knowledge of every Book in the Bible, and an accurate knowledge of the Doctrines of Salvation and Sanctification'. That was all, except that their candidates 'must be from those who have received the Baptism of the Holy Ghost themselves'. There was no shortage of applications and entrance requirements soon became more difficult, including the need for a two-year training period.[13] PMU chairman Cecil Polhill referred to the problems his organization had been finding with their new missionaries and said that 'some training was an absolute necessity' as previous experience had shown 'the mistake and undesirability of immature workers, however zealous and spiritual, going forth to a heathen land'.[14] All candidates to the PMU were required to answer a series of questions relating to (and give biblical support for) their doctrinal beliefs on salvation, sanctification, Spirit baptism, the 'second coming', the divinity of Christ, biblical inspiration, divine healing, baptism and the 'Lord's Supper', and 'eternal judgment'.

Successful candidates who were accepted for training mostly came from various working-class occupations and had only reached elementary or primary school education. They included a collier, a shipbuilding driller, a printer's compositor, a dental mechanic, two factory workers, a dressmaker and a needlewoman. Occasionally, successful applicants were a little more qualified, including an assistant librarian, book-keeper and a certified school-teacher. These were often given special privileges such as a shorter training period. Sometimes exceptions were made to the general rules for training and sending out. The PMU Candidates' Schedule for Fanny Jenner for example recorded that this 32-year-old 'fully qualified, trained, certified teacher, holding Government parchment', who had worked for the London City Council, was a devout Church of England member and involved with the YWCA, had lived with the Principal of the Women's Missionary Training Home, Mrs Crisp for nine years. 'During this time I have taken an active part in Christian work, especially at the YWCA', she wrote in her application for admission to the PMU, 'hence Mrs Crisp does not think it necessary for me to spend time in the training home.'[15] She was accepted on this basis and dispatched hastily to China. Most candidates, especially women, were required to be under 30 years old as it was deemed more difficult for those above 30 to make much progress in language learning, an essential for PMU missionaries.[16] Single candidates also had to declare whether they intended to marry or what was termed any 'understanding . . . although not amounting to a definite engagement'. In these and other policies the PMU followed the established practices of other mission societies like the CIM, on which most of their policies were modelled.[17]

The two PMU Training Homes in Hackney, London were more organized by 1915, although the Men's Home was soon closed on account of the war. 'We aim at a one or two years' course', the PMU brochure read, 'giving mainly a clear knowledge of the text of the Bible, and its simple interpretation . . . also a preliminary training in the theory and practice of evangelistic work.'[18] The women's training home had a similar purpose: 'a systematic study of the Scriptures under the light and teaching of the Holy Spirit' and 'considerable time for definite, intercessory prayer'. Lessons were also given in English, geography, and 'the peoples and religions of the world'. Candidates were given weekly tests on these subjects and they were also taught to use various musical instruments such as harmoniums, concertinas, a cornet, and even a mandolin. They were expected to engage in local ministry (but only among women) and a weekly 'tarrying meeting' for people to receive the Spirit was held in the home.[19]

But unlike many other Pentecostals at the time, the PMU did take its training course at their Missionary Training Homes very seriously. In 1913, the principal of the Men's Home H. E. Wallis wrote a spirited defence of the necessity of thorough training based on the New Testament model.

Some dear saints do not quite see the need of training for missionaries; a few moments reflection will show that such is hardly the case. Surely God *never* uses an untrained worker if He has *His* way. Each one of His true servants is trained and fitted by Himself. The man of GOD must be a thoroughly furnished man . . . Jesus patiently trained His disciples for three years. Paul's studies and university career, and deep knowledge of his people's history and hopes and aspirations, and his trained mind (1 Cor. xiv., 20) were, after the Holy Spirit had seized him, to make him eminently the apostle of the Gentiles . . . And God uses human instruments for the work of training His messengers . . . This 'teaching' must not be confused with the mere impartation of intellectual knowledge, but the real impartation of spirit-truth and the opening of the spiritual understanding to see the loveliness of Christ and the treasures of His Word, by exercise of the endowment for teaching Christ and the Holy Spirit have given . . . Again, seclusion and retirement are often one of God's methods of preparation, as in the cases of Moses, Elijah, John Baptist and Paul.[20]

And unlike most other Pentecostal missions at the time, the PMU enforced a strict policy on language learning. Missionaries were required to immerse themselves in it on their arrival, usually with the help of other missionaries and national helpers. If they did not make sufficient progress they could be recalled. Soon after her arrival in Yunnan, Ethel Cook described the process in a letter to the PMU secretary Mundell. She wrote that she was 'perfectly "at home", happy and well, working as hard as I can at the language, though I confess *some* days one does not seem to make much headway'. She had different kinds of lessons, including a class lesson with an experienced missionary, an individual reading lesson with a Chinese teacher and conversation lessons, where students obtained 'much amusement therefrom, as well as a little profit'. But, she sighed, 'our vocabularies are still *very* limited!!!'[21]

Gerrit Polman in Amsterdam also instituted a Bible school for the training of missionaries, in some respects significantly different from the English equivalent, especially in the language requirements and practical involvement in the local church. The course for the students was to include teaching in 1. Bible study; 2. a study of the 'various religions of heathendom'; 3. Geography; 4. English; 5. French; 6. German (optional). In addition there was 'instruction in the practical every-day matters a missionary should know – how to conduct meetings, to pay spiritual visits, tract distribution, personal dealing, etc.' The Amsterdam church

being always in full working order with meetings of some kind each
evening, whether Bible study, young people's gathering, holiness or healing
or baptism, and being by God's grace full of life as well as holy liberty, a
people who have great love for the missionary field, this church is in itself a
school of practical instruction, a field of work in which abundant exercise
may be had, and where experience may be obtained.

Students were to 'also share in those practical forms of house work, or hall
preparation, which suit them best as men or women, also in office work, the
sending out of our paper, *Spade Regen*, money, or parcels, to the missionary
field'.[22] Such were the modest requirements made of the missionary candidates 'of average ability' in Pentecostal circles in North America and Europe.

Training Local Leaders

Once the missionaries reached their destinations, they began their own
schemes of training 'native workers'. This was a principle long advocated in
evangelical missions. Sometimes the contribution of these workers was
properly acknowledged. One evangelical missionary writing of a revival in the
Congo in 1901 said that he had 50 African 'preachers and teachers', some of
whom he described as 'men of great power, and all of them have won many
souls'. He said that most of the 2,000 new converts at their mission station
had been brought in 'by the Christians themselves'.[23] John Paton, well-known
missionary in the Pacific islands wrote of 330 'native teachers and preachers of
the Gospel' helping a handful of western missionaries in New Hebrides at
'inland and distant villages'. He describes these 'earnest, faithful, devoted
men, praying and working for the salvation of the heathen wherever they are
placed, and doing all they can to help the Missionaries'.[24]

Pentecostals began to see the need for training these talented local people.
A. H. Post in Egypt wrote that the calling out and baptizing with the Spirit of
Egyptian workers for active service was one of the most encouraging signs of
the mission there. He later made a plea for the training and support of these
workers, saying that because 'they know the language and the customs and
notions and ideas of the people . . . the right native man can win more souls to
Christ than the American missionary can personally'.[25] PMU Canadian superintendent Allan Swift writing from Yunnan, China remarked, 'We have a few
good native workers who give their time at our evening meetings. The Lord
has well provided along this line.'[26] Another PMU missionary William Boyd
reported that at a visit to a religious celebration, 'We had native preachers with
us and they were always ready to preach the word.'[27] Ethel Cook wrote from
China of 'the pressing need for more workers – native helpers of established
character especially – to preach amongst the different tribes Peoples'.[28] George
Berg made training workers a priority in India, and even though he fell by the
wayside and returned to the USA, his trained workers, some of whom assisted
Robert Cook and other foreign missionaries, were pillars in South Indian
Pentecostalism. Arie Kok in northern Yunnan wrote, somewhat condescend-
ingly, that the Lord was 'training some natives to become messengers to their

own people'. His own earnest prayer was 'to work up the districts by native workers' in order to achieve 'a self-supported native Church, with Spirit-filled native workers'. But he thought that 'as long as the number of really-born-again people is small and the church is in her babyhood, she wants foreign help and foreign support'.[29] There was no shortage of either.

One of the most significant early Pentecostal documents was an article published by PMU leader Polhill, who was keen to implement a policy that would transfer the task of evangelization and church leadership to local people. In 1917 he outlined an in-service training course for local church leaders in which these leaders would be gathered from local churches to a central place where they would be trained for two-week periods at a time, 'thus ultimately combining theory with practice', he wrote. He then quoted from an African (CMS) mission periodical to 'emphasize the supreme fact that the natives themselves must be the chief factor in evangelization'. Africans were 'born missionaries', and would be 'ready to go out far and wide' with a little training and teaching. Every missionary should be 'the means in God's hands of sending out in a very short time numbers of well taught spiritual converts as missionaries to their own countrymen'. The article then quoted an African elder as saying in his sermon,

> It is not enough for me alone to believe, it is not enough for you all to come here every morning and listen to the things of God; we must all believe, and we must all pray for the Holy Spirit to enter our hearts so that we become strong in Him, that we ourselves may have His words put in our mouths so as to be able to go into the bush and teach our own brothers and friends who have never yet heard the good news.[30]

Polhill used further quotations to drive home his point about the 'tremendous limitations' of 'foreign evangelists' who are but a 'temporary makeshift'. The following was certainly important advice that, had it been followed for the rest of the twentieth century, might have made all the difference to the growth and maturity of national Pentecostal churches:

> All Christians ought to be missionaries; but in a most real sense the best missions are home missions . . . he is likely to do the least permanent good while it is he that controls the situation. So long as the native workers are his agents, his helpers, his nominees, the whole venture takes on a foreign aspect, Christianity itself appears as a foreign faith, and suffers under all the prejudice and suspicion which things foreign usually evoke. The larger advance will come when we have discharged our function as foreign missionaries by establishing in the several non-Christian lands indigenous, self-propagating churches, and have committed to them – either with or without subordinate assistance from us – the completion of the work of evangelization.
> Is not that day far nearer in not a few of our fields of work in Asia and Africa than we as yet commonly recognize? The Christians are reckoned by their thousands and tens of thousands. In nature and temperament they are far better qualified than we to present the message to their fellow country-

men. Intellectually they are often fully our equals. Spiritually the power that
works in us is the power that works in them also. Have we had sufficient
faith and courage to transfer to them the burden of responsibility and initiative, assured that as we do so the Holy Spirit of God will endue them with
new love and wisdom, and supply to them that steadfast and keen initiative
which we perhaps think they lack at present?[31]

These ideas did not usually catch on quickly in Pentecostal missions. Seldom
did foreign missionaries consider Africans and Asians by temperament 'far
better qualified', by intellect 'fully our equals', and having the same spiritual
power. Expatriate missionaries continued to see themselves as the indispensable focus of the work and attempted to control local preachers, often with
disastrous consequences. As a result their entire mission ventures, as Polhill
had warned, took on 'a foreign aspect' and became an object of suspicion and
prejudice. Such attempts that were made to follow Polhill's advice were few
and far between and they almost always involved the continual supervision of
the western missionary. Soon after his arrival in Kunming in 1916, PMU
missionary Boyd wrote of the 'native preachers' who accompanied the
expatriate missionaries to a religious celebration and were 'always ready to
preach the word'.[32] Later he wrote of the need to provide training for them so
that they could be sent to different outstations.[33] Fellow missionary Ethel Cook
wrote of the 'Native Helpers', some of whom worked hard in preaching and
teaching; and she listed what she thought were qualities found in the best
workers: 'polite, clean, &c, spiritually hungry – intelligent & well-informed
. . . & with ability & willingness to shepherd souls'.[34] Many of these Chinese
preachers were put in charge of stations; in fact, because most of the foreign
PMU missionaries lived in two main 'safe' centres, local preachers usually
staffed the outstations. Unfortunately, the missionaries often saw the 'native
workers' as paid employees, inferior servants of their mission who could
get by with much less support than they themselves needed. Allan Swift was
exercised about this, corresponding with the Council over getting more support for 'native evangelists', but was told that the PMU could not afford it.
Swift replied that 'so much depends on the Natives, and if we are unable to use
them through lack of means, our work is crippled'.[35] The Council itself
declared its commitment to providing for 'a new supply of Chinese evangelists'. The 'ultimate goal' of the PMU was 'to raise up men and women out of the
natives to evangelize and carry on the work', because 'missionary work
always fails unless it succeeds in reaching the natives to become workers'.[36]
    It took a while for Pentecostals in the North to grasp these principles, but
with support from gentle agitators like Polhill, Alice Luce and Samuel and
Addie Otis – and on the field, W. W. Simpson, Robert Cook, Gerard Bailly and
J. O. Lehman – gradually the idea grew that investment in 'native workers' was
more important than increasing the number of foreign ones. From about 1918
Samuel Otis pioneered the concept of 'Native Substitutes' and raised funds to
train and support 100 Asian, African and Latin American missionaries.[37]
It was a drop in the bucket, but it *was* a start. It was disappointing (but not
surprising) that expatriate missionaries who were asked by Otis to give the
names of the workers being supported were reluctant to do so. Perhaps they

thought of their workers as transferable commodities rather than as real people and comrades in the faith. There were also detractors who thought that 'natives' could not be trusted with finances, but generally Pentecostalism promoted the emergence of national churches. In most cases, however, it took many years before these churches were to gain any real autonomy. There was also the not-so-hidden assumption that 'native workers' could get by with much less and therefore more could be supported. John Norton was typical of this, writing,

> The native workers can live on so little. They sleep on the ground, eat the coarsest food, and while out in camp five men live in a tent not more than six feet square. No American missionary could stand it to rough it as they do. And then they can get at the people ever so much better than we foreigners. It surely is wise to have all the native workers we can get.[38]

Attitudes among American Pentecostals did not improve quickly. The AG in its second Missionary Conference in Chicago in 1918 resolved to recommend that 'the ordination of native workers be discouraged except where the matter can be arranged for and looked after by the proper committees on their respective fields and districts'. The report gave as the reason for this draconian move an instance of a 'native' who had 'attempted to assert authority over the missionary'. The same conference recommended to the General Council that 'bringing natives to this country to be educated' should be discouraged, and that no money should be sent directly to 'native workers on the field'.[39] One can only imagine the negative effect these rules would have on the long-term progress of a so-called 'indigenous church'.

The first Pentecostal missionary in Venezuela, Gerard Bailly, a former CMA missionary, worked for several years at establishing the first Pentecostal Bible School for Latin Americans at Hebron mission station outside Caracas in 1909, and he trained Pentecostal pastors from that country as well as from Puerto Rico. He did not charge fees and the School was run on a self-supporting basis, with students being employed in farm and other duties in the mission. Bailly made a plea for adequate support, referring to the 'serious drain on missionary funds' involved in the preparation, equipment, travel and language learning of foreign missionaries. He declared that the 'principal solution to the problem' was the 'properly equipped native'.[40] Although Bailly later found the newly constituted Assemblies of God appealing, he cautioned that 'scriptural submission one to the other' should 'not interfere with the free workings of a scriptural native church or pretend at a colonial government or lording it over God's heritage'. These were remarkable insights for 1915, as Bailly envisaged a Venezuelan church 'free from denominational and foreign trappings' that was 'brought forth into national and spiritual birth in Pentecostal manifestations and sovereign workings of the Holy Ghost'.[41] He was later responsible for assisting in the beginnings of such an independent Venezuelan church.

The indefatigable William Burton began his mission in the Belgian Congo in 1915 and operated on the principle of training African workers, but always under white supervision. As Burton expressed in a report in 1925, 'The great needs are Spirit-filled native evangelists, and a few white workers to superintend and help them.'[42] Burton, however, was not unaware of the benefits of having African leaders. His accounts of the work of such leaders in the Congo and South Africa provide uniquely fascinating stories of African initiatives in the early years of Pentecostalism in this continent. Nobody else from this era provided much information on African leaders, but Burton wrote books about some of them. As another former PMU worker, Percy Corry, put it in his foreword to one of these books, these accounts were 'a revelation of what can be done by consecrated, Spirit-filled, native leaders'. They showed the 'indigenous church' as 'directed and encouraged by Spirit-filled leaders, and as such it must command attention'. He went on to say that this was an example of what God could do 'if we allow Him to use us in a similar way in our own lands and to the people at our very doors'.[43] Burton's method was to select the best young men from the different stations who had shown their ability to evangelize and lead a church. Not more than 40 at a time, 'with their wives', were selected for the central training school, run by Burton himself, in the first years of the CEM. The course lasted 'for about two years' and its primary purpose was 'to make them Bible-lovers and to encourage them in personal holiness and fellowship with God. Brilliance of preaching and leadership are secondary to this.'[44] They accompanied the missionaries on their itinerating to learn on the job.

A photograph of two of the CEM's 'native overseers' Kangoi and Ngoloma, published in 1922, had the revealing caption, 'These men now take practically the same place and responsibility with regard to the young native churches as the white missionaries.' It continued, 'If anything occurred necessitating the withdrawal of white workers, the native church would still have steady godly men to whom to look for help and direction.'[45] Unfortunately, Burton did not follow through on this remarkably enlightened vision. Almost 40 years later, the CEM was still directed by an all-white Field Executive Council and had 65 European missionaries working in 14 mission compounds. Two missionaries were killed in the Congolese civil war, and Burton and his missionaries were evacuated in 1960, after 45 years of white leadership. The result of this seeming setback was that ten years later the churches left behind and now led by Africans had more than doubled in number.[46]

Some appreciated the potential of their so-called 'native workers'. Will Norton, an American missionary's son born in India, wrote of his six workers by thanking God for 'good Indian helpers', who were mostly men who had grown up in his father's mission. Some were even 'my own playmates in my childhood'. Others Norton had trained himself since he was old enough to take charge of a station. He commented on the indispensable role of these workers whom he knew well and could trust fully. He closed saying, 'But for their help we would have to close most of the work we have begun. I visit them in the cities where they are living, pray with them and then go on to the next place for the same purpose.'[47]

Although the missionary newsletters in the periodicals focused on the activities of the western missionaries, now and then we get glimpses of the multitude of 'native helpers' who were doing most of the work in evangelism and planting churches, and the stories of some of these have been traced in previous chapters. At the end of the nineteenth century, one article put the number of Protestant missionaries at 11,695, but stated that these missionaries were 'assisted by 65,000 native Christians who are engaged in active Christian service'.[48] So although these 'native workers' outnumbered the western missionaries by six to one (and in Pentecostalism the ratio was probably higher), they were often not recognized and many were forced to begin their own movements. But the growth in conversions and whatever success these missions had was largely due to the efforts of these local preachers and leaders. This emphasis on local leadership was the legacy of Pentecostal missions, who ultimately raised up national leaders who were financially self-supporting and whose new churches were nationalized much quicker than older mission churches had been.[49] In 1906, *Word and Work* reported the setting up of Indian missionary societies as 'one of the strongest proofs that the gospel has taken firm root in India'.[50] Pentecostal missionary Berntsen wrote from northern China: 'Although the number of missionaries has decreased greatly, the Chinese have taken hold of the work wonderfully.'[51] PMU missionary Elize Scharten made her first request for prayer to be 'that the Lord will raise up a great band of Spirit-filled evangelists in connection with the PMU work'.[52] Her colleague Nellie Tyler wrote, 'Perhaps the most encouraging work that the Lord is doing in our midst is the calling out of the native workers.' She said that 'one native worker filled with the spirit of God and a burning desire for the salvation of his people is of greater value than many foreign missionaries, for it takes a Chinese to fully understand a Chinese with their many strange customs and creeds'. The PMU workers were 'praying that the Lord will continue to raise up many native workers filled with the Holy Spirit who will be a praise and a glory unto Him Who hath called them'.[53]

Women in Ministry

The end of the nineteenth and the beginning of the twentieth century was an important period for changing social and religious expectations in the western world on the role of women. By the 1880s, training schools for evangelical missionary women were being founded and women like Phoebe Palmer, Catherine Booth, Carrie Judd Montgomery and Maria Woodworth-Etter were preaching in mass meetings on a regular basis. Montgomery's *Triumphs of Faith* was a significant vehicle for giving expression to women preachers and the majority of articles appearing there were written by women. It published an article 'Should Women Prophesy?' in 1886 giving a spirited defence of the rights of women in ministry.[54] The remarkable and sudden surge in the number of missionary candidates offering themselves for overseas service from the 1890s onwards was partly attributable to changing attitudes towards single women becoming missionaries in evangelical circles. Many, perhaps most of these missionary candidates were women. Coming from societies where their role was rapidly changing from a purely domestic function to that of one where women could embark on certain professional careers (at least in the middle classes), these women had volunteered for one of the few careers available in an ecclesiastical world that was still very much male-dominated. By 1900, published figures indicated that women Protestant missionaries were already 45 per cent of the 'foreign missionary' force: 6,970 out of 15,460. It is also significant that this same source gave the number of 'native laborers' (77,338) at over three times the total number of 'foreign missionaries'.[55]

John Alexander Dowie, whose Zionist movement so influenced early Pentecostal missions, was a clear supporter of women's ministry. In 1903 he wrote a reply to a letter from Alexander Boddy, who had asked why his leaders dressed up like Anglican bishops, and Dowie used the opportunity to defend the ministry of women. His women leaders wore the same 'costumes' as the men, he wrote, and believed that 'God has not only called men but women to the ministry, and what would apply to the robing of a man would also apply to that of the woman'. He went on:

> The Scripture says there is neither male nor female, but that all are one in Christ Jesus. In the former Dispensation women were Prophetesses, and in the Christian Dispensation women are also called to this office. God is no respecter of persons, and I, therefore, feel that women whom God has called should be ordained.[56]

Boddy did not declare his own views on the matter but it seems that in producing this letter ten years later he was either open to the possibility of women in ministry or in publishing the views of a disgraced heretic was diametrically opposed to it.

Women played an enormous role in the early Pentecostal movement as leaders and missionaries throughout the world, even though they faced enormous theological and social prejudice in their task.[57] Only a few women expressed their opinions publicly on the ministry of women. The Azusa Street revival set the record straight at the beginning with the comment (probably by Seymour) that it was 'contrary to the Scriptures that woman should not have her part in the salvation work to which God has called her'. Men had 'no right to lay a straw in her way, but to be men of holiness, purity and virtue, to hold up the standard and encourage the woman in her work, and God will honor and bless us as never before'. After all, the foundation for this ministry of women was the Spirit that had been poured out on the women as much as on the men: 'It is the same Holy Spirit in the woman as in the man', it declared. It then showed how the restrictions for women under the Old Testament had changed on the Day of Pentecost. Previously women were only allowed into the 'court of the women and not into the inner court', it continued. The anointing oil (signifying the Holy Spirit) was only poured on male kings, priests and prophets. But all this changed with Pentecost, when 'all those faithful women' were together in the upper room, 'God baptized them all in the same room and made no difference'. The result: 'All the women received the anointed oil of the Holy Ghost and were able to preach the same as the men.'[58] Pentecost had demolished all gender discrimination as far as *The Apostolic Faith* was concerned.

A glance at the financial records of those missionaries being supported by western Pentecostal agencies will reveal that there were more women than men on the mission field. The Stone Church in Chicago, for instance, one of the greatest supporters of missions in the early Pentecostal movement in North

America, sent donations in November and December 1919 to 32 single women missionaries and 26 men – and this did not include the missionary wives.[59] The training schools at that time had a majority of women, and the Great War had reduced the number of men applying even further – especially in Britain (where the men's training school for the PMU had to close) and in the USA. For instance, one of the best-known and best-equipped schools, Rochester Bible Training School in New York State, had ten women and four men in their class of 1917–18, and two years later there were seventeen women and three men.[60] Of course, one reason for this could be that the School was attached to Elim Tabernacle, which was led by women, and most Pentecostals were reluctant to allow women to teach men in those days. Nevertheless, Grant Wacker has estimated that two-thirds of the missionaries and half the travelling evangelists and healers in early Pentecostalism were women.[61]

Minnie Abrams also expressed her views on the ministry of women, in reporting on the Laymen's Missionary Convention in St Paul she attended in 1910. She was told there that 'the evangelization of the world was a man's job'. She said she was 'only one little woman', but that 'many a woman has undertaken a man's job in connection with her own and carried it through to success'. She thought that 'although the evangelization of the world is a man's job, you cannot do it without the women'.[62] Abrams was a champion of women's ministry in the Pentecostal movement. In recruiting women for her pioneering new mission in India, she wanted those who had 'been a success at home'. They should be 'educated and cultured women', she wrote, but above all they had to be 'women full of love and the Holy Spirit . . . women willing to settle down and plod, and hammer away until the rock breaks . . . who do not know what it is to be defeated in that which they undertake'. Unlike the PMU who, following CIM policy, wanted all their applicants (especially the women) to be under 30 in order to withstand better the rigours of language learning and pioneering missionary work, Abrams had quite the opposite opinion, preferring 'them at least thirty years of age for this pioneer work'.[63] There were other notable exceptions to the age rule. Annie Murray, who was in charge of the mission home in Bombay after Maud Orlebar's death in 1910 until her own death two years later, was a much older woman and blind. She would never have been accepted by any of the other mission societies.

In many of the countries to which the women missionaries went, the sight of women like this must have been truly remarkable. One woman wrote from Yunnan in 1915 that on market days people came in from the country 'to hear the Gospel and see the foreign woman'.[64] One wonders whether the message or the messenger was the main attraction. But these women often led the way, running mission bases and taking responsibilities that put them on an equal footing with men. They were also soon to discover the ways in which women were even more oppressed in some countries than they were in the West. This also affected the converts and church attenders. Christianity, particularly in India where it was often contrasted with Hinduism and Islam in this regard, was seen as the great equalizer, the religion that offered women freedom from harsh oppression. This theme often appeared in the writings of women missionaries. One remarked that the Hindu women of India 'were sunk in degradation from which only the Gospel of Jesus Christ can save them' and that the Muslim men similarly were 'appalling' in their 'oppression and degradation of women'. In particular, the practices of *purdah* (a lifelong seclusion that barred women from education or employment), child marriage and the caste system came in for heavy criticism.[65]

Women missionaries in Palestine spoke of the plight of the village women, many of them with 'bright intelligent faces', but only one in a thousand could read. They were raised with the belief that they were 'as truly beasts of burden as the donkeys' and that donkeys were 'often better cared for than they'.[66] In China there were far more men attending Christian services than women, one missionary explaining, 'Here in China as in other heathen lands the women have hard work to do and consequently have not the same liberty as the men.'[67] Ethel Cook expressed how women were enabled to be empowered in the Chinese context because 'some of the simple women are being taught by visions and dreams occasionally', giving an example of a woman who had 'wonderfully bright light in her room' while it was still dark. She went on, 'she knew God had given her His Spirit – and she certainly had a real quickening touch of God upon her'.[68] In Argentina, May Kelty found opposition to the ministry of women among the people and wrote wryly about how she wished they would 'interpret all the Scriptures as literally as those concerning women speaking in the church', adding, 'Pray that we may obey God and give messages when He shows us to'.[69]

Many of the early 'native workers' were also women. *Word and Work* reprinted an article speaking of the enormous contribution made to Christian mission by the Indian women Pandita Ramabai, Soonderbai Powar and Shorat Chuckerbutty. It declared that 'the best work done in India to-day' was 'upon purity principles of faith and prayer, and no leaders there are more mightily anointed than many of the native women'. These were 'women of peerless purity and power, the Deborahs of the darkened Empire'. Each of these women was a 'Spirit anointed prophetess of purity and faith principles' who had exposed herself to dangers on behalf of the 'oppressed and perishing'. Prayer had prevailed, and the work had 'developed into a permanent institution owned by God', the report concluded.[70]

These Indian women were outspoken in their demands for the equality of women in an unjust society, and of course, they had had the shining example of Pandita Ramabai who had led the way. Soonderbai Powar wrote that Indian women are 'never free' but were forced into obedience to men throughout their lives, first their fathers, then their husbands, finally their sons. Their obedience was forced on them and was not 'drawn by tender love and chivalrous attentions'. She blamed this bondage squarely upon the 'rules' of the Hindu religion, which she saw as 'a religion that has drawn out all that is selfish in man and made him see as his god nothing but his own ugly self; that has made woman nothing but a soulless animal to be used for the pleasure of man'.[71] At a convention in Rochester, New York in 1918 one of Ramabai's American assistants spoke of the contribution such Indian women had made to Pentecostalism. She pointed out that they were 'so filled with the Spirit and so taught of God' that expatriate missionaries had 'received Pentecost through their gracious ministry', and had 'been willing to learn the deeper truths of God through their words and holy examples'.[72]

The use of women with charismatic gifts was widespread throughout the Pentecostal movement and resulted in a much higher proportion of women in Pentecostal ministry than in any other form of Christianity at the time. This accorded well with the prominence of women in many pre-Christian religious rituals in Africa and parts of Asia, contrasting again with the prevailing practice of older churches which barred women from entering the ministry or even from taking any part in public worship. But in spite of all the important practical involvement of women in the leadership of Pentecostal churches and missions during this period, Pentecostal churches were not yet ready to come to terms with the theological implications of women in ministry. There were strong male, conservative voices in Pentecostalism advocating a restriction on the opportunities for women in ministry.

The last international conference in Sunderland in 1914 spent a great deal of time debating the issue 'Woman's place in the Church' and by any of today's standards their discussion would have been considered reactionary and conservative. All those whose opinions were published were men, except that of Wilhelmina Polman, whose position was as conservative as any of the men's was.[73] E. N. Bell, first chairman of the AG, wrote about the role of women missionaries in which he said that they were 'recognized in the New Testament only as "helpers in the gospel", as Paul puts it'. He thought that women missionaries should not itinerate alone but find permanent work in a station 'under the proper oversight of some good brother whom God has place in charge of the work'. Although he admitted that 'God has blessed' the work of women who had opened up stations of their own and had 'never objected to this', he confessed that he found 'no scriptural precept or example for such independent leadership by women'.[74] The first General Council of the AG in 1914 adopted a resolution on 'Rights and Offices of Women' to recommend to its ministers 'that we recognize their God-given rights, to be ordained, not as elders, but as Evangelists or Missionaries, after being approved according to the scriptures'.[75] Women delegates were not permitted to vote on this or any other resolution. Wacker has traced what he calls 'the tortured story of women's credentialing as ministers in the infant Assemblies of God' where restrictions on women's authority in this and other American Pentecostal denominations increased during the years following the First World War. Women could only become pastors in 1935 and even then only with significant restrictions.[76]

Such restrictions were not reflective of the reality of the prominent role played by women pastors and missionary leaders in early Pentecostalism. There were no such restrictions on women as missionaries, as somehow the patriarchs in their wisdom had decided that this was a position less threatening or authoritative in their organizations. Perhaps the geographical distance from the church headquarters made it a safe option. The praxis of Pentecostal missions and the stated position of the supporting churches did not always harmonize. But this was a time when women were still not fully franchised, educational opportunities were still denied them, and a general patriarchal attitude prevailed globally. Although the degree of gender discrimination has improved since those days, Pentecostal denominations are still struggling with these issues. Some Pentecostal organizations need to beware of decisions and actions limiting and quenching this most important ministry of women, who form the large majority of the church worldwide and without whose ministry Pentecostalism would have failed.

Missionary Hardships

The first Pentecostal missionaries certainly did not have it easy. Some of them, however, did not show the same commitment to long-term service as most of the others did and some went on world tours of the various places where Pentecostalism was established. Well-known early Pentecostal preachers made extended world tours, including Frank Bartleman, T. B. Barratt, Alexander Boddy and Daniel Awrey, who toured the Pentecostal work in Japan, China and India 'giving Bible readings'.[77] At the beginning of 1910 Awrey was in Canton and Hong Kong, where he set up a mission but did not stay there long. He continued his world tour, going to South America, back to North America and then dying of tropical disease in West Africa in 1913.[78] Frank Bartleman in 1910–11 met up with Awrey and his second and longer tour of Europe was interrupted by the Great War.[79] Long-term missionaries expressed their disquiet at the wholesale migration of untrained, poorly funded and inexperienced 'missionaries' from Pentecostal churches in the western world. John G. Lake expressed his disapproval most forcibly in a letter from South Africa. His views were not isolated ones. Nettie Moomau in Shanghai gave her reaction to his opinion, saying that many of these 'touring missionaries' did not accomplish much, but commented: 'If they have a real message, it is felt and known, but some drift about, and nothing is accomplished.' She declared her support for Lake in this matter, because there was 'no place for "kid-gloved" workers, but there is for real plow-horses who will stand through all the discouragement and darkness and opposition, and plow on in hope'.[80] E. N. Bell spoke for many early Pentecostals when he wrote in 1912:

> Our people are tired, sick, and ashamed of traveling, sight-seeing experimenting missionaries, who expect to make a trip around the world and come home. We are not willing to waste a cent of God's money on such. It is all right when necessary on account of serious illness or to stir up new interest by a visit to come home; but only to return soon. We want missionaries who go out to live and die on foreign fields . . . We want men to settle down to learn the language, to establish assemblies of saved people, to stay with these, teaching them and using them to reach their own people.[81]

It was clear by this time that the globetrotting Pentecostal adventurer was causing embarrassment for the movement as a whole. In Atlanta, *The Bridegroom's Messenger* wrote of the great dissatisfaction there was at 'the frequent travelling to and fro of missionaries' wasting precious time and money. It pleaded for 'steady, concentrated, determined effort' and a long-term commitment from the missionaries being supported.[82] The leader of the Pentecostal Mission in Southern Africa, George Bowie, wrote that it was 'a source of deep regret that many undesirable workers have gone to the foreign field, well-meaning, Christian men and women, but absolutely unqualified to learn the language or take charge of mission stations'. He said that the sending out 'of this class of people' had 'not only been an added burden to the real called missionary who has consequently been compelled to assume unnecessary responsibilities, but has been a great detriment to the work and a hindrance to the spread of the Gospel'. He deplored the fact that so often the financial contributions given to support missions and 'representing sacrifice and toil' had been 'unwisely given to those who have been mistaken in their call and were used in traveling to and fro, having no fixed work and accomplishing nothing'.[83]

This was a widespread problem during the first decade of Pentecostal missions. The issue was the expense involved in providing for the return fare and the effect this had on the morale and activities of remaining missionaries. Moorhead in India declared that ten Pentecostal missionaries were on their way home, none of whom had stayed longer than five years and that other denominations had 'fixed rules about furloughs' so that missionaries were 'not permitted to go and come at will'.[84] Similarly, Mary Norton wrote that many missionaries had been sent to India 'who ought never to have gone'. They had 'wrought havoc on the field, but no one could do anything about it because no one had any authority'. She complained of those who 'did absolutely no work and refused to make any effort to study a language, but who had money enough to travel about and see quite a good deal of the world'. She then showed how Pentecostal missionaries were treated by other missionaries: 'No wonder the board missions look down on us. They take good care of their missionaries and in return demand of them good work.'[85] Clearly, the leading of the Spirit in individual lives was becoming a challenge. Poor planning and organization, exacerbated by the globetrotting adventurers, were a strain on the limited finances of the fledgling movement. One of the reasons for the formation of the Assemblies of God in 1914 was to better organize missions, and to 'discourage wasting money on those who are running here and there accomplishing nothing'.[86] The problem, however, was not solved (in most cases) by the 1920s and Pentecostal missionaries continued to suffer from poor financial support and insufficient organization.

The initial cost of 'passage and outfit' for sending out PMU missionaries was between £65 and £70 in 1915. Each missionary was to be 'medically examined and the Doctor's report if not favourable to be forthwith forwarded . . . to the Hon. Secretary'.[87] This policy was in keeping with that of the CIM and pragmatic – people of weak constitution would not survive the rigours of a tropical climate with its attendant diseases. To some early Pentecostals who eschewed medical science such a policy would have been anathema.

Most of the early Pentecostal missionaries were entirely dependant upon the supporting churches, individuals, and especially the periodicals for their financial support. They did not have it easy and often there is oblique reference in their letters to the financial hardships experienced. Some were forced to return home through inadequate support; some were greatly weakened through inadequate food supplies as they faced the ravages of tropical disease and unsanitary living conditions. Because so many of these missionaries opened up schools and orphanages, the support needed was for many more than the missionaries themselves and they shared whatever they had with the children and workers in their care. Missionaries were restricted in their travelling and ability to move around and often they were unable to return for furlough because of the cost of purchasing the passage home. Some chose not to return at all. Special appeals were sometimes made in the periodicals for those missionaries unable to make ends meet through a lack of financial support.[88] Paul Bettex's pathetic letter describing his wife's death in Canton put part of the blame on the lack of financial support they were receiving from the American churches:

> When weak and faint for lack of food for days, I saw my earthly treasure coming to an end of her strength, I prayed agonizingly day by day for means to provide the much needed milk and cheap fruit she craved. I prayed and wrestled in agony with God because I knew and felt that five dollars might mean life or death to my dearest – but no help came. In those hours of spiritual conflict, I seemed to see the home saints in their comfortable homes looking on to see how long we could hold out without breaking. We had covenanted to fight it out to the death and she did.[89]

This tragic event seemed to spark off more intense calls for better organization of the number of new missionaries going out and their financial support. The periodicals described awful conditions of financial hardship like this one faced by Pentecostal missionaries on the field in an attempt to raise more funds for missionaries, but these appeals were not often successful in what was still a fledgling movement in the 'homeland'. It seems that there were far more missionaries going out from Pentecostal churches than there were funds to support them adequately. Some missionaries went out in haste, one writing to *Word and Witness* that he had been in China for eight months and had received only $12 in support. The editor, E. N. Bell, added a forthright note: 'This is because the brother did not get the support of the brethren in the home land before going.'[90] *The Latter Rain Evangel* made several earnest appeals for better organization in missionary support and had a telling comment on cases like that of Nellie Bettex, that Pentecostal people were 'grossly neglectful of our missionaries when they have not sufficient food to eat'. This amounted to 'indifference and lack of system in our giving' and had resulted in some missionaries who had gone out 'expecting the Pentecostal movement to stand behind them have been compelled to connect themselves with some missionary society in order to stay on the field'. Then the paper honed in on the specific tragedy:

> Nellie Clark Bettex was a noble woman who had left a position of honor and given up a salary that put her beyond [sic] any need of help. She was an able, consecrated worker that the foreign field could not afford to lose, and the thought of her untimely death in the prime of life, because her constitution was undermined by prolonged lack of food is touching in the extreme. It deeply stirs our hearts, and we can only hope that she has not died in vain. Whether or not she has been a martyr to our lack of system in supporting our

missionaries, let us earnestly pray that it may be a trumpet call to us all to 'keep not silence and give Him no rest' until we establish some method for the adequate support of the members of our Lord's body in heathen lands.[91]

Still the letters from missionaries reflected the financial difficulties they were facing on the field. Two young men from the Persian Pentecostal church in Chicago faced considerable hardship and persecution during the 18 months they itinerated in their homeland, and had to return to the USA through lack of financial support.[92] Another report on what was now called 'the missionary problem' was published of missionaries living on one meal a day of 'wild sago, boiled in water without salt and eaten without milk and sugar'.[93] Mrs D. L. McCarty, in Uttar Pradesh in India, wrote of the single women missionaries who did not want to join her because she had 'no comforts, no proper building to live in'. She lived in a 'good mud house, but the ceilings are not high', and she ate 'only native vegetables', but she said, 'I get along well'. She also wrote that she expected to stay in that village location 'till Jesus comes'.[94] J. M. L. Harrow placed the cause of death of two of his team in Liberia on the 'lack of nourishing food'.[95]

Calls for a more effective form of missionary organization began to be made. Turney in South Africa felt that the sporadic nature of the financial support was a good reason for better administration. He did not see how it was 'possible to avoid neglecting some parts of the work or some worthy workers, unless there is some responsible organization to whom these systematic offerings can be paid, and whose duty it is to disburse them to the different missionaries'. He pleaded for such an organization, because a missionary 'who went out from such a body would have a prestige in the eyes of the authorities which the lonely worker going out on his own initiative cannot have'.[96] By 1913 several periodicals were taking up the cause of the missionaries' financial hardships. Elisabeth Sexton published discussions relating to the appalling situation and lack of good financial management of funds sent to missionaries, including a letter from Bertha Dixon recently returned from China, and another concerned letter from a woman in Los Angeles suggesting practical ways in which local churches could systematically better support Pentecostal missionaries. Dixon was clearly greatly exercised about these issues, writing that the Pentecostal missionaries had gone out (quoting the words of Christ) '"without purse or script [sic]," that is, without boards or known financial backing at home' and had encountered frequent illness and death 'very early in their career'. Many had returned home after only a brief stay, partly because financial pressures were overwhelming, but the one who stayed hesitated to write home about difficulties and was 'practically a pioneer on the field'. Meanwhile, in the USA where (unlike in Britain) there was resistance to the setting up of any organization for united missionary effort, doctrinal disputes had exacerbated the problem and large financing of building projects in mission fields was missing. She thought that the time had come for a more concerted effort to be made regarding American Pentecostal missions.[97]

In an editorial, Sexton told her readers of the work of the paper keeping contact with 'about a hundred missionaries, and some native workers'. She wrote that The Bridegroom's Messenger was 'a missionary paper' and that by knowing the needs of these missionaries they were able to support them in prayer and send on financial support as it came in from readers. She urged 'faith missionaries' to be more revealing of their needs because 'the saints, who are standing with them, are in a measure identified with them in their work, their interests are ours, their needs are ours'. She urged better support for the missionaries because 'in every station the work is hindered for lack of sufficient means', and missionaries needed 'comfortable homes and plenty of nourishing food' and to be able to support 'the native workers'.[98] H. L. Lawler wrote an impassioned plea from Shanghai to readers of E. N. Bell's *Word and Witness*. He said that China's millions were suffering while many Americans known to this missionary who believed that 'Jesus is coming soon' had 'a fortune' to give but were not giving to missions, even though they shared a 'great responsibility' towards these people. He went on to say:

> I truly fear that the majority of the saints in the home land have not the real missionary spirit at heart. The sin and suffering on every hand is simply appalling. We are simply helpless for the lack of means. The work in this land is greatly hindered on account of lack of funds. The most of the Pentecostal Missions that we know any thing about in China are simply EXISTING, and that is about all ... We feel it a SIN for us to keep silent, when our brothers and sisters are suffering; yea, DYING for need of help.[99]

In 1918 Blanche Appleby spoke at the AG's Missionary Conference giving graphic details of the Pentecostal missionaries' difficult and unsanitary living conditions in South China, where not only were their homes small and crowded but there was a lack of privacy, adequate sanitation and healthy food.[100] These early Pentecostal missionaries were certainly finding their situation tough and some were getting bolder in letting their needs be known. The meeting forming the AG in April 1914 stated that the third reason for the organization was to better understand the needs of the mission field and see that missionaries were given fair treatment in support.[101]

The war years did not improve the situation, even though the USA was not directly involved in the war until 1917. In 1916 American missionaries all over the world were feeling the pinch, one writing from Liberia that 'the means for carrying on the work is the least we have known since the beginning'. Yet on the same page the leader of this mission, J. M. L. Harrow was appealing for more missionaries to join him.[102] Many missionaries had to return home for want of support for basic essentials. The AG reported that monthly income for missionaries in 1916 was one-third what it was two years earlier and published a special issue on missions in the hope of bolstering financial support. This was indeed a crisis, as there were 'missionaries who are on the field suffering for the need of actual bread and butter'. They were unable to return home because there was 'no money to travel' and unable to continue on the field because there was 'nothing to live on'. There was 'only one thing to do' and that was 'to starve and die, unless the Pentecostal people awake out of their lethargy, renew their consecration and bend their energies anew to come up to the help of the Lord for these worthy missionaries'.[103] The choice could not have been starker. Pentecostal missions were in crisis. The initial enthusiasm for getting missionaries out to the nations was waning seriously. In fact, the numbers of Pentecostal missionaries was increasing, but the supply of finances was not keeping up with the need, and prices were escalating.

There was another aspect of financing the work in the so-called 'foreign fields' that is still with us today and that is the matter of trust. Local people have not been trusted with finances to carry on the work of the missionaries after the missionaries have left. An early example of the prevalent attitude in the western churches comes from the Glad Tidings Tabernacle in New York where a report on the last missionary leaving Egypt (although Lillian Trasher was still there) continued to state that they had learnt 'from experienced missionaries that entrusting too much money to native workers not only hinders the work, but frequently means their own downfall'.[104]

By September 1917, when the AG held a missionary conference, important questions were being asked about the nature of Pentecostal missionaries going in the power of the Spirit without adequate training. Elisabeth Sisson, a former missionary and one of the most respected and experienced Pentecostal speakers and writers, addressed the issues in an article published in *The Weekly Evangel*. She wrote of 'much criticism' that the early Pentecostal missionaries had received because of alleged wasted money and lives of 'rash running into pioneer fields of novices in missionary operations'. They had not stopped to learn the lessons from the past two centuries that characterized the mission methods of the older boards – and if they had, they would have avoided many disasters. But God had 'poured out His Spirit so mightily and so suddenly' and this had been accompanied by 'such a missionary uprising among those of lowliest walks of life', while at home so few had understood 'the missionary pull and its responsibilities'. The failures of the missionaries had arisen because they had not received adequate prayer, sympathy and financial support from their home base. Through the neglect of the Pentecostals at home, she charged, they had 'really murdered many of our most precious missionary pioneers'.[105]

Sectarianism and Organization

The seeds of sectarianism within Pentecostalism were sown near the beginning of the movement in the USA. Division within American Protestantism was nothing new – there were already many denominations there by the end of the nineteenth century. Many of Pentecostalism's leaders came from small and newly emerging denominations such as the Christian and Missionary Alliance, the Burning Bush, the Peniel Mission, the Church of the Nazarene, the Holiness Church, the Salvation Army, and so on. A few were ministers in the more established churches such as the Baptists or the Methodists. Division was a way of life for early Pentecostals and their fiercely independent ecclesiology made it inevitable that further division would ensue. The Church was seen primarily as a gathering of believers and early Pentecostals vigorously sought to maintain this concept while resisting all attempts at institutional and hierarchical organization. The leading of the Spirit in an individual's life, combined with the perception of the priesthood of all believers and a sense of divine destiny, resulted in as many different opinions about how churches should be run, who should run them and what were their essential doctrines and practices.

A series of disputes in the first 12 years after the Azusa Street revival ensured the continuation of this process. Parham's break with Seymour in 1906, Seymour's breaks with Florence Crawford and Clara Lum in 1908 and in 1911 with Cook and Durham, the 'Finished Work' (1911) and 'Oneness' (1916) schisms, the creation of the Assemblies of God in 1914, all ensured that by 1918 American Pentecostalism would be as divided as the rest of Christianity was, if not more so. In that year further division followed the resignation of Fred Bosworth from the AG over the issue of initial evidence. Although this doctrine had been around and widely supported for over a decade, there was a good deal of flexibility about it. Many (like Bosworth) who spoke in tongues but did not think that it was the only evidence of Spirit baptism were prominent leaders in Pentecostal churches. Henceforth, the doctrine became enshrined in white American Pentecostal denominations and further alienated those who chose not to be so dogmatic, including the black Church of God in Christ. There were divisions within Holiness denominations too, the PHC publishing letters condemning the Church of God in 1917 for its exclusivity.[106] In any case, by 1920 there were already several emerging Pentecostal denominations. By that time, the CG in Cleveland, Tennessee (about to enter another painful schism), the Church of God in Christ, the PHC, the AG, the Pentecostal Assemblies of the World and several smaller groups had formed and were drawing battle lines. The independent churches that had characterized the beginnings of Pentecostalism were to survive (and thrive at the end of the twentieth century), but they were greatly depleted in the 1910s onwards by the new denominational affiliations. Bartleman, a passionate advocate of Christian unity, traces the origins of division in early American Pentecostalism. For him there was a simple explanation: it was the 'organized church', 'human manipulation' and 'party spirit' that had created the divisions that he so despised.[107] There were undoubtedly other factors: the repudiation of Parham by almost the entire Pentecostal movement because of his alleged misconduct in a sodomy charge, Parham's racism, the implicit racism and leadership ambitions behind many of the other divisions, and the excesses of some of its early leaders such as Levi Lupton, T. J. McIntosh and George Berg.

The 'initial evidence' was a non-issue in African American Pentecostal churches and in most European churches. Similarly, the 'finished work' issue was neither a big issue in Europe nor did the Oneness controversy make a great impact there. Perhaps it was more difficult for Pentecostals to survive the impact of dominant state churches, but the divisions there were relatively minor. Nevertheless, the die had been cast for divisions within European Pentecostalism too, aggravated by the Great War, and the movement soon lost both its early ecumenical character and its supporters in the older churches. In Britain, the Apostolic Church and the Elim Evangelistic Band (now the Elim Pentecostal Church) were in the process of formation by 1915 and within a decade the Assemblies of God in Great Britain and Ireland would follow. British (and South African) Pentecostalism was divided on the 'apostolic ministry' and church direction by spoken prophecy that separated the

'Apostolic' churches from other Pentecostals. The AFM and other South African Pentecostals entered a co-operative agreement in 1915 which did not include British missionary James Brooke of the Apostolic Faith Church for these reasons, and because his overseer in Bournemouth, W. O. Hutchinson, had declared himself 'First Apostle', following the tradition of Dowie and Sandford.[108]

Outside the western world, this division proliferated – and it is to be expected that converts saw the multiplication of independent churches as normal, given the example of the missionaries. Missionaries in the field wrote home in support of one or other of the opposing sides, as the dividing lines began to be more clearly drawn. Pentecostals tended to reproduce their divisions wherever they found themselves – despite many protestations that they were too busy 'saving souls' to have time for doctrinal pettiness. Several prominent Pentecostal missionaries in India and China made pronouncements against the so-called 'New Issue' while stating their dismay at the divisions occurring in American Pentecostalism.[109] Edward Barnes referred to the divisions that were making his life as a missionary in Nicaragua so difficult, relating to universal salvation, seventh-day observance, the doctrine of 'total annihilation' and the Oneness 'new issue'. He wrote that 'none of these persons stayed to work but only time enough to sow their special doctrines and passed on'. The result was 'dissension among the believers' so that 'the Spirit of God does not work'.[110] For many of these missionaries, the divisions in Pentecostalism were the 'enemy's strategy to benumb and almost to paralyze missionary interest in the clamor and preoccupation of doctrinal controversies'.[111]

But missionaries found themselves forced to seek new alliances, in some cases more out of financial necessity than conviction. Actually, the emerging Holiness and Oneness Pentecostal denominations in the USA in the 1910s could count the number of missionaries on one hand. At this time the Church of God in Christ, the CG and the Pentecostal Assemblies of the World had their main ministry outside North America in the British Caribbean, and the PHC had small operations in South China, South Africa and Guatemala. Part of the reason for this was organizational and limited financial resources. In contrast, the AG set out from its beginnings in 1914 to establish a strong organizational and financial support base for worldwide Pentecostal missions. Their General Council in 1917 required that all missionaries seeking credentials with the Council should subscribe to the Statement of Fundamental Truths, especially because of 'a very spirited discussion' about tongues as initial evidence, which position the AG 'unqualifiedly' adhered to.[112] Many Pentecostal missionaries all over the world (not only American missionaries, but a smaller number from Canada, Britain, the Scandinavian countries and a sprinkling of Latin Americans) found refuge from their financial and organizational nightmares in this new fellowship. In 1920 the AG's General Council in the USA listed 210 'endorsed missionaries' excluding 'native workers' (although the listing of a handful of Puerto Rican and Mexican missionaries made this somewhat of an anomaly). It had set up District Councils in India, Egypt, Japan and Liberia, obviously considered the most developed fields, and other fields included 'Africa', China, 'Latin America', Cuba, Puerto Rico, 'West Indies', Hawaii,

Alaska and 'Mexican Border'. Expatriate missionaries in India had gathered in conference in late 1918 in Saharanpur and organized the 'Indian Assemblies of God' in a desire 'to come together in greater unity', but without referring to any Indian leaders.[113] This early start in several different countries was one of the things that ensured that the AG would become by far the largest Pentecostal denomination globally, but the white domination in leadership also accelerated the schisms of independent churches.

There were a few national exceptions: although there were far more AG-affiliated missionaries in China than any other denomination by 1920, Oneness Pentecostalism had also made an early advance there. One of the earliest independent Chinese Pentecostal churches, the True Jesus Church (and later the Spirit of Jesus Church in Japan) embraced Oneness doctrine on their formation in 1919. Sometimes the issues of control and paternalism contributed towards the increasing schisms that took place between expatriate-controlled missions and emerging local leaders. The missionaries were sometimes aware of the tensions that their desire to control brought. Burton wrote of the 'Ethiopian spirit' (explaining that this meant 'Africa for the black man') that 'invariably creeps into unsupervised native evangelism', robbing the missionaries of all authority.[114] Missionaries did not take notice of comity arrangements or the presence of other churches in the places where they worked and when different Pentecostal denominations were working in the same place, they ignored each other. Juan Lugo in Puerto Rico was told by Protestant ministers to go and work in the Dominican Republic because there were 13 churches in town and too many missionaries in Puerto Rico. His response was probably characteristic of many Pentecostals at the time: 'sinners are going direct to hell at the doors of the churches', and long-time members of these churches were 'still smoking big cigars and even the pastors of the churches'. The Pentecostals, however, were providing the need of 'the true Gospel preached in the power of the Spirit'.[115]

Although missionaries from the West went out in independent and denominational Pentecostal missions, the overwhelming majority of missionaries have been national people 'sent by the Spirit', often without formal training. This is a fundamental historical difference between Pentecostal and 'mainline' missions. In Pentecostal practice, the Holy Spirit is given to every believer without preconditions. One of the results of this was, as Saayman observes, that 'it ensured that a rigid dividing line between "clergy" and "laity" and between men and women did not develop early on in Pentecostal churches' and even more significantly, 'there was little resistance to the ordination of indigenous pastors and evangelists to bear the brunt of the pastoral upbuilding of the congregations and their evangelistic outreach'.[116] Expatriate missionaries depended totally on their 'native workers' – they would have failed without them. This was one of the reasons for the rapid transition from 'foreign' to 'indigenous' church that took place in many Pentecostal missions, even when foreign missionaries held on tightly to the reigns of power. Leaders tended to come from the lower and uneducated strata of society and were trained in apprentice-type training where their charismatic leadership abilities could develop.[117] Being the only ones who could communicate effectively with local people, they developed their leadership abilities while the foreign missionaries sometimes sat helplessly on one side.

Early Pentecostal missionaries were bombarded with challenges arising from the fact that they were often people without any experience, training or adequate support going to distant lands simply because the Spirit had told them to. There were many drop-outs, deaths and pitiful stories as a result. Of course, there were also success stories of people who had accomplished much in a short time and some who had persevered for several years. Still, these were yet early days, and the Pentecostal missionary movement was barely a decade old. The divisions that ensued ensured that Pentecostalism would become one of the most diverse and diffuse movements in the entire history of Christianity.

Notes

1 *TF* 5:10 (Oct 1885), p.222.
2 *WW* 21:7 (Nov 1899), p.210.
3 *TF* 14:4 (April 1894), p.87.
4 *TF* 17:6 (June 1897), p.130.
5 *WW* 21:5 (Sept 1899), p.145.
6 *WW* 21:2 (June 1899), p.52.
7 *LRE* 2:11 (Aug 1910), p.13.
8 Letter, William J. Boyd to Cecil Polhill, 12 Oct 1912.
9 *LRE* 2:9 (June 1910), p.23.
10 McPherson, *Levi R. Lupton*, pp.106–7.
11 *WW* 24:7 (July 1902), p.120.
12 *LRE* 3:6 (Mar 1911), p.14.
13 *Conf* 2:1 (Jan 1909), p.14; 2:6 (June 1909), p.129.
14 *Conf* 2:11 (Nov 1909), p.253.
15 PMU Candidates' Schedule, Fanny Elizabeth Jenner, 2 July 1912.
16 *Conf* 2:1 (Jan 1909), 14; 2:6 (June 1909), 129; PMU Candidate's Schedules, 1911–20 (Donald Gee Archives).
17 PMU Candidates' Schedule, Ethel Mercy Cook, 8 Oct 1913.
18 Kay, 'Four-Fold Gospel', p.70.
19 *Conf* 4:3 (Mar 1911), p.68.
20 *Conf* 6:10 (Oct 1913), pp. 201–2.
21 Letter, E. Cook to T. H. Mundell, 8 Aug 1914.
22 *Conf* 7:4 (Apr 1914), p.78.
23 *WW* 23:9 (Sept 1901), p.277.
24 *WW* 25:8 (Aug 1903), p.245.
25 *LRE* 5:7 (Apr 1913), p 15; *WWit* 10:3 (Mar 1914), p.3.
26 Letter, A. Swift to T. H. Mundell, 2 Oct 1915.
27 Letter, W. J. Boyd to T. H. Mundell, 18 Feb 1916.
28 Letter, E. Cook to T. H. Mundell, 8 Aug 1914.
29 Letter, A. Kok to C. Polhill, 15 April 1914.
30 *FF* (May 1917), pp.4–6.
31 *FF* (May 1917), pp.6–7.
32 Letter, W. J. Boyd to T. H. Mundell, 18 Feb 1916.
33 Letters, W. J. Boyd to T. H. Mundell, 18 Dec 1916 and 12 June 1917.
34 Letter, E. Cook to T. H. Mundell, 15 Mar 1917.

35 Letter, A. Swift to T. H. Mundell, 24 Sept 1918.

36 Letter, T. H. Mundell to the Leighs, 18 Sept 1918.

37 *WW* 42:3 (Mar 1920), p.18.

38 *WW* 42:3 (Mar 1920), p.26.

39 *LRE* 10:9 (June 1918), p.16.

40 *LRE* 5:4 (Jan 1913), p.22.

41 *WWit* 12:5 (May 1915), p.5.

42 *Redemption Tidings* 1:4 (Jan 1925), p.12.

43 Burton, *When God Changes a Village*, p.vi.

44 Burton, *God Working*, p.106.

45 Moorhead, *Missionary Pioneering*, p.207.

46 Womersley, *Wm F.P. Burton*, pp.77, 113.

47 *WW* 42:10 (Oct 1920), p.14.

48 *WW* 21:1 (May 1899), p.18.

49 McClung, 'Spontaneous Strategy', p.77.

50 *WW* 28:4 (Apr 1906), p.117.

51 *UR* (May 1910), p.6.

52 *Conf* 6:1 (Jan 1913), p.23.

53 *FF* 39 (June 1916), p.10.

54 *TF* 6:12 (Dec 1886), pp.270–3.

55 *WW* 22:11 (Nov 1900), p.337.

56 Letter, J. A. Dowie to A. A. Boddy, 12 June 1903, reproduced in *Conf* 6:2 (Feb 1913), p.38.

57 Wacker, *Heaven Below*, p.158.

58 *AF* 12 (Jan. 1908), p.3.

59 *LRE* 12:3 (Dec 1919), pp.12–13.

60 *Trust* 17:2 (Apr 1918), p.9; 19:2 (Apr 1920), p.2.

61 Wacker, *Heaven Below*, p.160.

62 *LRE* 2:11 (Aug 1910), p.10.

63 *WW* 33:7 (July 1911), p.218.

64 Letter, E. Cook to T. H. Mundell, 8 Dec 1915.

65 *LRE* 6:3 (Dec 1913), p.4.

66 *BM* 134 (1 June 1913), p.3.

67 Letter, W. J. Boyd to T. H. Mundell, 26 Aug 1916.

68 Letter, E. Cook to T. H. Mundell, 6 Feb 1915.

69 *BM* 80 (15 Feb 1911), p.2.

70 *WW* 26:3 (Mar 1904), p.84.

71 Quoted in *LRE* 5:6 (Mar 1913), p.24.

72 *Trust* 17:7 (Sept 1918), p.11.

73 *Conf* 7:11 (Nov 1914), pp.208–9, 212–14.

74 *WWit* 10:1 (Jan 1914), p.2.

75 'Minutes of the General Council' (2–12 Apr 1914), p.7.

76 Wacker, *Heaven Below*, pp.165–8; Blumhofer, *Restoring the Faith*, p.174.

77 *Conf* 2:5 (May 1909), p.115.

78 *Pent* 2:4 (Mar 1910), p.3; *WWit* 9:10 (Oct 1913), p.2; Bartleman, *Azusa Street*, p.83.

79 Bartleman, *Azusa Street*, pp.146–9, 159; *Pent* 1:10 (Sept 1909), p.4; *WW* 36:10 (Oct 1914), p.311.

80 *UR* 2:3 (Nov 1910), p.7.

81 *WWit* 8:8 (20 Oct 1912), p.3.

82 *LRE* 5:6 (Mar 1913), p.15.
83 *LRE* 8:8 (May 1916), p.5.
84 *BM* 130 (1 Apr 1913), p.2.
85 *WE* 176 (10 Feb 1917), p.16.
86 *WWit* 9:12 (Dec 1913), p.1.
87 Letter, T. H. Mundell to E. J. G. Titterington, 15 Sept 1915.
88 *BM* 127 (15 Feb 1913), p.2.
89 *LRE* 5:4 (Jan 1913), p.17.
90 *WWit* 9:11 (Nov 1913), p.4;
91 *LRE* 5:4 (Jan 1913), pp.18–19.
92 *LRE* 5:11 (Aug 1913), p.4.
93 *LRE* 5:12 (Sept 1913), p.13.
94 *LRE* 5:10 (July 1913), pp.22–3.
95 *BM* 134 (1 June 1913), p.3.
96 *LRE* 5:8 (May 1913), p.24.
97 *BM* 131 (15 Apr 1913), p.2; 134 (1 June 1913), p.3.
98 *BM* 133 (15 May 1913), p.1.
99 *WWit* 9:8 (Aug 1913), p.2.
100 *LRE* 10:9 (June 1918), pp.19–23.
101 *WWit* 9:12 (Dec 1913), p.1.
102 *WE* 143 (10 June 1916), p.12.
103 *WE* 144 (17 June 1916), p.2.
104 *Midnight Cry* 4:2 (Mar 1916), p.4.
105 *WE* 209 (6 Oct 1917), pp.2–3.
106 *Advocate* 1:24 (11 Oct 1917), pp.2–3.
107 Bartleman, *Azusa Street*, pp.164–5.
108 *WE* 81 (18 Mar 1915), p.4.
109 *LRE* 8:2 (Feb 1916), pp.15–16.
110 *WE* 212 (27 Oct 1917), p.12.
111 *WE* 37:1 (1 Jan 1916), p.13.
112 *WE* 210 (13 Oct 1917), pp.2–3.
113 *LRE* 11:5 (Feb 1919), p.11; 'Combined Minutes', 1920, pp.37–8.
114 Moorhead, *Missionary Pioneering*, pp.11–12.
115 *WE* 169 (16 Dec 1916), p.12.
116 Saayman, 'Some reflections', p.43.
117 McClung, 'Spontaneous Strategy', p.76.

Table 1: The First Decade of Pentecostal Missionaries 1906–16

YEAR	COUNTRIES	FIRST MISSIONARIES TO ARRIVE
1905–6	India	Ramabai, Abrams, Garr
1906	Palestine, Leb'n, Syria	Leatherman
1907	Liberia	Hutchins, Farrow, Batman, McCauley, Harrow, etc.
	Angola	Mead
	Somalia	Slingerland
	Egypt	Ghali, Leatherman
	China	McIntosh, Garr, Law, Mok, etc.
	Japan	Ryan, etc.
	Nicaragua	Barnes
1908	South Africa	Hezmalhalch, Lake, Lehman, etc.
	Kenya	Miller
	Guatemala	Bradley
	Venezuela	Bailly
1909	Chile	Hoover
	Argentina	Francesconi, etc.
	El Salvador	Mebius
	Philippines	Leatherman
	Bolivia	Clark
	Bahamas	Barr
1910	Brazil	Vingren & Berg, Francesconi
	Sierra Leone	Hare
	Lesotho	Lion
	Swaziland	Taylor, Gourlay
	Sri Lanka	Wanigasekera, Hettiaratchy
	Turkey	Gerber
	Algeria	Hebden
1911	Persia	Lazarus & Baddell
	Fiji	Starkenberg & Johnson
	Ecuador	Cragin
	Antigua	Jamieson
1912	Tunisia	Planter
1913	Mexico	Valenzuela
	Tanzania	Wittich
	Zimbabwe	Hitchcock, Wallis
1914	Zambia	Vernon
	Congo	Johnstone
	Peru	Stevens
	Jamaica, Montserrat	Jamieson
1916	Puerto Rico	Lugo, Feliciano

Conclusions: The Missionary Nature of Pentecostalism

By 1926, only two decades after the revivals that gave birth to the movement, Pentecostal missionaries were found in at least 42 countries outside North America and Europe. The first of these missionaries to operate in these different countries are listed in Table 1 on the previous page. This was indeed a remarkable achievement, especially in view of the lack of central organization and co-ordination, the naivety of most of these missionaries and the physical difficulties and opposition they encountered. It is possible, however, to understand the present global proliferation of Pentecostalism from these rather chaotic beginnings and to discern what were the essential characteristics that made it ultimately the most successful Christian missionary movement of the twentieth century. This book has set out to accomplish this task, and it remains for us to outline its significant findings.

Charismata or 'spiritual gifts' and ecstatic or 'enthusiastic' forms of Christianity have been found in all ages, albeit sometimes at the margins of the 'established' Church, and they have often been a characteristic of the Church's missionary advance, from the early Church to the pioneer Catholic missionaries of the Middle Ages. Protestantism as a whole did not favour such enthusiasm, however, and it took new revival movements in the nineteenth century, especially of the Methodist and Holiness type and among radical Protestants who espoused similar ideas, to stimulate a restoration of spiritual gifts to accompany an end-time missionary thrust. The many and various revival movements at the turn of the twentieth century had the effect of creating a greater air of expectancy for Pentecostal revival in many parts of the world. The signs that this revival had come would be similar to the earlier revivals: an intense desire to pray, emotional confession of sins, manifestations of the coming of the Spirit, successful and accelerated evangelism and world mission, and especially spiritual gifts to confirm that the power of the Spirit had indeed come.

Missionaries from these various revival movements went out into faith missions and independent missions, some joining Holiness and radical evangelical organizations like the CMA and then becoming Pentecostal. The coming of the Spirit was linked to a belief that the last days had arrived and that the 'full gospel' would be preached to all nations before the coming of the Lord. Considerations of religious pluralism, colonialism and cultural sensitivity were not on the agenda of those who rushed out to the nations with this revivalist message believing that they had been enabled to speak those languages they needed for the task. The stage was set for the coming of a new Pentecost to spread across the world in the twentieth century. The means by which these Pentecostal fires would spread would be a global network of these same faith missionaries and so-called 'native workers' whose devotion to Christ and enthusiastic zeal were unrivalled by most of their contemporaries. The Pentecostalism emerging was essentially a missionary movement of unprecedented vigour.

There are several aspects of this study that require further research. Historians speak of the need to formulate a new history written in deliberate reaction to traditional history and its paradigms, a history concerned with the whole of human activity, 'history from below' rather than 'history from above', history taken from the perspective of the poor and powerless rather than from that of the rich and powerful. So in the writing of Pentecostal history there needs to be 'affirmative action' to redress the balance, where the contribution of national workers, pastors and evangelists is emphasized rather than that of foreign missionaries. Scholars, especially outside the western world, must plumb the depths of oral histories and written archives to illuminate that which has been concealed or unknown for so long. Consequently, the work of western missionaries who came from countries of power and wrote newsletters for their own specific purposes is put into correct perspective. We cannot ignore the failings of these missionaries and give exaggerated importance to those whose role was often catalytic rather than central. Asia, Africa and Latin America have their own Christian heroes who should be more visible in the writing of Pentecostal histories. Information on western missionaries to Africa, Asia, the Pacific, the Caribbean and Latin America is disproportionate to their role and contribution, mainly through the scarcity of written information on national leaders. I fear that this book might not have greatly changed that perception. A serious and extensive revision of global Pentecostal history needs to be done in which the enormous contributions of these pioneers is properly recognized, so that some classical Pentecostals in particular shed their assumption that Pentecostalism is a made-in-the-USA product that has been exported to the rest of the world. The revising of the history of Pentecostalism in the twenty-first century should be undertaken, not by emphasizing the missionary 'heroes' of the powerful and wealthy nations of the world, but by giving a voice to the people living in the world's most marginalized parts. We can listen to the 'margins' by allowing the hitherto voiceless and often nameless ones to speak, if that is ever really possible. We can recognize the contribution of those unsung Pentecostal labourers of the past who have been overlooked in the histories and hagiographies. Assumptions at the World Missionary Conference in Edinburgh in 1910 were that Christianity would not flourish without white missionary control.[1] Providentially, early Pentecostalism gave the lie to that assumption and probably became the main contributor to the reshaping of Christianity itself from a predominantly western to a predominantly non-western phenomenon during the twentieth century.

In any debate about the origins of global Pentecostalism, one has to reckon with some of the central assumptions of this book. These are that: 1. the Azusa Street revival in the USA and the Mukti revival in India were part of a wider series of revivals and had equal significance in the early promotion of Pentecostal beliefs and values throughout the world; 2. the missionary networks, especially that of the CMA, were fundamental in spreading Pentecostalism internationally; 3. the Pentecostal periodicals that were posted to missionaries in the 'field' were not only significant in spreading Pentecostalism internationally but were the foundation of the meta-culture that arose in global Pentecostalism in its earliest forms; and 4. the various centres and events in early Pentecostalism were part of a series of formative stages in the emergence of a new missionary movement that took several years to take on a distinctive identity.

Although Pentecostals have been around for only a century, today they are among the most significant role players in Christian missions, with perhaps three-quarters of them in the Majority World.[2] According to the controversial statistics of Barrett et al., in 2006 60 per cent of the world's Christians (1,288 million) were in Asia, Africa, Latin America and Oceania, while those of the two northern continents (including Russia) constituted only 40 per cent. When this is compared to 1900, when 82 per cent of the world Christian population was found in Europe and North America, we have dramatic evidence of how rapidly the western share of world Christianity has decreased in the twentieth century. According to the same statistics, if present trends continue two-thirds of the world's Christians will live in the South by 2025. But it is not only in terms of overall numbers that there have been fundamental changes. Christianity is growing most often in Pentecostal and Charismatic forms, and many of these are independent of both western 'mainline' Protestant and 'classical Pentecostal' denominations and missions. What Andrew Walls describes as the 'southward swing of the Christian centre of gravity' is possibly more evident in Pentecostalism than in other forms of Christianity.[3] In 2000 Barrett and company estimated a total of 523 million, or 28 per cent of all Christians to be Pentecostal and Charismatic. This number is divided into four groups: 1. 18 million 'peripheral quasi-Pentecostals', 3 per cent of the total; 2. 66 million 'denominational Pentecostals', 12 per cent; 3. 176 million 'Charismatics' (including 105 million Catholics), 32 per cent; and 4. the largest group of 295 million 'Neocharismatics (Independents, Postdenominationalists)', a massive 53 per cent of the total.[4] These figures, of course, are highly debatable but do give an indication that something highly significant is taking place in the global complexity of Christianity as a whole and of Pentecostalism in particular.

Although I give considerable space in this book to the first 'Pentecostal' and 'Apostolic Faith' missionaries from the West, for me the terms 'Pentecostals' and 'Pentecostalism' include a wide variety of movements where the emphasis is on receiving the Spirit and practising spiritual gifts, especially prophecy, healing and speaking in tongues. The terms include what eventually became Pentecostal denominations, Charismatic renewals in the older churches and a wide range of independent churches – over half the numbers in Barrett's statistics. However we interpret these terms and statistics, we need to acknowledge and celebrate the tremendous diversity in Pentecostalism. This has amounted to a twentieth-century reformation of Christianity that has precipitated a resurgent interest in pneumatology and spirituality. Whereas older

Protestant churches bemoan their ever-decreasing membership and possible demise in the West in the early twenty-first century, a most dramatic church growth continues to take place in Pentecostal and independent Pentecostal-like churches, especially outside the western world. During the 1990s, it was estimated that the Majority World mission movement had grown at 17 times the rate of western missions.[5] Countries like South Korea, Nigeria, Brazil and India have become major Christian missionary-sending nations, many of whom are Pentecostal. Half the world's Christians today live in developing, poor countries, where forms of Christianity are very different from what western 'classical Pentecostals' might wish them to be. These Christians have been profoundly affected by several factors, including the desire to have a more contextual and culturally relevant form of Christianity, the rise of nationalism, a reaction to what are perceived as 'colonial' and foreign forms of Christianity, and the burgeoning Pentecostal and Charismatic renewal. These factors play a major role in the formation of independent churches throughout the world. Unfortunately, there are still areas of the world Pentecostal movement dominated physically, financially and ideologically by foreign missionaries.

Simon Coleman's study of a Charismatic church in Sweden has demonstrated the globalization of Charismatic Christianity by reference to three dimensions: 1. the use of the mass communications media to disseminate its ideas; 2. a social organization that promotes internationalism through global travel and networking, conferences, and mega-churches that function like international corporations; and 3. a 'global orientation' or global Charismatic 'meta-culture' that transcends locality and denominational loyalty and displays striking similarities in different parts of the world.[6] Although Coleman had in mind late twentieth-century Pentecostalism, all three of these features can also be discerned in early Pentecostalism. Key to understanding this was the role of the periodicals. With reference to the first feature, the periodicals provided the mass media for the spread of Pentecostal ideas. They also formed the social structures that were necessary during this time of creative chaos, the second feature. International travel was an increasing feature of the early missionaries and their networks and conferences the means by which their message spread. One cannot read these different early periodicals without noticing how frequently a relatively small number of the same Pentecostal missionaries are referred to in all the periodicals. Division and schism was to come later; but the periodicals promoted a unity of purpose and vision that has since been lost. And third, this internationalism, this global 'meta-culture' of Pentecostalism was evident in these years through the influence of both the periodicals and the missionary networks. At the same time, Pentecostal missionaries like Burton saw the globalization that occurred by which native peoples were adopting western ways as 'a marvelous, an unparalleled opportunity for presenting the realities of Christ' to replace the now discarded old beliefs in witchcraft, fetishes and charms.[7]

From its beginnings, Pentecostalism throughout the world is both transnational and migratory, or 'missionary' in its fundamental nature. In these processes the various movements remain stubbornly consistent, for they see the 'world' as a place to move into and 'possess' for Christ. Transnationalism and migration do not affect their essential character, even though their adherents may have to steer a precarious course between contradictory forms of identity resulting from the migratory experience. Pentecostalism developed its own characteristics and identities in different parts of the world during the twentieth century without losing its transnational connections and international networks. The widespread use of the mass media, the setting up of new networks that often incorporate the word 'international' in their title, frequent conferences with international speakers that reinforce transnationalism and the growth of churches that provide total environments for members and international connections are all features of this Pentecostalism, which promotes this Charismatic global meta-culture constantly.

The extent to which globalization and migration have affected the shape of this very significant religious sector is something that requires a much more careful analysis than this study offers, but is surely an important task for future research. The shapes of the new Pentecostalisms that have emerged as a result of the globalization process, how they differ from the older networks of denominational Pentecostalism and specifically what the features of this global shift of centre to the South means for Pentecostalism have yet to be precisely described. Another area that needs further investigation is the extent to which Pentecostalism has permeated and affected the beliefs, values and practices of other Christians, seen especially in the popular Christianity that dominates public events like weddings and funerals. Only when these investigations have taken place will we be better able to understand those external forces that forge the religious identities of people in our contemporary societies and the increasingly important role of Pentecostalisms in this pluralistic world.

This study has set to demonstrate that Pentecostalism in its many and various forms has been from its beginnings a migratory faith. Its earliest propagators at the start of the twentieth century were driven by an ideology that sent them from North America and Western Europe to Asia, Africa and Latin America within a remarkably short period of time. A particular ideology of migration and transnationalism has been a common feature of all types of Pentecostalism. André Droogers has outlined three broad but common features of transnational Pentecostalism that are helpful in understanding the ideology that makes Pentecostals feel part of a global community. These are: 1. the central emphasis on the experience of the Spirit, accompanied by ecstatic manifestations such as speaking in tongues; 2. the 'born again' or conversion experience that accompanies acceptance into a Pentecostal community; and 3. a dualistic worldview that distinguishes between the 'world' and the 'church', between the 'devil' and the 'divine', between 'sickness' and 'health'.[8] These were all features of early Pentecostalism, abundantly evident in the publications of the time and illustrated throughout this book.

The most significant event for global Protestant Christianity outside the rise of the Pentecostal movement in the early twentieth century was the birth of the ecumenical movement, beginning with the great World Missionary Conference held in Edinburgh in 1910. For the Pentecostals and radical evangelicals, this event was hardly noticed. They were not invited to attend and their work was unrecognized, but these were very early days for them. I have only found one commentary on this epochal event made by Pentecostals at the time. Elisabeth Sexton in a 1910 editorial in *The Bridegroom's Messenger* titled 'Increasing Missionary Activity' referred to the Edinburgh Conference of less than three months earlier as 'undoubtedly the greatest missionary gathering the Christian world has ever known'. She noted that although the increasing number of missionary societies (aided by the laymen's movement) pointed to an 'auspicious outlook for great results for God' in this age unlike any other, she doubted whether any activity 'not representing the fullness of the Gospel, with full redemption in Christ Jesus for body, soul and spirit' would achieve the expected outcome. She wondered whether the unity reported on in Edinburgh was 'by the working of the blessed Spirit of God, uniting them in Christ' or was merely 'apparent unity out of respect for the great occasion'. She lamented what she saw as 'compromise' in allowing a Roman Catholic to address the conference – unless Catholics had 'greatly changed', she added. She felt that concessions had been made 'regarding heathen religions in recognising certain moral good in them'. Such concessions would 'dishonor God and weaken the cause of Christ'. She reiterated her conviction that the only 'equipment for effectual missionary service' was 'Holy Ghost power' and 'uncompromising faithfulness to the full Gospel truth'. Without this there was 'little hope for great results for God as the outcome of this great missionary conference'.[9] This commentary illustrates what were some of the fundamental issues already developing in Pentecostal circles making it highly suspicious of and uncooperative with the wider Christian world, especially in the case of the ecumenical movement and Catholicism. Thankfully, this is beginning to change.

Pentecostalism has always been a missionary movement in foundation and essence. It emerged with a firm conviction that the Spirit had been poured out in 'signs and wonders' in order for the nations of the world to be reached for Christ before the end of the age. Its missionaries proclaimed a 'full gospel' that included individual salvation, physical healing, personal holiness, baptism with the Spirit, and a life on the edge lived in expectation of the imminent return of Christ. For this message, its pioneers were prepared to lay down their lives and many of them did. This book has made it abundantly clear that they were very human vessels of this 'full gospel' who cannot be emulated in many respects – especially when it comes to attitudes to other religions and cultures and matters of race. But we should not throw out the baby with the bathwater. The selfless dedication and sacrifices in the face of immense difficulties of these courageous women and men of early Pentecostalism (among countless others) can only be greatly admired. Without them we would be the poorer, and the composition of global Christianity today would certainly look very different and probably in a state of permanent decline. Thank God that such women and men filled with the Spirit were willing to pay the price that altered the course of Christian history.

Notes

1 Stanley, 'Twentieth Century World Christianity', p.77.

2 The term 'Majority World' is adapted from the *New Internationalist* and is used to refer to Asia and the Pacific, Africa, South America and the Caribbean.

3 Walls, 'Of Ivory Towers and Ashrams', p.1.

4 Barrett, Johnson and Crossing, 'Missiometrics 2006', p.28; *DPCM*, pp.286–7.

5 Jaffarian, 'Are there more non-western missionaries than western missionaries?', p.132.

6 Coleman, *The Globalisation of Charismatic Christianity*, pp.66–9.

7 Moorhead, *Missionary Pioneering*, pp.81–2.

8 Droogers, 'Globalisation and Pentecostal Success', pp.44–6.

9 *BM* 69 (1 Sept 1910), p.1.

References

Primary Literature

'Combined Minutes of the General Council of the Assemblies of God', 1914–25, Flower Pentecostal Heritage Center, Springfield, Missouri, USA.

'Constitution and By-Laws of the General Council of the Assemblies of God', 1927–39, Flower Pentecostal Heritage Center, Springfield, Missouri, USA.

First Baptist Church, Los Angeles, Records, Volume IX (1905), 29 May, 31 May.

First New Testament Church, *Weekly Bulletin*, 8–15 July 1906.

Fritsch, Cora, Letters to her various family members, 1909–10.

The Hongkong Government Gazette, 22 May 1886.

Hong Kong Government, 'Registrar General's Report for the Year 1892', Hong Kong, 1 June 1893.

Los Angeles Times, 8 June 1905, 14 July 1906, 17 July 1906, 23 July 1906.

'Minutes of the General Council of the Assemblies of God', 1914–19, Flower Pentecostal Heritage Center, Springfield, Missouri, USA.

Pentecostal Missionary Union, Letters from various missionaries, 1911–25, Donald Gee Centre, Mattersey, Notts, UK.

Pentecostal Missionary Union, Letters from T. H. Mundell, Secretary, 1914–25, Donald Gee Centre, Mattersey, Notts, UK.

Pentecostal Missionary Union, Council Minutes, 1909–24, Donald Gee Centre, Mattersey, Notts, UK.

Pentecostal Missionary Union, Candidate's Schedules, 1911–20, Donald Gee Centre, Mattersey, Notts, UK.

Periodicals

The Apostolic Evangel (Royston, Georgia & Falcon, N. Carolina), 1907, 1909.

The Apostolic Faith (Los Angeles, California), 1906–8.

The Apostolic Light (Spokane, Washington), 29 August 1907.

Bombay Guardian and Banner of Asia, 7 November 1905.

The Bridegroom's Messenger (Atlanta, Georgia), 1909–16.

Confidence (Sunderland, England), 1908–20.

Flames of Fire (London, England), 1911–18.

The Holiness Advocate (Goldsboro & Clinton, N. Carolina), 1901–7.

The Latter Rain Evangel (Chicago, Illinois), 1908–20.

Leaves of Healing (Chicago & Zion City, Illinois), 1894–1906.

Live Coals (Mercer, Missouri & Royston, Georgia), 1904–7.

The Midnight Cry (New York), 1911–20.

Missionary Review of the World (July 1906).

Mukti Prayer-Bell (Kedgaon, India), September 1907.

The Pentecost (Indianapolis, Indiana & Kansas City, Missouri), 1908–10.

The Pentecostal Evangel (Springfield, Missouri), 1913–20, earlier *The Christian Evangel* (Plainfield, Indiana; Findlay, Ohio & St Louis, Missouri), 1913–15, 1918–19 and *The Weekly Evangel* (Springfield, Missouri), 1915–18.

The Pentecostal Holiness Advocate (Falcon, N. Carolina), 1917–20.

Pentecostal Truths (Hong Kong, China), 1908–17.

The Pentecostal Witness (Edinburgh, Scotland), 1924.

Redemption Tidings (Stockport, England), 1924–30.

Things New and Old (London, England), 1921–5.

Triumphs of Faith (Buffalo, New York & Oakland, California), 1881–1920.

Trust (Rochester, New York), 1908–32.

The Upper Room (Los Angeles, California), 1909–11.

Word and Witness (Malvern, Arkansas), 1912–15.

Word and Work (Framingham, Massachusetts), 1899–1920 .

Secondary Literature

Adhav, Shamsundar Manohar, *Pandita Ramabai* (Madras: Christian Literature Society, 1979).

Alexander, Kimberley Ervin, *Pentecostal Healing: Models in Theology and Practice* (Blandford Forum, Dorset: Deo Publishing, 2006).

Allen, Roland, *Missionary Methods: St Paul's or Ours?* (Grand Rapids, MI: Eerdmans, 1962).

Anderson, Allan, 'The Lekganyanes and Prophecy in the Zion Christian Church', *Journal of Religion in Africa*, XXIX:3, October 1999 (285–312).

Anderson, Allan, *Zion and Pentecost: The Spirituality and Experience of Pentecostal and Zionist/Apostolic Churches in South Africa* (Pretoria: University of South Africa Press, 2000).

Anderson, Allan, 'Signs and Blunders: Pentecostal Mission Issues at "Home and Abroad" in the Twentieth Century', *Journal of Asian Mission* 2:2, September 2000 (193–210).

Anderson, Allan, *African Reformation: African Initiated Christianity in the 20th Century* (Trenton, NJ & Asmara, Eritrea: Africa World Press, 2001).

Anderson, Allan, 'Christian Missionaries and "Heathen Natives": The Cultural Ethics of Early Pentecostal Missionaries', *JEPTA* 22, 2002 (4–29).

Anderson, Allan, *An Introduction to Pentecostalism: Global Charismatic Christianity* (Cambridge: Cambridge University Press, 2004).

Anderson, Allan, 'Revising Pentecostal History in Global Perspective', in Anderson and Tang, *Asian and Pentecostal*, 157–83.

Anderson, Allan, 'The Dubious Legacy of Charles Fox Parham: Racism and Cultural Insensitivities among Pentecostals', *Pneuma* 25:1 (Spring 2005), 51–64.

Anderson, Allan and Walter J. Hollenweger (eds.), *Pentecostals after a Century: Global Perspectives on a Movement in Transition* (Sheffield: Sheffield Academic Press, 1999).

Anderson, Allan and Edmond Tang (eds.), *Asian and Pentecostal: The Charismatic Face of Christianity in Asia* (Oxford: Regnum & Baguio City, Philippines: APTS Press, 2005).

Anderson, Robert M., *Vision of the Disinherited: The Making of American Pentecostal-ism* (Peabody, MA: Hendrickson, 1979).

Ashcroft, B., G. Griffiths and H. Tiffin (eds.), *The Post-Colonial Studies Reader* (London & New York: Routledge, 1995).

Austin, Alvyn, '"Hotbed of Missions": The China Inland Mission, Toronto Bible College, and the Faith Missions – Bible School Connection', in Bays and Wacker, *Foreign Missionary Enterprise*, 134–51.

Barratt, T. B. *When the Fire Fell and an Outline of my Life* (Oslo, 1927); in Dayton (ed.), *Work of T. B. Barratt*.

Barrett, David B., Todd M. Johnson and Peter F. Crossing, 'Missiometrics 2006: Goals, Resources, Doctrines of the 350 Christian World Communions', *International Bulletin of Missionary Research* 30:1, 2006 (27–30).

Bartleman, Frank, *Azusa Street* (S. Plainfield, NJ: Bridge Publishing, 1925, 1980).

Bays, Daniel H., 'Indigenous Protestant Churches in China 1900–1937: A Pentecostal Case Study', in Kaplan, *Indigenous Responses*, 124–43.

Bays, Daniel H., 'The Growth of Independent Christianity in China, 1900–1937', in Bays, *Christianity in China*, 307–16.

Bays, Daniel H., (ed.), *Christianity in China: From the Eighteenth Century to the Present* (Stanford, California: Stanford University Press, 1996).

Bays, Daniel H., 'The Protestant Missionary Establishment and the Pentecostal Movement', in Blumhofer, Spittler and Wacker, *Pentecostal Currents*, 50–67.

Bays, Daniel H. and Grant Wacker, 'Introduction: The Many Faces of the Missionary Enterprise at Home', in Bays and Wacker, *Foreign Missionary Enterprise*, 1–9.

Bays, Daniel H. and Grant Wacker (eds.), *The Foreign Missionary Enterprise at Home: Explorations in North American Cultural History* (Tuscaloosa: University of Alabama Press, 2003).

Bebbington, David, *Patterns in History: A Christian Perspective on Historical Thought* (Leicester: Apollos, 1990).

Bergunder, Michael, *Die südindische Pfingstbewegung im 20. Jahrhundert. Eine his-torische und systematische Untersuchung*. Studien zur Interkulturellen Geschichte des Christentums 113 (Frankfurt am Main: Peter Lang, 1999).

Bergunder, Michael, 'Constructing Indian Pentecostalism: On issues of methodol-ogy and representation', in Anderson and Tang, *Asian and Pentecostal*, 177–214.

Blair, William N. and Bruce Hunt, *The Korean Pentecost and the Sufferings which Followed* (Edinburgh: The Banner of Truth Trust, 1977).

Blumhofer, Edith L., *Restoring the Faith: The Assemblies of God, Pentecostalism, and American Culture* (Urbana & Chicago: University of Illinois Press, 1993).

Blumhofer, Edith L., '"From India's Coral Strand": Pandita Ramabai and U.S. Support for Foreign Missions', in Bays and Wacker, *Foreign Missionary Enterprise*, 152–70.

Blumhofer, Edith L., Russell P. Spittler and Grant A. Wacker (eds.), *Pentecostal Currents in American Protestantism* (Urbana & Chicago: University of Illinois Press, 1999).

Bond, G., Johnson, W. and Walker, S. S. (eds.), *African Christianity: Patterns of Religious Continuity* (New York: Academic Press, 1979).

Booth-Clibborn, Arthur S., *Blood Against Blood* (New York: Charles C. Cook, 1914).

Boyd, Gladys, *A Chinese Rainbow: Remarkable Missionary Experiences in Yunnan* (London: Victory Press, 1944).

Bundy, David, 'The legacy of William Taylor', *International Bulletin of Missionary Research* 18:4, 1994 (172–6).

Bundy, David, 'Thomas Ball Barratt: From Methodist to Pentecostal', *JEPTA* 13, 1994 (19–40).

Bundy, David, 'Historical and Theological Analysis of the Pentecostal Church in Norway', *JEPTA* 20, 2000 (66–92).

Burgess, Stanley M. 'Pentecostalism in India: An Overview', *AJPS* 4:1, 2001 (85–98).

Burgess, Stanley M. and Eduard M. van der Maas (eds.), *New International Dictionary of Pentecostal and Charismatic Movements* (Grand Rapids, MI: Zondervan, 2002).

Burpeau, Kemp Pendleton, *God's Showman: A Historical Study of John G. Lake and South African/American Pentecostalism* (Oslo: Refleks Publishing, 2004).

Burton, W. F. P., *When God Changes a Man* (London: Victory Press, 1929, 1937).

Burton, W. F. P., *God Working With Them* (London: Victory Press, 1932).

Burton, W. F. P., *When God Changes a Village* (London: Victory Press, 1933).

Burton, W. F. P., *When God Makes a Pastor* (London: Victory Press, 1934).

Cartledge, Mark (ed.), *Speaking in Tongues: Multi-Disciplinary Perspectives* (Milton Keynes, UK: Paternoster, 2006).

Chesnut, R. Andrew, *Born Again in Brazil: The Pentecostal Boom and the Pathogens of Poverty* (New Brunswick, NY: Rutgers University Press, 1997).

Coleman, Simon, *The Globalisation of Charismatic Christianity: Spreading the Gospel of Prosperity* (Cambridge: Cambridge University Press, 2000).

Comaroff, Jean, *Body of Power, Spirit of Resistance: The Culture and History of a South African People* (Chicago & London: University of Chicago Press, 1985).

Corten, André and Ruth Marshall-Fratani (eds.), *Between Babel and Pentecost: Transnational Pentecostalism in Africa and Latin America* (Bloomington, IN: Indiana University Press, 2001).

Cox, Harvey, *Fire from Heaven: The Rise of Pentecostal Spirituality and the Reshaping of Religion in the Twenty-first Century* (London: Cassell, 1996).

Creech, Joe, 'Visions of Glory: The Place of the Azusa Street Revival in Pentecostal History', *Church History* 65 (1996), 405–24.

Dayton, Donald W. (ed.), *The Work of T. B. Barratt*, 'The Higher Christian Life' Series (New York & London: Garland Publishing, 1985).

Dayton, Donald W., *Theological Roots of Pentecostalism* (Metuchen, NJ: Scarecrow Press, 1987).

De Kock, Leon, *Civilising Barbarians: Missionary Narrative and African Textual Response in Nineteenth-Century South Africa* (Johannesburg: Witwatersrand University Press, 1996).

Dempster, Murray A., Byron D. Klaus and Douglas Petersen (eds.), *Called and Empowered: Global Mission in Pentecostal Perspective* (Peabody: Hendrickson, 1991).

Dempster, Murray A., Byron D. Klaus and Douglas Petersen (eds.), *The Globalization of Pentecostalism: A Religion made to Travel* (Oxford: Regnum, 1999).

Deng Zhaoming, 'Indigenous Chinese Pentecostal Denominations', in Anderson and Tang, *Asian and Pentecostal*, 437–466.

De Wet, Christiaan R., 'The Apostolic Faith Mission in Africa: 1908–1980. A case study in church growth in a segregated society', PhD thesis, University of Cape Town, 1989.

Dongre, Rajas K. and Josephine F. Patterson, *Pandita Ramabai: A Life of Faith and Prayer* (Madras: Christian Literature Society, 1963).
Droogers, André, 'Globalisation and Pentecostal Success', in Corten and Marshall-Fratani, *Between Babel and Pentecost*, 41–61.

Espinosa, Gastón, 'Ordinary Prophet: William J. Seymour and the Azusa Street Revival', in Hunter and Robeck, *Azusa Street Revival*, 29–60.
Evans, Eifon, *The Welsh Revival of 1904* (Bridgend, UK: Evangelical Press of Wales, 1969).

Faupel, D. William, *The Everlasting Gospel: The Significance of Eschatology in the Development of Pentecostal Thought* (Sheffield: Sheffield Academic Press, 1996).
Frodsham, Stanley H., *'With Signs Following': The Story of the Latter-Day Pentecostal Revival* (Springfield, Missouri: Gospel Publishing House, 1926, 1928).
Fuller, Mary L. B., *The Triumph of an Indian Widow: The Life of Pandita Ramabai* (New York: Christian Alliance Publishing Co., 1927).

Goff, James R. Jr., *Fields White unto Harvest: Charles F. Parham and the Missionary Origins of Pentecostalism* (Fayetteville, AR: University of Arkansas Press, 1988).
Goff, James R. Jr. and Grant Wacker (eds.), *Portraits of a Generation: Early Pentecostal Leaders* (Fayetteville, AR: University of Arkansas Press, 2002).

Haliburton, Gordon M., *The Prophet Harris: A Study of an African Prophet and his Mass Movement in the Ivory Coast and the Gold Coast 1913–1915* (London: Longman, 1971).
Hanekom, Chris, *Krisis en Kultus* (Pretoria: Academica, 1975).
Hastings, Adrian, *The Church in Africa 1450–1950* (Oxford: Clarendon, 1994).
Hastings, Adrian, 'The Clash of Nationalism and Universalism within Twentieth-Century Missionary Christianity', in Stanley, *Missions, Nationalism*, 15–33.
Hedlund, Roger E., 'Indigenous Pentecostalism in India', in Anderson and Tang, *Asian & Pentecostal*, 215–244.
Hinnells, John R. (ed.), *The Routledge Companion to the Study of Religion* (Abingdon, UK & New York: Routledge, 2005).
Hobsbawm, Eric, 'Introduction: Inventing Traditions', in Hobsbawm and Ranger, *Invention of Tradition*, 1–14.
Hobsbawm, Eric, *The Age of Empire 1875–1914* (London: Abacus, 1987).
Hobsbawm, Eric and Terence Ranger (eds.), *The Invention of Tradition* (Cambridge: Cambridge University Press, 1984).
Hodges, Melvin L., *The Indigenous Church* (Springfield: Gospel Publishing House, 1953).
Hollenweger, Walter J., *The Pentecostals* (London: SCM Press, 1972).
Hoover, Willis Collins and Mario G. Hoover, *History of the Pentecostal Revival in Chile* (Santiago, Chile: Imprenta Eben-Ezer, 1930, 2000).
Hudson, Neil, 'Strange Words and Their Impact on Early Pentecostals – A Historical Perspective', in Cartledge, *Speaking in Tongues*, 52–80.
Hunter, Harold D., 'A Journey Toward Racial Reconciliation: Race Mixing in the Church of God of Prophecy', in Hunter and Robeck, *Azusa Street Revival*, 277–96.
Hunter, Harold D. and P. D. Hocken (eds.), *All Together in One Place: Theological Papers from the Brighton Conference on World Evangelization* (Sheffield, UK: Sheffield Academic Press, 1993).

Hunter, Harold D. and Cecil M. Robeck Jr. (eds.), *The Azusa Street Revival and its Legacy* (Cleveland, Tennessee: Pathway Press, 2006).

Isichei, Elizabeth (ed.), *Varieties of Christian Experience in Nigeria* (London: Macmillan, 1982).

Jacobsen, Douglas, *Thinking in the Spirit: Theologies of the Early Pentecostal Movement* (Bloomington, IN: Indiana University Press, 2003).
Jaffarian, Michael, 'Are there more non-western missionaries than western missionaries?', *International Bulletin of Missionary Research* 28:3 (July 2004), 131–2.

Kalu, Ogbu U. (ed.), *The History of Christianity in West Africa* (London & New York: Longman, 1980).
Kaplan, Steven (ed.), *Indigenous Responses to Western Christianity* (New York & London: New York University Press, 1995).
Kay, Peter K., 'The Four-Fold Gospel in the Formation, Policy and Practice of the Pentecostal Missionary Union (PMU) (1909–1925)', MA dissertation, Cheltenham and Gloucester College of Higher Education, 1995.
Kay, William K. and Anne E. Dyer (eds.), *Pentecostal and Charismatic Studies: A Reader* (London: SCM Press, 2004).
King, Joseph H., *Yet Speaketh: Memoirs of the Late Bishop Joseph H. King* (Franklin Springs, GA: Publishing House of the Pentecostal Holiness Church, 1949).
King, Richard, 'Orientalism and the Study of Religions', in Hinnells, *Study of Religion*, 275–90.
Kosambi, Meera (ed. and trans.), *Pandita Ramabai through her Own Words: Selected Works* (New Delhi: Oxford University Press, 2000).
Kydd, Ronald A. N., *Healing through the Centuries: Models of Understanding* (Peabody, MA: Hendrickson, 1998).

Lake, John G., *Adventures in God* (Tulsa, OK: Harrison House, 1981, reprinted).
Land, Steven J., *Pentecostal Spirituality: A Passion for the Kingdom* (Sheffield: Sheffield Academic Press, 1993).
Law, E. May, *Pentecostal Mission Work in South China: An Appeal for Missions* (Falcon, NC: The Falcon Publishing Co., 1915).
Lederle, Henry I., *Treasures Old and New: Interpretations of 'Spirit-baptism' in the Charismatic Renewal Movement* (Peabody, MA: Hendrickson, 1988).
Lee, Young Hoon, 'The Holy Spirit Movement in Korea: Its Historical and Doctrinal Development', PhD thesis, Temple University, Philadelphia, 1996.
Lewis, Donald M. (ed.), *Christianity Reborn: The Global Expansion of Evangelicalism in the Twentieth Century* (Grand Rapids, MI & Cambridge, UK: Eerdmans, 2004).
Lindsay, Gordon, *John G. Lake: Apostle to Africa* (Dallas: Christ for the Nations, 1972).
Lukhaimane, E. K., 'The Zion Christian Church of Ignatius (Engenas) Lekganyane, 1924 to 1948: an African experiment with Christianity', MA thesis, University of the North, Pietersburg, South Africa, 1980.
Ma, Wonsuk and Robert P. Menzies (eds.), *Pentecostalism in Context* (Sheffield: Sheffield Academic Press, 1997).
Macchia, Frank D., 'The Struggle for Global Witness: Shifting Paradigms in Pentecostal Theology', in Dempster, Klaus and Petersen, *Globalization of Pentecostalism*, 8–29.

Mair, Jessie H., *Bungalows in Heaven: The Story of Pandita Ramabai* (Kedgaon, India: Pandita Ramabai Mukti Mission, 2003).

Martin, David, *Pentecostalism: The World their Parish* (Oxford: Blackwell, 2002).

McClung Jr., L. Grant (ed.), *Azusa Street and Beyond: Pentecostal Missions and Church Growth in the Twentieth Century* (South Plainfield, NJ: Bridge, 1986).

McClung Jr., L. Grant, 'Spontaneous Strategy of the Spirit', in McClung, *Azusa Street and Beyond*, 71–81.

McClung Jr., L. Grant, 'Truth on Fire: Pentecostals and an Urgent Missiology', in McClung, *Azusa Street and Beyond*, 47–54.

McGavran, Donald A., 'What makes Pentecostal churches grow?', in McClung, *Azusa Street and Beyond*, 121–3.

McGee, Gary B., *This Gospel shall be Preached: A History and Theology of Assemblies of God Foreign Missions to 1959* (Springfield, Missouri: Gospel Publishing House, 1986).

McGee, Gary B., 'Pentecostals and their Various Strategies for Global Mission: A Historical Assessment', in Dempster, Klaus and Petersen, *Called and Empowered*, 203–24.

McGee, Gary B., 'Pentecostal Missiology: Moving beyond triumphalism to face the issues', *Pneuma* 16:2 (Fall 1994), 275–82.

McGee, Gary B., '"Power from on High": A Historical Perspective on the Radical Strategy in Missions', in Ma and Menzies, *Pentecostalism in Context*, 317–36.

McGee, Gary B., '"Latter Rain" Falling in the East: Early-Twentieth-Century Pentecostalism in India and the Debate over Speaking in Tongues', *Church History* 68:3 (1999), 648–65.

McGee, Gary B., 'Minnie F. Abrams: Another Context, Another Founder', in Goff and Wacker, *Portraits of a Generation* (2002), 87–104.

McGee, Gary B., 'The Calcutta Revival of 1907 and the Reformulation of Charles F. Parham's "Bible Evidence" Doctrine', *Asia Journal of Pentecostal Studies* 6:1 (2003), 123–143.

McPherson, Aimee Semple, *This is That: Personal Experiences, Sermons and Writings* (Los Angeles: Echo Park Evangelistic Association, 1923).

McPherson, C. E., *Life of Levi R. Lupton* (Alliance, OH: author, 1911).

Menzies, Robert P., *Empowered for Witness: The Spirit in Luke-Acts* (Sheffield: Sheffield Academic Press, 1994).

Meyer, Birgit, *Translating the Devil: Religion and Modernity among the Ewe in Ghana* (Edinburgh: Edinburgh University Press, 1999).

Moorhead, Max W. (ed.), *Missionary Pioneering in Congo Forests: A Narrative of the Labours of William F.P. Burton and his Companions in the Native Villages of Luba-land* (Preston, UK: R. Seed & Sons, 1922), also revised in Womersley and Gerrard, 2005.

Murray, Andrew, *The Full Blessing of Pentecost* (Basingstoke: Marshall Morgan and Scott, 1954, republished).

Noll, Mark A., 'Evangelical Identity, Power, and Culture in the "Great" Nineteenth Century', in Lewis, *Christianity Reborn*, 31–51.

Nongsiej, T., 'Revival Movement in Khasi-Jaintia Hills', in O. L. Snaitang (ed.), *Churches of Indigenous Origins in Northeast India* (Delhi: ISPCK, 2000), 20–39.

Oosthuizen, Gerhardus C., *The Birth of Christian Zionism in South Africa* (KwaDlangezwa, South Africa: University of Zululand, 1987).

Overy, Richard (ed.), *The Times History of the World*, new edition (London: Times Books, 1999).

Parham, Charles F., *A Voice Crying in the Wilderness* (Baxter Springs, Kansas: Apostolic Faith Bible College, 2nd edn 1910).

Parham, Charles F., *The Everlasting Gospel* (Baxter Springs, Kansas: Apostolic Faith Bible College, 1st edn 1911).

Parham, Charles F., 'The Latter Rain', in Kay and Dyer, *Pentecostal and Charismatic Studies*, 10–13.

Park, Myung Soo, '"The Korean Pentecost": A Study of the Great Revival of 1903–1910 in Relationship to Contemporary Worldwide Holiness Revival Movements', in Yrigoyen, *Global Impact*, 185–200.

Park, Myung Soo, 'The Fourfold Gospel and Korean Churches', *Journal of Asian Evangelical Theology* 12 (2004), 73–94.

Penney, John Michael, *The Missionary Emphasis of Lukan Pneumatology* (Sheffield: Sheffield Academic Press, 1997).

Porter, Andrew (ed.), *The Imperial Horizons of British Protestant Missions 1880–1914* (Grand Rapids, MI & Cambridge, UK: Eerdmans, 2003).

Robeck, Cecil M. Jr., 'Pentecostal Origins in Global Perspective', in Hunter and Hocken, *All Together in One Place*, 166–180.

Robeck, Cecil M. Jr., *The Azusa Street Mission and Revival: The Birth of the Global Pentecostal Movement* (Nashville, TN: Thomas Nelson, 2006).

Robert, Dana, *Occupy Until I Come: A.T. Pierson and the Evangelization of the World* (Grand Rapids, MI & Cambridge, UK: Eerdmans, 2003).

Rosell, Garth M. and Richard A. G. Dupuis (eds.), *The Original Memoirs of Charles G. Finney* (Grand Rapids, MI: Zondervan, 2002).

Saayman, Willem A., 'Some reflections on the development of the Pentecostal mission model in South Africa', *Missionalia* 21:1 (April 1993), 40–56.

Said, Edward W., *Culture and Imperialism* (London: Vintage, 1994).

Sanneh, Lamin, *West African Christianity: The Religious Impact* (London: Hurst, 1983).

Sanneh, Lamin, *Translating the Message: The Missionary Impact on Culture* (Maryknoll, NY: Orbis, 1989).

Saracco, Norberto J., 'Argentine Pentecostalism: Its History and Theology', PhD thesis, University of Birmingham, 1989.

Shew, Paul Tsikidu, 'Pentecostals in Japan', in Allan Anderson and Edmond Tang (eds.), *Asian and Pentecostal: The Charismatic Face of Christianity in Asia* (Oxford: Regnum, 2005), 489–510.

Somaratna, G. P. V., *Origins of the Pentecostal Mission in Sri Lanka* (Mirihana-Nugegoda: Margaya Fellowship of Sri Lanka, 1996).

Spivak, Gayatri Chakravorty, 'Can the Subaltern Speak?' in Ashcroft, *et al.*, *The Post-Colonial Studies Reader*.

Stanley, Brian, *The Bible and the Flag: Protestant Missions and British Imperialism in the Nineteenth and Twentieth Centuries* (Leicester, UK: Apollos, 1990).

Stanley, Brian (ed.), *Missions, Nationalism, and the End of Empire* (Grand Rapids, MI & Cambridge, UK: Eerdmans, 2003).

Stanley, Brian, 'Twentieth Century World Christianity: A Perspective from the History of Missions', in Lewis, *Christianity Reborn*, 52–83.

Sundkler, B. G. M., *Zulu Zion and Some Swazi Zionists* (London: Oxford University Press, 1976).
Sung, S. H., 'History of Pentecostal Mission, Hong Kong & Kowloon', in *Pentecostal Mission, Hong Kong & Kowloon 75 Anniversary 1907–1982*, 8–10.

Tasie, G. O. M., 'Christian Awakening in West Africa 1914–18: A study in the significance of native agency', in Kalu, *History of Christianity in West Africa*, 293–306.
Tasie, G. O. M., 'The Prophetic Calling: Garrick Sokari Braide of Bakana', in Isichei, *Varieties of Christian Experience*, 99–115.
Taylor, Geraldine, *Pastor Hsi: A Struggle for Chinese Christianity* (Singapore: Overseas Missionary Fellowship, 1900, 1949, 1997).
Taylor, Malcolm John, 'Publish and be Blessed: A Case Study in Early Pentecostal Publishing History', PhD thesis, University of Birmingham, 1994.
Thompson, Steve and Adam Gordon, *A 20th Century Apostle: The Life of Alfred Garr* (Wilkesboro, NC: MorningStar Publications, 2003).
Tomlinson, A. J., 'Brief History of the Church that is Now Recognized as the Church of God' (1913), in Kay and Dyer, *Pentecostal and Charismatic Studies*, 7–9.
Tomlinson, Homer A. (ed.), *Diary of A.J. Tomlinson* (New York: Church of God, World Headquarters, 1949).
Torrey, R. A., *The Holy Spirit: Who He Is and What He Does* (Westwood, NJ: Fleming H. Revell, 1927).
Turner, Harold W., *History of an African Independent Church (1) The Church of the Lord (Aladura)* (Oxford: Clarendon, 1967).

Wacker, Grant, 'Are the Golden Oldies Still Worth Playing? Reflections on History Writing Among Early Pentecostals', *Pneuma* 8:2 (1986), 81–100.
Wacker, Grant, *Heaven Below: Early Pentecostals and American Culture* (Cambridge, MA: Harvard University Press, 2001).
Wagner, C. Peter, *Look Out! The Pentecostals are Coming* (Carol Stream: Creation House, 1973).
Wagner, C. Peter, 'Characteristics of Pentecostal Church Growth', in McClung, *Azusa Street and Beyond*, 125–32.
Walker, Sheila S., 'The Message as the Medium: The Harrist Churches of the Ivory Coast and Ghana', Bond, Johnson and Walker, *African Christianity*, 9–64.
Walker, Sheila S., *The Religious Revolution in the Ivory Coast: The Prophet Harris and the Harrist Church* (Chapel Hill, NC: University of North Carolina Press, 1983).
Walls, Andrew F., 'Of Ivory Towers and Ashrams: Some reflections on theological scholarship in Africa', *Journal of African Christian Thought* 3:1 (June 2000), 1–5.
Watt, C. Peter, 'The Assemblies of God: A Missiological Evaluation', MTh thesis, University of South Africa, 1991.
Webster, James B., *The African Churches among the Yoruba 1888–1922* (Oxford: Clarendon, 1964).
Wilson, Everett A., *Strategy of the Spirit: J. Philip Hogan and the Growth of the Assemblies of God Worldwide 1960–1990* (Carlisle: Regnum, 1997).
Womersley, David and David Garrard (eds.), *Into Africa: The Thrilling Story of William Burton and Central African Missions* (Nottingham, UK: New Life Publishing & Preston, UK: Central Africa Missions, 2005).
Womersley, Harold, *Wm F.P. Burton: Congo Pioneer* (Eastbourne, UK: Victory Press, 1973), also revised in Womersley and Gerrard, 2005.

Woods, Daniel, 'Failure and Success in the Ministry of T.J. McIntosh, the first Pentecostal Missionary to China', *Cyberjournal for Pentecostal Charismatic Research* 12, 15 April 2003, http://www.pctii.org/cyberj/cyberj12/woods.html.

Woodworth-Etter, Maria, *Signs and Wonders* (New Kensington, PA: Whitaker House, 1997, republished).

Yrigoyen, Charles, Jr., *The Global Impact of the Wesleyan Traditions and Their Related Movements* (Lanham, MD: The Scarecrow Press, 2000)

Index of Names and Subjects

Berg, George & Mary 6, 54, 60, 81, 95–7, 102, 172, 211, 226, 242, 263, 266, 282
Berg, Daniel 204–5, 288
Bernauer, Estella 139–40
Berntsen, Bernt & Magna 30, 54, 64, 132, 133, 134, 142, 219, 271
Beruldsen, Christina, John & Thyra 125, 212, 234
Bethel Pentecostal Assembly, Newark 52–3, 129, 132 see also Pentecostal Mission, South Africa
Bettex, Paul & Nellie Clark 116, 117, 120, 278
Boddy, Alexander A. 11, 28, 31, 38, 51, 52, 56, 61–3, 65, 86, 87, 99, 112, 123, 124, 132, 158, 159, 172, 202, 225, 226, 228, 245, 250, 272, 276
Bolivia 193, 199, 200, 202, 288
Booth-Clibborn, Arthur 38, 56–7, 127, 224–5
Bowie, George 172, 182, 276
Boyd, William & Fanny Jenner 127–8, 129, 130, 264, 266, 268
Bradley, Amos & Effie 193, 195, 248, 288
Braide, Garrick Sokari 162, 165–6
Brazil 6, 68, 193, 201, 204–6, 288
Brelsford, George S. 54, 56, 155–6, 216, 236
British Israelism, see Anglo-Israelism
Brooke, James 172, 173, 283
Brown, Elisabeth 153
Brown, Marie Burgess & Robert 38, 52
Bryant, Daniel 168
Buddhism, Buddhist 102, 214, 235, 237, 239, 244, 247
Burton, William F.P. 6, 174, 175, 177, 178, 182–5, 215, 216, 219, 225, 237, 239, 242, 245, 246, 249, 253, 255, 269–70, 284, 292

Cashwell, Gaston B. 64, 112, 113
Caste 48, 76, 77, 78, 92, 94, 248, 274
Ceylon, see Sri Lanka
Ceylon Pentecostal Mission 98, 103
Chawner, Charles & Emma 170, 251
Chile 20, 21, 51, 88, 116, 153, 193, 200, 201–4, 205, 288
China, Chinese 3, 7, 8, 10, 11, 13, 14, 26, 29, 30, 32, 33, 39, 42, 47, 48, 51, 52, 54, 55, 56, 59, 61, 62, 63, 64, 68, 76, 78, 86, 109–38, 142, 202, 213, 214, 218, 219, 220, 227, 232, 233, 234, 235, 237, 238, 243, 244, 245, 246, 247, 248, 255, 264, 266, 271, 274, 276, 278, 279, 280, 283, 284, 288

China Inland Mission 25, 30, 33, 39, 54, 90, 111, 124, 125, 126, 128, 131–2, 133, 212, 220, 263, 264, 273, 277
Christian and Missionary Alliance 22, 25, 26, 36, 37, 47, 54, 61, 63, 67, 80, 85, 86, 87, 88, 89, 90, 93, 95, 96, 111, 113, 114, 115, 125, 126, 129–31, 132, 133, 136, 153, 156, 195, 199–200, 202, 212, 269, 281, 289, 291
Chuckerbutty, Shorat 90, 91, 194, 274
Church Missionary Society 20, 28, 90, 95, 96, 102, 158, 166, 194, 246, 267
Church of God (Cleveland, Tennessee) 6, 22, 98, 153, 157, 195, 196, 197, 198, 199, 201, 282, 283 see also Indian Pentecostal Church of God and Pentecostal Church of God
Church of God of Prophecy 198
Church of God in Christ 22, 52, 159, 282, 283
Clark, Earl W. 199, 202, 288
Clifford, Walter 103, 234
Cole, Anna Deane 55, 121
Colleges, theological see Schools, Bible/missionary training
Colombia 193
Colonialism, see Imperialism
Congo 6, 15, 20, 33, 63, 149, 151, 173, 182–5, 215, 227, 235, 237, 239, 242, 245, 249, 250, 251, 261, 266, 269, 270, 288
Congo Evangelistic Mission 182–5, 270
Cook, Ethel 127–8, 129, 130, 214, 227, 237, 239, 265, 266, 268, 274
Cook, Glenn 52, 282
Cook, Robert & Anna 97–8, 215, 266, 268
Cooper, Archibald 170, 172, 178, 181
Coote, Leonard 140
Côte d'Ivoire 162, 163–4
Cragin, Howard & Catherine 199–200, 288
Crowther, Samuel Ajayi 34, 162
Cuba 193, 196, 197, 283
Cumine, Joseph 91
Cumine, Robert Charles 96, 97

De Alwis, Alwin 102–3
Deane, Anna 55, 116, 119, 120, 121, 255
Deliverance (from demons) 39, 47, 91, 92, 137, 153, 215, 236, 240, 241 see also Exorcism
Demon, demonic 25, 27, 30, 39, 47, 55, 91, 134, 137, 214, 222, 233, 234, 235, 239, 241, 259 see also Satan, Satanic

Hitchcock, George & Johanna 173, 288
Ho Maan Leung 115, 116
Ho Si Tai 115, 116, 117, 120
Holiness Movement 19–22, 24
Hong Kong 12, 14, 52, 55, 56, 59, 62, 90, 111–23, 125, 126, 137, 138, 152, 217, 218, 221, 233, 243, 276
Hong Kong Pentecostal Mission 12, 14, 112, 117–22, 125
Hoover, Willis 21, 51, 66, 88–9, 201–4, 205, 288
Hoste, D.E. 132
Hsi, Shengmo 39, 125
Hudson, Henry 198
Hutchins, Julia 48, 59, 157, 158, 159, 288

Imperialism 4, 11, 14, 15, 18, 31–5, 75, 76, 85, 109, 246–7, 249, 256
Independency, independent churches 5, 14, 15, 21, 30, 34–5, 38–9, 51, 98, 103, 111, 116, 121, 123, 133, 136–8, 151, 158, 161–7, 169, 174, 178, 179, 180–1, 194, 195, 197, 199, 203, 240, 246, 251, 269, 281, 282, 283, 284, 291, 292
India, Indian 3, 6, 7, 8, 10, 11, 14, 19, 20, 21, 24, 26, 27–9, 30, 31, 34, 47, 51, 52, 53, 54, 58, 59, 60–1, 62, 64, 66, 67, 68, 75–101, 103, 109, 111, 113, 114, 115, 119, 124, 125, 129, 152, 156, 172, 194, 201, 202, 203, 214, 216, 217, 218, 221, 222, 232, 233, 234, 236, 237, 242, 243, 244, 246, 247, 248, 251, 253, 254, 255, 263, 266, 270, 272, 273, 274, 276, 277, 279, 283, 284, 288
Indian Pentecostal Church of God 98
Ingram, James 198–9
Iraq 92, 152
Irving, Edward 19, 38
Islam, Muslim 92, 149, 151, 154, 157, 221, 233, 234, 236, 238, 247, 263, 273, 274
Israel 149, 152, 158, 165, 222 see also Palestine
Ivory Coast see Côte d'Ivoire

Jamaica 196, 198, 288
Jamieson, Robert & Elisabeth 198, 288
Japan, Japanese 11, 12, 14, 30, 32, 52, 54, 55, 58, 60, 68, 109, 111, 112, 118, 135, 138–41, 152–3, 220, 232, 247, 248, 276, 283, 284, 288
Jesus Family 137
Jing Dianying 137
Johnson, Agnes 141

Johnson, Berger 200, 201
Johnson, William 160, 161, 163
Johnstone, Fred 182, 183, 250, 288
Jordan 152, 153, 178
Juergensen, Carl, Friderike, Marie, Agnes & John 140
Junk, Thomas 42, 51, 54, 55, 64, 134–5, 142, 255

Kangoi 184, 270
Keller, Otto & Marian 158
Kelley, George & Margaret 115–6, 117, 246
Kelty, May 12, 196, 200, 248, 274
Keswick conventions, movement 23–4, 28, 36, 38, 79, 219–20
Kgobe, Elias 173, 174
Kil, Sun Ju 29–30
Kim, Ik Du 30, 141
King, Joseph H. 98, 102, 114, 121
Kirschner, Edith 92
Klaver, Pieter 127–9, 245
Kok, Arie 126, 127, 128, 242, 248, 266–7
Korea 29–30, 32, 78, 109, 140–1, 167, 292

Lake, John G. 6, 38, 50, 54, 56, 168–78, 181, 215, 243, 252–3, 254, 276, 288
Language learning 14, 27, 46, 57, 62, 64, 65, 93, 102, 114, 117, 125, 127, 134, 158, 182, 183, 217, 241, 263, 264, 265, 269, 273, 276, 277
Law, May 56, 111–2, 114, 115, 116, 122, 138, 247, 288
Leatherman, Lucy 6, 51, 53–4, 59, 85, 98, 152–3, 155, 193, 201, 288
Lebanon 85, 152
Lehman, Jacob 54, 168, 169, 171, 172, 174, 181, 214, 263, 268, 288
Lekganyane, Engenas 179–80
Leonard, Charles 64, 153, 226
Le Roux, Pieter L. 38, 168–72, 174, 179, 180
Letwaba, Elias 172, 174–7, 179, 252, 253
Lewer, Alfred 130, 244–5
Lewini, Anna 103
Liberia 6, 20, 21, 51, 54, 55, 59, 60, 68, 152, 157–61, 162–4, 184, 201, 217, 279, 280, 283, 288
Lion, Edward Motaung 171, 177–9, 180, 288
Livingstone, David 25, 32, 34, 149
Lo Heung Lun 116
Luce, Alice 90, 194–5, 246, 268

Simpson, William W. & Otilia 125, 130–3,
    136, 142, 214, 224, 268
Slaybaugh, Edgar T. 171, 172, 173, 174,
    243
Smale, Joseph 47–8
Smith, Rudolph 198
Smith, Sarah 155, 157
Smith, Stanley 125, 126
Sorcery, see Witchcraft
South Africa 6, 15, 17, 19, 20, 50, 52, 54,
    56, 58, 61, 63, 68, 162, 167–81, 182, 183,
    184, 215, 216, 217, 221, 226, 243, 246,
    251–2, 254, 255, 270, 276, 279, 282–3, 288
Spirit Baptism see Baptism in the Spirit
Sri Lanka 54, 87, 89, 90, 96, 101–3, 111,
    156, 214, 234, 248, 288
Starkenberg, Alma 141
Statistics 4, 26, 111, 180, 291
Stone Church, Chicago 12, 38, 53, 66, 86,
    87, 90, 99, 102, 160, 173, 250, 272
Sunderland conventions 3, 28, 63, 102,
    156, 228, 275
Sun Yat-Sen 109, 135, 247
Sung Teng Man 122
Sweden, Swedish 3, 12, 20, 25, 41, 51, 55,
    59, 82, 194, 202, 204, 205, 292
Swift, Allan & Carrie 129, 130, 218, 244,
    266, 268
Syria, Syrian 34, 95, 96, 152, 288

Takigawa, Ichitawo 140
Tanimoto, Yoshio 140
Taylor, William (Bishop) 20–1, 80, 157,
    160, 201, 246
Taylor, William & Mary 138, 140, 141
Tibet, Tibetan 59, 89, 109, 124–8, 130, 213,
    222, 234, 235, 247, 248, 253–4
Toe, Jasper 160
Tomlinson, Ambrose J. 198
Tongues, speaking in 7, 14, 17, 18, 19, 22,
    24, 25, 27, 28, 29, 30, 37, 39, 40–2, 46,
    47–9, 50, 53, 57–65, 66, 67–8, 80–7, 89,
    92, 93, 95, 112, 113, 131, 132, 137, 154,
    157, 159, 162, 163, 166, 181, 199, 202,
    204, 213, 221, 261, 282, 283, 291, 293
Torrey, Reuben A. 23, 24, 29, 79
Trasher, Lillian 155–7, 221, 263, 281
Trevitt, Frank & Maggie Millie 125–6,
    132, 218, 234
Trinidad 198

True Jesus Church 123, 133, 137, 284
Turkey, Turkish 54, 58, 152, 153, 154, 222,
    247, 288 see also Ottoman Empire
Turney, Henry M. & Anna 141, 167–8,
    170–1, 172, 174, 181, 221, 243, 263, 279

Upper Room, Los Angeles 12, 63, 120,
    124, 153, 172, 199
Urshan, Andrew 55, 154, 238

Valenzuela, Romanita Carbajal de 194,
    288
Venezuela 193, 199, 200, 269, 288
Vernon, Roy & Blanche 173, 288
Vingren, Gunnar 6, 204–5, 288

Wallis, William 173, 288
Wanigasekera, D.E. Dias 90, 91, 96, 102,
    288
War, the Great (First World War) 14, 15,
    34, 75, 97, 118, 122, 124, 127–9, 152, 153,
    154, 155, 156, 198, 222, 223–8, 243, 236,
    249, 251, 256, 264, 273, 275, 276, 280, 282
Wei, Paul 137
Welsh Revival 27–8, 29, 31, 47, 48, 65, 79,
Wesley, John 19, 20, 21, 22, 30, 35, 49, 203
Williams, Amos & Lizzie Millie 125–6,
    217
Witchcraft, sorcery 151, 167
Witchdoctor 164, 184, 216, 235, 237, 239,
    240, 241, 292
Women, ministry of 6, 15, 77, 88, 271–6
Wood, Alice 64, 200–1
Woodworth-Etter, Maria 37, 199, 221,
    271
Worldview 5, 238, 240, 293

Young Men's Christian Association
    (YMCA) 89, 117, 127, 138
Young Women's Christian Association
    (YWCA) 90, 91, 264

Zambia 173, 288
Zhang, Barnabas 137
Zhang Lingshen 137, 142
Zimbabwe 168, 173, 174, 176, 288
Zion Christian Church 39, 179, 180, 252
Zion, Zion City, Zionist 38, 39, 40, 42, 53,
    154, 167, 168–9, 170, 171, 175, 178,
    179–80, 181, 272

Lightning Source UK Ltd.
Milton Keynes UK
UKOW06f1308280716

279425UK00005B/150/P